Staatlichkeit und Governance in Transformation

Weltordnung, regionale Integration und nationalstaatliche politische Systeme im Vergleich

herausgegeben von

Prof. Dr. Gisela Müller-Brandeck-Bocquet
Prof. Dr. Hans-Joachim Lauth
Prof. Dr. Michèle Knodt
Prof. Dr. Marianne Kneuer

Band 8

Michèle Knodt | Natalia Chaban | Louise Nielsen

Bilateral Energy Relations between the EU and Emerging Powers

Mutual Perceptions of the EU and Brazil, China, India and South Africa

Nomos

The Deutsche Nationalbibliothek lists this publication in the Deutsche Nationalbibliografie; detailed bibliographic data are available on the Internet at http://dnb.d-nb.de

ISBN 978-3-8487-2159-7 (Print)
978-3-8452-6259-8 (ePDF)

British Library Cataloguing-in-Publication Data
A catalogue record for this book is available from the British Library.

ISBN 978-3-8487-2159-7 (Print)
978-3-8452-6259-8 (ePDF)

Library of Congress Cataloging-in-Publication Data
Knodt, Michèle / Chaban, Natalia / Nielsen, Louise
Bilateral Energy Relations between the EU and Emerging Powers
Mutual Perceptions of the EU and Brazil, China, India and South Africa
Michèle Knodt / Natalia Chaban / Louise Nielsen
300 p.
Includes bibliographic references.

ISBN 978-3-8487-2159-7 (Print)
978-3-8452-6259-8 (ePDF)

1st Edition 2017

Table of Content

List of Figures

List of Tables

Acknowledgements

Our team of authors is grateful for the generous support provided to the two projects that informed this book by the Volkswagen Foundation, Riksbankens Jubileumsfond and Compagnia di San Paulo, as well as by the Jean Monnet Lifelong Learning Programme of the European Commission.

We are indebted to all our interview respondents and participants in the survey who kindly agreed to collaborate with us and dedicated their time and energy to support research. Without their contribution, this book would have been impossible. We are also grateful to our research assistants Katharina Kleinschnitger and Lai Suet-yi for their meticulous and thorough work. Dr. Lai's efforts warranting media data collection in a nine-location setting, and Ms. Kleinschnitger's help with the production of this volume are greatly appreciated. Special thanks go to Franziska Krauß and Yvonne Grosch for all their administrative and coordination support.

In the course of the two projects that informed this book we have received constructive and enriching feedback concerning different aspects of the project from Romy Chevallier, Ole Elgström, Erik Oddvar Eriksen, José Goldemberg, Andreas Goldthau, Anna Herranz-Surrallés, Martin Holland, Rajendra K. Jain, Andrew Judge, Ligia Noronha, Andreas Nölke, Johan P. Olsen, Jörn Richert, Ummu Salma Bava, Anke Schmitt-Felzmann, Elizabeth Sidiropoulos, Helen Sjursen, Nathalie Tocci, Richard Youngs and Yang Xiepu. Special thanks goes to Amy Verdun who was our co-leader in the project supported by the Jean Monnet Lifelong Learning Programme.

The support and hospitality of GIZ offices in China, India, Brazil, and South Africa as well as the research centre GovInn at the University of Pretoria in South Africa and its director Lorenzo Fioramonti. Marcelo Vitali and Aline Cardoso Barabinot of Orbiz (São Paulo) and Jessica Bain of University of Leicester (UK) also contributed to the project. All their contributions were invaluable and allowed us to advance our research.

Our strongest words of gratitude go to an incredibly talented group of researchers who worked with us analyzing media. It is not a secret that successful completion of our projects is due to their hard work and dedication: Anastasia Chebakova, Carolina Guimaraes, Berengere Greenland, Olga Gulyaeva, Juan-José (JJ) Miranda, Shreya Pandey, Nadine Piefer and Tatiana Shaban.

Many thanks go to all our colleagues who contributed to this volume through inspiring and passionate discussions and valuable feedback at various conferences and workshops.

Finally, we would like to thank our fantastic families for their ongoing support, love and patience!

Michèle Knodt, Natalia Chaban and Louise Nielsen

Introduction
Situating the EU and BICS in Global Energy Governance: Mutual Perceptions and Normative Recognition

In December 2015 in Paris, the conference of the parties of the United Nations Framework Convention on Climate Change (UNFCCC COP) concluded a historic agreement – to keep the increase in global average temperature to well below 2°C. This internationally binding climate agreement has brought a new dynamic into global climate efforts. It has also served as a wake-up call for a rapid transformation of the world's energy system (UNFCCC 2015). It is a dynamic investment signal in the switch towards renewable energy, with the prospect that a wide-ranging decarbonization will foster an energy transition. Interpreted in light of the great "global transformation" (WBGU 2011: 71-73), the agreement will create dynamics that ensure fair participation in and distribution of renewable energy worldwide (Jänicke 2013). Thus, it paves the way towards global climate policy making, to be performed jointly and in cooperation with emerging powers, including Brazil, India, China and South Africa (BICS), as analysed in this book. We witnessed a first joint effort, an announcement to ratify the Paris agreement by the United States (US) and China in September 2016. On the eve of the G20 summit in Hangzhou, after weeks of intense negotiations by Chinese and US officials, the world's largest emitters of greenhouse gases presented their historic effort. Then-US President Barack Obama said, in the presence of Chinese President Xi Jinping and the then United Nations Secretary-General Ban Ki-moon, that "China and the United States are prepared to show leadership and to lead by example" (The Guardian 2016).

Although the US commitment to the Paris Agreement is currently being questioned by the newly elected US President Donald Trump, the joint move has been strategically symbolic and significant. It showed that political action on a bilateral base is needed to move the Paris agreement beyond buzzwords. In particular, new forms of political cooperation at the climate/clean energy nexus in bilateral dialogues between the Western countries including the European Union (EU) and emerging powers provide ample opportunities for implementing the Paris agreement. Although climate issues are embedded in a global climate regime, the UNFCCC, the clean energy complex is only in its nascent stage (Andonova/Chelminski 2016).

Global energy issues are organized in a highly fragmented structure consisting of at least 24 international energy organizations (Baccini et al. 2011), and governance is organized along regional lines (e.g., International Energy Agency [IEA]) and according to type of energy resources (e.g., OPEC, IEAE, IRENA[1]). In addition, decisions on energy mix and transformation remain at the national level, even in the EU. Therefore, bilateral cooperation is bound to play a more important role for national governments and the EU in the policy field of energy than in climate policy due to the lack of an alternative international discursive arena.

Thus far, the EU has not yet undertaken a high-profile initiative such as the one carried out but the US and China. Nevertheless, the EU and China committed themselves to work together in the energy field (European Council 2015: 3) and signed the EU-China Energy Roadmap 2016-2020 in June 2016. It documents common energy and climate challenges including security of energy supply, energy infrastructure and market transparency (European Commission 2016b). In addition, the EU and India adopted a 'Joint Declaration between the EU and India on a Clean Energy and Climate Partnership' at the Summit 2016 (Joint Declaration 2016). Despite these most recent initiatives, the EU's efforts to communicate and cooperate with emerging powers on energy issues appear challenged, not yet tapping their full potential. Until recently, bilateral dialogues between the EU and emerging powers were performed separately for climate and energy policy. In particular, the EU has shown very poor performance in the dialogues (Knodt et al. 2015). They are characterized by mutual mistrust, minor interests of the emerging powers in them and different perceptions of the norms and goals underlying the respective dialogues. It appears that the EU is very good in 'talking at' instead of 'talking with' its external energy partners. The EU engages in top-down, one-way communication, projecting interests, norms and values rather than developing a horizontal dialogue-led two-way communication process between equal partners (Chaban et al. 2016). Smith (2013) investigates more closely the EU's role as an external actor and the current challenges attached to this role. He states:

1 The Organization of the Petroleum Exporting Countries (OPEC), International Atomic Energy Agency (IEAE) and International Renewable Energy Agency (IRENA) address oil, nuclear and renewable energy issues, respectively.

> [T]he EU's approach and actions are now under question and challenged as never before, thanks to a concatenation of internal and external forces that has thrown into question the EU's capacity to adapt to and profit from a reshaped world arena (Smith 2013: 670).

In this light, bilateral relations between the EU and the BICS attract increasing scholarly attention. This dynamic research field is informed by a view that

> the EU's individual strategic partnerships with Brazil, Russia, India, China and South Africa are the most complex in terms of common goals, interests and global strategies (Gratius 2013: 2)

– a challenge that suggests an ongoing academic insight. The interest is rather new, with many research gaps remaining. Although the EU's respective Strategic Partnerships with the BICS have been explored in various studies, there is a lack of comprehensive *comparative in-depth* analyses of these relationships.[2] In addition, the energy area of cooperation has been overlooked in the relevant literature (Knodt et al. 2015). Mapping the literature on the EU's bilateral relations with the BICS demonstrates a certain imbalance. Research on the EU-China relationship is prolific (see among others Men 2014; Yuan/Orbie 2014; Mergenthaler 2012; Shambaugh et al. 2008). In comparison, the EU's relations with Brazil, India and South Africa is a less popular topic (On Brazil, see Santander 2015; Whitman/Rodt 2012. On India, see Winand et al. 2015; Jain 2014b, 2007; Jaffrelot 2006. On South Africa, see Oliver/Fioramonti 2010). Importantly, these three countries' relations with the EU are increasingly in the literature's focus not least due to the recognition of the "growing regional presence" (Williams et al. 2009: 92) of India, Brazil and South Africa. Relevant research suggests the rise of the Global South and confirms the increasing importance of South-South cooperation,

> whatever shape the world political order takes in future, it is going to be one in which at least parts of the Global South are going to play a far more active role (Williams et al. 2009: 100).

Studies also reflect on the diplomatic success by these emerging powers – for instance, in international trade (Narlikar 2003; Oehler-Şincai 2011). These developments are argued by scholars to place the EU at risk of being marginalized. Related to our analysis is a conclusion by Renard and Grevi

---

2 One exception is a PhD Dissertation by Natalie Hess analysing the EU's Strategic Partnerships with Brazil, India and South Africa (2013).

on the lack of linkages between Strategic Partnerships and the international negotiations on climate change (Renard/Grevi 2012b: 9).

The EU's search for a new role in a polycentric world has been an ongoing process that affects not only the EU's self-image and institutional structure but also how relations with other major powers are (re)shaped (Keukeleire/Bruyninckx 2011). To enhance – or at least maintain – its global profile, the EU uses its Strategic Partnerships as a 'privileged mode' of interactions with major emerging powers. In the aftermath of the Iraq War in 2003 and the crisis in transatlantic relations between the EU and the US, the Strategic Partnerships were viewed by the EU as a tool to enhance 'multilateral bilateralism', in contrast to the US' unilateralism. For the BICS, the recognition of a multipolar world order and, thus, their status as major powers in it might have been a main motivation to engage in Strategic Partnerships with the EU (Keukeleire et al. 2011).

Although able to initiate its Strategic Partnerships, the EU is often criticized for its lack of strategic approach in its relations with the B(R)ICS (see Allen/Smith 2012; Renard 2010, 2011; Gratius 2013). Grevi and de Vasconcelos, who viewed the BRIC as potential partners to the EU in fulfilling its 'effective multilateralism', identified several challenges attached to these relations. More specifically, they noted the diversity among the BRIC, the lack of performance by the EU and the diverging priorities between the EU and the BRIC (2008: 155).

This book contributes to the literature on EU-BICS relations from a novel perspective; it explores *mutual perceptions* of the EU and the BICS. In our research, we are inspired by the following premise:

> To gain a richer understanding of today's world power, it is important to look not only at the actions of states themselves but also at the international systems and ideas that link them together (Williams et al. 2009: 93).

Relevant scholarship has demonstrated that an informed insight into the understanding of EU governance worldwide demands a systematic comparative and empirically-informed consideration of the EU's actions and interests with its values, ideas, norms and identities. Works in the field of EU foreign policy and international relations also increasingly warn against a Eurocentric bias and challenge EU scholars to overcome an exclusive focus on EU projections to the world. They call for the inclusion of a multifaceted inquiry into the EU communication with and reception by global partners. In-depth nuanced understanding of a globalizing multipolar reality is needed in a world that is characterized by networks and communications –

including the field of global energy governance. As such, we prioritize informed systematic research reflections on dialogue, cooperation and collaboration – through the lens of mutual perceptions – in addition to the scope of the EU's projections of its positions and actions. This premise grounds our work on the EU as a global energy governance actor within the tenets of the constructivist approach. This approach accentuates the idea of reality being socially constructed and international relations being a product of human interactions in a social world. Importantly, in this approach, social values, norms and language are all viewed as possessing a crucial role because they shape and help understand changes in world structures (Fierke 2010: 179-180).

More specifically, our research is grounded in the interpretative framework (see Chapter 1). Starting with consideration of how the EU projects its actions and ideas to its external partners (the BICS in our case) through various structures and discourses, we progress to analyse how the EU's actions – together with projected ideas, values and identities – are perceived, imagined and recognized by the EU's key international interlocutors in the energy realm.

Our emphasis on perception and recognition is not accidental. Although powers must be "recognized by others to have certain special rights and duties" (Bull 1977: 196), perceptions and images – key elements in the reception process – are important explanatory factors in understanding a nuanced interaction among the global actors. Our consideration of the EU's identity – and preference-shaping interactions with BICS within the global energy governance structures – is complemented by our innovative analysis of external images and perceptions of the EU and its policies. Research anchors within interpretative constructivism prescribe a complex architecture for our research questions and diverse methods of analysis, which are described briefly below (and in detail in Chapter 1).

The aim of this book is to identify, understand and compare *mutual perceptions* of the EU and the emerging powers in energy policy. Considering the complexity of the external energy governance of the EU and the BICS, our main question is, what mutual perceptions do both sides hold of each other as energy actors? In a set of sub-questions we ask: What controversies in the energy field are highlighted by those perceptions? What are the perceived dominant norms and their hierarchies in the bilateral energy dialogues? What is the EU's self-perception of its roles as an energy actor in respective dialogues? What are the emerging powers' views of the EU? What are the self-perceptions of the emerging powers' and their role in global energy governance? What are the EU's views of the respective emerging powers? What are the views of the respective emerging powers of each other? How do these many perceptions compare with each other? Finally, we ask how these insights and comparisons can be useful for the policy- and decision-makers involved in the energy interactions.

We argue that an understanding of mutual perceptions between the EU and BICS in the energy field is a function of many factors. Some of them are specific to the EU. These factors can be influenced by many achievements of Europe who arguably projects to the world images of a 'sustainable', 'green', 'technologically advanced' and 'environment- and climate-concerned' actor. However, they also might be tainted by the EU's multiplying crises and, internal to the EU, critical reflections on the place and role of the idea of European integration:

The absence of a new *raison d'être*[3] and the conceptual vacuum about Europe's future, the elite crisis and the leadership deficit on the level of Member States and EU institutions, the widespread fatigue concerning future EU reforms and further rounds of enlargement, the political elites' fear of 'power castration' and the citizens' perception of an 'apolitical Europe', as well as the consequences of Europe's relative economic decline are the key reasons for the EU's loss of dynamism and attractiveness (Emmanouilidis 2012: 84). Reflective of these changes, recent surveys demonstrate a growing lack of trust in the EU (see, for example, the survey conducted by *Der Spiegel* in 2016 [Der Spiegel, 07.08.2016]).

Importantly, these internal problems and negative attitudes are visible to the EU's external partners. They are believed to influence the EU image in the world and, potentially, external relations of the EU in many fields, including energy. Moreover, although the EU is viewed as navigating stormy waters in its political, economic and social areas, the world is witnessing "China's rise to power together with other Southern countries, such as India, South Africa and Brazil" (Wilson et al. 2009: 93). Inevitably, EU-specific factors will interact with global ones (including the EU's role in the COPs) and with the 'local filters' of external partners – their location-specific policies, priorities, attitudes and experiences (see Chaban/Magdalina 2014). In the BICS case, these 'local' visions of the EU are also marked by BICS' growing confidence and self-perception of their global importance and feeling of belonging to a new 'powerful club' – the 'club of emerging powers'.

---

3 Raising the question of "the future added value of European integration" (Emmanouilidis 2012: 88).

As such, the EU perceptions also must be understood in relation to how BICS are seeing themselves and each other.

The book addresses a novel subject in EU external perception studies – comprehensive comparative analysis of issue-specific images of the EU as a global energy actor. Although several relevant studies address general perceptions of the EU (for review of this field see Lucarelli 2014; Chaban/Holland 2014, 2015; Elgström/Chaban 2015), only occasionally do they explore EU perceptions in the energy field.[4] Moreover, the book focusses on the many intersections between self-perceptions and perceptions of the Other and on 'mirror' perceptions. Our book contributes innovatively to EU external perception studies by focussing on these multiple visions.

Most EU perception studies consider only one perspective – 'outside looking in'. EU perceptions in BICS have been studied by many. The relevant literature includes large-scale comparative projects that addressed the BICS, among other cases. See, for example, 'EU Global Perceptions' (online), led by Natalia Chaban and Martin Holland (Holland et al. 2007; Chaban/Holland 2008, 2013, 2014; Chaban et al. 2009; Holland/Chaban 2010, 2014), FP6 project 'EU external perceptions' led by Sonia Lucarelli and Lorenzo Fioramonti (Lucarelli 2010) and FP7 project EuroBroadMap (online) led by Clarisse Didelon-Loiseau and Claude Gasland. Among the most recent studies is a 2015 project supported by the EEAS in which the four BICS countries were studied in the project on EU perceptions in ten EU Strategic Partners (PPMI/NCRE/NFG 2015). Both India and China are the focus of the project 'Asian Perceptions of the EU' (Stumbaum et al. 2015) and an individual author Lisbonne-de Vergeron (2011). China's perceptions of the EU is perhaps among the most popular topics in EU external perception studies (Shambaugh et al. 2008, FP7 project 'Disaggregating EU Perceptions' (online), Zhang 2011; Lisbonne-de Vergeron 2007, 2011; Zhou 2007 to list only few). India's perceptions of the EU were investigated by Jain and Pandey (2010, 2013), Lisbonne-de Vergeron (2006, 2011), and Winand (2014), among many others. Views on the EU from Brazil and South Africa might be a less popular subject; nevertheless, they were studied in the project led by Lucarelli and Fioramonti and in the 2015 project 'Analysis of EU external perceptions', commissioned by the EEAS (PPMI/NCRE/NFG 2015). South Africa was also the focus of the project 'EU Global Perceptions', led by Chaban and Holland (their 2006-2007

4 One exception is the Special Issue 'External Images of the EU – Energy Power across the Globe' of *Comparative European Politics* (2016, online first) edited by Chaban, Knodt and Verdun.

study on EU images as a development actor). Country chapters in this book will review relevant 'EU external perceptions' literature in greater detail. Here, we would like to note that although diverse and rich, these studies have typically given modest attention to images of the EU as an *energy* actor – a scholarly deficit rectified by this book – and rarely considered mutual perceptions.

Importantly, 'mirror' perception studies have occurred. For example, the research project 'Asia in the Eyes of Europe' (ASiE), supported by the Asia-Europe Foundation (ASEF), addressed public perceptions of Asia in the EU, aiming to "track the existing landscape of perceptions of Asia within the EU" (Bersick et al. 2012b: 13). More specifically, the project focussed on the perceptions of Asia in general, and the awareness of regional integration processes in Asia in particular, in seven EU Member States (Bersick et al. 2012). Perceptions of the two leading Asian actors China and India – the two case studies in our volume – were explored in this study. One follow-up project to ASiE was a research project on China's perceptions in the EU by Tshinghua University ('China in the Eyes of Europe', online). In general, analysis of images of China in the eyes of Europe remains a popular research subject. Ingrid d'Hooghe's 2010 study of China's soft power in Europe focussed on three EU Member States (the UK, Germany and France) and presented a comprehensive analysis of several public opinion polls conducted in these three European states by various reputable organizations. Among those polls were a 2008 monthly poll by the Financial Times/Harris, the Pew Global Attitude Project with yearly large-scale surveys (2005-2008), the BBC World Service Polls 2008 and 2009, and the 2006 German Marshall Fund poll 'The Transatlantic Trends'. Research into Europe's perceptions of India, Brazil and South Africa remains limited. Some insights come from large-scale public opinion surveys (e.g., the Bertelsmann Stiftung Survey [2006] or annual BBC Worlds Service poll by GlobeScan/PIPA). However, those studies do not focus on the images of these powerful players as energy actors. All of the studies listed above tend to leave energy out of their focus.

Inspired by existing studies, our book offers an innovative multi-layered research design backed by a comprehensive and systematic comparative approach. Based on tested empirical algorithm, it considers both EU perceptions in the four BICS ('outside looking in') and perceptions of each BICS in Europe ('mirror perceptions' in the three selected EU Member States – France, Germany and the UK). Moreover, it also briefly touches on three additional dimensions: 1) self-perceptions of each BICS as energy actors; 2) BICS' perceptions of other emerging powers of BICS; and 3) perceptions of the EU in the eyes of three EU Member States (European self-perceptions). The complex matrix of mutual perceptions is backed by a call to study meanings emerging in Self-Other interactions through multiple intersections. One must compare 'Self about the Other' vs. 'Other about Self' meanings and complement them with insights into 'Self about Self in relation to Other' and 'Other about Other in relation to Self' perspectives (Greimas' 'semiotic square' model adapted by Chaban (1997, 2016) to study images of the Others).

The value of this book is also in its attention to multiple opinion-forming discourses, namely elite discourse (opinions of stakeholders involved in the global energy governance and respective EU-BICS energy dialogues in the EU and BICS) and media discourse (influential newspapers in each location that lead and shape the agenda of public and business debate on policy issues). Some theoretical models credit these discourses with heightened capability to create, spread and activate frames of foreign policy and international actors. Among such models is a communication studies 'cascading activation framing theory' proposed by Robert Entman (2003, 2004). The communication studies field has a plenitude of theories to explain the influence of media on the public and elites. However, our book chooses the cascading activation framing theory to inform our research because it brings together elites (government administration and other levels), the media and the public in one analytical schema and predicts how frames related to foreign policy can be spread through different levels. Importantly, it argues the centrality of news media in communicating and influencing the public and government and other elite levels. Entman considers media more than "passive receptacles for government propaganda" (2010: 428; see also Brand 2012) and argues scope conditions for media to spread and activate certain frames about foreign partners in a given society. Chapter 1 details the primary analytical positions and constructs that informed our research.

Among those analytical frameworks considered in Chapter 1 is a Normative Power Europe (NPE) theoretical approach. Although recognizing that NPE is currently challenged, we still consider it relevant in different ways for our research. Our application of the NPE framework in this book is inspired by the "third wave" of its theorization (Nicolaïdis/Whitman 2013), characterized by a critical approach to the NPE concept. The main problem in this 'wave' is tripartite:

> structural changes in international relations problematizing Europe's capacity for normative power; ontological and epistemological contestation of normative power Europe; and a contestation of Eurocentricity seen to be intrinsic to normative power Europe (Whitman 2013: 186).

These three directions guide our analysis of EU global energy governance through the perceptions lenses. In it, we prioritize the concepts of receivers of normative messages, recognition, and perception of norms specific to the energy field – *security of supply*, *sustainability* and *competitiveness* – that are viewed (or not viewed) as having influence and impact. This book systematically considers interaction between the norm-senders and norm-receivers; norm-receivers' agency, identity and cultural filters; the resonance or clash between normative visions; perceived Eurocentric bias; and a two-way communication of normative meanings through various discourses.

Chapter 1 also describes a combination of methods to analyse the data – media content analysis, elite discourse analysis, and network analysis. The data for this book came from two transnational comparative research projects, both completed in 2015. One was a three-year project on 'Challenges of European Energy Governance with Emerging Powers' (EnergyGov), which analysed the EU energy dialogues with Brazil, India, China and South Africa. The project was funded by the Volkswagen Foundation and led by TU Darmstadt. It involved the University of Aarhus, Peking University, Stiftung Wissenschaft und Politik (SWP), the University of Cambridge, South African Institute of International Affairs (SAIIA), Fundación para las Relaciones Internacionales y el Diálogo Exterior (FRIDE), The Energy and Resources Institute (TERI), Gesellschaft für Internationale Zusammenarbeit (GIZ), Federal University of Rio de Janeiro and the University of Zurich. Data provided by this project come from 150 interviews conducted from February 2012 to December 2013. These interviews involved EU officials in Brussels and the EU Delegations in the BICS; officials from EU Member States (primarily from Denmark, Germany, Spain and the UK); Chinese, Indian, Brazilian and South African government officials; and representatives of business associations, NGOs, chambers of commerce, development agencies, other European and emerging power business actors and representatives of state-owned enterprises. The interviews were performed in Bangalore, Beijing, Berlin, Brasilia, Brussels, Cape Town, Copenhagen, Eschborn, Johannesburg, Hannover, London, Madrid, Mumbai, New Delhi, Pretoria, Rio de Janeiro, and São Paulo by 15 researchers of the project team. Furthermore, a survey on BICS-EU Energy Relations was conducted with data quoted from EnergyGov, Darmstadt, 2014.

The second project was a two-year project, 'External images of the EU as a Normative Energy Power: BRICS vis-à-vis the EU' (EXIE). It examined influential news media discourses of the BRICS and the EU's 'Big 3' (France, Germany and the UK) framing the EU's place in the global energy landscape vis-à-vis BRICS. Images of the EU as an energy actor were also traced in the social medium of Twitter (case study 'EU Sustainable Energy Week 2013'). This project was supported by the Jean Monnet Lifelong Learning Programme of the European Commission. It was led by the University of Canterbury (New Zealand) and co-led by TU Darmstadt (Germany) and the University of Victoria (Canada). It also involved the University of Pretoria (South Africa) and the University of Leicester (UK). Media data analysis was conducted by an international team of 10 researchers. Data are quoted from EXIE 2015.

Chapter 2 presents an overview of strategic cooperation between the EU and each of the BICS, with Strategic Partnerships critically considered an instrument in the EU's external relations arsenal. The literature in the field argues that relations between the EU and the BICS tend to follow similar patterns in terms of trade agreements, cooperation agreements, and the establishment of Strategic Partnerships (Keukeleire/Bruyninckx 2011: 385). These similarities are reflected upon. However, the chapter also notes major differences and challenges in the relations between the EU and each of the BICS.

Chapter 3 provides an insight into the development of European energy governance. In particular, it focusses on how the interpretation of and discourses about the three normative frames of *security of supply*, *sustainability* and *competitiveness* shape the energy policy in the EU's multi-level system and which actors are involved. The chapter concludes with its main finding – a competition and dissonance between the *energy security of supply* and *sustainability* frames resulting in a current deadlock for the EU's energy policy.

Empirical findings on the mutual perceptions of the EU and BICS on energy policy are presented in four country chapters: Chapters 4-7. These chapters follow an identical outline to ensure comparability across the four cases. Each chapter starts with detailing the energy policy and energy mix of a respective BICS country. Next, is a section on the EU-BICS bilateral energy relationships. After reviewing the relevant literature on the reality of relations, the chapters then dissect the EU-BICS mutual perceptions in the energy field and perceptions of the EU energy relations with a respective BICS country. These perceptions are sourced from media and elite discourses of each of the BICS, the EU and its three selected Member States. Here the focus is on the leading topics in mutual perceptions, images of the normative orientation of EU-BICS energy relations, views on roles in the energy domain and evaluations assigned to each other as energy actors. These chapters also explore perceptions of other global energy actors vis-à-vis the EU and BICS.

Finally, Chapter 8 summarizes the empirical findings comparatively across the four cases and in the Conclusion discusses the scholarly significance and practical importance of this research for EU-BICS energy cooperation.

Concluding this Introduction, we underline that our research belongs to a growing body of literature oriented towards analysing the EU as a global actor.

> Such a sustained and substantial interest reflects both the empirical importance of the EU in the international arena and the analytical challenge of addressing what is a distinctive if not unique type of internationally acting body (Hill/Smith 2011b: 4).

This "distinctive if not unique" character of the polity was stressed by the EU's new Global Strategy (EUGS) of 2016 – the EU's declaration of its visions and strategies in addressing the world. The EUGS lists energy insecurity as one of its key security challenges – a condition that is argued to "endanger our people and territory" (EEAS 2016a: 9). In this light, and specifically concerning the EU's dealings with external partners far from its borders, the EUGS declares that

> [t]hrough our energy diplomacy, we will strengthen relations worldwide with reliable energy-producing and transit countries, and support the establishment of infrastructure to allow diversified sources to reach European markets (EEAS 2016a: 22).

However, energy security is not the only normative priority for the EU in the global energy arena.

> On energy, we will encourage multilateral mechanisms aimed at ensuring sustainable energy patterns both by developing our own sustainable policies and by deepening dialogue with major energy consumers and producers (EEAS 2016a: 42-43).

The EU's actions with reference to energy and the related field of climate change were specifically mentioned when the EUGS described EU relations with geopolitical regions in which the four BICS are the political and economic leaders. Outlining priorities in its relations with Africa, the EU states:

> We will build stronger links between our trade, development and security policies in Africa, and blend development efforts with work on migration, health, education, *energy and climate*, science and technology, notably to improve food security (EEAS 2016a: 36, emphasis added).

The EU's multilateral ties with the Community of Latin American and Caribbean States (CELAC) – of which Brazil is a member – are promised to be enhanced in many ways, including energy.

> We will step up political dialogue and cooperation on migration, maritime security and ocean life protection, *climate change and energy*, disarmament, non-proliferation and arms control, and countering organised crime and terrorism (EEAS 2016a: 37, emphasis added).

For India and South Asia in general, the EUGS indicates that it "will deepen cooperation on counterterrorism, anti-trafficking and migration, as well as enhance transport, trade and *energy connectivity*" (EEAS 2016a: 38, emphasis added). China is the only country in our case that was not mentioned by the EUGS explicitly in terms of energy. However, a related theme – climate change – was listed.

> The EU will also deepen trade and investment with China, seeking a level playing field, appropriate intellectual property rights protection, greater cooperation on high-end technology, and dialogue on economic reform, human rights and *climate action* (EEAS 2016a: 38, emphasis added).

These visions and objectives echo an earlier argument by Renard/Biscop (2012a), who examined the EU as an actor on the global stage with a specific focus on the changing world order, and the "EU's possible *active* role in shaping this changing global environment" (Renard/Biscop 2012b: xv, emphasis in original).

Perhaps an even larger signification of the EUGS is its overall vision of the EU's external action with energy diplomacy as a constituent part of it:

> New fields of our joined-together external action include energy diplomacy, cultural diplomacy and economic diplomacy. A more prosperous Union requires economic priorities to be set in relations to all countries and regions and integrated into the external dimensions of all internal policies. A more prosperous Union calls for greater coordination between the EU and Member States, the EIB and the private sector. We must become more joined together across internal and external policies (EEAS 2016a: 49).

We believe that our research presented in this book explores a key requirement in achieving this ambitious vision – an ability to listen attentively to how the EU is imagined and how its messages and interactions are understood by key global partners and internal stakeholders. Here, we agree with Christopher Hill and Michael Smith; the

> actual or potential gap between understandings about the EU's international performance and impact is likely to be implicated in more-general estimates of the EU's success or failure in international relations (Hill/Smith 2011b: 15).

In this respect, this book provides lessons for future EU-BICS energy cooperation.

Chapter 1
Theory and Methodology: Concepts and Operationalisations

1.1 Theoretical Approach

Studying EU external governance and International Relations (IR) is necessarily complex and interdisciplinary. Different theoretical approaches and models are expected and natural, each adding a new dimension to understand European integration and Europe's links to the world. This also holds true for the area of energy governance on which this volume is focussed. We define energy governance as a "form of coordination and cooperation, involving a variety of actors within a multi-level system" (Müller et al. 2015a: 18-19) – it

> seeks to regulate inter- and transnational energy relations thereby involving a combination of soft steering instruments, policy diffusion, communicative arrangements and diplomatic activities.

As relevant scholarship demonstrates, developing informed insights into the understanding of EU governance worldwide demands a systematic, comparative consideration of the EU's actions and interests, as well as its values, ideas, norms and identities. Works in the field of EU foreign policy and international relations also increasingly warn against a Eurocentric bias and challenge EU scholars to overcome an exclusive focus on EU projections to the world. They call for multifaceted inquiry into the Union's communication with and reception by global partners. An in-depth, nuanced understanding of the EU's place and role in a globalizing multipolar reality is needed in a world that is characterised by networks and communications – including the field of global energy governance. As such, we argue for prioritising informed reflections on dialogue, cooperation and collaboration, in addition to the insights on the EU's monologues and projected positions and actions. These premises ground our work on the EU as a global energy governance actor within the tenets of the constructivist approach. This approach accentuates the idea of reality being socially constructed and international relations being a product of human interactions in a social world. Importantly, in this approach, social values, norms and language are all seen to play a crucial role, as they shape and facilitate understanding changes in world structures (Fierke 2010: 179-180).

Specifically, our research is grounded within the framework of interpretative constructivism – an approach that emphasises the "centrality of intersubjective cognition and norms in the definition of the social structure" (Schimmelfennig 2001: 58). Carta and Morin (2014: 7) echo this definition stating,

> by discursively interacting within a given structure, agents endogenously construct social reality, and, in turn, interactions with the structural context contribute to reconstructing their preferences and interests.

Starting with a consideration of how the EU projects its actions and ideas to its external partners (the emerging BICS powers, in our case) through various structures and discourses, we then analyse how the EU's actions – together with projected ideas, values and identities – are perceived, imagined and recognised by the Union's key international interlocutors in the energy realm. Our emphasis on perception and recognition is not accidental. While powers need to be "recognized by others to have certain special rights and duties" (Bull 1977: 196), perceptions and images – key elements in the reception process – are important explanatory factors in understanding nuanced interaction among IR actors. Thus, our consideration of the EU's identity – and preference-shaping interactions with the BICS within global energy governance structures – is complemented by our analysis of external images and perceptions of the EU and its policies. Innovatively, EU external perceptions in the BICS are systematically compared not only to the EU's self-perceptions, but also to the BICS self-perceptions, and their external perceptions in the eyes of the EU and other BICS.

The rationale behind this complex 'matrix' of mutual perceptions stems from Onuf's description of international politics as a "world of our making" (1989, cited in Rüger 2012: 131). Following it, we recognise that existing international political structures are established through a process of interaction. This process takes place according to the "logic of appropriateness" (March/Olsen 1989), which suggests that actors interact based on shared values and norms. The roles of actor identity are important in this regard:

> These understandings – which can be called cultures, mentalities or discourses – are not simply subjective reflections of an objective, material reality, but rather emerge out of social interaction processes, through socialization, debate and sometimes coercion (Griffiths 2011: 159).

Hence, "[r]elations are a product of a historical process and interactions over time" (Fierke 2010: 182) and shaped by their mutual constitution (Nielsen 2014: 25). In our research, this level of theorisation is critical to understand a European External Energy Policy – a policy at the EU level. It is also helpful in searching for the answers to the questions concerning

> the type of actor that the EU constitutes regarding its policies towards the rest of the world and whether this actor is constituted by certain norms and values (Aydin-Düzgit 2015: 138).

In our case, the three norms we focus on are typical for the energy field, namely *security of supply*, *sustainability* and *competition* (elaborated in Chapter 3).

We also share the view that foreign policy may be conceived of as a

> discursive practice that constructs particular subject identities for states, positioning them vis-a-vis one another and thereby constructing a particular reality in which certain policies become possible (Doty 1993: 305, as cited in Aydin-Düzgit 2015: 138).

Within this constructed world, states – an original focus of the political scientists in this regard – possess a corporate identity, which means how they perceive themselves in relation to others (Griffiths 2011: 157). It is quite possible for actors to have several social identities (Ibid.), and these can change, as understandings of the world are reproduced and changed through discourses and actors' responses to them (Brand 2012: 217-218). Thus, discourses play an immense role in the creation of knowledge (Brand 2012: 214). As Wæver states:

> Discourse analysis does not claim that discourse is all there is to the world, only that since discourse is a layer of reality where *meaning is produced and distributed*, it seems promising for an analysis to focus on it (1999: 200, as cited and emphasised by Brand 2012: 235).

Importantly, discourse is a lens that allows us to focus on ideas. According to Schmidt (2008: 306, as cited in Carta/Morin 2014: 7), we are dealing with

> the representation of ideas (how agents say what they are thinking of it) and the discursive interactions through which actors generate and communicate ideas (to whom they say it) within given institutional contexts (where and when they say it).

In this light, Carta and Morin conclude, "the term discourse enmeshes textual and contextual elements, components of agency and structure" (Carta/Morin 2014: 7).

Constructivist theory can be drawn upon for studies at the macro and micro levels, as states, institutions and individuals are all acknowledged as actors. It is therefore also suitable when looking at the public sphere (Rüger 2012: 121, cited in Nielsen 2014: 26). Extending these arguments from their foci on states to the EU as a *sui generis* polity, our research assesses the potential effects of European External Energy Policy discourses on the relevant discourses of the EU's BICS partners – influential news media and elite opinion discourses in this book. We argue that these discourses provide a valuable source of reflection on how the EU and its energy interactions with the BICS are imagined and perceived inside the EU and in the BICS. Importantly, the BICS (or any other international agent) will also use the same discourses to communicate their own self-images vis-à-vis the EU as their important Other. Here, we argue that such a complex constellation of self- and Other-images and perceptions represents a crucial indicator to identify and assess EU recognition and reception as a global energy actor in the eyes of the BICS. Images are also interpreted here as "road maps" and "focal points" (Goldstein/Keohane 1993) that influence how policy-makers define a certain situation and give them clues on how to relate to their environment, how to diagnose a situation and which actions to choose (Cottam 1994; Shimko 1991 as cited in Chaban et al., forthcoming).

In summary, our book contributes to a constructivist direction in EU foreign policy studies that has

> gained momentum since the changes in the security architecture following the end of the Cold War and the step taken towards a more integrated foreign policy the EU (Aydin-Düzgit 2015: 137).

Our research, which is anchored within interpretative constructivism characterised by inherent duality, prescribes a complex architecture for our research questions and hypotheses, as well as diverse methods of analysis. With this book, we reiterate a view that any understanding of the world, and global energy governance in it, is based upon "collective interpretations, practices and institutions of the actors themselves" (Fierke 2010: 183). We add to this formula a need to explore external perception, recognition and reception, complemented by insights into self-visions and 'mirror' views. In combination, they serve as crucial determinants of external policy choices (including EU external energy policy) – ideas and perceptions count as important explanatory factors of the identity and role of the EU in foreign political issues (Rüger 2012: 132). Lucarelli and Fioramonti (2010: 1) echo this statement and suggest that

> self-rhetorical representation, public debate and mirror images are fundamental components of a political identity in the making like the EU/European one.

Understanding the perceptions of the "other" side can provide a "basis for improved communication and provide guidance on policy adjustments" (Wetterqvist 2009: 16, as cited in Chaban/Holland 2010: 128).

This chapter now turns to outline an analytical framework – the Normative Power Europe theoretical approach – that informs our investigation and provides explanatory power with respect to the two analytical foci described above: 1) the role of norms in the definition of the social structures of global energy governance and 2) the representation of ideas through particular discourses that constitute a layer of reality where the meanings of the EU as a global energy actor are produced and distributed.

1.2 Understanding External Energy Governance from a Normative Perspective

Social constructivist/discursive approaches often inform studies of EU external governance that seek to identify what type of actor the EU is. Many of these works ask if the EU's actorness is shaped by certain norms and values. Such works are typically informed by the analytical approach of 'Normative Power Europe' (NPE) (Manners 2002, 2006; Manners/Whitman 2003; Diez 2005, 2013; Lucarelli/Manners 2006; Sjursen 2006; Khasson et al. 2008; Gstöhl 2009).

A concept and a critical approach, NPE originally emerged as a means of understanding the post-Cold War world – and the EU as an actor in it (Manners 2002). NPE's definition as the 'ability to shape conceptions of "normal" in international relations' in the early 2000s (Manners 2002: 239) was conceived in the context of the EU's 'big bang' enlargement following the collapse of the Soviet Union. To gain entry into the EU, the then-candidate countries (many of which belonged to Europe's 'communist camp' during the Cold War) were transforming and moulding themselves to fit the canon of norms and values characteristic of NPE: democracy, human rights, rule of law, peace, liberty, social solidarity, good governance, anti-discrimination and sustainable government. This set of norms is not accidental. According to Manners, these particular normative values are a result of shared events in history (two devastating and degrading world wars in Europe), shared political space (the creation of a supranational EU), and a shared legal foundation driven by elites (the EU backed by treaties).

NPE has proved to be a popular and long-lived analytical tool that possesses explanatory power for understanding the EU's actorness in a changing, globalising multipolar world. As it enters its second decade, the NPE approach is regularly used to theorise on international relations beyond state-centred politics and beyond oppositions of hard *vs.* soft power, or military *vs.* civilian power (Whitman 2013). Manners' pioneering vision also made it possible to theorise on the EU in terms of its international identity, and the place and role of norms and values in it, while distinguishing the two aspects of normative power: "being normative and acting in a normative way" (see Whitman 2013).[5] These conceptual innovations remain relevant in understanding and explaining how the EU shapes and communicates its policies towards its global partners, including the BICS in the energy governance field.

Yet, we argue that NPE has overlooked the theorisation of the agency and identity of a *receiver* of the normative messages in the diffusion process (also noted by Diez 2005; Merlingen 2007; also Björkdahl et al. 2015; Scheipers/Sicurelli 2008). A receiver may identify itself as a proud owner and an eager sender of its own normative visions, which may differ from NPE. A receiver may react to the sent norms on a continuum, from adopting and adapting, to resisting and rejecting (Björkdhal et al. 2015). A multipolar, increasingly globalising world, characterised by networking and communication, including the global energy scene, dictates an urgent need to explore and conceptualise the norm-receivers, and their interactions with the norm-senders, to assess NPE's impact on third parties. This volume asks whether EU ideas and values, as a normative global energy actor, resonate with four receivers (the 'emerging' powers of the BICS) and whether and how the negotiation of normative meanings between the EU and BICS takes place. Norm re-interpretation and norm changes by receivers are expected – all of them are increasingly confident international actors that wish to be heard and understood by others. This multi-level elaboration of the process by which European norms are transferred within interactions with third countries – the emerging powers of the BICS in this case – is a highlight of this book.

The existing literature indicates that the EU's images as a normative actor are often contested in the 'mirror' of its external partners, particularly amongst the emerging powers. Our previous findings (Chaban et al. 2016; Chaban/Knodt 2016; Chaban/Knodt 2015; Knodt et al. 2015) indicate that emerging powers are only partially receiving EU normative messages in the field of energy governance. They also indicate a preference to have a different dialogue with the EU (in which 'the EU is talking with' rather than 'talking at' them) and often see themselves as norm-senders. Some of them

5 Whitman clearly differentiates between the two: "The former is a result of the nature of the EU or of its hybrid polity embracing intergovernmental and transnational governance, whereas the latter involves behaving in an ethically good manner" (Whitman 2013: 176).

communicate these in a more powerful and forceful manner (China, India); some of them are softer, with a weaker external message (Brazil, South Africa). Importantly, this volume considers China, India, Brazil and South Africa, as well as the EU, as normative foreign policy actors. This vision follows March and Olsen's 'logic of appropriateness' (March/Olsen 1989) – as mentioned above – based on their identity in their respective (normative) foreign policy actions.

This volume argues that the status of being and acting like a normative power is validated foremost by the *recognition* of such power in the eyes of others. By prioritising the issue of the external *recognition* of normative power, we echo an argument by Kavalski (2013), who stated '*to be* a normative power is oftentimes less important than to *appear to be* a normative power' (Kavalski 2013: 250). This is where our volume offers novel contributions. By assessing the EU's external images as a normative global energy actor, we trace the degrees and patterns of the EU's recognition as a normative power in external energy governance in the eyes of the BICS. We also identify what facets of the BICS' external energy governance are seen by the European receivers and what norms are perceived to be projected globally (and onto the EU) in the energy realm. Recognition, then, is suggested to underlie specific reactions – from the BICS to the EU, and from the EU to each of the BICS. Recognition is shaped by images and perceptions that are conceptualised by the relevant literature to be powerful 'cultural filters' (Björkdahl et al. 2015; Chaban et al. 2015; Chaban/Pardo 2015). Manners defines 'cultural filters' as "the interplay between the construction of knowledge and the creation of social and political identity by the subjects of norm diffusion" (Manners 2002: 245). His definition is informed by the work of Kinnval, who argues that cultural filters affect the impact of international norms and political learning in third states and organisations, leading to the learning, adaptation or rejection of norms (Kinnval 1995). Thus perceptions, explored systematically and empirically, can be instrumental in assessing global resonance of the EU and the BICS as senders of the 'normative' messages in the external energy governance field.

Following our earlier research (Chaban et al. 2016), our application of the NPE framework in this book is inspired by the 'third wave' of its theorisation (Nicolaïdis/Whitman 2013). This 'wave' invites scholars to undertake a "critical approach to Manners's concept as the starting point rather than an attempt to operationalise the notion of normative power Europe" (Whitman 2013: 186). Within this tradition, scholars are challenged to factor in

> structural changes in international relations problematising Europe's capacity for normative power; ontological and epistemological contestation of normative power Europe; and a contestation of Eurocentricity seen to be intrinsic to normative power Europe (Whitman 2013: 186).

Our volume addresses these three needs, applying them to a specific case of EU normative interactions – global energy governance. While IR research recognises the difficulty in measuring power and influence, our research, informed by a critically revised NPE approach and the concept of recognition within it, allows us to trace what norms have some perceived impact. The key in our quest for answers is a systematic consideration of interaction between the norm-senders and norm-receivers; norm-receivers' agency, identity and cultural filters; the resonance or clash between normative visions; perceived Eurocentric bias; and a two-way communication of normative meanings through various discourses.

1.3 Discourses and Representation of Ideas: Production of Meaning

Our next analytical focus – informed by interpretive constructivist approach discussed above – is the processes of the formation and distribution of normative meaning within influential opinion-making discourses. The focus of this book is on the discourses of an opinion-forming news media and influential elite opinion.[6] We examine how the BICS's elite stakeholders view EU as an external energy actor and how the EU stakeholders perceive the BICS in the energy field. For both groups, we explore how they perceive the interactions between the respective locations and the EU in the energy domain. We also assess media discourse – in the BICS and in Europe – used to communicate the EU and the BICS and their energy-related interactions. Our aim is to assess critically whether the EU's external energy governance is noticed, recognised and publicised and how EU images compare to the images of the four BICS. Our analysis of interactions through the lenses of messages, images, perceptions and frames reiterates the importance of communication between powers in an age of global governance.

Theoretical models informing our team's quest to explain complex processes of meaning formation and contestation – specifically, the meanings of the EU and the BICS as a global energy governance actors guided by a

---

6 We are clear that the international perceptions and expectations of actors can be evaluated through different types of sources, including official documents, interviews, media and surveys (Rüger 2012: 135).

normative identities – lay the foundation for a set of operationalisations used to craft the methods of analysis. These are detailed below – a content analysis of media images, with its categories grounded in cascading activation framing theory, a survey and interviews, and network analysis of elite opinions. The methods employed are characterised by their mixed use of qualitative and quantitative techniques.

1.3.1 Production of Meaning: Media Discourses

Theoretical framework

Our choice of the news media discourse rests on the premise that

> [f]or most of the foreign policy audience, the really effective political map of the world – that is to say, their *operational* map of the world – is drawn by the reporter and the editor, not by the cartographer (Cohen 1967: 13, emphasis in original).

The press is also considered to function as an observer in its search and presentation of foreign policy issues and as a catalyst that the public uses to satisfy its interests in foreign policy (Bersick et al. 2012b: 4-5). Importantly, the news media are able to influence not only the general public but also elites. Livingstone famously proposed the so-called 'CNN effect' (Livingstone 1997), which suggests among other interpretations that policy-makers react to the reality created by the news media, rather than to reality itself.

Media's significance in opinion formation is acknowledged in the studies of EU external perceptions. Media analysis has attracted attention from individual researchers and from large-scale multinational projects. Two foundational projects in the field of external perceptions of the EU – the transnational project 'EU Global Perceptions' led by Chaban and Holland (32 locations, 2000-present) (online, see also Holland et al. 2007; Chaban/Holland 2008, 2013, 2014; Chaban et al. 2009; Holland/Chaban 2010, 2014) and the 2006 FP6 GARNET project 'The External Image of the European Union' (16 countries) (online, see also Lucarelli 2007; Lucarelli/Fioramonti 2010) – prioritised the study of EU media imagery.[7] The former project 'EU Global Perceptions' is recognised as undertaking the most comprehensive media research in EU perceptions field. Its ongoing media analysis includes content analysis of verbal and visual images of the EU and targets various

7 This project considered external media representations of the EU by examining the press along the left–right continuum or government–opposition classification.

media (press, television and social media). It compares media images across time, studies the news production practices and surveys newsmakers' perceptions of the EU. This project's theoretical and methodological premises informed a large-scale media study of EU images in ten Strategic Partners of the EU commissioned by the European External Action Service, including the BICS (PPMI/NCRE/NFG 2015). Media analysis methods tested by the project 'EU Global Perceptions' inform media analysis in our volume. Importantly, our book contributes innovatively to media studies of EU images. First, it explores EU images from an issue-specific (energy) angle rather than an actor-focussed (EU) approach. Second, it traces the media's framing of the EU in an area of global energy governance overlooked by earlier research. Third, it systematically compares images of the EU produced by BICS media to the images of the BICS produced by European media (EU and EU Member States), a novel approach in EU perception studies.

Over the decades, a number of communication theories[8] have argued that the news media have powerful potential to shape opinions within and across societies. Diverse media theories hypothesise that news media are able to tell their audiences *what to think, what to think about* and *how to think about it.* Informed by these questions, and grounded in the cascading activation framing theory (Entman 2003, 2004), our study examines how the EU's meanings as a global energy actor are formed and spread through the media. This choice of this theory is intentional, as Entman's model was conceived to understand how meanings related to foreign policy are activated and diffused within a given society. Thus, we found the model to be instrumental in explaining how messages on external energy policy are formed, disseminated and activated at different levels in the EU and the BICS.

As its name suggests, the central analytical concept in the cascading activation framing theory is the concept of framing. While there is no scholarly consensus on how to define 'framing', this analysis follows a popular definition formulated by Entman in his earlier work:

> To frame is to select some aspects of a perceived reality and make them more salient in a communicating text, in such a way as to promote a particular problem definition, causal interpretation, moral evaluation, and/or treatment recommendation (Entman 1993: 52).

---

8 Among the most influential, we list agenda-setting theory (began in a seminal work by McCombs and Shaw (1972) and currently possessing a group of followers), media dependency theory (Ball-Rokeach/DeFleur 1976), and the common knowledge paradigm (Neuman et al. 1992).

This definition was further elaborated within Entman's theoretical model. For Entman, framing is "the central process by which government officials and journalists exercise political influence over each other and over the public" (Entman 2003: 417). In addition, framing is key to understanding of the process of political communication within a given society, especially successful political communication. Effective political communication, according to Entman,

> requires the framing of events, issues, and actors in ways that promote perceptions and interpretations that benefit one side while hindering the other (Entman 2003: 417).

The model further delves into the consideration of such 'successful' frames, arguing that they are consistent with the schemas that dominate the political culture: "the most inherently powerful frames are those fully congruent with schemas *habitually* used by most members of society" (Entman 2003: 422, emphasis original).

The theory also stresses the inevitability of contestation over the public framing of ideas, emphasising the limited cognitive facility at all levels of the 'cascade' – from administrative elites on the 'top' of the cascade (who are endowed with the utmost power to initiate the ideas), to non-administrative elites (including media professionals who create and disseminate news frames), to the general public. Elites on all levels "operate under uncertainty and pressure, with mixed motives and varying levels of competence and understanding" (Entman 2003: 420). Specifically, journalists will continue to

> work in accordance with established mental maps and habits and rarely undertake a comprehensive review of all relevant facts and options before responding (Entman 2003: 420).

Returning to our main research foci of global energy governance (a complex and ever-changing field) and the EU (a complex and unique polity), we share Entman's premise that "what passes between levels of the cascade is not comprehensive understanding but highlights packaged into selective, framed communications" (Entman 2003: 421). Thus, a systematic analysis of framed communication – at different societal levels, but foremost on the media level – is critical for understanding how elites and general publics in the BICS and the EU imagine global energy governance and what EU and BICS roles are supported or opposed.

Within the model, the media are credited with a central role. Ideas concerning foreign policy and international relations are argued to emerge at the top level, with the national administration. This level is considered the most powerful in activating 'selective, framed communications' on foreign policy issues that are then spread 'down the cascade' to other elites (including media elites). Researching perceptions of the EU as NPE among Asian newsmakers, Chaban/Holland (2015: 288) cited Entman (2003: 420) who suggested that the interaction between newsmakers and administrative and non-administrative elites is a

> key transmission point for spreading activation of frames, and it is not always easy to determine where the line between 'elite' and 'journalist' should be drawn, or who influences whom Entman (2003: 420)

also notes an important element of communication exchanges among newsmakers and acknowledges the so-called "cueing system": prestigious and influential national media outlets generate and supply selective communication highlights to "other national media, to regional newspapers and to local papers and television stations". Chaban/Holland (2015: 288) reiterated Entman's idea that effectively, in a given society, a limited number of opinion makers "exercise more sway over the spread of ideas than all but the most powerful public officials" (Entman 2003: 420).

The resulting news frames produced by journalists are then spread through the media to the general public, who are argued to have the weakest ability to form and spread ideas on foreign policy. As in a real cascade or waterfall, it is easier for information to flow from the top downwards than in reverse (Chaban 2016, forthcoming). Yet, the public is nevertheless able to provide feedback to influence elites on external policies, and it primarily does so through media. As such, even though each level in the metaphorical 'cascade' makes a contribution to the mix and flow of ideas, we consider the media to play the key role in the spreading and activation of ideas on foreign policy and international relations, both up and down the metaphorical cascade.

Our research presented in this volume also focuses on 'selective, framed communications' in the media and makes clear that the framing is not arbitrary. Notions of power and strategy are seen as informing the framing of decisions by newsmakers. In their study of external media professionals' perceptions of the EU, Chaban/Holland (2015: 289) quoted Entman (2003: 422) who argued that newsmakers are aware of their "capacity to ask questions and to decide precisely which words and images to assemble and transmit". Yet, there are other considerations beyond those of power. Framing decisions are also triggered by journalists' motivations concerning decisions of what to present and how to present it, as well as "economic pressure and incentives; professional customs, norms, and principles; and normative values" (Entman 2003: 422, as cited in Chaban/Holland 2015: 289). The last element clearly links cascading activation framing theory to models that study normative power and flows of communication around such power (see also Chaban/Holland 2015). Significant for this book is the theory's point on the notion of 'successful frames' based on congruence with the schemas that dominate political culture. This point necessarily brings us to the question of norms and values that constitute this culture and are shared by its members – as discussed above.

Methods

Content analysis is among the most popular research methods in analysing news media. Characterised by its approach of evaluating content from different text sources in a systematic and consistent manner, it offers an opportunity to study both manifested and latent content (e.g. newspaper articles can also be analysed in the sense of what is *not* reported [Häder 2006: 319]). The abundant literature in the field of content analysis agrees that the approach's main strengths are minimum interference by a researcher in the production of the primary data, thereby limiting researcher bias; its intersubjective traceability (Früh 2011: 27); its ability to analyse materials dating back in time (Häder 2006: 325) to trace changes in content over time; and its openness to qualitative, quantitative and mixed approaches in research design and data analysis.

For our analysis, we selected prestigious, leading newspapers in each BICS country and in Europe (leading newspapers in three EU Member States – France, Germany and the UK – and a pan-European weekly, *The European Voice*[9]). While each BICS country in our sample uses various channels for news (print, broadcast and internet), leading newspapers remain prominent opinion-shapers and primary sources of news for national elites, educated citizens, other domestic media, at both the regional and local levels, and external observers. Online editions of influential newspapers have given a second life to this media genre despite gloomy predictions of newspapers becoming extinct due to competition from broadcast and internet channels. Bearing in mind the ability of prestigious and influential national media outlets to trigger the "cueing system" (Entman 2003: 420) discussed above, our analysis focuses on two prominent national dailies in

---

9 *Politico* as of April 2015.

each of the BICS and each of the three EU Member States we consider (Table 1.1) a popular prestigious newspaper and a leading business daily. In addition, the European sample also includes a prestigious national analytical weekly in each location. The size of the sample is justified by the reality of a large comparative project (to remind our readers, the data came from transnational project "EU External Perceptions" (EXIE) described in the Introduction). In such projects, "the sample should be kept narrow in scope and nature in order to facilitate realistic execution of a large scale, transnational, comparative project" (Sreberny-Mohammadi et al. 1985: 10). Paramount to our analysis is that the chosen papers are among most important opinion-shapers and agenda-setters in our respective locations, boasting high circulation, nationwide distribution and international reputations. Their journalists and editors are recognised as respected and influential opinion-formers, members of the national elites.

Table 1.1: All outlets observed, by country

	Country	**Prestigious national daily**	**Business**	**Weekly**
BRICS	Brazil	Folha de Sao Paulo	Valor Economico	
	Russia*	Kommersant	Vedomosti	
	India	The Times of India	The Economic Times	
	China	People's Daily	21st Century Business Herald	
	South Africa	The Star	Business Day	
The EU	Germany	Süddeutsche Zeitung	Handelsblatt	Der Spiegel
	France	le Figaro	les Echo	Le Nouvel Observateur
	The UK	The Guardian	The Financial Times	The Economist
	The EU		European Voice	

*Russian data is not analysed in this volume
Source: EXIE, 2015.

The choice of different types of papers – specifically popular prestigious and business papers – was critical to ensure the diversity and quality of media sources in our limited sample, as well as comparability across all BICS and European locations. Business papers were included because energy matters and relations are topics that are typically closely intertwined with economic and financial matters that resonate within national business communities. The popular prestigious papers (be they dailies or weeklies) address energy matters within a broader context, in addition to economic considerations. These newspapers feature large national readerships and are examples of quality press institutions with respected domestic and international reputations. Where possible, we selected the papers to include various political perspectives.

The period of observation spans over five years: 2009-2013. The year 2009 was chosen as our starting point because that year marked crucial changes for the EU in global politics, with the emergence of the European sovereign debt crisis and the failed Copenhagen Conference of the Parties (COP) to discuss the United Nations Framework Convention on Climate Change (UNFCCC). The UNFCCC conferences were chosen because they represent a global forum that traditionally addresses issues of sustainability, including in the energy domain. As global energy governance is highly fragmented, there is no international organisation or forum in which all of our countries are involved in an equal manner, which is a necessary prerequisite for comparison. At the COP 15 in Copenhagen, for the first time, the BICS challenged the EU's role as a sender of normative messages about climate change and sustainability. The challenge that the BICS made to the EU and the EU's underperformance during the summit captured global media attention. The following COPs were often seen as an arena for the EU to revise and redeem its reputation (2013 was selected as an end point following the framework of the research projects that inspired this book). We contend that a five-year sample (with a focus on one month of coverage surrounding the conferences to ensure comparability across years) represents a sufficient time frame to trace changes in 'normative' meanings assigned to the EU and in the framing of the EU as an energy counterpart for the BICS.

In each BICS and EU case, we observed coverage of the EU and/or the BICS and energy matters during the two weeks of the COP, as well as one week before and after the climate summit. This time period was expected to feature numerous reports in which the EU and the BICS will appear in interaction within these international negotiations. The discussions at the COPs offer a common frame in which climate and energy issues are discussed. This is because of the distinctive feature of energy relations; they have a strong 'nexus quality': energy as a policy field is an almost canonical crosscutting issue, standing in very close connection to climate policies. Since we elected to monitor in our analysis one month of coverage surrounding the conferences, we also expected a certain bias in the findings. Namely, we predicted *sustainability* issues to dominate the coverage of the global energy governance and the EU's role in it. Yet, as this volume will demonstrate, it was not global but *local* priorities that led the framing of energy issues in general and of the EU and other global actors in particular. As such, despite our initial expectations, the research reported in this book revealed only limited implications of the sampling period on the framing in question – *sustainability* was often not the most dominant frame in the BICS or EU cases under analysis.

Table 1.2: Collected sample in the EXIE project (2009-2013)

Location	**'Energy' field**	**'The EU as an actor' field**
Brazil	587	307
Russia**	962	578
India*	567	192
China	1633	571
South Africa	405	385
Total BRICS	4154	2033
France	881	307
Germany	773	654
UK	752	424
The EU	198	168
Total European	2604	1553

*India was observed during the period 2011-2013 due to data access limitations. To compensate, our analysis included an additional two week period of observation on the coverage of EU-India Energy Summit (two weeks, 16.01.-17.02.2012): 53 articles

**Russian datasets are not analysed in this book

Source: EXIE, 2015.

Two conceptual fields were analysed: *images of the EU* as an actor in various policy areas (including energy) and the representations of *the semantic field 'energy'* with all actors in this field (including the EU and the BICS). This volume elaborates on the data collected within the latter field, leaving the former field to future investigations (except for brief references in the country-specific chapters). The chosen approach allowed us to compare images of the EU as a global energy actor (and media frames of its external energy governance) with the images of other main actors (and media frames of their energy governance). Special attention was given to the images of the BICS appearing alongside the EU and their interactions. Since the new multipolar world is a world of networking and communications, the project was specifically interested in the communication patterns between the EU and the BICS as well as within the BICS group concerning energy matters. We studied these *relations* in terms of framing. The analysis also took note of other actors that appeared in the coverage when the EU and the BICS were mentioned (e.g., the US). As such, the data facilitate a multi-vector portrayal of the global networks of the EU and the BICS when newsmakers report about these key international actors in the field of energy relations and the key messages that they send and receive.

Electronic databases storing daily editions of the papers were searched with key words, allowing for high precision in collecting the data. For the dataset on the thematic field 'energy', the key search terms were 'energy', 'oil', 'gas', 'coal', 'fossil', 'nuclear', 'biofuel', 'biomass', 'solar', 'wind', 'hydro', 'tidal', 'renewable', 'thermal', 'EEP'/'European Energy Policy'. Other key search terms, in addition to the list above, were: the EU (and/or its major institutions of the European Commission, European Parliament, European Central Bank, European Court of Justice, EU Council and/or EU Presidency) and/or any of the BICS countries, or the terms 'BRIC' or 'BRICS'. Despite the limited time period under observation, the EXIE project (discussed in the Introduction) collected a large volume of newspaper articles, yielding a dataset with 10,344 news items from all locations in the project (Table 1.2). In this volume, we focus only on four BICS cases and four European cases using the 'energy matters' dataset – 3,245 articles in the former case and 2,604 articles in the latter collected by the project. Textual and visual data were the focus of analysis in this project; however, this volume will examine only the textual framing of the EU and BICS as global energy actors.

To answer the leading research questions of this book, our analysis had to focus only on those articles that reported the EU and BICS as an *energy actors*. This requirement led to a smaller final sample (Tables 1.3 and 1.4).

Importantly, low numbers are a finding in itself, and it is discussed in a greater detail in the country chapters.

A crucial aspect of any content analysis protocol is the formulation of categories for the analysis. The categories used in this volume are distinctly theory-driven, grounded in cascading activation framing theory. Specifically, the model differentiates between frames that have greater capability to "stimulate support of or opposition to the sides in a political conflict" (Entman 2003: 417) and frames that fail to stir the activation of ideas. According to Entman (2003: 417, emphasis original), the former – or, as we call them here, 'capable' – frames are those that 1) resonate culturally within and across different levels in the network (meaning that they are "*noticeable, understandable, memorable,* and *emotionally charged")* and 2) are characterised by magnitude (including "*prominence* and *repetition*"). This volume will examine media content with the goal of identifying EU frames that may be described as more 'capable' than others – i.e., more visible, locally resonant and emotionally loaded (Table 1.3). Our analysis also asks which EU framings were 'weaker' – i.e., of peripheral visibility, not locally grounded and/or not emotionally charged. Finally, we were interested in identifying 'latent' frames – facets of the EU and its BICS counterparts that did not appear in media coverage of energy matters.

Table 1.3: Samples of articles referencing the EU as an energy actor in the BICS "energy-related" news

Location	**Country-specific samples**
Brazil	78
India	29
China	87
South Africa	14

Source: EXIE, 2015.

Following the content analysis method presented by Chaban et al. (2016), *visibility* was operationalised in this volume in two respects – the *volume* of coverage and *degree of centrality*. *Volume* was measured through the number of stories that contained the key search terms. To complement *volume* as a measure of visibility, we also employed the notion of the *degree of centrality*. In this category, we assessed whether the actors – the EU and the

BICS – were mentioned with a minor reference (only once and peripherally), a secondary one (the coverage of several actors in a news story is balanced, with none dominating), or a major one (the actor was the leading, dominant actor of the story). *Degree of centrality* was introduced to ensure a more nuanced assessment of actors' media visibility.

Table 1.4: Samples of articles referencing BICS as an energy actor in the European "energy-related" news

	Brazil as energy actor	India as energy actor	China as energy actor	South Africa as energy actor
France	63	97	217	36
Germany	74	59	241	22
UK	117	143	336	66
The EU*	1	3	12	1

*The overall low number of articles from the *European Voice* meant that only China's images were analysed in this book
Source: EXIE, 2015.

Local resonance was operationalised in terms of *sources*, the *foci of domesticity*, *thematic frames*, *issues, contexts and types of energy* and *actors*. The *sources* (journalists, opinion-makers or news agencies) were assessed in terms of their origin – local *vs.* international sources. This category also accounted for non-attributed news items. We hypothesised that locally sourced news would possess greater potential for being 'understandable' to and generate local resonance among domestic audiences, as they are often 'anchored' in local contexts and feature familiar personalities. Linked to this idea is our next category – *the focus of domesticity*. In it, we identified the focus of the story according to a four-part framework: whether the news story was situated within domestic, regional, external or global contexts.[10]

The *thematic frames* category was included to assess evidence concerning the normative agenda on global energy matters. Importantly, our analysis assessed not the framing of the entire article but of every key actor reported in the article (the EU and/or the BICS). A tripartite framework of the

10 This category was not used in the analysis presented in this volume.

three specific energy 'frames' guided our analysis in this category – *competitiveness*, *security of supply* and *sustainability*. Special attention was paid to the identification of additional thematic frames and alternative interpretations or framings, particularly in the locations that were conceptualised as receivers of the EU's normative messages. Within those frames, further analysis determined leading energy *contexts*, *issues,* and *types* (Table 1.5) and the state and non-state *actors* associated with them.

The visibility and framing of an actor in relation to two *types of energy – renewables* and *non-renewables* – was assessed. The former category captured reportage on oil, gas, coal, nuclear and fossil fuels. The latter assessed the coverage of renewables in general, as well as wind, solar, hydro, biofuels, biomass, thermal and tidal. We also examined reporting on the actors in relations to the following *issues* – investments, prices, urbanisation, emissions, energy policy/governance, energy access, energy efficiency, energy saving, energy infrastructure, cooperation, and sustainable development. Finally, we assessed the *contexts* of the media representations of the EU and BICS as energy field actors – economy, politics, development, environment, climate change, safety, culture and normative.

Emotional charge was operationalised through the evaluation category. Our analysis first generated generic evaluations by employing the following set of perspectives: *positive*, *positive-to-neutral*, *neutral*, *neutral-to-negative*, negative or *mixed.* To confirm the generic assessment and to retrieve location-specific emotive images, we also assessed evaluations associated with metaphorical categorisations of the actors (defined within the tenets of the Conceptual Metaphor Approach [Lakoff/Johnston 1980]). Analyses of news texts and evaluations within them were performed by pre-trained researchers, who are educated native speakers able to identify subtle nuances in connotations.

Data collected according to these categories were then analysed using both qualitative and quantitative techniques. This mixed approach is essential for the multi-level assessment and measurement of 'capable' *vs.* 'weak' frames in terms of visibility, local resonance and emotive charge.

Table.1.5: Categories of analysis as operationalisations

Visible			Understandable						Emotionally charged	
Volume	**Degree of centrality**	**Sources**	**Actors**	**Frames**	**Focus of domesticity***	**Contexts**	**Issues**	**Types**	**General evaluation**	**Metaphor**
Number of articles	Major Minor Secondary	Local International N/A	European Union European Commission European Parliament European Central Bank European Court of Justice EU Council EU Presidency Eurozone EU Member States BRICS/ BRIC Brazil Russia India China South Africa Other	Sustainability Competitiveness Security of supply Other	Local Regional 3rd country Global	Politics Economy Development Environment Climate change Safety Culture Normative Social affairs	Invesments Prices Urbanisation Emissions energy policy/ governance energy access energy efficiency energy saving energy infrastructure cooperation sustainable development	*Non-renewables:* Oil Gas Coal Nuclear Fossil *Renewables:* Renewable(s) Wind Solar Hydro Biofuels Biomass Thermal Tidal	Positive Neutral-to-positive Neutral Neutral-to-negative Negative	Positive Neutral Negative

*This category is not elaborated in this volume

1.3.2 Production of Meaning: Elite Opinion

In his 1976 seminal work, *Perception and Misperception in International Politics*, Robert Jervis links images and perceptions to the behaviour of actors in external affairs, famously stating,

> it is often impossible to explain crucial decisions and policies without reference to the decision makers' beliefs about the world and their images of others. That is to say, these cognitions are part of the proximate cause of the relevant behaviour (Jervis 1976).

As such, our choice of the elite discourse rests on the assumption that

> decision makers act in accordance with their perception of reality, not in response to reality itself. [...] In any event, all decision-makers may be said to possess a set of images and to be governed by them in their response to foreign policy problems. Indeed, elite images are no less "real" than the reality of their environment and are much more relevant to an analysis of the foreign policy flow (Brecher 1968: 298).

Unsurprisingly, many studies of external perceptions of the EU have prioritised analytical insights into the views of elite 'movers and shakers' around the world (for reviews, see Chaban/Holland 2015; Elgström/Chaban 2015). The analysis of elite opinion undertaken in the three foundational projects in the field of EU perception studies: 1) Chaban and Holland's project "EU Global Perceptions" discussed above, which covered 32 locations and sourced original data from elite and public opinion polls, in addition to news media (online; see also Holland et al. 2007; Chaban/Holland 2008, 2013, 2014; Chaban et al. 2009; Holland/Chaban 2010, 2014); 2) the 2006 FP6 GARNET project, 'The External Image of the European Union,' which covered elites in 16 countries, five international organisations, and several multilateral settings (online; see also Lucarelli 2007; Lucarelli/Fioramonti 2010); and 3) the project, 'New Roles for the EU in International Politics?' that researches perceptions of international negotiators in various multilateral settings such as the UN Forum on Forestry, the Conference on International Trade in Endangered Species of Wild Fauna (CITES) and the World Trade Organization (2004-2006) (Elgström 2006, 2007a, 2007b, 2008, 2010; Kilian/Elgström 2010; Bäckstrand/Elgström 2013). Of special interest here is Elgström's ongoing study in multilateral settings at the UNFCCC COPs (Kilian/Elgström 2010), which follows the impact of developments at the COP 15 in Copenhagen (2009) on the EU's reputation. In addition, there are a number of other studies of EU perceptions in individual countries or geopolitical regions. These include a Southeast Asian focus group survey of elite opinion (EuropeAid Final Reports 2003, 2007), reflections from Australia (Murray 1999, 2002), Japan and the US (Tsuruoka 2006), India

(Lisbonne-de Vergeron 2006) and China (Lisbonne-de Vergeron 2007). Several studies have also considered images of the EU in the multilateral UNFCCC COPs (Gupta/Grijp 2000; Karlsson et al. 2011). The reality of a globalising, multipolar world has inspired a number of the most recent EU external perception studies to explore EU images and perceptions among stakeholders from emerging powers: China (FP7 project 2009-2011), India (Jain 2009), and Russia (Secrieru 2010; EuropeAid 2010). Studies comparing views from emerging powers are also increasingly popular, for example comparative studies of elite views from China and India (Lisbonne-de Vergeron 2011; see also work by NFG Research Group 'Asian Perceptions of the EU' [online] during the period 2011-2014). Reviewing these many studies reveals an evolution of the images of the EU in the area relevant for our analysis. While the pre-Lisbon/pre-Euro debt crisis period was marked by a recognition and perception of the EU's emerging leadership in combatting environmental damage and climate change. According to Chaban and Holland (2015: 679),

> [p]ost-2009 surveys of global elite opinion indicate a shift towards more negative and sceptical external perceptions […] The EU's failure in the 2009 UN CCC cast a negative shadow on the vision of the EU as an international leader in climate change.

Our volume contributes innovatively to literature on perceptions of the EU, focusing on elite opinion research. First, it elaborates on perceptions in the previously overlooked issue area of energy governance. Second, it compares mutual elite perceptions between the EU and each BICS. Third, it employs a combination of several methods to trace and assess elite opinion in the EU/Member States and the BICS on energy interactions.

Analysing EU-BICS energy governance relations from a 'normative' perceptive requires research methods that combine quantitative and qualitative approaches. Research on norms demands a distinct perspective on the meaning and use of language, a demand that can best be satisfied by drawing on qualitative approaches. Research on governance structures requires some 'explorative' methodology, as well as more detailed heuristics derived from multi-level governance approaches, thereby allowing the institutional structures, informal and flexible stakeholder relations and the broader regulatory frameworks to be taken into account. Therefore, a combination of several methods informs this part of our analysis – semi-structured expert interviews, a cross-country survey based on a structured questionnaire, a network analysis and document analysis. These research instruments complement one another, thereby allowing us to identify image of external energy governance using several empirical tools (Müller et al. 2015a: 26).

Qualitative, semi-structured expert interviews with the key actors from Europe (the EU and Member States – the UK, Denmark, Spain and Germany) and the BICS provided insights into elite perceptions of the content, structures, highlights and challenges of energy cooperation. In total, 150 interviews were conducted from February 2012 to December 2013 and involved EU officials in Brussels and the EU Delegations in the BICS; officials from the above listed EU Member States; Chinese, Indian, Brazilian and South African government officials; and representatives of business associations, NGOs, chambers of commerce, development agencies, and business actors representatives of state-owned enterprises from EU Member States and emerging powers. The interviews were conducted in Bangalore, Beijing, Berlin, Brasilia, Brussels, Cape Town, Copenhagen, Eschborn, Johannesburg, Hannover, London, Madrid, Mumbai, New Delhi, Pretoria, Rio de Janeiro, and São Paulo by 15 pre-trained researchers. Here, we used a semi-structured set of questions, partly corresponding to those from our survey (discussed below) but adapted to the respective roles and expertise of our interview partners. Specific emphasis was placed on institutional knowledge of governance structures. Furthermore, we emphasised the importance of constructivist thinking on perceptions, as "decision makers act in accordance with their perception of reality, not in response to reality itself" (Brecher 1968: 298). This method complemented the structured questionnaires, as it enabled us to gain first-hand insights, trace personal experiences of the respondents and elicit recommendations, which then formed the basis for our subsequent analysis. Employing qualitative interpretative methods for our analysis and to improve the reliability of the research, the collected data were then analysed using content analysis methodology (Chaban et al. 2009; Müller et al. 2015a: 27).

The survey[11] contained 25 questions – 22 closed and 3 open questions. It consisted of five sections, which asked respondents for their personal views on 1) participation in EU-Emerging Powers cooperation on energy issues, 2) procedural aspects of EU-Emerging Powers cooperation on energy issues, 3) the importance of events and fora during EU-Emerging Powers cooperation on energy issues, 4) the EU and Brazil/India/China/South Africa as dialogue partners, and 5) secure, competitive and sustainable energy policy. A pilot study was conducted in India and Brussels. It was conducted with the participants in the four EU-BICS Energy Dialogues. We identified

11 All data were collected and stored with the project leaders at the Technische Universität Darmstadt, Germany. When referring to the evaluation of our survey data in the following chapters, the source reads EnergyGov, Darmstadt, 2014.

all relevant participants who were engaged in the Energy Dialogues on a regular basis. In addition to the English version, the questionnaire was also translated into Portuguese and Mandarin. Overall, 143 questionnaires were completed, for an average response rate of 52 per cent. Individual response rates range between 39 and 73 per cent. While the response rates were rather similar in the cases of China (49 per cent), South Africa (45 per cent), and India (39 per cent), Brazil's rate was markedly higher, at 73 per cent (Müller et al. 2015a: 27).

The survey included a network question to allow us to use the provided information as a heuristic tool to describe the energy dialogues and map relevant stakeholders in EU-emerging powers cooperation on energy issues (Schneider et al. 2009). In analysing the network data, we used relational data processed with the assistance of social network analysis (SNA). Emerging in the late 1980s, SNA has become a standard form of analysis, especially in inter-organisational research. In brief, the essentials of the method are as follows. Based on own knowledge of the case at hand and on prior expert interviews with representatives of those organisations that are particularly familiar with a specific policy domain and this domain's participants, the researcher begins by drafting an organisation list, which is then presented to actors that form part of that list. Depending on the exigencies of the research project, a number of questions are then asked to the respondents. In our case, we limited our attention to only two types of information: first, the reputation of domestic and supranational public and non-state organisations within the energy policy domain and, second, the exchange of strategically important information among these organisations. Respondents were presented lists of other organisations, both public and non-state, domestic and European (35 in India, 40 in South Africa, 41 in Brazil and 49 in China), and asked to mark the most relevant actors for cooperation between emerging powers and the EU on energy issues. For each national case, this produced networks containing confirmed and unconfirmed, i.e., reciprocal and unilateral, reputational ties together with the rank orderings of actors in terms of prominence. In this volume, we present both types of information, that on reciprocal relations and that on unilateral choices. Concerning the information on individual institutions and organisations, such as, these actors' positions in terms of in-degree and betweenness centrality, we considered all ties in our networks independent of whether they are unilateral or reciprocal (Müller et al. 2015a: 27).

The same procedure was conducted for the second question, where the same organisations were asked to identify those actors with whom they maintain regular contacts in terms of information exchange. This, again, resulted in the production of several binary square matrices containing relational data on the extent to which any two actors maintained more or less frequent ties of resource exchange. The responses to these questions were then stored in rectangular data matrices that, after initial elaborations, contain entries ranging between 1 and 3 depending on whether actor "I" choses actor "j" (1), actor "j" choses actor "I" (2), or both chose one another, the latter meaning that we have a reciprocal relationship of, mutual reputation and mutual exchange. With the aid of the appropriate software (ucinet), both of these types of matrices – on reputation and information exchange – were then subjected to a visual representation procedure, thereby generating network graphs that present basic information in a way that allows it to be easily grasped and described (for a visual version of the networks, see Piefer et al. 2015a). This volume contains the condensed description of the results. Conclusions on the form of EU-BICS energy cooperation are drawn from the mapping of relevant stakeholders combined with insights into the structure of information exchange. Furthermore, the comparison of the different country networks allows for interpretations of which actors occupy central positions in a given structure, who is actually 'the spider in the web' and the most prominent gatekeepers or brokers in energy cooperation (Müller et al. 2015a: 27-28).

In a final step, we subjected our data to a blockmodelling procedure to discover more about relational performance across different types or categories of organisations. To do so, we re-grouped our data matrices according to the affiliation of our network members into one of four categories: respective BICS public, respective BICS non-state[12], EU public, and EU non-state institutions and organisations. We then partitioned the matrix and calculated the density values for each of the resulting four sub-matrices. Each partition obtaining a density value equal to or higher than the density of the respective overall network was assigned a value of '1' such that the resulting 4x4 image matrices could now be redrawn as very simple graphical representations (see Piefer et al. 2015a). Thus, we are able to state

12 For this volume as well as for the EnergyGov project, non-state actors are defined as all actors that are not part of the public administration (public actors) and follow a business, agency, association, or NGO logic. We are aware that defining actors in these two categories is not an uncontestable endeavor, as we would e.g. include state-owned companies which are organizational hybrids that combine an entrepreneurial for-profit orientation with varying forms and degrees of public ownership and accountability to politicians (see Müller et. al 2015a: 18).

which actor category is more active in attempting to reach other actor groups.

The theoretical and methodological positions described here inform the logic and structure of the four country-specific chapters in this volume (Chapters 4-7). After setting the scene, each chapter starts with a detailed consideration of the respective BICS country's energy policy and energy priorities. This lays the foundation for understanding the BICS countries' energy dialogues with the EU, which are elaborated next. Within this context, we discuss the first set of our "perceptions" findings – elite perceptions of the energy dialogue detected through the network analysis, elite interviews and the survey, and the analysis of the relevant documents. Then, we shift to the analysis of the mutual images as energy actors found in media and elite discourses. We first analyse visibility, issues, types and contexts of the EU's energy-related images in the BICS media and BICS' images in European media. We proceed by comparing these to the elite perceptions of the motivations to engage in cooperation on energy issues. In the following section, we discuss normative media framings of the EU and BICS as energy actors, comparing media findings vis-à-vis elite normative framings of the EU and BICS. The next section of each chapter explores to what extent the two actors perceive one another to be willing and able to cooperate. Here, we assess evaluations of the EU as an energy actor in the BICS media and of BICS in the European media. We contrast these findings with the perceived roles of the EU and BICS in the energy dialogue traced through elite interviews and the survey. In the final section, each chapter details how actors other than the EU and BICS appear alongside the EU and BICS in the field of energy governance (in media and elite discourses). Chapter conclusions elaborate on where our findings indicate challenging clashes and promising resonances in mutual perceptions and how these can obstruct or advance the EU's energy dialogue with the respective BICS country.

Chapter 2
EU Strategic Partnerships with the BICS in a Changing World: Great Expectations or Problematic Reality?

2.1 Introduction

In a provocative argument, Whitman and Rodt suggested, “The EU and its Member States are becoming less important in an increasingly multi-polar world” (2012: 42). Yet, they also argued that both the EU and its Members “want to remain relevant beyond their borders” (Ibid.). To achieve this aim, they “need to establish and maintain constructive relationships with existing and emerging powers on the world stage” (Ibid.). Informed by this argument, the following chapter explores the EU’s relations with four emerging powers – Brazil, India, China and South Africa – and lays the foundation for our specific focus on the EU’s energy relations with the BICS considered in subsequent chapters.

One of the leading frameworks for the EU’s future – “Europe 2020 – A Strategy for Smart, Sustainable and Inclusive Growth” – declared the overarching aim for the EU: to strengthen the EU’s economy to combat the economic crisis. The Strategy listed priorities for the EU in achieving this aim: new opportunities for employment, education, combatting poverty, research and innovation and – important for our research – climate preservation and sustainable energy. Naturally, these priorities are impossible to achieve in isolation from the rest of the world, which is characterised by rising economic interdependence, external competition, and mounting security challenges. In this context, the EU recognises the need for a consistent response in its external political actions (European Commission 2010). This argument is also predominant in the EU’s new Global Strategy on Foreign and Security Policy – “Shared Visions, Common Action: A Stronger Europe” (EEAS 2016a). One response to the new global economic divides and power shifts has been the EU’s establishment of Strategic Partnerships: the EU identifies a group of established and emerging powers (great and middle) that the EU designates as Strategic Partners and invests in relations with them. Currently, this group includes (in alphabetical order) Brazil, Canada, China, India, Japan, Mexico, Russia, South Korea, South Africa and the US. Dialogues with these countries are multifaceted (trade, international security matters, cultural exchange, research, etc.), with energy being an intrinsic aspect of each facet. The emerging powers in this group (including the BICS) present a so-called 'strategic interest' for the EU – to the EU, these relations need to be viewed from a political rather than a technical perspective (European Commission 2010: 23).

Despite similar structures and elements, the ten Strategic Partnerships (SP) differ dramatically from one another, thus raising critical questions about the EU's definitions of them. Furthermore, the EU adopts a confusing attitude towards these partners. The EU highlights the importance of "mutual recognition" while simultaneously discussing "the adaption of our rules and standards" by the partners (European Commission 2010: 23). These observations are echoed by Ferreira-Pereira, who notes the ambiguity inherent to these Strategic Partnerships:

On the one hand, the establishment of an Strategic Partnership is generally associated with the existence of shared world views, but on the other hand, the EU is seen as behaving as if its own rules and visions of the world must be universally accepted, something that limits its own understanding of others' views (Ferreira-Pereira 2015: 651).

The former EU President Van Rompoy once famously noted, "Until now, we had strategic partners, now we also need a strategy" (Council of the European Union 2010). What does a new EU Global Strategy tell us about Strategic Partners? The new EU Global Strategy persists in the ambiguity. It formulates, on the one hand, strategic approaches:

> In pursuing *our goals*, we will reach out to states, regional bodies and international organisations. [...] We will *partner selectively* with players whose cooperation is necessary to deliver global public goods and address common challenges (EEAS 2016a: 18, emphasis added).

On the other hand, several Strategic Partners are never mentioned (e.g., Brazil, Mexico and South Africa). The EU Global Strategy mentions "principled pragmatism" (EEAS 2016a: 8) in the EU's external actions – "we [the EU] will engage in a practical and principled way [...]" (EEAS 2016a: 4). Yet, the nature of the EU's mission with respect to the Strategic Partners in its external action remains unclear, perhaps indicating that the concept is losing its attractiveness for the EU. Some would say, looking at the missing Strategic Partners in the new Global Strategy, that the EU does not assign priority to these relationships. Nevertheless, importantly for this volume, energy is one of the main themes in the EU Global Strategy and is considered in many contexts: developing a new generation of trade agreements, defence and security (traditional and non-traditional) ENP, development, diplomacy (and specifically energy diplomacy), and scientific cooperation (EEAS 2016a).

This chapter examines in greater detail the bilateral relations between the EU and Brazil, India, China and South Africa. While the official framework for these relations entails a common set of parameters across the four BICS (trade agreements, cooperation agreements, etc.) (Keukeleire/Bruyninckx 2011: 385), there are major differences among the four countries in their interactions with the EU. These are explored throughout this chapter, after we examine the institute of EU Strategic Partnerships in general.

2.2 The Strategic Partnerships of the European Union

In its external relations, the EU engages at the multilateral, interregional and bilateral levels. The Strategic Partnerships are situated at the bilateral level, but they are also regarded as important tools in gaining allies in an effective multilateral order within the UN framework (Keukeleire/Delreux 2014: 300). While the Strategic Partnerships with the US and Canada date back to 1995 and 1996 (and that with Japan to 2001), the Partnerships with Brazil (2007), South Africa (2007), Mexico (2010) and South Korea (2010) are of more recent vintage. The Strategic Partnerships with China and Russia were initiated in 2003, while the EU and India formed a Strategic Partnership in 2004. Further concrete Strategic Partnerships were suggested by former High Representative Catherine Ashton with Egypt, Israel, Indonesia, Pakistan, and Ukraine (Rettman 2010), such steps have, however, not yet been taken. The EU-Ukraine Association Agreement, signed in spring 2014, is yet to be fully ratified. The main obstacle is the negative vote by the referendum in the Netherlands in April 2016 (Van der Loo 2016). Indonesia is mentioned in the EU Global Strategy, with the aim of expanding the EU's partnerships (EEAS 2016a: 38). Israel is only mentioned in relation to the Israeli-Palestinian conflict (EEAS 2016a: 34), while neither Egypt nor Pakistan are mentioned. "Like-minded and strategic partners in Asia, Africa and the Americas" (EEAS 2016a: 43) are, however, referred to with respect to facing global challenges but without reference to any specific country.

The establishment of the Strategic Partnerships is argued to be a response to global power shifts and an effort by the EU to better position itself in a globalised world (Gratius 2013: 1). The increased attention and importance given to new and emerging powers reflects global power changes and are symbolic of "the political will of the EU to be part of the new global game"

(Gratius 2013: 2). Yet, the concept of 'strategic' partnership remains unclear, as the EU still lacks a clear definition of this term (Knodt et al. 2015a: 6). The sceptical opinion of the former President of the European Council, Herman Van Rompuy, quoted above, is shared by EU external action professionals. While one EU diplomat rather positively stated, "It's like love – no one can define it. You only know what it is when you experience it," another diplomat, striking a more critical note, noted that the term is being used "without anyone ever really defining what it meant and whether, indeed, the others regard us as their Strategic Partners" (cited in Rettman 2010). The confusion seems to be long-lived. In 2003, the European Security Strategy stated that the EU "should look to develop strategic partnerships, with Japan, China, Canada and India" (European Council 2003: 14). This overlooked the fact that the EU at that time had already established Strategic Partnerships with Japan and Canada, with the latter dating back to 1996.

To complicate the story, how the EU chooses its Strategic Partners is not necessarily straightforward. Some scholars even argue that this grouping reflects the EU's

> inability to agree and decide which third actors are genuine strategic partners and consequently its inability to behave strategically in relation to these partners (Keukeleire/Bruyninckx 2011: 389).

However, the EU's commitment to the idea of Strategic Partnerships shows that the EU has

> indicated its desire for these arrangements to deliver comprehensive, contractual, rule-based relationships with its strategic partners in the long term (Whitman/Rodt 2012: 36).

As such, the Strategic Partnerships seem to be an aspiration rather than a reality:

> In most cases, the 'strategic partnership' with the emerging or re-emerging powers is rather a goal to be pursued through a gradual process of interaction than a reflection of reality (Keukeleire/Delreux 2014: 291).

A rhetorical façade hides the lack of clear means of implementing the objectives and political goals within the Strategic Partnerships and often consists of a vague and general catalogue of common political aims (Ibid.).

Yet, to overcome these shortcomings – and in light of the 'Europe 2020 Strategy' – the Partnership Instrument was agreed upon as a "new and complementary instrument providing direct support for the Union's external policies" (Regulation (EU) No 234/2014, 11.03.2014). It has been conceived as a tool to cope with major global challenges (including energy security, climate change and environmental protection) and to support the EU's strategic interests. The Partnership Instrument contains four main objectives: the provision of policy support for the EU's external relations and responses to global challenges; projection of the internal dimension of Europe 2020; the improvement of market access, trade, investments and business opportunities for EU companies; and the promotion of public diplomacy and academic cooperation.[13] This has been seen as an important step by the EU to improve its Strategic Partnerships. Yet, it remains to be seen whether this initiative will actually enhance the quality of strategic relations. Keukeleire and Delreux (2014: 291) have argued, that in most cases, the launch of Strategic Partnerships has not been able to either facilitate achievement of a common vision or to create shared values in international politics. Some commentators have also noted that it has not affected the external perceptions of the EU in a positive manner (Ibid.). However, our book would argue for a more cautious attitude in this regard. The 2015 survey of public opinion on the EU in ten EU strategic partners (PPMI/NCRE/NFG 2015) demonstrated that the majority of the general public in the BICS countries has a positive view of the EU (consisting of 'very positive' and 'somewhat positive' responses): 59 per cent in Brazil, 56 per cent in China, 63 per cent in India, and 53 per cent in South Africa.[14] Respondents in the BICS also generally chose positive descriptors when they were asked to describe the EU: strong, efficient and multicultural in Brazil; multicultural, modern and strong in China; modern, strong and efficient in India; and strong, modern and multicultural in South Africa (PPMI/NCRE/NFG 2015).[15]

Finally, most respondents across the BICS countries perceived that EU's leadership role in world affairs as both desirable and likely. In terms of desirability, between 50 per cent and 60 per cent of respondents in Brazil and China, and between 60 per cent and 70 per cent in India and South Africa argue for the EU's strong leadership role (PPMI/NCRE/NFG 2015). In

13 Available at: http://ec.europa.eu/dgs/fpi/what-we-do/partnership_instrument _en.htm [05.05.2016].

14 The public opinion samples in the BICS countries were: 1210 respondents in Brazil, 1410 in China, 1056 in India, and 1169 in South Africa (PPMI/NCRE/NFG 2015), available at: http://ec.europa.eu/dgs/fpi/documents/showcases/eu _perceptions_study_executive_summary_with_country_fiches.pdf [05.08.2016].

15 Please note that the "multicultural" descriptor was seen ambiguously, with potentially negative connotations, as 2015 was shaped by the migration crisis and the EU's handling of it.

terms of likelihood, in the four BICS countries between 60 per cent and 70 per cent of respondents agree that the EU is likely to take a strong leadership role in the world affairs five years from now (PPMI/NCRE/NFG 2015).

These rather positive perceptions indicate that the institution of Strategic Partnership has strong potential to resonate with the publics of the BICS countries. Nevertheless, as addressed above, the EU lacks clear definitions and an actual 'strategy' for its Strategic Partnerships with its selected partners.

2.3 EU-BICS Strategic Partnerships

EU strategic relations with the BICS, which are among the EU's ten Strategic Partners, have thus far been marred by major challenges and limitations. First, these emerging powers share the aspiration to 'counterbalance' to the global dominance of the Western powers. Due to their increasing economic and political importance, these actors are seen as possessing growing influence at the global level. They also forge alliances among themselves to make their voice heard internationally. Second, these emerging powers consider themselves to be increasingly important players in 'South-South' cooperation. In this context, the BICS can all be seen as competitors of the EU in the search for markets, resources, and political influence (Keukeleire/Delreux 2014: 293-294). Third, the EU's commitment to the "promotion of international norms and multilateralism" (Sautenet 2012: 134) vis-à-vis the priority given to the ideas of national sovereignty and non-intervention within the BICS (Keukeleire et al. 2011: 1) challenges their relations:

> The BRIC countries have a preference for non-legally binding political commitments, do not have a particular preference for all-inclusive multilateralism, and generally start from a realist perspective on sovereignty (hard sovereignty) (Keukeleire/Bruyninckx 2011: 398).

The BICS' preference to follow the paradigm of a "*multilateralism à la carte*" (Saxer 2012: 70) contradicts the EU's orientation toward "effective multilateralism" based on "[t]he development of a stronger international society, well-functioning international institutions and a rule-based international order" (European Council 2003: 9). These features often lead to tensions in cooperation with the EU, making true 'Strategic Partnerships' difficult to achieve.

However, as we have seen in this chapter thus far, despite or even due to these challenges, the EU believes that it needs to cooperate more closely with these emerging powers. This is also due to the EU's changing role in international politics and the rising importance and influence of the BICS.

In the "Implementation of the European Security Strategy", all of the BICS are mentioned as countries of interest to the EU (European Council 2008). In the EU Energy Security Strategy, both India and China are mentioned as major consumers, and in the context of the EU being a major global energy consumer, as relevant international partners for cooperation with the EU (European Commission 2014a). Important for our research, there are several idiosyncratic contexts for energy interactions between the EU and its Strategic Partners. Among the four BICS, China especially is seen as major economic competitor, specifically in the area of green technology (European Commission 2010: 14-15).

2.3.1 Brazil-EU Relations

Diplomatic exchanges between the EU and Brazil date back to the 1960s. Initially, the relations between Brazil and the EU were mainly framed through the EU-Mercosur cooperation and focussed on economic issues (Piefer et al. 2015a: 34). The relationship between the EU and Mercosur was institutionalised through an interregional framework agreement in 1995, with the EU supporting the idea of regional integration in South America. With the accession of Spain and Portugal to the European Economic Community (EEC) in 1986, bilateral cooperation with Brazil was advanced. New attention to Brazil was formalised through the Framework Cooperation Agreement with the EEC in 1992. This cooperation addressed by broad areas, covering political, economic, social and technical issues. Through financial assistance, the EEC supported economic reforms, social development and environmental protection in Brazil. An Agreement for Scientific and Technical Cooperation was signed in 2004 (Whitman/Rodt 2012: 34).

In 2007, the bilateral relations were intensified through a Strategic Partnership, which was supported in a major way by the Portuguese EU Presidency at that time (Knodt et al. 2015a: 6; Whitman/Rodt 2012: 34; Santander 2015: 183-184). This Strategic Partnership stresses cooperation in the following areas: promotion of effective multilateralism, sustainable energy, Mercosur integration, general stability in South America, and the global fight against climate change and poverty. The Joint Action Plan signed in 2008 focuses on peace and security through an effective multilateral system; sustainable development; regional cooperation; science, technology, and innovation; and people-to-people contacts and cultural exchanges (European Commission 2014b).

The new action plan covering 2012-2014 involves diverse areas of cooperation, including "general UN matters, drugs, tourism, space cooperation, disaster risk preparedness and small and medium-sized enterprises (SMEs)" (EEAS 2011). The focus of the last area is on regular Brazil-EU Business Summits, including SMEs, as well as opportunities for exchanging best practices (Council of the European Union 2011: 12). In 2013, the first meeting of the EU-Brazil Sector Dialogue on Drugs was held, focusing on common approaches towards "the global drug problem" (Council of the European Union 2014: 11). Energy, education, climate change and the environment are further issues covered in the more than 30 sectorial dialogues that exist within the framework of the EU-Brazil partnership. The most recent dialogue – signed in 2014 – is on International Cyber Policy.[16] This dialogue concerns Internet Governance, where Brazil and the EU aim at establishing an inclusive, transparent, multi-stakeholder model of Internet Governance. One initiative within this agreement is to lay a direct cable from Brazil to Portugal, instead of through the US, and thereby save costs and achieve cheaper data transmission (Council of the European Union 2014; Lazarou 2015). More concrete initiatives should appear in the new Joint Action Plan (2015-2017). However, this Joint Action Plan has not yet been finalised. A high-level meeting, which was scheduled for 2015, has been postponed until 2016 due to the ongoing EU-Mercosur negotiations on an Association Agreement[17] (and has thus far not taken place). Despite this delay, relevant documents dated from 2015 show some progress in the bilateral relationship, especially regarding Internet Governance, as well as cooperation in environmental and sustainability issues (Lazarou 2015; EUBrasil 2015). In November 2015, the Head of EU Delegation to Brazil, João Gomes Cravinho, stated:

> Our relationship (Brazil – EU) is becoming more political. I.e, we exchanged more and more ideas, express concerns and gain the advice of each on matters of political matters. (EUBrasil 2015).

Yet, the current political and economic situation in Brazil necessarily affects these bilateral relations, as they imply considerable uncertainty regard-

---

16 Available at: http://europa.eu/rapid/press-release_STATEMENT-14-235_en.htm [21.05.2016].

17 Available at: http://en.mercopress.com/2015/08/28/brazil-eu-summit-next-year-following-exchange-of-proposals-with-mercosur [20.05.2016].

ing Brazil's near-term development. Brazil is facing a deep economic recession, which began with a massive corruption scandal at the oil company Petrobras. President Dilma Rousseff was suspended in spring 2016 and impeached in August 2016 following accusations of corruption (Reuters 2016).

One reason for the shift in the EU's attention from Mercosur to Brazil is the lack of progress in Mercosur-EU relations, the increasing importance of Brazil as actor on the international scene, and the influence of Portugal (Ferreira-Pereira 2015: 649). Mercosur and the EU were unable to intensify their cooperation, as the EU had expected they would. The EU's expectation of exporting its model of regional cooperation was not met, as the Latin American countries were reluctant to abandon their national sovereignty *á la* the EU's *sui generis* model (Whitman/Rodt 2012: 34; Santander 2015: 182-183). According to the EU, Mercosur had failed to create a collective bargaining body, and the EU began to doubt the effectiveness of regional institutions and their power in international relations (Santander 2015: 185). Closer cooperation had been hoped for, especially on trade and other economic issues, yet negotiations have been progressing slowly. Nevertheless, Mercosur can still be considered an important ally of the EU in the promotion of regional integration and interregionalism (Ferreira-Pereira 2015: 649). Negotiations on an Association Agreement with Mercosur were initiated in 2000; however, these were suspended in 2004 (European Commission 2014b). For several years, these negotiations were considered deadlocked (Keukeleire/Delreux 2014: 293), yet they were reopened in 2010. The EU-Brazil Joint Action Plan from 2011 evinces a strong commitment to the strengthening of EU-Mercosur relations. A goal to achieve "an ambitious, balanced and comprehensive EU-MERCOSUR Association Agreement" (Council of the European Union 2011: 3) remains in place. The agreement faced challenges not least due to different visions of priorities. For the EU side, the most crucial emphasis should have been on the protection of intellectual property rights. For the Mercosur member states, the focus was agriculture (Santander 2015: 193). Since the end of 2015, the two parties have been close to exchanging offers, which finally took place in May 2016.[18] Yet, as a consequence of European farmers' protests against the negotiations (due to higher competition on meat prices and standards),

18 http://en.mercopress.com/2016/05/12/eu-and-mercosur-exchanged-market-access-offers-beef-and-ethanol-excluded-as-sensitive-products [31.07.2016].

'sensitive' issues, such as meat and ethanol, were excluded from the exchange offers (Burke-Kennedy 2016).[19]

From the EU side, stronger engagement with Brazil can be seen as a recognition of global shifts in power. In the Implementation of the European Security Strategy, Brazil is highlighted as one of the Strategic Partnerships that has grown in significance since 2003 (European Council 2008). In a communication from the Commission on EU-Latin America relations, Brazil is described as a major player with considerable influence in regional affairs (European Commission 2005). Brazil has established an active and wide-ranging diplomacy, resulting in growing international visibility, strengthened relations with Northern powers and increased 'South-South' cooperation. It has achieved more influence in international affairs and raised its profile in multilateral fora (Santander 2015: 186-187). These characteristics make Brazil an attractive and interesting actor to the EU.

Due its economic rise, Brazil has also become one of the largest donors aiding poor countries (Santander 2015: 186). This makes Brazil a potential partner for the EU in the form of triangular cooperation. In a Joint Statement from 2011, both actors express the desire for closer cooperation on coordinating a global partnership on development aid (Council of the European Union 2011). The EU stated its readiness to promote triangular cooperation with Brazil in developing countries (particularly in Portuguese-speaking Africa and Timor-Leste), in such sectors as health, energy, agriculture, education, justice and security (European Commission 2014b: 3).

The EU's intensified cooperation acknowledges Brazil's increasing importance in world politics. Brazil's opposition to the liberalisation of agricultural trade in the current WTO negotiations has encouraged the EU to enter into dialogue with Brazil to reach a consensus. Importantly, the EU considers Brazil an ally on international issues, due to shared values in several areas (Whitman/Rodt 2012: 36-37), including support for human rights – the EU-Brazil Human Rights Dialogue is held annually in Brasilia. The EU and Brazil appear to be like-minded actors regarding the protection of human rights, abolition of the death penalty, protection of children's rights, fight against discrimination, and freedom of religion and belief (European Commission 2014b: 2). However, despite these shared values, little has

19 However, the chief negotiator of Mercosur, Uruguayan Foreign Minister Rodolfo Nin Novoa, stated that these issues are part of the negotiations, yet without any specific volumes or time span: http://en.mercopress. com/2016/05/13/uru guay-says-beef-and-ethanol-are-included-in-mercosur-eu-proposals-but-with-no-volumes-or-time-span [31.07.2016].

been achieved in reaching common positions and joint action in international politics (Santander 2015: 192-193).

Regarding trade, South America as a whole, and Brazil in particular, are markets of great interest to the EU. Despite declining trade volumes due to the economic crisis, the EU represented Brazil's largest trading partner in 2015, followed by China and the US. For the EU, Brazil is the tenth largest trading partner. The EU is the largest foreign investor in Brazil, representing half of the latter's FDI flows between 2008 and 2012.[20]

The US's traditional profile and influence in South America and China's rising political and economic presence in the region, particularly in Brazil, challenge the EU's position. The growing presence of China in Latin America is of particular note for the EU. China is exhibiting greater importance in South America not only economically but also politically. China's increasing presence on the continent has begun to have notable impacts, e.g., China has granted market economy status to several countries, including Brazil (Santander 2015: 188). For Brazil, its relations with the EU are in this sense strategic, as they can help to counterbalance its relations with the US and China (Santander 2015: 190-191). Despite competing actors, such as China and the US, and the difficult inter-regional negotiations between the EU and Mercosur, the EU still strives to gain better access to the Brazilian market. Renewable energy is one area where Brazil is regarded as a country with considerable potential (Whitman/Rodt 2012: 36).

Brazil still regards the EU as a major economic power, especially in the area of technical cooperation. Nevertheless, under most presidents until Luis Ignacio "Lula" da Silva, Brazil had a generally sceptical and negative view of the EU, as it has mainly been regarded as a player that routinely creates trade complications for Brazil (Gomes Saraiva 2012: 45-46). However, some EU Member States – especially Germany, France, Italy, Spain and Portugal – are considered important (economic) partners (Ibid.). In recent years, the EU's ongoing economic crisis has negatively influenced perceptions of the EU in Brazil: "The crisis has […] harmed the EU's image abroad – particularly in Brazil, where media often depict it as a 'continent on the verge of collapse'" (Santander 2015: 192). The author continues with an argument on how this perception influences the behaviour of Brazilian officials – they become "less inclined to work closely with EU representa-

20 http://ec.europa.eu/trade/policy/countries-and-regions/countries/brazil/ [01.08.2016].

tives on a daily basis" (Santander 2015: 192). To be fair to Brazilian officials, the mix of European voices – that of the EU in developing a Strategic Partnership and that of the EU Member States in interacting with Brazil in parallel to the EU – is sometimes difficult to understand. Intentions conflict and messages are unclear. Nevertheless, Santander suggests that despite this polyphony, the Brazilian official side acknowledges the EU's undertakings towards common foreign policy (2015: 190).

The EU and Brazil cite one another as strategic partners. Yet, this rhetoric clashes with reality, as the two do not recognise one another as crucial partners. Brazil is omitted from several EU official documents on external relations (for example, the European Security Strategy [Whitman/Rodt 2012: 40], the Europe 2020 Strategy and EU Global Strategy of 2016), suggesting that the EU keeps overlooking Brazil as a significant partner. This is despite the normative alignment between the two actors and Brazil's foreign policy goals echoing those of the EU. To Brazil, bilateral relations with the EU Member States have always been regarded as more important than its relations with the EU (Piefer et al. 2015a: 39). Nevertheless, Brazil's decision to join a Strategic Partnership with the EU has delivered benefits – according to Whitman and Rodt, this Strategic Partnership has led to Brazil exercising growing importance in its immediate geopolitical region (2012: 40).

2.3.2 India-EU Relations

The relations between India and the EU were institutionalised with a Cooperation Agreement on Partnership and Development in 1994. This agreement still serves as the framework for EU-India cooperation. In 2000, the first EU-India summit was held (Jaffrelot 2006: 330), and one year later, a 'Joint Initiative on the Enhancement of Investment and Trade' was signed (Sautenet 2012: 130). In 2001, the EU-India Science and Technology Cooperation Agreement was signed, and in 2004, a Human Rights Dialogue was established. In 2010, the two partners adopted a Joint Declaration on International Terrorism (EEAS 2016b), and a Joint Declaration on Research and Innovation was agreed to in 2012.

The Strategic Partnership between India and the EU was launched in 2004, "to enable both sides to better address issues of common concern in the context of ever-increasing globalisation" (EEAS 2016b). This Partnership was established one year after the publication of the European Security

Strategy in 2003, which highlighted India as one of the EU's important partners (Knodt et al. 2015: 6). It was initiated alongside a Joint Action Plan, which came into force the following year and was reviewed in 2008 (Keukeleire/Delreux 2014: 292; Sautenet 2012: 130). This Joint Action Plan entails a broad range of areas of cooperation, such as security issues, migration, education, climate change, trade and, important for our study, energy (Council of the European Union 2005).[21] Annual high-level meetings were held until 2012 (Allen/Smith 2015: 169). However, none were held for the next four years. The summits resumed only in March 2016. The latest (2016) summit adopted the "EU-India Agenda for Action", featuring a concrete roadmap for the next five years, covering several areas. These include foreign policy, security, exchange, energy and climate change. Implementation of this agenda is to take place through the different instruments existing within the dialogue, for example the Partnership Instrument, as well as through the relevant joint working groups (European Council 2016). The impact of this agenda is a subject for future investigations. Thus far, EU-India relations have produced numerous agreements but lacked concrete realisation. As Winand and Vicziany note:

> The problem is perhaps not so much in having an exhaustive relationship covering every aspect of EU–India relations, as in implementing the various agreements that have been concluded (Winand/Vicziany 2015: 3).

The EU and India have also agreed to cooperate in various areas at the international level. These include counter-terrorist cooperation, democracy and defence of human rights. However, cooperation on international issues is often hindered by a lack of consensus between the two and, moreover, is often regarded as having only symbolic value. This is demonstrated by several international negotiations in which the EU and India were involved. For example, the EU and India adopted diverging positions in the WTO's Doha round, the reform of the UN Security Council and the nuclear non-proliferation negotiations (Keukeleire/Bruyninckx 2011: 388). Despite a common desire for further cooperation on peacekeeping missions, different views hindered this development (Jain 2014a: 16). In addition, the two actors seem to view international politics in different ways. While the EU strongly believes in the importance of institutions or norms, India has a different approach and does not believe that institutions alone can secure international peace (Mohan 2006: 260). Furthermore, the aim of India to reform international institutions is not supported by EU Member States, which are keen to

21 See Chapter 6 for specific details of the EU-India Energy Dialogue.

maintain their positions in various international organisations and are unwilling to make individual national concessions (Allen/Smith 2015: 167). Despite these diverging views at the international level, both the EU and India aim to strengthen their bilateral economic cooperation (as evidenced by numerous sectorial dialogues and regulatory policies), development cooperation (mutual support for the millennium development goals), intellectual and cultural exchanges, and the improvement of institutional frameworks (Jaffrelot 2006: 330). Finally, climate change and the environment are increasingly important areas of cooperation (Gratius 2013: 5).

The EU remains India's largest trading partner, while India is the EU's the ninth largest trading partner (EEAS 2016b).[22] Additionally, the EU is an important foreign direct investor in India (Allen/Smith 2015: 168-169). FTA negotiations between the two have been ongoing since 2006 and were supposed to enter their final phase in 2011 (Chaban/Elgström 2014: 182). Yet, despite 14 rounds of negotiations, they have not yet come to a successful conclusion (Allen/Smith 2015: 169). These 'deadlocked' negotiations are credited with escalating tensions in the bilateral relations, as well as with having a negative influence on other areas of cooperation, including energy (Piefer et al. 2015a: 50).

The sovereign Euro debt crisis is argued to have negatively influenced progress in the FTA negotiations (Allen/Smith 2015: 169), but it is not the sole issue. Some scholars describe this FTA as too ambitious, covering market access for goods, services, investment, intellectual property, and social provisions related to sustainable development (Allen/Smith 2015: 169). India was keen to leave non-trade issues out of the negotiations. Yet, the EU, and especially the European Parliament, has been pushing for an ambitious and legally binding sustainable development chapter. The agreement is also seen to affect the regulations on intellectual property rights on medicines, which would have negative consequences for low-income groups in India. This triggered protests by civil society groups – in the EU and India – during the various rounds of negotiations (Legg 2014: 349-351). The EU admits

22 In the aftermath of the Brexit referendum, it is important to recall that the UK represents a significant share of EU-India trade flows: In the current fiscal year, more than 25 per cent of India's exports to the EU went to the UK. The UK is the largest investor in India among the G20, and the UK is the top destination for India's investments. This will also have an impact on current free trade negotiations between the EU and India: http://www.thehindu.com/business/Economy/uk-starts-trade-talks-for-postbrexit-deal-with-india/article8824943.ece [31.07.2016].

that progress is still needed in several areas of the FTA negotiations, including market access for some goods and services, sustainable development and government procurement (EEAS 2016b).

The relations between India and the EU are challenged by the exaggerated attention that the EU has given to China. After having neglected India and its potential as a rising economy, the EU has become increasingly aware of India as a strategic partner, with the aim of improving the balance in its relations between India and China (Piefer et al. 2015a: 47). At first glance, prioritising China over India seems somewhat paradoxical. When it comes to common social and political values, the EU and India are sometimes called "natural partners" (Coulon 2006: 347) – India and the EU share democratic values. EU officials also stress the shared beliefs between the EU and India (Winand/Viczianky 2015: 4). Nevertheless, the infrastructure of the EU-India Partnership is not nearly as developed as that between China and the EU, and far below its potential in general (Allen/Smith 2015: 172). Prior to 2008, the relations between India and the EU were generally economic and commercial. Scholars of EU-India interactions doubt whether the relationship has gone beyond these issue areas, despite the comprehensive nature of the strategic partnership. EU Member States often seem reluctant to agree on collective interests towards India (Allen/Smith 2015: 169).

Scholarship on India's changing role in international politics stresses India's links to the US, overlooking India-EU interactions. Exceptions are a recent work by Winand, Vicziany and Datar from 2015 and several publications by Jain, which also specifically focus on EU perceptions in India (see, among others, Jain 2015, 2014a, 2014b, 2007; Jain/Elsenhans 2006 and Jain and Pandey's studies on EU perceptions in India in 2015 and 2014). Relevant research argues that India is somewhat dismissive of the EU's role in international affairs (Allen/Smith 2015: 167-168) and does not perceive the EU as a "major security actor" (Allen/Smith 2015: 170) (see also Lisbonne-de Vergeron 2006). The EU appears to have lost influence, not only due to the economic crisis but also because the EU is no longer perceived to be a frontrunner in various research areas (Jaffrelot 2006: 329) (this is important for our research). Dismissive attitudes seem to be mutual –

> [...] a declining Europe finds it convenient to remain skeptical of India's rise and is in any case limited in what it can achieve, particularly in security issues (Allen/Smith 2015: 168).

India's security concerns (including issues related nuclear arms) are among the most sensitive areas in EU-India interactions. Unsurprisingly, India finds more enthusiastic support from other international actors in its aim to become a leading international power (Jaffrelot 2006: 329). For example, the relations between India and the US are seen as strong and of strategic importance to India. Relations with China are also of immediate strategic interest to India (Allen/Smith 2015: 171). In addition, the policy and academic discourses frame ASEAN+3 as being increasingly important to India in geopolitical terms. Yet, India has little to gain from the EU's engagement in South East Asia through ASEAN, due to the EU's very limited impact in the region (Allen/Smith 2015: 171). The EU is seen to lack a strategic vision and imagination in its outreach to the South East Asia; it also fails to recognise that India is searching for allies in the region to counterbalance China's growing influence in Asia (Allen/Smith 2015: 172).

In its interactions with the EU, India tends to differentiate between relations with the EU from relations with individual EU Member States. Despite a plethora of official declarations on EU-India relations, India still perceives some EU Member States as much more engaged in their diplomatic relations with India than the EU (Allen/Smith 2015: 171). Problematically, EU Member States' interactions and bilateral agreements with India tend to undermine the role of the EU as a single actor, harming the EU's reputation as a "viable and worthwhile interlocutor" (Allen/Smith 2015: 168). In several instances, a dialogue initiated by the EU and India was followed by bilateral dialogues between India and individual EU Member States (Allen/Smith 2015: 171).

Hence, as we have seen, EU-India relations feature a set of challenging moments. Core issues such as the promotion of democracy and intervention in national sovereignty are also challenging the partnership, as these are viewed differently by the two sides (Winand/Vicziany 2015: 5). Here, India regards the EU's criticisms of its internal policies on human rights, the Kashmir conflict and child labour as unwanted interference in its national affairs (Jaffrelot 2006: 332, on human rights see also Jain 2014a: 13-14).

To conclude, the current dialogue between the EU and India indicates that better mutual awareness and understanding are needed to enhance the existing Strategic Partnership. Immediate areas of concern include the need for the EU to listen more attentively to India's security concerns, as well as to address the problematic reception of and reaction to the EU's normative messages towards India. The relationship is also in need of concrete milestones – research in the field calls for specific timelines, measurable indicators and achievable goals in the official agreements between the EU and India (Joshi/Ganeshan 2015: 154). Jain argues in a similar vein:

> The two sides [...] need to focus on a smaller number of longer-term strategic priorities than cluttering the agenda, but this is not always easy as many dialogues seem to take on an inherent institutional life of their own (Jain 2014a: 10).

Whether the recently adopted "EU-India Agenda for Action-2020" will improve the course of relations remains to be seen.

2.3.3 China-EU Relations

Among the BICS, the partnership between the EU and China is the most extensive and institutionalised (Mergenthaler 2012: 253). It features several annual meetings and over 50 sectoral dialogues. Three pillars characterise EU-China relations: the 'Political dialogue', 'Economic and sectoral dialogue' and 'People-to-people dialogue'. The engagement of the EU with China dates back to 1975, when the EC established diplomatic relations with China. This was followed by the first trade agreement between the EEC and China in 1978 (Mergenthaler 2012: 255) and then by a Trade and Economic Cooperation Agreement in 1985.[23] At present, the latter agreement remains the only legal framework between China and the EU (Mergenthaler 2012: 256).

With its Communication titled "Building a Comprehensive Partnership with China" (COM 1998), the Commission presented its fundamental aim for the EU-China relationship. The Communication, the resulting Council conclusions and the Report on the Implementation of the Communication (European Commission 2000) stressed the Union's fundamental interest in strengthening relations with China and developed five aims: (1) Engaging China further, through an upgraded political dialogue, in the international community; (2) supporting China's transition to an open society based upon the rule of law and the respect for human rights; (3) further integrating China into the world economy by bringing it more fully into the world trading system and by supporting the process of economic and social reform underway in the country, including in the context of sustainable development; (4) making better use of existing European resources; and (5) raising the EU's profile in China. In reaction to a change in government, which took office in March 2003, and with it the coming to power of a new generation of Chinese leadership, the Commission launched another policy paper, "A

23 http://eeas.europa.eu/china/index_en.htm [01.08.2016].

maturing partnership – shared interests and challenges in EU-China relations", which was embedded in the wider EU-Asia strategy of 2001 (European Commission 2001). The paper also called for increasing the emphasis on the EU-China relationship in the light of a forthcoming Chinese policy paper in which the Chinese side intended to reflect on the China-EU relationship (Knodt et al. 2012).

The decades since 1985 have shown that the relationship has deepened. This is mainly due to increasing economic interactions, accompanied by a further institutionalisation of the dialogue (Mergenthaler 2012: 256). Current interactions feature numerous areas of cooperation, but the main driver of the bilateral partnership is trade. In 2015, the EU was China's largest trading partner, and for the EU, China was the second-largest trading partner after the US.[24] The EU is also among the main sources of foreign direct investment to China. The EU's main imports from China are industrial and consumer goods (machinery and equipment, footwear and clothing, furniture and lamps, and toys), while the EU exports machinery and equipment, motor vehicles, aircraft, and chemicals.[25] Services, however, constitute only 1/10 of total trade (Ibid.). This leads to the EU having a rather high trade deficit with China – meaning that the value of the EU's imports from China exceeds that of its exports to China. This is mainly a result of low-cost Asian value chains but is also partly due to remaining market restrictions in place in China (Ibid.). The EU's non-recognition of China as a market economy and its imposition of anti-dumping duties represent the next set of challenges to be addressed in this asymmetrical bilateral trade relationship (Lai/Shi 2016).

Political dialogue between the two partners was initiated in 1994 to enable communications on common concerns. Since 1998, annual summits have been held and covered a wide range of topics, including security issues

---

24 See http://ec.europa.eu/trade/policy/countries-and-regions/countries/china/ [01.08.2016]. It has though to be kept in mind that EU-China trade relations are also based to a great extent on the UK-China trade relations with the UK being the second biggest European exporter to China (with a big distance after Germany). Thus, Brexit will also change the EU-China relationship. China already approached the UK with the proposal of a UK-China free trade agreement in August 2016: http://exporthelp.europa.eu/thdapp/display.htm;jsessionid=055D6975D0B2CD3B0BF2F7DEE00D6E13?page=st%2fst_Statistics.html&docType=main&languageId=en [29.09.2016].

25 http://ec.europa.eu/trade/policy/countries-and-regions/countries/china/ [01.08.2016].

and climate change. In 2008, the first High Level Economic and Trade Dialogue Mechanism was held and was followed by other high-level dialogues, e.g., on strategic and foreign policy issues in 2010 (Nielsen 2014). In 2003, the Strategic Partnership was officially launched through a Joint Statement (Sautenet 2012: 126). Earlier that year, the EU had expressed its aim to develop this Strategic Partnership with China (European Council 2003: 21). With the Strategic Partnership progressing well, the EU sought to create a more comprehensive strategy with respect to China, especially after several discussions, e.g., on the arms embargo in 2003/2004, during which diverging opinions among the individual EU Member States had become clear (Mergenthaler 2012: 265). In 2013, negotiations on a comprehensive EU-China Investment Agreement were launched. The focus was on the liberalisation of investments, and the aim of the Agreement was to provide a secure and simpler legal framework for both Chinese and European investors.[26] In July 2016, the 18th China-EU Summit was held in Beijing[27], shortly after the publication of the Joint Communication on "Elements for a new EU strategy on China" (European Commission 2016a). The strategy also highlights the 'Comprehensive Agreement on Investment' and the EU's aim to complete negotiations on this in the near future (European Commission 2016a: 2).

The sectoral dialogues cover several issues, including trade, economics, the environment, human rights and energy. The dialogue on energy was established in 1994. It is described as "one of the most constructive areas of cooperation"[28] and entails six areas of cooperation: renewable energy, smart grids, energy efficiency in buildings, clean coal, nuclear energy, and energy legislation.[29] Close cooperation in this area seems natural due to China's rising energy demand. Furthermore, it is an area with considerable investment potential for the EU (see Chapter 5 for a detailed description of the EU-China energy dialogue).

Finally, the EU-China High Level People-to-People Dialogue was initiated in 2012. It focuses on exchange among youth and in education, culture, research, gender equality, and multilingualism (European Commission

---

26 http://ec.europa.eu/trade/policy/countries-and-regions/countries/china/ [22.05.2016].

27 http://eeas.europa.eu/top_stories/2016/130716_mogherini_eu-china_summit_en.htm [01.08.2016].

28 http://eeas.europa.eu/delegations/china/eu_china/energy/index_en.htm [01.08.2016].

29 https://ec.europa.eu/energy/en/topics/international-cooperation/china [01.08.2016].

2015a). In 2014, a 'Tour of China' was held, during which the EU and its Member States presented research priorities and exchange opportunities. At present, Europe is the second-most attractive destination for Chinese students who study abroad (Nielsen 2014; EEAS 2015).

Recent publications from the EU confirm the increasing awareness of China within EU structures and a growing recognition of China's importance in general and in the energy field in particular. In 2013, an "EU-China 2020 Strategic Agenda for Cooperation" was published (EEAS 2013). It presented a framework for EU-China relations until 2020 with a particular focus on four areas: peace, prosperity, sustainable development, and people-to-people exchanges. In the context of this Agenda, and for the first time, sustainable development was mentioned as major issue in EU-China cooperation (Yuan/Orbie 2014: 338). In 2014, "Roadmaps for International Cooperation" were issued. In this document, China is mentioned alongside the EU's other strategic partners, focusing on cooperation on research and innovation (European Commission 2014c). In 2016, the EU-China Roadmap on energy cooperation (2016-2020) was agreed upon (European Commission 2016b). In June 2016, the previously mentioned new EU strategy on China was published by the Commission (European Commission 2016a), as a response to China's changing role and increasing influence in global politics. The EU Council adopted the new strategy on China in July 2016 (Council of the European Union 2016). In the document, the EU expressed its need to develop its *own* strategy towards China (referring to the EU-China 2020 Strategic Agenda) (European Commission 2016a: 2). The strategy addresses – beyond the Agreement on Investment mentioned above – further key concerns in EU's approach towards China: engagement with China in its ongoing reforms (e.g., in the social, economic and environmental areas [implying mutual benefits]); the promotion of reciprocity (e.g., fair competition); stronger connectivity between Europe and China (digital, people-to-people, trade, infrastructure); the promotion of global goods, sustainable development and international security; and consistency in EU's policy towards China and the promotion of rule of law and human rights (European Commission 2016a: 2).

China's president Xi Jinping visited EU headquarters in March 2014. This was the first visit by a Chinese president to Brussels, and it can be seen as a sign of China's will to improve its relations with the EU (despite economic and political hurdles, namely, the European debt crisis and the meeting of European leaders with the Dalai Lama). Shortly after this visit, China published its second policy paper on the EU. In China's 'New Type of Relations between Major Powers', the EU is acknowledged as one of the major actors (Lai/Shi 2016). In June 2015, China and the EU celebrated the 40th anniversary of their diplomatic relations. The summit addressed how to improve trade relations between the two actors and ensure safety for European consumers. It also discussed international security issues, exchange, energy and climate change (EEAS 2015). However, the relationship continues to be challenged by a set of issues. For the EU, the most pressing issues in its cooperation with China are access to the Chinese market and the questions concerning intellectual property rights. For China, the most immediate issues are the ongoing sanctions imposed by the EU on (the sale of) weapons and its status as a market economy (Bieling 2014: 388).

Despite these challenges, for China, the Strategic Partnership with the EU indicates long-term, stable cooperation, characterised by dialogue on an equal footing, mutual benefits and 'win-win' outcomes (Zongze 2008: 289). The relations with the EU are described as 'comprehensive' and trusting. Wen Jiabao, the former Premier of China, specifically underlined in 2004 the importance of mutual trust:

> [T]his includes respecting each other's choice of development model [and] transcending ideology and differences in social systems improving understanding (Shambaugh et al. 2008: 308).

However, according to the relevant literature, the EU's occasionally slips into a posture of "talking at" China (as reflected in several official EU documents), while China seeks an equal bilateral relationship (Men 2014: 6). These sensitivities are particularly visible when the EU communicates normative messages towards China. When the EU is engaging in "exporting-values", Chinese reactions indicate resistance and rejection. This is especially apparent in the case of Tibet, in which the EU has not been able to act as a normative power in opposition to China's policy (Shen 2015: 234). The EU's discourse on Tibet has been shaped much more by China's position than vice versa. China's clear and persistent opinion that the EU has no legitimacy in opposing China and that the case of Tibet is clearly part of China's domestic affairs has influenced the EU's behaviour (Shen 2015: 237-239). EU policy-makers have focussed on the human rights situation in Tibet instead of questioning the political status of Tibet, which seems to underplay

> Western audiences' demand for criticism of China, while permitting Chinese officials to consider such criticisms as mild enough not to threaten China's fundamental interests in Tibet (Shen 2015: 233).

Furthermore, the EU faces a conflict between its economic interests in China and its normative concerns and sympathy for Tibet. Hence, EU institutions (European Parliament vs. European Commission) and EU Member States have expressed conflicting opinions on the case of Tibet and behaviour towards China, which has weakened the position of the EU (Shen 2015). This issue, which led China to cancel a 2008 summit in response to the Dalai Lama's visit to Europe, remains an obstacle in creating a strong EU-China partnership (Shen 2015; Chan 2010: 142).

Despite the challenges posed by the Tibet case and past interruptions of the political dialogue due to the Tiananmen events in 1989, "both sides always showed a clear interest in re-establishing and intensifying the political dialogue" (Algieri 2008: 76). Furthermore, the EU seems to have achieved some success when communicating on a normative basis in other policy areas. Specifically, in interactions with China in the social field, covering employment, social welfare, health and education, the EU has been able to reach to local receivers of norms. This was achieved through adopting a pragmatic approach, namely, by more closely linking social issues with economic aspects and anchoring them within the sectoral dialogues instead of employing the levers of political dialogue. Through cooperation and dialogue, the EU has been able to encourage China to undertake economic and social reforms and make an effort to promote social norms and policies (Yuan/Orbie 2014: 348).

Following the familiar pattern discussed above, the EU-China relationship is impacted by China's engagement with individual EU Member States. This is especially apparent in the case of Germany and the UK, which are currently engaging in assertive and pragmatic diplomatic relations with China. Another source of interference in EU-China relations comes from European institutions. The EU's complex institutional structure, and the fact that several actors tend to represent the EU in its external relations, complicate EU-related matters for China (Men 2014: 17). The EU acknowledges this issue in its new strategy on China and states, "The EU must project a strong, clear and unified voice in its approach to China" (European Commission 2016a: 4), an aspect that is addressed several times throughout the strategy.

In summary, despite its long history and the mutual recognition of one another's importance, the relationship between the EU and China should address the remaining challenges and not shy away from differences. The former EU Commissioner of Trade, Peter Mandelson, once noted the following:

> The EU and China are interdependent in more ways than we are different. We have to deal with the differences frankly and constructively. But the interdependence is a fact of twenty-first century life. This reality should drive us to see this dialogue, and others that it complements, as the most important work we do.[30]

2.3.4 South Africa-EU Relations

Diplomatic relations between South Africa and the EU can be traced back to the anti-Apartheid struggle. The former South African President, Mbeki (1999-2008), had sought stronger cooperation with the EU (Keukeleire et al. 2011: 24). The relationship between the EU and South Africa was institutionalised in 1999, with the adoption of a Trade, Development and Cooperation Agreement (TDCA). This agreement came into force in 2004 and covers cooperation in trade, development cooperation, economic, social, and cultural issues, as well as political dialogue (European Commission 2006). South Africa, due to its commitment to the transition towards democracy, became a valuable partner for the EU. It has also become a key partner for the EU in its overall relations with Africa.

South Africa places a high value on its economic relations with the EU, which is its most important trading partner. Exports from South Africa to the EU have been growing and also become more diverse.[31] Regarding foreign investment in South Africa, the EU is responsible for approximately 75 per cent of total investment in the country. After years of negotiations, an FTA between the two partners was signed in 2010, but the first free trade area had already been implemented in 2000 (Keukeleire/Delreux 2014: 293). This makes South Africa one of the first countries in the world to sign a free trade agreement with the EU (Fioramonti 2016). In 2014, an Economic Partnership Agreement (EPA) between the EU and the South African Development Community was settled after longer negotiations. It covers improvements in market access, as well as agriculture and development cooperation. However, in this document, the chapter on sustainable development appears to be more symbolic in nature and does not offer concrete, in-depth regulations on environmental and labour issues (European Commission 2015b). The EPA was signed on 10 June 2016 between the EU and the

30 http://europa.eu.rapid/press-release_IP-08-648_en.htm?locale=en [12.10.2014].

31 http://ec.europa.eu/trade/policy/countries-and-regions/countries/south-africa/ [23.05.2016].

SADC EPA Group (Botswana, Lesotho, Mozambique, Namibia, South Africa, and Swaziland [initially excluding Angola but with the possibility of the country joining the agreement in the future]).[32]

The Strategic Partnership between the EU and South Africa was announced in 2006 and implemented in 2007. Former President Thabo Mbeki in particular sought this closer cooperation with the EU (Knodt et al. 2015: 6). For the EU, this decision was motivated by South Africa's role in regional and international politics, as confirmed by Louis Michel, the former EU Commissioner for Development and Humanitarian Aid:

> South Africa has taken on a pivotal role in Southern Africa and throughout the continent, which is reflected in its international profile and its commitment to multilateralism (European Commission 2006).

During the period 2008-2013, annual high-level meetings were held and 18 sectoral dialogues established, including dialogues on migration, human rights, health, education, and energy (see Chapter 7 on the South Africa-EU Energy Dialogue; Piefer et al. 2015a: 43; ESPO 2013). However, in 2014 and 2015 no high-level meetings were held, and thus far in 2016, only a ministerial meeting has taken place.

At the EU-South Africa Summit 2013, an agreement between EURATOM and South Africa on peaceful use of nuclear energy was signed. The summit also discussed employment, youth job creation, and exchange possibilities. In this context, the idea to create an Employment and Social Affairs Dialogue was expressed (Council of the European Union 2013). In February 2016, a ministerial dialogue was held between the South African Minister of International Affairs and Cooperation, Matie Nkoana-Mashabane, and the EU's High Representative for Foreign Affairs and Security Policy, Federica Mogherini, to reaffirm existing dialogues (EEAS 2016c). Regarding development cooperation, the EU and its Member States are the largest donors in South Africa (European Commission 2006), accounting for 70 per cent of all external assistance funds.[33] In this issue area, the focus of cooperation is on jobs, education and capacity building. These are linked to the three main goals in South Africa's National Development Plan – Vision 2030 (Council of the European Union 2013). On international political issues, common peacekeeping missions and a regular security dialogue are important areas of cooperation (Keukeleire et al. 2011: 26).

---

32 http://ec.europa.eu/trade/policy/countries-and-regions/regions/sadc/ [20.08.2016].

33 http://ec.europa.eu/trade/policy/countries-and-regions/countries/south-africa/ [23.05.2016].

Yet, despite this increasingly multifaceted cooperation and the relationship having been upgraded to a Strategic Partnership, the two partners do not seem to stand on equal footing in it. This was most obvious in the trade negotiations, e.g., in the first rounds of negotiations on an FTA in the late 1990s (Fioramonti 2016). South Africa's dependency on EU development aid (which is the greatest among the BICS) is argued here to shape the EU's somewhat superior views on and approaches towards South Africa. The EU tends to perceive South Africa as a developing country, not a strategic partner beneficial for the EU. For example, South Africa shows great potential for EU investments (Piefer et al. 2015a: 44). Undeniably, such perceptions negatively influence bilateral relations. The relations have also been negatively influenced by the EU's and South Africa's differing approaches towards Zimbabwe (sanctions and cooperation, respectively). Moreover, South Africa opposed the EU in negotiations between the EU and the ACP (African, Caribbean and Pacific) Group of States on the reform of trade relations (Olivier/Fioramonti 2010: 107).

South Africa also cooperates bilaterally with individual EU Member States. In general,

> an Emerging Power such as South Africa tends to favor bilateral relations not only with individual European countries but also in the context of South-South cooperation (Maupin 2015: 207).

From a European perspective, the stronger focus on South-South cooperation might be regarded with some concern. As the UK research director at Chatham House states:

> In a multi-polar world, South Africa obviously needs to diversify its relationships to reflect new global trade and political realities, but this does not need to occur by neglecting old relationships that remain strategic (Vines 2013).

Among the EU Member States, the UK is seen to have particularly strong historical, economic and cultural ties with South Africa (Kalaba 2016).

The Strategic Partnership between South Africa and the EU has gained some attention, especially regarding the institutionalisation of their trade relations. Their cooperation has also developed to encompass other areas beyond trade (e.g., international security matters, energy and social affairs). Yet, the progress seems to be slow, and the EU tends not to view South Africa as an equal partner (Piefer et al. 2015a: 44). At the same time, South Africa is diversifying its international partners, with a greater focus on South-South cooperation, specifically on its relations with China.

2.4 Conclusions

The institution of Strategic Partnerships between the EU and BICS can be seen as the EU's response to changing structures and new divides in the global economy and geopolitical landscapes. The aim of the EU is to preserve its role as an important and necessary actor on the international stage. Yet, the rise of emerging powers has changed the relative bargaining power of the EU in international institutions and pressed the EU to search for and create alliances with new relevant actors, including the BICS. However, scholars argue that Strategic Partnerships have not led to a more effective multilateral order. Hence, some question the relevance of these Partnerships.

In defence of the Partnerships, they are still relatively young phenomena in historical terms. Their effects in the BICS are compounded by much older influences, which include Europe's colonial past in general and the colonial legacy of some EU Member States in particular. It is also obvious that EU Member States' role and dominance in world politics also influence the success of the Partnerships (Laatikainen 2015: 563). Importantly, contemporary and historical influences have unique impacts on the EU's relations with each of the BICS countries. Thus, it is crucial for the EU to assess the views and perceptions in each BICS country – regarding the role of the EU and its Member States, as well as of other emerging and established powers, in global regimes and international institutions and concerning the locations in question – instead of hewing to Eurocentric (and sometimes out-of-date) positions. The BICS place a high value on national sovereignty and non-intervention in international affairs, mainly due to their colonial history. In their dialogue with the EU, they prioritise mutual benefits and equality in interactions. The divergent positions taken by the EU and BICS within international organisations and during various negotiations indicate a major gap between the so-called Strategic Partners. In our book we propose to look into mutual perceptions as one explanation behind this gap.

Among the most recent crises to have affected the EU, the sovereign Euro debt crisis has negatively influenced cooperation between the EU and BICS.[34] The worldwide financial crisis has led to protectionist measures, in general, which makes closer cooperation difficult (Allen/Smith 2012: 166). However, perhaps even more damaging are persistent perceptions of the EU

34 It remains to be seen how Brexit will affect EU-BICS cooperation.

as a weakened global economic actor. Here, in Einstein's words, imagination becomes more important than knowledge. Despite increased cooperation between the EU and BICS in several areas in recent decades, knowledge gaps remain on both sides. Specifically, for the EU, the lack of knowledge is further compounded by Euro- and Western-centric perspectives on foreign policy and global governance. Successful Partnerships are argued here to depend on whether the EU is willing to listen to, understand and recognise perspectives from the outside in its dialogue with BICS. This book will evaluate this with regard to a specific dialogue: energy.

Chapter 3
EU Energy Governance

3.1 Introduction

EU energy governance has developed from its origins during the first days of the European integration project, with the initial institutions being the European Coal & Steel Community (ECSC) and the European Atomic Energy Community (EURATOM). The latest treaty – the Treaty of Lisbon (2009) – also has an article on energy policy. Energy governance is among the core objectives of EU energy policy, with the aim of creating an Energy Union at the European level.

Looking back at the history of European integration, concerns related to energy sources represented the basis for the ECSC and EURATOM. Both facilitated peaceful cooperation among Member States in post-War Europe, contributed to a common market for coal and steel, and supported the European nuclear power industry to secure the energy supply. It should be noted that they were not established with the goal of creating common energy policy. It was only in the 1980s, after the European Commission had extended its competences to environmental policy – which then incorporated energy issues – that a common energy policy came into view. The 1980s were also characterised by the enlargement of the European Single Market, which led to common consideration of the issues of electricity, petroleum and natural gas. In addition, the European Commission became involved in energy infrastructure programmes involving cross-border construction in the early 1990es (see Fischer 2009; Knodt et al. 2015a: 57). The founding documents of all these developments contained and stressed the three normative frames of *security of supply*, *sustainability* and *competitiveness*. Yet, the three normative frames received different degrees of attention and guided European action in different ways over the history of European integration. Despite historical differences, the three of them entered the Treaty of Lisbon in 2009.

One of the main innovations of the Lisbon Treaty lies in its pioneering attempt to introduce a contractual basis into energy policy within the European treaties. Article 194 TFEU mandates the following:

> In the context of the establishment and functioning of the internal market and with regard for the need to preserve and improve the environment, Union policy on energy shall aim, in a spirit of solidarity between Member States, to (a) ensure the functioning of the energy market; (b) ensure security of energy supply in the Union; (c) promote energy efficiency and energy saving and the development of new and renewable forms of energy; and (d) promote the interconnection of energy networks.

Article 194,2 states:

> Without prejudice to the application of other provisions of the Treaties, the European Parliament and the Council, acting in accordance with the ordinary legislative procedure, shall establish the measures necessary to achieve the objectives in paragraph 1. [...] Such measures shall not affect a member state's right to determine the conditions for exploiting its energy resources, its choice between different energy sources and the general structure of its energy supply.

Finally, Article 192,2 outlines that the Council within a

> special legislative procedure and after consulting the European Parliament, the Economic and Social Committee and the Committee of the Regions, shall adopt [...] measures significantly affecting a Member State's choice between different energy sources and the general structure of its energy supply (Art. 192,2 TFEU) (cited in Knodt et al. 2015a: 58-59).

In the post-Lisbon period, numerous green and white papers, as well as roadmaps and other papers concerning energy governance, have been issued by the Commission, revealing its determination to proceed with the idea of an Energy Union. Thus far, this concept is not without controversy, and has triggered heated debates between, on the one hand, the northern and western Member States, which would like to deepen the *sustainability* frame within the Energy Union, and their Central and Eastern European counterparts on the other, which call for energy security and insist on Member State sovereignty in the national energy mix. The present-day energy discourse remains highly politicised and Member State-specific. This inevitably feeds into European energy policy in general and its external dimension in particular.

In addition to the importance of the above-mentioned energy frames, one of the formative characteristics of EU energy policy is its crosscutting nature – energy is a matter addressed more than one Directorate-General (DG) of the European Commission, which leads to heterogeneous and fragmented energy governance.

This chapter assesses the development of European energy governance. In particular, it focuses on how the interpretation of and discourses about the three normative frames of *security of supply*, *sustainability* and *competitiveness* shape energy policy within the EU's multi-level system and what actors are involved. The contribution ends with concluding remarks, which reflect on the main finding of competition between the energy *security* and *sustainability* frames that resulted in the present deadlock in the EU's energy policy.

3.2 Competitiveness, Security of Supply and Sustainability: Normative Frames of EU Energy Governance

The three frames of *competitiveness, security of supply* and *sustainability* form the "strategic backbone of the EU energy policy" (Van Vooren 2012: 268). They play different roles in the development of EU energy policy. Although the three frames are given equal treatment within the Lisbon Treaty, they have attracted different degrees of attention throughout the history of European integration. In this section, we discuss the three normative frames in terms of their background and impact on energy governance in European energy policy.

3.2.1 Linking the *Competitiveness* and *Security of Supply* Frames: Market Perceptions

As mentioned above, energy policy was a critical input into the foundation of the European Community in the 1950s. It was a central aspect of two of the three founding treaties – the Treaty of Paris (1951), which established the European Coal & Steel Community (ECSC), and The Treaty of Rome (1950), which established EURATOM. The former created a common market for coal and steel among its Member States, with the objective of avoiding competition among European nations over national resources. The latter followed a similar logic: EURATOM was designed to facilitate the establishment and growth of European nuclear industries and create a special market for nuclear power within the European Economic Community. Together with the expansion of internal markets to include energy and the liberalisation of energy markets within the Single Market Programme during the 1980s (McGowan 1989), these developments demonstrate that the *competitiveness* frame occupies a dominant position within the ECSC/EEC/EC/EU framework. This argument is echoed by Herranz-Surrallés, who notes that EU energy policy was "born with the main goal of eliminating the barriers to free and fair competition in the energy markets" (Herranz-Surrallés 2015: 4).

In the 1990s, the *competitiveness* frame was a catalyst in advancing EU energy policy. The Green Paper "For a European Union Energy Policy" (European Commission 1995a) appears to be a direct reaction to the completion of the Single Market initiative (1993) on the one hand and the preparation of the Intergovernmental Conference (1996) on the amendment of the Treaties to launch energy policy as a new policy field. Although the Green Paper addresses the three frames, it begins with a statement on "overall competitiveness". Arguably, this clearly demonstrates the priority assigned to this particular frame – not least due to the liberal market mind-set and orientation of the time. The justification for the prioritisation of the competitiveness objective was that "it gives companies in the sector the international dimension necessary for security of supply" and "ensures the development of the whole economy" (European Commission 1995a: 16). The second-most popular frame was *security of supply*. Among the three frames, *sustainability* was third, typically labelled 'environment' (European Commission 1995a: 27) – the environmental discussions in the 1990s called for including 'environmental issues' into such papers when discussing competitiveness. *Security of supply* was defined as

> ensuring that future essential energy needs are satisfied by means of sharing of internal energy resources and strategic reserves under acceptable economic conditions and by making use of diversified and stable externally accessible sources (European Commission 1995a: 22).

The text calls for synergies among the three frames – albeit with the acknowledgement that they are 'contradictory' and that it will be difficult "to balance the different elements in such a way that the essential objects can be satisfied" (European Commission 1995a: 5).

The White Paper, "An Energy Policy for the European Union" (European Commission 1995b), that followed the Green Paper of the same year reflected the discourse and position of the internal market. The *competitiveness* frame was again at the top of the agenda. Environmental protection was mentioned in tandem with *competitiveness*, with environmental issues being framed by a market logic:

If the Commission is to continue to work on fiscal instruments by helping the Member States to restructure their own taxation policies with a view towards convergence while talking account of the aim of reducing taxation pressure on business; this must not undermine efforts to meet environmental challenges by taking into account energy efficiency at consumer-product level (European Commission 1995b: 4).

Energy security was in the same way interlinked with consumer markets. The emergence of the *security* frame was also interlinked with energy markets and the perception of international energy threats (McGrowan 2011). In 1968, 'the Six-Day War' in the Middle East had an impact on oil supply (Fischer 2011: 112). Thereafter, energy security became an issue within the European Community. Perceptions of international oil supply scarcities and high prices threating vulnerable Member States dictated a set of political actions. In the aftermath of the 'Six-Day War', the European Commission issued a directive that imposed an obligation on Member States to maintain minimum stocks of crude oil and/or petroleum products (Council of the European Community 1968) as an instrument to enhance security of supply. The directive obligates Member States to store crude oil and/or petroleum products at a level equal to at least 65 days of average daily domestic consumption in the preceding calendar year. These storage requirements were increased after the oil crisis of 1973/74. In this case, the European regulation was superseded by international regulation from the newly founded (in 1974) International Energy Agency (IEA) within the framework of the OECD. It extended the regulation for stocks to last up to 90 days. The storage of crude oil and petroleum was an obvious preventative measure to avoid energy shortages and provide energy security. Nevertheless, the Commission's effort to mandate larger reserves, i.e., regulations that require Member States to secure oil and gas reserves far in excess of the IEA mandate, failed. The Commission also expressed concerns with the growing dependence of the Union on external energy sources. In 2000, the EU's external energy dependence had increased, with the EU meeting up to 50 per cent of its energy needs through imports. At the beginning of a new millennium, 45 per cent of the EU's oil was imported from the Middle East and 40 per cent of its natural gas imports came from Russia. The Commission stated in a Green Paper on energy security that the EU did not have the power to influence international markets and that this 'weakness' was "highlighted by the sharp rise of oil prices at the end of 2000" (European Commission 2000a). Thus, the Commission proposed an increase in the reserve requirement. However, the Council and the European Parliament rejected the proposal, arguing that there was a low risk of supply disruption and thus that such an effort was not necessary (Herranz-Surrallés 2015: 10; Knodt 2016).

Energy security again appeared on the EU's agenda some years later during the disputes over gas deliveries between Ukraine and Russia (2006) and between Belarus and Russia (2007). Those conflicts affected the EU, especially because of the accession of new Member States, which entered the

EU in 2004. All Eastern European countries, but especially the Baltic States and Poland, were dependent on Russian oil and gas, which in some cases represented nearly 100 per cent of supply. Any conflict between Russia and transit countries such as Ukraine would immediately jeopardise Poland's energy supply. Poland strengthened its emphasis on the *security* frame in run-up to the Lisbon Treaty – it initiated a pan-EU debate, demanding solidarity from the other European Member States in the event of a supply disruption to ensure energy security for Polish citizens. This external threat and the move by Poland strengthened common European energy activities (Geden 2007) and advanced the *security of supply* frame. The Commission addressed the issue in its Green Paper on a European Strategy for Sustainable, Competitive and Secure Energy in March 2006 (European Commission 2006a), the Commission communication 'An energy policy for Europe' (European Commission 2007) and its comprehensive Energy Action Plan for the period 2007-2009 (European Council 2007). In the Green Paper "A European Strategy for Sustainable, Competitive and Secure Energy" (European Commission 2006a), the Russian-Ukraine gas conflict was reported as an emerging topic given initial indications of an impending energy crisis. The green paper introduced the Strategic EU Energy Review, which offered a clear European framework for national decisions on the energy mix to avoid supply crises and ensure energy security for the EU (European Commission 2006a: 9), starting in 2007 with its first Strategic Energy Review, the Communication entitled 'An Energy Policy for Europe' (European Commission 2007). The Communication clearly promoted the EU's prioritisation of energy security, with a focus on minimizing the EU's vulnerability with respect to imports, shortfalls in supply and possible energy crises (European Commission 2007: 3-4). It attempted to cope with "expected exponential increases in global demand; rising and volatile prices; and climate change" (Van Vooren 2012: 268). In its communication, the Commission reminded readers that 'it remains important for the EU to promote diversity with regard to source, supplier, transport route and transport method' and called for the establishment of effective mechanisms to "ensure solidarity between Member States in the event of an energy crisis" (European Commission 2007: 10).

A linkage between the solidarity and *energy security* frames can also be found in the Energy Action Plan for the period 2007-2009, announced by the European Council (European Council 2007). The Presidency Conclusion notes that the Action Plan was not only established to complete the EU's internal market for gas and electricity and achieve a more interconnected and integrated market but also to "address the crucial issue of security of energy supply and the response to potential crisis" (European Council 2007: 14). The European Council underlined

> the need to enhance security of supply for the EU as a whole as well as for each Member State' through different measurements, such as effective diversification of energy sources and transport routes as well as effective crisis mechanisms including the date collection, reviewing and assessment (European Council 2007: 18).

Thus, the Action Plan directly aligned with the measures listed in the energy strategy of the Commission from 2007. Within the *security* frame, the Action Plan especially focussed on infrastructure measures to link the Central and Eastern European countries, as well as Spain and Portugal, with the rest of the Union (European Commission 2007: 9). Among the important infrastructure measures mentioned in the Plan are

> the power link between Germany, Poland and Lithuania; connections to off-shore wind power in Northern Europe; electricity connections between France and Spain; and the Nabucco pipeline, bringing gas from the Caspian to central Europe (European Commission 2007: 9).

With regard to the external dimension, the Action Plan highlighted the EU's relationships with Russia, Central Asia, Africa and the BIC countries (Brazil, India and China) (European Council 2007: 19). The Commission's Second Strategic Energy Review, launched in November 2008, on 'An EU Energy Security and Solidarity Action Plan' (European Commission 2008) again stressed the priority of the *energy security* frame and the strong link with the solidarity frame. In this document, the Commission proposed a five-point EU Energy Security and Solidarity Action Plan that again listed (1) infrastructure needs and the diversification of energy supplies, (2) external energy relations, (3) oil and gas stocks and crisis response mechanisms, (4) energy efficiency and (5) making the best use of the EU's indigenous energy resources (European Commission 2008: 3).

At present, the two frames divide the European Union's Member States. We now turn to the latest security aspects of energy policy development and discuss them in relation to the *sustainability* frame.

3.2.2 The *Sustainability* and *Security* Frame: A Dividing Line through the EU

When the concept of sustainability was placed in the context of the *competitiveness* frame, the term 'environmental issues' entered the discourse surrounding the three energy frames. In that context, *sustainability* was the weakest of the three frames, as illustrated by a 1995 communication from the Commission (European Commission 1995a). However, since then, the *sustainability* frame has gained increasing prominence – and this is due to its being placed in the context of climate policy at the international level. As international debates on the greenhouse effect and global warming grew, energy policy became closely linked to climate issues. This was clearly expressed in a 1997 communication from the Commission. The document linked the issue to the upcoming 'Third Conference of the Parties to the United Nations Framework Convention on Climate Change' (COP 3), then to be held in Kyoto in December 1997 (European Commission 1997a), and stated that the "European Union has recognized the urgent need to tackle the climate change issue" (European Commission 1997b: 4).

In this context, the *sustainability* frame first appeared in the second Green Paper on energy issues in 2006. The Commission's 2006 Green Paper, 'A European Strategy for Sustainable, Competitive and Secure Energy' (European Commission 2006a), stated that European energy policies should strive to fulfil three main objectives (as cited in Knodt et al. 2015b: 64-65).

'Sustainability: (i) developing competitive renewable sources of energy and other low carbon energy sources and carriers, particularly alternative transport fuels, (ii) curbing energy demand within Europe, and (iii) leading global efforts to halt climate change and improve local air quality.

Competitiveness: (i) ensuring that energy market opening brings benefits to consumers and to the economy as a whole, while stimulating investment in clean energy production and energy efficiency, (ii) mitigating the impact of higher international energy prices on the EU economy and its citizens and (iii) keeping Europe at the cutting edge of energy technologies.

Security of supply: tackling the EU's rising dependence on imported energy through (i) an integrated approach – reducing demand, diversifying the EU's energy mix with greater use of competitive indigenous and renewable energy, and diversifying sources and routes of supply of imported energy, (ii) creating the framework which will stimulate adequate investments to meet growing energy demand, (iii) better equipping the EU to cope with emergencies, (iv) improving the conditions for European companies seeking access to global resources, and (v) making sure that all citizens and business have access to energy' (European Commission 2006a: 17-18).
With regard to *sustainability*, the Green Paper asked,

> how can a common European energy strategy best address climate change, balancing the objectives of environmental protection, competitiveness and security of supply? (European Commission 2006a: 5).

This focus was further advanced by the German presidency in the first half of 2007. In preparation for the spring European Council meeting in 2007, the Commission presented the communication 'An Energy Policy for Europe' (European Commission 2007). In the communication, the Commission elaborated on and justified the combination of the three frames, beginning with the *sustainability* frame, as follows: First, the Commission admitted that its present energy policies are not sustainable, as energy accounts for 80 per cent of the EU's greenhouse gas emissions. Second, the Commission warned that dependency on external energy sources is growing rapidly. This was regarded as a major risk for the security of supply (European Commission 2007). Third, the Commission predicted that price volatility and rising energy prices on international markets would increasingly affect the EU. Therefore, the Paper called for a common internal energy market. Such a market would need to stimulate competition and investment to ensure substantial benefits from the liberalisation of energy markets (Knodt et al. 2015b: 65).

This position was vigorously advocated by the German government, which stated at the beginning of its presidency:

> A focus of the European Spring Council 2007 during the German EU Council Presidency will be the adoption of an Action Plan on an 'Energy Policy for Europe' containing measures categorized in the order of their priority importance (German Government 2007).

At the helm of the EU, Germany explicitly linked energy measures to the challenges associated with climate change: "the European Council will therefore conduct an integrated debate on energy and climate policy" (German Government 2007). During its summit in March 2007, the European Council decided to "develop a sustainable integrated European climate and energy policy" (European Council 2007: 1). The summit was shaped by the vision and determination of Chancellor Merkel to advance the EU in combating climate change. Merkel's ambitious initiative was also driven by high expectations regarding the upcoming G8 summit in Heiligendamm (Germany), where climate change was at the top of the agenda. The key outcome of this vision was a decision by the European Council to "develop a sustainable integrated European climate and energy policy" (European Council 2007: 1).

The focus of this new turn is the serious consideration of the crosscutting nature of energy policy. Importantly, this is closely linked to climate policy, with the aim of reducing emissions and expanding renewable energy and energy efficiency, under the slogan of '20-20-20 by 2020'. This goal represents a reduction of at least 20 per cent in greenhouse gases by 2020 relative to 1990 levels, ensuring that renewable energy represents 20 per cent of EU energy consumption by 2020 and reducing primary energy use by 20 per cent relative to projected levels – to be achieved through energy efficiency (Knodt 2016). The European Council prepared the EU to take the lead in forthcoming UN climate negotiations. It was agreed that a reduction of up to 30 per cent reduction would be supported by Member States if a global agreement with comparable commitments by other countries was successfully negotiated (Oberthür/Pallemaerts 2010: 45). To implement the European Council's decision from March 2007, the Commission prepared a set of legislative proposals – the so-called 'climate and energy package' of 23 January 2008. These were rapidly approved by the Council and the European Parliament. The proposals included a set of measures to promote renewable energy and provide regulations for the EU emissions trading system (ETS) and the development of low-carbon technologies, including carbon capture and storage (CCS). In addition, binding targets for Member States were agreed. The remaining controversial issues – especially on the levels of CO_2 reduction – were postponed to the EU Summit in December 2008.

The Summit in December 2008 witnessed the beginning of the divide between the 'new' and 'old' EU Member States on the issue of sustainability. The Central and Eastern EU states had low expectations regarding the likelihood that the COP 15 in Copenhagen would end with substantial results, whereas most of the northern and western EU Member States had hopes for this international agreement. At the time, with France occupying the EU Presidency, French president Nicolas Sarkozy had to offer the 'new' Member States lower CO_2 targets in and exceptions for affected industries to secure an agreement among Member States (Financial Times online, 14.12.2008). In addition to opposition from the Central and Eastern European Member States, the German government was also reluctant to support ambitious plans and argued for exceptions for Germany's industry. It seems that the bold intentions concerning energy and climate commitments made in March 2007, which shaped the EU's energy policy with respect to sustainability perspective, were already being challenged. Higher targets were positioned within the framework of the then-upcoming UN global agreement in Copenhagen on climate change for the period after 2012 (European Council 2008b). The outcomes of the Copenhagen Climate Change Conference of 2009 were disappointing for the northern and western EU Member States, which had argued for CO_2 reduction targets to respond to climate change. In addition, the financial and economic crisis had already begun. It shifted attention away from environmental and sustainability issues, as did the next conflict between Russia and Ukraine over natural gas. The latter issue again placed the spotlight on the *security of supply* frame. On January 1, 2009, Russia halted gas supplies to Ukraine following the unresolved disagreements over payments from the Ukrainian gas company Naftogaz to the Russian natural gas company Gazprom. The Czech Prime Minister, Mirek Topolanek, whose country held the EU Presidency at that time, argued for a European solution to diversify energy supply. However, there was disagreement over which gas pipeline project to realise to diversify advance energy security by diversifying energy supplies. The Presidency, together with the Commission, announced support for the Nabucco pipeline project (bringing gas from the Caspian region to Central Europe). On the other side, Member States such as Germany and Italy were arguing for the EU to support other pipeline projects – the North-Stream and South-Stream pipeline projects bypassing Ukraine – advanced by Russia with participation of Germany (North-Stream) and Italy (South-Stream). In January 2009, the dispute culminated in a letter from German Chancellor Angela Merkel to Commission President Jose Manuel Barroso and Topolanek. In it, Merkel used energy security rhetoric to support her argument that the diversification of the energy supply entailed more than relying on the EU's own projects and withdrawing from co-operation with Russia. It is of "great significance" that the Nabucco, Nord Stream and South Stream pipelines should be "politically desired and supported by all EU Member States', she wrote in her letter (cited in Spiegel International online, 29.01.2009).[35] The European Parliament supported the European Commission, which in its turn supported the Nabucco project, which was seen as a step to curtail dependency on Russia (Herranz-Surrallés 2015: 11).

Arguably, the *sustainability* frame lost its prominence relative to the frames of *competitiveness* and *security of supply* in the following years (Fischer 2014: 1). In its Roadmap 2050, the Commission considered the gaps in the implementation of its 2020 framework and presented various scenarios for European energy policy (European Commission 2011). However, there was no real advance towards the successful implementation of the agreed goals. The EU's energy policy has become stuck. Only in 2013 did the Commission initiate another initiative to advance the targets agreed upon in 2008 and 2009. It published a Green Paper (European Commission 2013) and launched a public consultation on the content of a new energy

35 http://www.spiegel.de/international/europe/europe-split-over-energy-security-merk el-calls-on-eu-to-support-baltic-gas-pipeline-a-604277.html (03.06.2016).

policy framework for 2030. It contained an emission reduction target of 40 per cent relativc to 1990 levels by 2030 and stipulated that renewable energy should represent approximately 27 per cent of total energy use by 2030. Some months later, in July 2014, the Commission also proposed a new energy efficiency target, calling for an improvement of approximately 30 per cent by 2030 (European Commission 2014).

This communication sparked heated disagreement on the EU's climate and energy policy positioned within the *sustainability* frame. The debate was held in the European Council, which was responsible for deciding on such long-lasting strategic decisions according to the preciously stipulated framework for 2020. Two camps, which had already begun to form in 2008, have emerged in the discussion. On the one side, Member States such as Germany and Denmark lead a group of environmentally and climate friendly governments in the EU and have supported the package proposed by the Commission. On the other side, the Visegrád states (Poland, Slovakia, the Czech Republic and Hungary), Bulgaria and Rumania, under the leadership of the Polish government, opposed the new targets and insisted on national sovereignty over decisions on their national energy mix and a limited role for the EU. The latter camp pleaded for greater emphasis on the *security* frame instead of pushing for sustainability targets (Fischer 2014: 2-3). To achieve a compromise, the Polish government proposed a new concept. Donald Tusk, the then Polish Prime President and the current President of the European Council, proposed the creation of an energy union.[36] The concept placed the *energy security* frame back at the centre of the pan-EU discussion. The Central and Eastern European Member States framed European energy policy through the narrative of a Central or Eastern European household without heating in winter due to Russian gas policy. They linked the discussion with the European solidarity frame, and Tusk asked for a new policy under the umbrella of a European Energy Union. This agenda rapidly attracted a growing number of supporters, not least due to the Ukraine crisis. Even without being mentioned explicitly, the Russian-Ukrainian crisis served as the foundation for the agenda to gain supporters (Fischer/Geden 2015a) and deepened the divide between the sustainability-informed visions held by northern and western EU Member States vis-à-vis the Central and Eastern European Member States, which are oriented towards solidarity in

36 Tusk revisited an old idea proposed Jacques Delors and the then-president of the European Parliament, Jerzy Buzek, from 2010, who pleaded unsuccessfully for a European Energy Community to integrate the Central and Eastern European Member States into a common system of energy security.

the area of energy supply. Unsurprisingly, a final agreement was reached with a high degree of ambiguity in its conclusions. Namely, the targets for 2030 prescribe 'at least' a 40 per cent reduction in greenhouse gas emissions relative to 1990 levels, as proposed by the Commission, 'at least' 27 per cent of energy consumption being covered by renewable energy and 'at least' 27 per cent in energy savings compared with the business-as-usual scenario. The last figure falls short of the Commission's proposal of 30 per cent. In addition, the extent to which the decision can be revised is ambiguous. Specifically, the European Council's conclusions mentioned a review of the framework after the 2015 Paris Climate Change Conference. The two 'camps' interpreted this in different ways. Whereas the northern and western Member States hoped for greater reductions in greenhouse gas emissions, the Member States from Central and Eastern Europe expected an unsuccessful outcome of the international negotiations. Thus, both sides were willing to agree. Finally, the European Council, addressing the sentiments from the 'eastern camp', stated,

> these targets will be achieved while fully respecting the Member States' freedom to determine their energy mix. Targets will not be translated into nationally binding targets (European Council 2014: 5).

To obtain consent, there extensive concessions were granted to the governments of Central and Eastern Europe in the form of financial compensation and exemptions from the regulations (Fischer 2014: 3-5; Knodt 2016).

When Jean-Claude Juncker, as newly elected President of the European Commission, presented his political vision in his opening statement to the European Parliament (15.07.2014), energy was mentioned as a topic of concern. According to Juncker, energy is one of the ten priorities of the Commission.[37] His views reveal that energy security is his highest priority – he explicitly called for the formation of a "Resilient Energy Union" (Juncker 2014: 5). Juncker stressed that Europeans need to 'pool our resources, combine our infrastructures and unite our negotiating power vis-à-vis third countries' (Ibid.). Renewables were mentioned as the second-most important issue. However, this source of energy was framed within the *competitiveness* frame – as an "industrial policy imperative" (Juncker 2014: 6) to make energy affordable. Finally, energy efficiency was highlighted within the frame of *sustainability*. In conclusion, Juncker noted that in an 'increasingly competitive world, Europe will only be able to thrive if we get it right on Energy Union' (Juncker 2014: 26). Important for our research,

37 http://europa.eu/rapid/press-release_SPEECH-14-546_en.htm [10.10.2016].

cooperation with other countries does not seem to be an important issue within this Energy Union. This was emphasised by the fact that Juncker's political manifesto did not mention either 'Strategic Partnerships' in general or the BICS in particular.

Juncker embraced the idea of an Energy Union after his election in 2014. He commissioned the Vice President of the Commission, Maroš Šefčovič, (responsible for the Energy Union) and the Commissioner for Climate Action and Energy, Miguel Arias Cañete, to draft a framework for the Energy Union (Fischer/Geden 2015). The aim is to use this project to better align the three frames and create a stronger and more independent energy actor – the EU. In a brief follow-up, in February 2015, the new Commission issued a communication called 'Energy Union Package. A Framework Strategy for a Resilient Energy Union with a Forward-Looking Climate Change Policy' (European Commission 2015). In this communication, the Commission offered its vision of a European energy system while employing the three frames – being secure, sustainable, and competitive – extended to the production of affordable energy. The Commission made it explicit that "achieving this goal will require a fundamental transformation of Europe's energy system" (European Commission 2015: 2). Fundamentally, it will have to steer away from the 28 different national regulatory frameworks towards one common European framework. The Commission's strategy contains five dimensions that were adopted by the European Council in March 2015 (European Council 2015: 1): (1) energy security, solidarity and trust; (2) a fully integrated European energy market; (3) energy efficiency contributing to moderation of demand; (4) decarbonizing the economy; and (5) research, innovation and competitiveness.

To bridge the gap between the Member State 'camps' and gain greater acceptance for the Energy Union, Vice President Šefcovic toured all of the Member States from May 2015 until January 2016 and introduced the concept of the Energy Union, featuring the three frames. Moreover, the Commission launched several legislative acts to implement the five dimensions. Among these are Emissions Trading System (ETS) Reform, the summer package to redesign the electricity market, gas supply security, the sustainable energy security package, intergovernmental agreements in energy (IGAs), liquefied natural gas (LNG) and gas storage, and energy infrastructure investments. The European Council decision in March 2015 also stipulated that the European Commission would be required to generate reports, with the first report deliverable in November 2015. In this report, the Commission described the first nine months of the Energy Union as a success.

A closer examination shows that many of the listed projects and implemented instruments had already been agreed upon before the Energy Union and were not affected by the dissonance among the different frames. However, both recently launched and future legislation, as well as further strategies, are predicted to reveal conflicts within the European Parliament and the Council as well as within the European Council (Knodt 2016).

With the aim of balancing the *sustainability* frame, the Commission released its Energy Security Strategy (European Commission 2014a). As part of the Strategy, the EU Member States and some non-Member States conducted a stress test in 2014. The test showed that through the cooperation of all Member States and due to already improved infrastructure connecting the east, consumers would remain supplied even in the event of a six-month gas disruption. As a result of the test, short-term measures were implemented and EU Member States were asked to prepare regional energy security preparedness plans that were reviewed and adopted in 2015. The Strategy also addressed long-term measures. It proposed actions in areas such as ensuring energy efficiency, completing the energy market, diversifying supply, speaking with one voice in external energy policy, strengthening emergency and solidarity mechanisms and protecting critical infrastructure (European Commission 2014a).

3.3 European Union-Member State Coordination in Energy Governance

The Lisbon treaty regulations confirm that EU Member States are important actors in energy policy that are fully responsible for their national energy mix. The conflicts described above provided insight into major national differences in the framing of European energy governance. They also suggest that the coordination of EU and Member State energy activities play an important role in the EU's energy governance.

One of the tests of such coordination is the EU's and its Member States' synergies (or lack of thereof) in global energy governance. Our research discussed in this book will show that cooperation on energy matters by the EU and Member States with third countries, such as Brazil, India, China and South Africa, took place in an uneven manner. In some instances, the EU and Member States were in agreement, yet at times they rivalled one another. Moreover, there is a serious lack of information on Member States' external energy-related activities in the DG Energy. An overwhelming majority (86.1 per cent) of the EU actors in our survey reported that it is very important to ensure coordination of bilateral Member State-third-country dialogues vis-a-vis the dialogues between the EU and third countries. Such coordination is paramount for EU external energy governance. Yet, there is still significant room to improve it (EnergyGov, Darmstadt, 2014; Knodt et al. 2015b: 59-60).

In its conclusion of the summit held on 4 February 2011, the European Council specifically mentioned the problem of a lack of coordination: 'there is a need for better coordination of EU and Member States' activities with a view to ensuring consistency and coherence in the EU's external relations with key producer, transit, and consumer countries' (European Council 2011: 4). The European Council invited the Commission to submit a communication on energy supply and international cooperation on further improving the coordination between Member States and the EU. The European Commission responded and introduced an information exchange mechanism with the EU Member States (Decision 994/2012/EU in Official Journal of the European Union 2012). According to the new mechanism, Member States have to inform the Commission of all of their new and existing international agreements (IGAs) with third countries in the field of energy. Otherwise, they risk sanctions. IGAs provide a political framework for bilateral energy governance between a Member State and a third country to create a stable environment for business, e.g., for investors in the construction of energy infrastructure. The exchange mechanism should now cover intergovernmental agreements that have an impact on the internal energy market or on the security of the Union's energy supply. The Commission requests that it be informed of future intergovernmental agreements to be negotiated between Member States and third countries. Member States have the option to invite the Commission to participate in the negotiations as an observer or an assistant. There is also an option for a Member State to oppose the participation of the Commission in the negotiations. The regulation states, 'The Commission should also have the possibility to participate as an observer at its own request, subject to the approval of the member state concerned'. In addition, the Commission should facilitate and encourage coordination among Member States. With this measure, the EU aims for greater transparency. This should allow the Commission to take coordinated action on behalf of the EU and promote a common voice in energy issues. However, this measure could also lead to more intense tensions among the Member States, as the Commission could exert pressure on them (Interview Brussels, November 2012). Currently, most EU Member States oppose this regulation, as they regard it as harmful to confidentiality and sovereignty in establishing energy supply agreements (EURactiv 2012). Nevertheless, they have complied and informed the Commission of their

IGAs. As a result, a database of more than 114 IGAs has been created (European Commission 2013a, 2015c). In February 2016, the Commission proposed a change to the IGA agreement to the European Parliament and the Council. It will introduce a mandatory ex ante compatibility check by the Commission for any IGA agreement. The Commission's impact assessment and a stakeholder consultation had shown that current ex post assessments of the IGAs' compatibility with EU law is problematic. Of the one-third of IGAs considered incompatible, none has been re-negotiated. The Parliament and Council are slated to discuss this proposal in 2016.

The Commission has undertaken additional initiatives to enhance information exchanges among the Member States on external energy relations. It has created discussion forums: for instance, monthly discussions in the Council's Energy Working Party, where the Commission updates the Member States on EU activities and/or prepares common EU positions. Formal meetings of the Energy Council have continued to include international energy relations on the agenda when discussions are held at the ministerial level. The establishment of a Strategic Group for International Energy Cooperation (Commission, EEAS and Member States' Energy and Foreign Affairs Ministries) allows for the identification and discussion of common priorities, which could lead to the development of joint initiatives and positions vis-à-vis third countries and regions (European Commission 2013a; Knodt et al. 2015b: 60).

Beyond these examples, the institutionalisation of energy governance is leaving most of the crucial competences – specifically, the energy mix – to national level policy-makers. This inevitably challenges the implementation of the Energy Union. As demonstrated above, the Commission has attempted to address the reality of the EU not possessing a single 'European energy framework' but 28 national frameworks. Through the Energy Union, the Commission announced its intention to introduce a new governance mode – a mode that is similar to the so-called Open Method of Coordination. Thus, the Commission chose the model that grants the most autonomy to Member States and introduced national Energy and Climate Plans that all Member States have to fulfil and requires them to document their national implementation strategies according the five dimensions of the Energy Union. First drafts of these plans are to be delivered by the Member States in 2017.

3.4 Horizontal Energy Cooperation at the EU level: The Crosscutting Issue of Energy Policy

As a policy field, energy is an almost canonical example of a crosscutting field. It relates not only to climate policies but also to environmental policy, development cooperation, trade policies, and foreign and security policies (Müller et al. 2015a: 18). The use of the three frames that shaped the development of the EU's energy governance (internal and external) can also be found along the horizontal dimension, by examining different EU actors. Among these are a number of DGs of the Commission and the EEAS.[38]

Within the Commission, DG Energy is the leading DG on EU energy policies. It has the main responsibility for all energy-related issues, including drafting internal and external EU energy strategies and policies. Nevertheless, when framing processes in external energy policy, different Commissioners establish their own focal points. Former Energy Commissioner Piebalgs (2004-2010) focussed on the linkages with development policy as a main component of the EU's external policy. He began a diplomatic campaign to diversify energy supplies in response to the discussion of the supply threat caused by Russia-Ukraine gas dispute. His successor, Oettinger (2010-2014), prioritised Russia to an even greater extent and paid close attention to the countries included in the European Neighbourhood Policy. Subsequently, he strengthened the framing of energy policy within the *security* perspective. DG Energy under Commissioner Dominique Ristori (2014-present) is assisted by two additional members of the Commission. Vice President of the Commission, Maroš Šefčovič, was appointed to advance the Energy Union by facilitating the framing of energy policy within all three frames (Knodt 2016). In addition, Miguel Arias Cañete was made responsible for climate action and energy – a post that underlines the close relationship between the climate and energy topics and indicates commitment to the *sustainability* frame. DG Climate Action and DG Environment have always been closely linked with DG Energy, as there are considerable overlaps in the policies and discourses of the three DGs regarding the *sustainability* frame. The discussions on the Commission's new Green Paper 'A 2030 Framework for Energy and Climate Policies' (European Commission 2013b), as well as the Energy 2020 and 2030 strategies elaborated above, illustrate the close linkages between those issues. The inclusion of the term "energy" in the name of DG Climate is indicative. Nevertheless,

38 For the presentation of the different DGs, see Knodt et al. 2015a: 61-64.

the *sustainability* frame, which is logically elaborated and implemented by DG Climate, has been contested in disputes on the European Council between central and eastern Member States (those are stressing *energy security* frame) and northern and western Member States (those supporting DG Climate Action in sustainability terms). One such example is the decrease in CO_2 emissions reductions included in the energy and climate package from January 2008. This was further discussed at the December 2008 summit in Brussels, where Stavros Dimas, the then-Commissioner for Environment, proposed rigid measures for CO_2. His proposal, which was developed within the *sustainability* frame, was not only challenged by the *energy security* frame of the central and eastern Member States but was also contested by Günter Verheugen, Vice President of the Commission responsible for enterprise and industry, via the *competitiveness* frame. Verheugen's framing was supported by other DGs such as Competition, Economic and Financial Affairs, Trade, Transport and Justice, Freedom and Security. This alliance succeeded in convincing the then-President of the Commission, Barroso, to protect the competiveness of energy-intensive industries and thus challenge the *sustainability* frame within the Commission's proposal (Dreger 2014; Knodt 2016).

For DG Trade, external energy issues and the external competitiveness dimension are among the few topics that are not yet part of a consistent liberalisation strategy. This DG's activities concentrate on returning this topic to the liberalisation discourse. Neither the multilateral negotiations at the World Trade Organization (WTO) nor the expansive bilateralism between the EU and third countries currently cover energy issues on a regular basis. The only initiative that actually sought to extend WTO standards to the field of energy policies, the Energy Charter Treaty (ECT), is losing relevance and undergoing substantial revisions after the withdrawal of Russia.[39] It is obvious that DG Trade is framing energy policy in terms of *competitiveness* from an external perspective. It concentrates on embedding energy into bilateral FTAs and lobbying for a sectoral approach at the WTO (Knodt et al. 2015b: 61-62).

DG Development and Cooperation (DevCo) is the partner of DG Energy in energy projects implemented under the development heading in third countries. It is an extremely relevant actor in the EU's external energy policy. As DG Energy has very few resources for external governance, it often

39 July 2009 Russia withdrew from the ECT due to its objections regarding the dispute settlement mechanisms and investment protection provisions.

depends on DG DevCo to implement energy projects in third countries. In the current financial framework (2014-2019), the emerging BIC powers considered in this book (not South Africa) are no longer classified as 'developing' countries, and thus, they will be phased out of development cooperation. This will inevitably change the cooperative pattern between DG DevCo and DG Energy. DG DevCo is supporting the *sustainability* and *security* frames but is also bringing in social aspects. In many cases, such as in cooperation with South Africa, the *energy security* frame is interpreted somewhat differently in light of development policy: Energy security is closely linked to the energy poverty discussion, with a focus on access to electricity (Knodt et al. 2015b: 62; Knodt 2016).

A new energy actor at the EU level is the European External Action Service (EEAS). Created under the Lisbon Treaty, the EEAS is designed to be the overall coordinator of the EU's external energy governance. On a strategic level, it frames energy relations as 'energy diplomacy' and thus attempts to streamline aspects of EU external energy policy under general external relations. In an internal non-paper on energy and EU foreign policy (EEAS 2012), the EEAS acknowledges the changing dynamics and power relations in energy governance and seeks to support the EU's external energy relations by ensuring policy coordination. It sees itself as bridging political and business interests. Thus far, the EEAS has lacked issue-specific competencies because it does not have a clearly defined role in the EU's institutional system. The EEAS' understanding of energy governance as 'energy diplomacy' is not yet accepted as an advantage by other institutions that agree on the approach to governing energy. 'Energy diplomacy' would imply a more flexible way of connecting public and non-state energy actors, in both the EU and third countries. This might dwarf the competencies of other EU actors involved, as long as the roles and competencies are not clearly defined (Knodt et al. 2015b: 63-64).

With its Communication, 'A Framework Strategy for a Resilient Energy Union with a Forward-Looking Climate Change Policy' (European Commission 2015), of 25 February 2015 and the respective European Council decision in March 2015 (European Council 2015), the EU gave special recognition to the importance of the external dimension of the Energy Union, especially with regard to the December 2015 climate negotiations in Paris. It is declared that the new Energy Union should not be seen as an inward-looking project. The communication highlights the goal of establishing strategic energy partnerships with (future) production and transition countries and regions (Algeria, Turkey, Azerbaijan, Turkmenistan, the Middle East and Africa) (European Commission 2015: 6). Stronger cooperation with Norway (a supplier of oil and gas), the US, Canada and, especially, Ukraine (through a Strategic Partnership on energy) are also mentioned. Energy cooperation with third countries within the fields of renewables and energy efficiency is mentioned only in one sentence, without any details or any mention of the BICS (European Commission 2015: 21). Following up, the Foreign Affairs Council, on 20 July 2015, determined the EU's 'Energy Diplomacy'. The key priorities for the Energy Diplomacy Action Plan are shaped by the *security* and *sustainability* frame, with particular focus on the diversification of sources, suppliers and routes, energy partnerships and dialogues, nuclear safety and energy architecture and multilateral initiatives including the International Renewable Energy Agency (IRENA).

This institutional mapping shows that the energy governance network of EU institutions is a polyphonic structure in which different EU actors support different framings of the EU's energy policy. It is clear that the EU does not 'speak with one voice' in energy governance – energy is and will remain crosscutting issues. In addition, new actors enter the governance – such as the EEAS – and attempt to introduce their own energy frame, understood as one combining the frames of *energy security* and *sustainability*. Institutional fragmentation, as well as inadequately defined roles and responsibilities (e.g., the positioning of the EEAS), may foster competition among the various EU actors involved, and this may result in competing frames and policy incoherence. See, for example, Selianko and Lenschow (2015) for their analysis of the Energy Efficiency Directives. They examine the implications of intra-institutional coordinative discourse and focus on the preparatory stage of policy-making. Their findings suggest that even in an institutional context that is formally favourable to policy coordination, such as in the Energy Efficiency Directive, policy coherence may fail in highly politicised contexts (Knodt 2016).

3.5 Conclusions

Within the EU's energy policy, the three frames of *security*, *sustainability* and *competitiveness* play a central role. This chapter showed that the development of the EU's energy policy has been and continues to be framed by different and occasionally competing frames during different periods of the European integration process. EU Energy policy began with eliminating barriers between energy markets. Resulting from various energy supply crises, the EU's energy policy came into existence in response to the need to secure the energy supply. In recent years, following disputes between Russia and Ukraine that created major concerns regarding supply shortages, central and eastern EU Member States advanced the alternative narrative of solidarity. They called for solidarity among all Member States to prevent the negative consequences of their energy dependency. Moreover, they have defended exclusive national competences with respect to the energy mix. In contrast, northern and western Member States have supported the *sustainability* frame, which links energy with the challenges of climate change. It was initially facilitated by the German presidency 2007 in light of the G8 agreement of climate change in 2007 and the UN climate negotiations at the 2009 Copenhagen summit (Knodt 2016).

As this chapter demonstrated, over the last ten years, the EU's energy policy discourse has taken place in a highly politicised context. At the level of EU Member States, Germany and Denmark lead a group of environment- and climate-oriented governments informed by the *sustainability* frame, while the Visegrád states (Poland, Slovakia, the Czech Republic and Hungary), together with Bulgaria and Romania, have advanced the *energy security* frame. At the EU level, the crosscutting nature of energy policy means that different frames are supported by different DGs in a competitive manner. Moreover, EU institutions also occasionally attempt to introduce additional frames (for example, the EEAS's 'energy diplomacy' frame).

The Commission, under Juncker's leadership, is attempting to bridge the gap between the Member State 'camps' and to ensure concord and balance among the three frames through the creation of the Energy Union. The external dimension is at present focussed mainly on the EU's Neighbourhood countries with a view towards diversifying the energy supply and routes. Yet, less attention is currently being devoted to the EU's main competitors among the 'emerging' powers.

Chapter 4
Invisible Partners and Potential Benefits: EU-Brazil Mutual Perceptions as Energy Actors

4.1 Introduction

Brazil's reputation of a 'green energy power' largely stems from its clean energy matrix; in 2012, 42.2 per cent of its primary energy came from renewable sources (EPE 2013). Rubens Ricupero, former Environment Minister of Brazil, emphasized that "Brazil has everything to be an environmental power, which is, by the way, the only area in which our aspiration to be a great power is realistic" (quoted in Sotero/Armijo 2007: 61). Brazil's vast natural resources – which include the utmost biodiversity and the world's largest rainforests – back this statement. Over the last 40 years, Brazil has successfully transitioned from an oil-import-dependent nation to a mostly energy-independent country due to using renewable energy sources (Ribas/Schaeffer 2015: 173). It is logical to assume that Brazil's orientation on renewable energy should make the country a close and natural partner of the EU in the energy domain (Guimaraes/Piefer 2016). Moreover, the normative basis of a larger framework of EU-Brazil relations generates opportunities for normatively framed energy cooperation. Strong cultural and historic ties – specifically with several EU Member States – might further facilitate Brazil-EU relations. However, despite these conditions, energy cooperation between the EU and Brazil remains nascent, with the EU-Brazil Energy Dialogue staying below its potential (Piefer et al. 2015a: 39).

This chapter argues that understanding mutual perceptions of the EU and Brazil in the area of energy policy can shed light on how the EU and Brazil conduct their energy dialogue within external energy governance. We also aim to understand controversies in this dialogue that could be explained through the perceptions and images of each other.

4.2 Brazil's Energy Policy

Despite the current economic recession and the latest political crisis in Brazil,[40] this largest South American country has been showing impressive economic growth rates in recent decades. These rates are inevitably linked to increasing energy demands in Brazil. Brazil's energy consumption rose 40 per cent in 2005-2015, making Brazil the seventh largest energy consumer in the world (BP 2015, 2016; Enerdata 2016). Remarkably – and given its fortuitous environmental circumstances – Brazil is close to attaining its goal of being energy independent. Brazil also shows its strong engagement in fighting climate change and achieving an international climate agreement. It is responsible for less than 1.3 per cent of the world's total CO_2 emissions from fuel combustion and from energy use (Ribas/Schaeffer 2015: 174). In Paris COP 21, Brazil played a key role in the negotiations and formulation of the 2015 agreement. It affirmed its commitment to high reductions of greenhouse gas emissions (WBG 2016).

Since the 1970s, Brazil has undergone immense changes concerning its energy mix and production. Once, it was largely dependent upon oil imports. Today, it has turned for the most part into an independent energy actor due to its own energy production (particularly renewable energy). Hydroelectric power plants and ethanol supply energy to Brazil's electric and transport sector to a great extent, and newly discovered pre-salt oil reserves add to Brazil's energy independence (Ribas/Schaeffer 2015: 173). Brazil has been predicted to become an "important oil-exporting nation with one of the cleanest energy matrices" (Ribas/Schaeffer 2015: 178). However, these encouraging advances have slowed down due to Brazil's current weak economic growth and the most recent corruption scandal of Brazil's largest oil company, Petrobras (described below) (EIA 2015). Currently, oil accounts for almost 50 per cent of Brazil's energy consumption (see Figure 4.1).

Brazil began to use renewable energy as a reaction to the oil crises in the 1970s. To reduce its exposure to oil prices and oil imports, Brazil developed one of the largest ethanol fuel-production sectors, ranking second after the US. The ethanol strategy was solving two problems at the same time. On the one hand, it reduced Brazil's dependence upon oil imports (the country was importing 80 per cent of its oil in the 1970s). On the other hand, it

40 In May 2016, President Dilma Rouseff was removed from office, facing impeachment and suspicion of corruption. In August 2016, she was impeached.

offered an alternative for Brazil's sugar industry as a main export commodity. When prices on sugar had collapsed worldwide, the sugarcane-based ethanol production offered a new opportunity for Brazil's sugar producers. In 1975, the Brazilian government launched the National Ethanol Fuel Program (Proalcool), aimed at subsidizing the national gasoline supply with Brazilian ethanol production (Hira/de Oliveira 2008). Accompanied by other governmental strategies – such as providing tax exemptions on ethanol-fuelled cars and subsidies to finance a distribution network and pegging the ethanol prices at the gas stations – the government enabled the development of a solid market for ethanol. Together with improvements in the production chain, sugarcane-based ethanol production increased 6 per cent per year on average from 1980. Hence, costs sank significantly and became fully competitive with gasoline on the international markets by 2004 (Goldemberg 2007; Goldemberg et al. 2008). Although government interventions have not occurred since the late 1990s, the industrial production of sugarcane-based ethanol has increased to a significant degree (Ribas/Schaeffer 2015: 174-175). As a side product, Brazilian sugar mills already combined their production with biomass facilities (based on bagasse – a by-product of sugarcane processing), producing their own electricity. In the late 1990s, a power sector deregulation in Brazil made it possible to feed their surplus into the grid.

As home to one of the largest dams in the world, Brazil is also a forerunner in hydropower, with most installed capacity coming from hydro sources. Hydropower currently accounts for 28 per cent of Brazil's energy consumption and 80 per cent of electricity production (Figure 4.1). The hydropower plants, most of which are located in the north and the west of Brazil, are coordinated over large interconnected transmission networks that can be called on short notice to react to demand changes. The networks thus provide the energy supply a certain degree of flexibility (IEA 2013: 309-310). However, the discussion on the construction of 'Belo Monte', a hydropower dam affecting indigenous areas in the Amazonian rainforest, has led to social uprisings and strong international criticisms. Construction of hydropower dams remains a controversial issue challenged socially and environmentally. Nevertheless, the current National Energy Plan 2030 outlines government's commitment to further advances in hydroelectric power generation. Yet, construction of new power plants in the Amazon rainforest region has become difficult due to the many socio-environmental restrictions. The new hydroelectric power plants tend to be smaller and hence more susceptible to the effects of rainfall.

Figure 4.1: Brazil's energy consumption (2015)

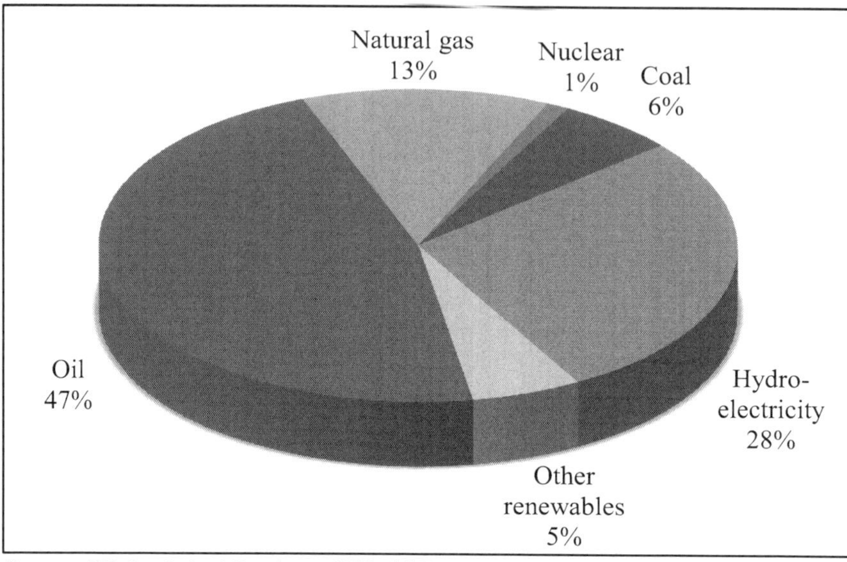

Source: BP Statistical Review of World Energy 2016.

The Brazilian government has also implemented two important policies to push forward renewable energies. The first innovative strategy, starting in 2002, was the PROINFA Programme (Incentive Programme for Alternative Electric Generation Sources), which consists of a feed-in tariff system. The second was the setting up of the auction system. This instrument allows the government to intervene in technologies that will be allowed to participate as supply in the auctions (IRENA 2015: 3).

In summary, since the 1970s, Brazil has undergone radical changes concerning its energy mix and production. Over the last 40 years, it has successfully transitioned from an oil-import-dependent nation to a relatively energy-independent country with immense renewable resources (Ribas/Schaeffer 2015: 173-174). In addition to renewable energy sources, Brazil recently discovered major oil resources in its offshore territories, in which huge 'pre-salt' oil fields have been located deep under a thick layer of salt. These reserves are anticipated almost to triple the country's oil production by 2021, and Brazil is expected to become an important oil-exporting nation (Ribas/Schaeffer 2015: 177-178). Thus, the highest overall energy investment in Brazil in the next ten years will be in oil and gas. For the area of power generation specifically, Brazil is investing primarily in small hydro, wind, biomass and solar facilities. Among those technologies, wind power constitutes the fastest-growing source of electrical power in Brazil as laid down in the most recent Ten-Year Energy Expansion Plan of the Brazilian Ministry of Mines and Energy (published December 2015) (MME/SPE 2015). It remains to be seen to what extent the current economic and political crisis will affect these developments.

Institutionally, Brazil's energy governance is quite fragmented. The National Council for Energy Policy (CNPE) was created in 1997 as an advisory body for the President on national policies and strategies for overall energy policy in Brazil. The Council consists of eight ministers and three representatives appointed by the President of Brazil. It is chaired by the Minister of Mines and Energy (MME), whose Ministry formulates the guidelines and policies for the national energy sector (the MME is the key ministry responsible for energy policies). It is supported by two regulatory federal agencies: ANEEL (Agency for Electric Energy) for the electricity sector and ANP (Agency for Oil, Gas and Biofuels) in the oil and gas sector. ANEEL, created in 1996, is financially and politically independent. As such, the agency addresses all electricity topics delegated to it by the MME and the federal government (ANEEL 2013). ANP, created in 1997, addresses issues related to the assurance of oil, natural gas and biofuels supply and establishing technical standards (ANP 2016). Furthermore, since 2004, the Power Research Company (EPE) has had the mission of developing an integrated long-term plan for the energy sector in Brazil. Moreover, the Ministry of the Environment (MMA) is involved in renewable energy policy-making and the Ministry of External Relations (MRE) in energy foreign policy, such as the energy dialogues with the EU.

The Brazilian energy sector comprises a large number of private, national and international companies. Two large, state-owned enterprises are linked to the MME: Petrobras for oil and gas and Eletrobras for the power sector (Ribas/Schaeffer 2015: 181). Currently, the Brazilian electric sector is facing a deep crisis not least due to the problems challenging Eletrobras and Petrobras in their role in Brazilian energy governance.[41] Another key actor is the Brazilian Development Bank (BNDES) – it channels and provides the

41 Since 2014, Petrobras has been involved in a corruption scandal, the so-called Operação Lavo Jato (Operation Car Wash). Construction companies are claimed to have been overcharging orders from Petrobras and transferring the surpluses to Petrobras executives and politicians. In the aftermath, the involvement of Eletrobras is being investigated as well: http://newsroom.ucla.edu/stories/what-s-behind-brazil-s-economic-and-political-crises;http://www.bloomberg.com/news/articles/2015-12-22/in-petrobras-s-shadow-one-company-races-to-contain-graft-probe [22.06.2016].

right incentives for private investments in portfolio investment, including energy. Brazil's medium-term renewable energy targets are laid down its ten-year energy expansion plans (PDEE). The PDEEs are updated annually. The National Energy Plan 2030 (PNE) from 2006/7 is running out next year, and the National Energy Plan 2050 is currently being developed.

Overall, the Brazilian energy market is growing and has the potential to thrive if it overcomes its bottlenecks. The obstacles include a lack of long-run strategic policy planning, a lack of infrastructure investment, and other issues discussed above. However, Brazil's energy policy also aims at strengthening and reforming its energy governance and the development of long-term plans to provide the proper incentives to all energy stakeholders. Brazil is challenged by a need to balance exploiting new energy resources and pursuing and sustaining a strong energy sector attractive to investors while considering the socio-economic effects of new hydro dam projects, securing its green energy mix and ensuring its current low carbon-emissions status.

4.3 EU-Brazil Energy Dialogue

The diplomatic relations of the EU and Brazil date back to the 1960s, when cooperation was focussed almost entirely on economic issues. The interregional framework agreement between the EU and Mercosur was considered the cornerstone of the bilateral relationship until the consensus on a Strategic Partnership in 2007 was reached. Annual meetings are being held (the 2015 high-level meeting was postponed and scheduled for 2016 but has not yet occurred), and the number and content of the dialogues have expanded over the years (see Chapter 2). The dialogue on energy was established in 2009 with the foci on several areas of mutual interest, such as energy supply, renewable energies, energy efficiency, technology and infrastructure (European Commission 2007b).

These priorities were already stressed in the first meeting of the EU-Brazil energy dialogue in November 2009 at which both sides agreed to exchange experiences and technical consultations on regulatory issues for competitive energy markets, including investment opportunities, and on energy efficiency and demand management (Council of the European Union 2009). The latter area should be addressed through participation in the multilateral International Partnership for Energy Efficiency Cooperation (IPEEC). An important topic in the Partnership is joint efforts in second-generation biofuels and the promotion of EU-Brazil industrial cooperation on low carbon technologies. This topic also covers clean coal and research and cooperation on nuclear energy and nuclear safety. Furthermore, indirect land use change and other topics in the areas of renewable energies and climate change are discussed in the dialogue. Three new areas have been included over the years: offshore safety, ocean energy and trilateral cooperation with African (Mozambique and Kenya) countries on bioenergy (Piefer et al. 2015a: 34).

The EU-Brazil dialogue builds a broad base for energy interactions because both partners have large internal markets with high-energy demands and a clear focus on renewable energies. Yet, paradoxically, the two partners do not appear to share much interest in each other's energy matters. For the EU, the European Neighbourhood countries are much more the focus of DG Energy. For Brazil, South-South cooperation is stressed. The EU-Brazil Dialogue Support Facility was initiated to facilitate and support exchanges between the relevant stakeholders engaged in the specific sector dialogues (Ribas/Schaeffer 2015: 179). The Facility claims that 'the importance of Brazil as a strategic partner of the EU in energy matters should increase as Brazilian oil production grows' (EU-Brazil Dialogue Support Facility Homepage 2013).

The main topic – however at the same time the main controversy – in the EU-Brazilian dialogue is biofuels. Brazil attributes a great priority to biofuels in its external energy relations and aims for its second-generation biofuels to be certified according to EU standards to secure better market access opportunities in Europe, Africa and Asia. However, reluctance towards the full certification process is observed from the EU side because of severe concerns about the quality of Brazilian biofuels. In response, Brazil now aims for an equivalence agreement recognizing the compatibility of Brazilian legislation and European sustainability requirements for biofuels (Interviews Brasilia, December 2013). The Brazilian side also tried to push forward this topic in the context of trilateral cooperation with African partners. For Brazil one aim of such cooperation with the EU was to have its standards certified through this rather implicit approach. Both partners were planning trilateral cooperation projects in the bioenergy sector with Africa (as declared in the Joint Action Plan (2011) and in the declaration of the EU-Brazil Summit in 2013). However, an envisaged trilateral project with Mozambique was not realized due to the EU's concerns with respect to the biofuel standards (Piefer et al. 2015a: 34-35).

This chapter now turns to an analysis of the interactions and exchanges of the actors involved in the Brazil-EU energy dialogue. Here, we start with assessing actors' perceived importance of each other in this dialogue. This perception is measured by using the methodological tool of social network analysis (see Chapter 1 for a description of the methods used). The network of the Brazil-EU energy dialogue is found to be the densest and most central among the four energy dialogue networks considered in this book.[42] The network analysis reveals that a wide range of public and non-state actors from Brazil and the EU are involved in Brazil-EU energy cooperation. The most significant finding – found in all cases in this volume – is that the most important actors[43] in the importance and the exchange networks are perceived to be local actors (Brazilian actors in this case). MME, MRE, the Ministry for Development, Industry and Commerce (MDIC),[44] the Sugarcane Producers' Union (UNICA), Planalto/the Brazilian Presidency and Petrobras are considered among the top five in the importance and exchange networks. This fact is no surprise, because the Department of Energy of the MRE is formally responsible for the dialogue in cooperation with the MME. The latter has an interesting position in the institutional setup. As its name implies, its responsibilities include mines and energy. In our interviews in Brasilia (December 2013), some respondents alluded to the distinction of MME being focussed on mining. This focus is about resource extraction and the exploitation of energy sources, arguably a more fossil fuels-oriented agenda. The Ministry of Environment (MMA) is considered another key actor in the Brazil-EU energy dialogue on issues of renewable energies and energy efficiency, although it is not formally the main responsible partner. MMA ranks 6th in the betweenness centrality and thus is perceived as one of the main actors. This finding is somewhat predictable – the first energy-related issues in Brazil-EU cooperation were initiated by MMA within the dialogue on the Environmental Dimension of Sustainable Development.

The formal responsibility for energy issues is viewed as being with MME, which explains its high importance and very central position in the network without being as engaged in the dialogue as MRE and MMA are. The organization with the highest-in-degree centrality values in the EU-Brazilian exchange network on energy issues is Petrobras (27.5), closely followed by MDIC, UNICA, and MRE (25.0). These rankings imply that these organizations are chosen by at least one-quarter of the respondents as important exchange partners. MME (22.5) also forms part of the five most important organizations in terms of exchange, although this organization's

42 Density of 0.29 and a centrality of 25.8 in the importance network (EnergyGov, Darmstadt, 2014).

43 Detailed findings of the network analysis; see Piefer et al. 2015a.

44 Ministério do Desenvolvimento, Indústria e Comércio Exterior.

position is much less remarkable. In the case of the Brazil-EU energy dialogue, our data clearly reveal a broker – the Ministry for Development, Industry and Commerce (MDIC). This point is interesting because the MDIC has not been one of the most prominent actors. Its responsibilities include addressing crosscutting issues in energy and foreign investments (Piefer et al. 2015: 35-37).[45]

The European Commission's DG Energy was mentioned among the top five – and the only – EU actors in the *importance* network (not in the *exchange* network). The External Action Service (EEAS) and DG Trade were not found among the top five. However, DG Trade was located more centrally in comparison to other European actors (with the exception of DG Energy). This location may be explained by the historic focus on trade diplomacy within the scope of the EU-Mercosur dialogue. DG Development and Cooperation (DevCo) and the Delegation of the European Union to Brazil (DelBRA) are valued as important and are seen to be involved in regular exchanges; however, they are not perceived to be as central as are the other three EU actors. It was DG DevCo and not DG Energy that was financing the energy-related programmes, when bilateral development cooperation between the EU and Brazil have been taking place. In their interviews in Brasilia (December 2013), the Brazilian stakeholders mentioned that the coordination between the two DGs was confusing at times; DG Energy would say "yes", whereas DG DevCo would say "no" to project proposals and vice versa. From 2014 onwards, all new activities are funded by the new Partnership Instrument and the Industrial Cooperation+ Instrument (ICI+). Brazil is now only one country among many from the group of emerging economies and industrial countries, in the European neighbourhood and other parts of the world, that is entitled to receive funding through these two instruments (Piefer et al. 2015a: 37).

Perceptions of the position and role of *non-state* actors are also of note. Petrobras, the country's largest state-owned energy company linked to the MME, was predictably viewed as playing an important role. This perception intensified with the country's recent pre-salt oil discoveries. UNICA – the Sugarcane Producers' Union – was viewed as another important actor, with many other dialogue participants regularly exchanging information with it

45 The Ministry of Planning was not part of the network analysis. However, it might have been identified as a broker because it is responsible for the Dialogue Support Facility, which is financed by the development cooperation budget of DG DevCo with aims to enhance all sectoral dialogues, which are currently stagnating (Piefer et al. 2015a: 35-37).

(see Figure 4.12). Considering the strong focus on biofuels in the Brazil-EU energy dialogue, this perception was expected. The perceived role of UNICA and Petrobras as brokers is noteworthy. The important position given to the Brazilian Confederation of National Industries (CNI) – as a representative of the private sector – can be explained by the role the private sector plays in most issues of the dialogues on, for example, biofuels, renewables, offshore safety and energy efficiency. Finally, many actors report regularly exchanging information with Greenpeace, which can be attributed to the NGO's lobbying and information function (Piefer et al. 2015a: 37).

Next, we examine how diverse actors (*public* and *non-state*, in Brazil and in the EU) reflect on the EU's role and behaviour in energy cooperation with Brazil. Four categories of actors (domestic public, domestic non-state, EU public, and EU non-state) appear to maintain relatively dense relationships within their respective categories in terms of the exchange of strategically important information. However, this statement is not true for *non-state* EU actors. Brazilian domestic actors are clearly considered the most active actors concerning both the 'sending' and the 'receiving' of information, which could be explained by the specific time of our analysis. As mentioned above, from 2012 until the end of 2013, Brazilian actors tried to engage with the EU on the certification of Brazil's second generation of biofuels according to EU standards – or else an equivalence agreement. *Public* EU actors are addressed more by Brazilian *public* and *non-state* actors than vice versa, whereas *non-state* actors at the EU level are addressed very much below average. This point indicates that Brazilian *public* and *non-state* actors view the EU's public actors to be important and exchange information with them, whereas the EU *public* actors see themselves primarily cooperating internally, not even with the European private sector. A vision of the good reciprocal relationship between the Brazilian *public* and *non-state* actors does not appear surprising given that some of the main Brazilian energy companies are partially state-owned whereas others also maintain close linkages to ministries. European *non-state* actors appear better connected than are EU *public* actors, inviting us to seek further explanations for the EU's role in the network and to identify the potential to improve cooperation and mutual understanding (Piefer et al. 2015a: 38-39).

The network analysis – complemented by the results of the survey and interviews – leads to the conclusion that Brazil-EU energy cooperation is seen having a muted profile and remains below its potential. Overall, the EU is not perceived to be the most important partner for Brazil. In contrast, bilateral relations with EU Member States have always been recognized as more important. The view that the EU as an energy actor is not very visible marked the opinion of Brazilian actors and even some EU Member States' representatives in Brasilia.

Energy relations between Germany and Brazil have changed radically since their first energy agreement in 1975 (on the peaceful use of nuclear energy). Today, renewable energies and energy efficiency take central place in the Strategic Partnership (established in 2008) between the two countries (BMZ 2016). Several official documents and agreements serve as a basis for their cooperation in the areas of energy and climate. Among these are the German-Brazilian Energy Agreement (2008), the German-Brazilian Memorandum on Climate Change (2009), the Brazilian-German Committee on Climate Change, the Cooperation for Sustainable Development, and the Brazilian-German Joint Statement on Climate Change signed before the UNFCCC Climate Summit in Paris 2015 (Westphal 2015: 94; BMUD 2015). The latest document showcases a joint commitment to a binding agreement at the then upcoming climate summit and further emphasizes bilateral cooperation in fighting deforestation, ensuring low-carbon development and promoting renewable energies (BMUD 2015). Concrete projects and regular meetings indicate substance and mutual commitment to these agreements. Specifically, the Brazilian energy ministry has become more active in this respect. The German Society for International Cooperation (GIZ), the Banking Group Kreditanstalt für Wiederaufbau (KfW), and the International Climate Initiative (IKI) all have projects in Brazil (Westphal 2015: 94). Despite this booming interaction, Brazil and Germany still view sustainable development and renewable energies differently – a difference that is challenging their energy cooperation. Whereas Germany promotes renewable energies to replace fossil fuels, Brazil focusses more strongly on the economic and agricultural development attached to renewable energy sources (Ibid.).

Brazil's rising importance in global energy flows and its reputation as a frontrunner in biofuel production and an increasingly significant energy exporter make it an attractive energy partner to the UK. The first high-level energy dialogue occurred in 2011, with the then Prime Minister David Cameron confirming the enhancement of this dialogue in 2012 (Kim 2015: 107). Relations between the two are in general viewed as friendly, including their energy relations. The dialogue focusses on sustainable development (e.g. low carbon development, renewables, and sustainable bioenergy). Both sides also aim at stronger commercial relationships. The UK's energy relations with Brazil are thus largely driven by the private sector. This sector has a strong interest in entering the Brazilian energy market, despite difficulties presented by Brazil's local content policy. Conversely, Brazilian energy companies are also interested in accessing the newest energy technology in Europe; e.g., Petrobras has a London office (Kim 2015: 107-108). The UK-Brazil Economic and Financial Dialogue (EDF) in 2015 confirmed its willingness for a stronger economic relationship, including transport and energy issues (HM Treasury/Osborne 2015).

The Strategic Partnership between France and Brazil was established in 2006, followed by an Action Plan in 2008. The main area of cooperation lies in defence and the common border (between Brazil and French Guiana) shared by the two countries. Strong energy relations have thus far not been developed. Predictably, nuclear energy is the main cooperation area. It was a part of the Action Plan, together with sustainable development (Ministry of Foreign Affairs 2016a). In the area of nuclear cooperation with France, transfer of technology, particularly concerning the development of nuclear submarines, is a key interest to Brazil (Vaz 2014: 11). In 2013, the Franco-Brazilian Economic Forum (2013) occurred, focussing on science and technology and on the interests of the private sector (Minstry of Foreign Affairs 2016b).

The potential of Brazil as an energy partner for the EU and its Member States is obvious; Brazil is likely to become the fifth largest economy within the next 20 years, and its internal market is almost the size of the EU's. In this context, the EU has acknowledged that Brazil remains one of its closest strategic partners in terms of normative orientation and foreign policy goals. The Strategic Partnership initiated in 2007 can be considered a clear response of the EU to Brazil's economic rise and its increasing political presence on the international scene. However, at the same time, Brazil has been reorienting its foreign policy. Traditionally, Brazil has focussed on the US and the EU in its external relations. Today, Brazil's foreign policy stresses its direction towards an increasing "BRICSalization" and South-South cooperation (Gratius 2012; Santander 2015: 186-187). In the energy field, Brazil moved towards being a very self-confident cooperation partner for the EU, with clear visions of how the energy dialogue can serve its own domestic interests in a broader geopolitical context (Piefer et al. 2015a: 39). Worryingly, Brazil has not been mentioned in the new EU Global Strategy (EEAS 2016a), perhaps indicating that the EU is not considering Brazil among its top strategic partners in the world.

4.4 EU-Brazil Energy Perceptions in Media and Elite Discourses

The great potential for EU-Brazil bilateral energy relations has not yet led the two partners to truly close cooperation, as argued above. We propose that one explanation for this omission lies in how the two actors view each other in the energy governance field. Our chapter now details mutual images and perceptions found in media and elite discourses. The findings highlight that there is little awareness of the energy dialogue between the two and, to some extent, there are vague and mismatched images of the EU and Brazil as energy actors. As detailed in Chapter 1, the Brazilian and European presses were observed over five years (2009-2013), one month each year surrounding the period of the annual Conference of the Parties to the UNFCCC (COP). Setting the frame of analysis in Brazil, we observed daily coverage of energy matters and of the EU as an energy actor (on its own and interacting with BICS) in the prestigious influential daily *Folha de Sao Paulo* and a respectful leading business newspaper *Valor Economico*. In Europe, we monitored the leading presses of three EU Member States – Germany (*Süddeutsche Zeitung, Handelsblatt* and *Der Spiegel)*, the UK (*The Guardian, The Financial Times* and *The Economist*) and France (*Le Figaro*, *Les Echos* and *Liberation*). Additionally, we observed the pan-European *European Voice.* However, the *European Voice* is omitted from the following analysis because Brazil as energy actor was reported in only one article in the observed periods. European news reporting Brazil in the energy field was almost exclusively written by local authors (65 news stories out of 69 in the German case, 97 out 117 in the UK case, and 60 out of 63 in the French case). The Brazilian press reporting the EU as an energy actor demonstrated a greater openness to engage international sources – 39 locally sourced news stories vs. 12 stories of international origin and 16 of mixed origin (local and international sources employed).[46] The presence of international news sources (often explained by the news making practices and newsgathering systems in a given location) may lead to a greater diversity of views and different voices when framing an international energy counterpart. Dominance of the local sources, conversely, is ripe with the potential to ground an external energy actor in domestic discourses, policies and priorities. However, it also offers the possibility that local concerns and

46 In 17 articles in the UK sample, 3 in the French sample and 4 in the Brazilian sample, sources were not acknowledged.

interpretations will overshadow the perspectives original to the Other's views.

Overall, Brazil was not a very visible energy actor in our European 'energy' sample. In comparison, it was the most visible in the UK press, in which 16 per cent of the articles addressed Brazil as an energy actor. In the German media, the visibility was 10 per cent, and in the French case, it was only 7 per cent (Figure 4.2). Comparing Brazil's visibility to the visibility of India, China and South Africa, Brazil was the second most reported BICS after China in the German case. In the French and UK samples, both China and India were given more attention. Analysis of the intensity in Brazil's representations shows that France and the UK both reported on Brazil from a predominantly minor perspective. In German media, however, Brazil is more visible from secondary and major perspectives. A higher degree of intensity is argued here to add to the relatively higher prominence of Brazil as an energy actor communicated by the German press.

In Brazilian newspapers under observation, the EU as an energy actor was found to have low visibility. The EU appeared in only 13 per cent of a sample of 587 articles that referenced the concept of "energy" (see Chapter 1). Importantly, in several of these articles, the EU was only indirectly connected to energy matters, being framed within a more general economic theme (Guimaraes/Piefer 2016). Moreover, the EU as an energy actor was reported from a predominantly minor perspective (Figure 4.2). Hardly any of the energy-related news occurred in Europe; energy-related news was much more likely to be framed in Brazil's domestic context. Finally, energy was a minor point in the articles in which the EU appears (Ibid.). We argue that these visibility patterns indicate that Brazilian leading press presented the EU as almost an invisible energy actor, potentially prompting its readers to assign a low salience to this actor in the energy field.

Figure 4.2: Visibility of the EU and Brazil in Brazilian and European media

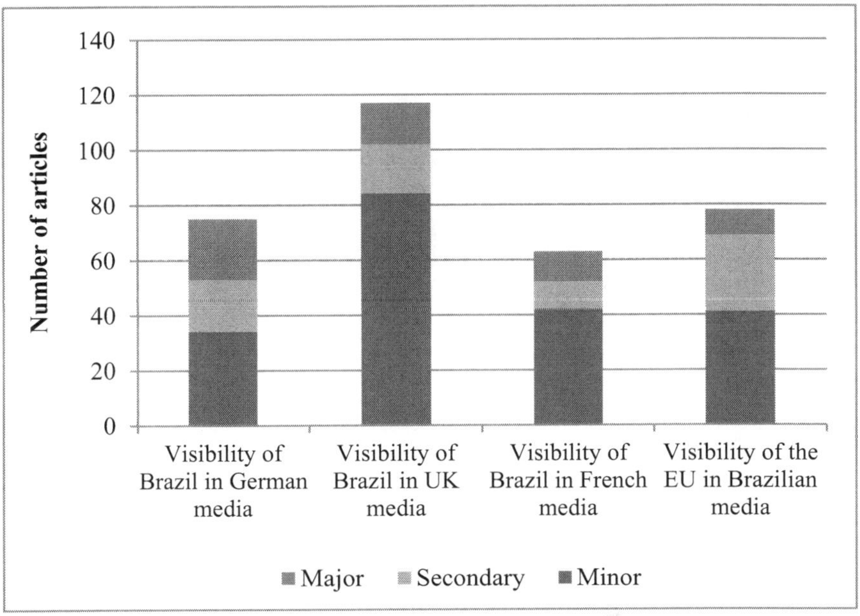

Source: EXIE, 2015.

We also assessed media visibility of other actors presented as involved in energy matters, together with the EU or Brazil. Although the EU has acknowledged the rising economic importance of Brazil by upgrading the status of their bilateral cooperation to a Strategic Partnership, Brazil, as an increasingly confident actor, has turned its attention towards other global actors such as Russia, India, China, and countries in South-South cooperation (Piefer et al. 2015a: 39). This turnabout has been reflected in how the media framed the "energy" field in our period of observation.

In the monitored Brazilian media, the US was the most visible external energy actor, significantly more prominent than the EU. The stories reporting the US focused on energy-related trade disputes, exports of ethanol, shale gas exploration, and investment opportunities and on diplomatic relations in energy governance (Guimaraes/Piefer 2016). The US was also addressed in Brazil's domestic context, in which shale gas was mentioned as an important new energy source for Brazil (Ibid.). The US appeared in the reportage on its own national energy politics, its interaction with Brazil and on the global level, showing the local media's recognition of the

US as a significant actor in international politics and in the specific field of energy. Although the US was often portrayed as a minor actor, it continued to be employed as a reference point and is argued here to be an actor commanding a great deal of media attention in Brazil.[47] China was the second most visible external energy actor reported. This profile arguably illustrates Brazil's increasing attention towards China in the energy field, together with an acute interest in China's current economic development and its involvement in Africa. Importantly, China was framed as an important investor into the Brazilian energy sector (Guimaraes/Piefer 2016). In the specific EU sample, these priorities of external energy actors are also reflected. The US and China were the second and third most reported actors together with the EU. Brazil appeared as the most visible actor together with the EU, indicating a strong domestic focus of energy news stories in Brazilian media (Table 4.1).

For Brazil, energy dialogue with EU Member States is viewed as more important than with the EU itself (Ribas/Schaeffer 2015: 190). Referring to Grevi and Renard (2012), Ribas and Schaeffer note that it is not easy for Brazilian actors to address EU draft documents that are the result of an internal consensus-building process and are thus very difficult to amend (Ribas/Schaeffer 2015: 189). Brazilian actors and even some EU Member States' representations in Brasilia state that the EU is not very visible, which emphasizes the greater importance given to EU Member States (Piefer et al. 2015a: 39). It is not surprising that in the Brazilian leading press, France, Germany and the UK – the three most important EU Member States – were the most frequently mentioned EU Member States in the energy context.

Similar actors were visible in the three cases of EU Member States' presses under observation (Table 4.1). In the three countries, we have China as the most visible 'other' actor appearing together with Brazil, and the US as the second most visible. In the monitored German press, Germany itself was as visible as China, whereas France appeared as the third most visible actor in the French media. In the UK media, however, India was more visible than the UK itself. The appearance of China, the US and India among the most visible actors reported together with Brazil – not the EU and only partly its Member States – framed Brazil in European news as somehow detached from the European energy policy.

---

47 The US was not used as search word in the media analysis. It is assumed that the visibility of the US is even higher.

Table 4.1: The most visible 'other' actors appearing together with Brazil and the EU in the media

German media	UK media	French media	Brazilian media
China/Germany	China	China	Brazil
US	US	US	US
India	India	France	China

Source: EXIE, 2015.

Turning our focus to the elite survey data, we observed that all of the Brazilian *public* and most of the *non-state* actors directly engaged in energy matters consider the bilateral energy dialogue important – 93 per cent. This statistic shows a gap between the informed and involved stakeholders' perceptions of the EU as an energy actor and the low profile assigned to the EU by the influential Brazilian press, inviting further consideration of the reasons behind the low media visibility of the EU as an energy actor. In contrast, surveyed EU actors assigned less importance to energy cooperation with Brazil. Although EU *non-state actors* valued the dialogue as being important, EU *public* actors were less enthusiastic (somewhat paralleling European media's low attention to Brazil in the energy field). More than 40 per cent of the EU *public* actors disagree that the EU-Brazil energy dialogue is important (EnergyGov, Darmstadt, 2014).

The differences in the perception of the dialogue are linked to differences in the perceived effect of the dialogue on Brazilian and EU energy policy. Although more than 80 per cent of Brazilian *public actors* perceive that the dialogue affects Brazilian energy policy, only 50 per cent of EU *public* actors consider the dialogue to affect European energy policy. The opinions of the EU *public* actors are also divided 50/50 concerning the effect of the dialogue on Brazilian energy policy. *Non-state* actors have different perceptions. *EU non-state* actors perceive that the dialogue has an effect on European energy policy, whereas fewer than 50 per cent of the *Brazilian non-state* actors consider the dialogue to affect domestic policy (EnergyGov, Darmstadt, 2014).

Clearly, perceived importance and impact of the dialogue are greatly connected. *EU public* actors give less attention to the dialogue because it is perceived to have only a small effect. Conversely, Brazilian *public* actors perceive the dialogue's effect on their domestic energy policy and hence consider the dialogue important. Although the EU elites' opinion parallels low media coverage of Brazil as an energy actor in European media, the case of Brazil low media attention but higher importance assigned to the EU as an energy actor by stakeholders – invites special consideration. One potential explanation is the sheer complexity of the EU as a *sui generis* energy actor that is challenging to report on in an attractive, 'sellable' manner by the newsmakers. Here, when considering energy *issues*, *types* and *contexts* in media discourses are critical. We turn now to the energy *issues* most visible in the coverage of Brazil and the EU in the respective media.

4.4.1 Topics of EU-Brazil Energy Perceptions in Media and Elite Discourses

Several energy *issues* are visible in both Brazilian and European media when each covers the other political entity as an energy actor (Table 4.2). The most visible topics on both sides are *investments*, *energy policies/governance* and *emissions*. The degree of visibility does however differ between the two sides. In the Brazilian press, *energy policies/governance* is the most visible issue assigned to the EU, followed closely by *emissions*, *investments* and *energy infrastructure*, and then *prices*. Visibility of such issues as *energy policies/governance* and *emissions* was linked to the time period of our analysis (around the COPs) marked by attention to climate negotiations and framed within the sustainability debate. In this light, the visibility of the *investments* and *prices* issues is standing out because it frames EU energy matters within a very different – competitiveness – theme. The *energy infrastructure* issue frames them within a security of supplies context.

In the observed European media, *investments* (indicative of *competitiveness* frame) dominated the German reportage of Brazil as an energy actor, with almost one-half of the articles mentioning Brazil related to investments. Keeping in mind that Brazil is often reported as a major or secondary actor by the German press, *investments* then can be considered a characteristic feature in Germany's portrayal of Brazil as an energy actor. More specifically, that portrayal created the image of Brazil as a potential market for business interests (the finding that echoes positive perceptions among *EU non-state* actors towards Brazil discussed above). The UK press presented a balanced portrayal of Brazil, with competitiveness (*investments*, *prices*) and sustainability (*emissions*, *sustainable development*, and *energy policies/governance*) being the most visible frames. In the French press, *emissions* dominate in the reportage of Brazil, followed by *infrastructure*. This quick comparison indicates that the European and Brazilian press frame each other in common terms through a prism of a shared set of *issues* presented by the press as the most visible and thus potentially the most salient. These shared priorities – on sustainability issues, securing access to energy sources and dominance of the economic interests of the private sector – can become a promising common ground for increased cooperation. However, our elite opinion analysis suggests that this potential appears to be overlooked, particularly by the European partners.

Table 4.2: Visibility of energy issues in European and Brazilian media

European media reporting Brazil as an energy actor			**Brazilian media reporting the EU as an energy actor**
German media	**UK media**	**French media**	**Brazilian media**
Investments	Emissions/ Investments	Emissions	Energy policies/ Governance
Energy policies/ Governance	Prices/ Energy efficiency/ Energy policies/ Governance	Energy infrastructure	Emissions/ Investments/ Energy infrastructure
Energy access	Cooperation/ Sustainable development	Investments	Prices

Source: EXIE, 2015.

Turning now to the media's mutual representations of the *non-renewable* and *renewable energy types*, we see that *non-renewable* energy sources by far dominated Brazil's portrayal in the European press, whereas the observed Brazilian media placed more emphasis on *renewable* energy sources when looking towards the EU. European newsmakers appear to be more focussed on oil – a focus greatly influenced by the discovery of the pre-salt oil that catapulted Brazil up as an oil producing country. The Brazilian media focus on *renewables* renders Brazil's interests in the EU as an energy cooperation partner in the area of renewables. We should not forget that Brazil is not 'green' because it has always been seeking sustainable energy; the 'greenness' of its energy mix came as a side effect when Brazil tried to ensure its energy supply. Brazil is viewed in terms of renewables because it wants to sell its biofuels to the EU Member States.

Examining specifically *non-renewable energy sources*, *gas* and *oil* were the two most visible energy *types* for both actors in the eyes of each other's media (Table 4.3). In the case of Brazil, *gas* was even more visible than was *oil* when the EU was reported. This media priority is not a surprise, because these two sources remain the most used fossil fuels to produce energy in general (Figure 4.1). The visibility of *coal* in the German and UK media and the focus on *nuclear* energy in the French media are arguably reflections of their own domestic energy mixes. Supporting this argument, *coal* was not highly visible in the Brazilian media; indeed, coal constitutes only 5 per cent of the Brazilian energy mix. It appears that when the two sides report on each other, they tend to echo their own energy priorities in the portrayals of the Other.

Table 4.3: Visibility of non-renewable energy types in European and Brazilian media

European media representations of Brazil as an energy actor			**Brazilian media representations of the EU as energy actor**
German media	**UK media**	**French media**	**Brazilian media**
Oil	Oil	Oil	Gas
Gas	Gas	Gas	Oil
Coal	Coal	Nuclear	Fossil

Source: EXIE, 2015.

Examining the *renewable energy* types in comparison with the *non-renewable* energy types, the former were much less visible in the observed European media when Brazil was reported. Among the different types of *renewables*, *wind* energy and *renewables in general* were the most visible in the German and UK samples on Brazil. French press had *solar* as the most dominant renewable energy source attached to Brazil, followed by *renewables in general*. Brazil attached similar priorities when reporting the EU, focussing on *wind* energy and *renewables in general* (Table 4.4). Framing each other in terms of *renewables in general* and *wind* energy specifically indicates another potential to build common ground in the dialogue. This focus appears to reflect the latest positive developments of the wind sector in Brazil, which is a special interest of Germany and the UK.

To support this argument, *hydropower* was the third most visible energy type in the German reportage on Brazil sample, in recognition of the significant role hydropower plays in Brazil's electricity production. Interestingly, only a handful of such articles addressed the environmental and social challenges brought to life by the hydro dam constructions in Brazil – and not as the focus of the articles. Most articles framed *hydropower* from an economic angle, that is, in the context of investments and economic benefits for Brazil. *Hydropower* was also visible in the monitored UK media, however to a lesser extent. *Hydropower* had a minimal profile in the French sample (only two articles). Other *renewable* energy sources key to the Brazilian energy mix (e.g., *biomass* and *biofuels*) had only limited visibility in the European reportage of Brazil. In contrast, *biomass* was the third and *biofuels* the fourth most visible energy issue in the observed Brazil press reporting the EU as an energy actor, once again confirming that representation of the Other is often a subject of domestic energy priorities. However, in the Brazilian case, the most visible *renewable energy* types diverged from the overall Brazilian 'energy' sample which focussed on *biomass*, *biofuels* and *hydropower* (all clearly domestic energy priorities). It was noticeable that in the EU 'energy' sample, *hydropower* was mentioned by the observed Brazilian papers in one article only. Importantly, the discrepancies point to gaps in 'framing' and 'imagining' each other and potentially to obstacles in the dialogue. Arguably, EU Member States cannot offer much to Brazil with respect to hydropower because Brazil has the more advanced technology in that field. Similarly, Brazil does not need much from the EU in this area. Also, the EU does not want to let Brazilian biofuel products in, and no Member States are interested in them. We suggest that the perceived low dependencies on each other lead to such low media profiles of these renewable sources.

Insights into the *context* of the energy news echo our analysis of the visibility of the energy *issues* (Table 4.5). In both German and UK media under observation, *economics* was by far the most dominant context for Brazil's energy-related actions (related to the high visibility of *investments* in news about Brazil). *Politics* was also a part of the UK and German media reflections on Brazil; however, it was much less visible when compared with the Brazilian press reflections on the EU. The French newspapers in our sample focussed attention on neither *politics* nor *economy*. Here, *environment* and *climate change* were the dominant contexts for profiling Brazil's energy matters. In the monitored Brazilian media, *politics* was the most visible *context* when the EU was reported as an energy actor (this context related to the most visible energy issue reported for the EU, namely *energy policies/governance*). Brazilian articles on the EU as an energy actor were also often framed in the context of *economics*. In all cases – European and Brazilian – *climate change* and/or *environment* were visible contexts, showing a close interlink between energy, climate change and environmental issues. *Development* as a context for the EU in the Brazilian media was slightly less visible than *climate change*; it was the fourth most visible context, with only one article of difference. In the UK media, it was also the fourth most visible context, but less significant than in the Brazilian case. In contrast, this context was highly peripheral in German and French cases (only two and one articles, respectively).

Table 4.4: Visibility of renewable energy types in European and Brazilian media

European media reporting Brazil as an energy actor			**Brazilian media reporting the EU as an energy actor**
German media	**UK media**	**French media**	**Brazilian media**
Wind	Renewables, in general	Solar	Renewables, in general
Renewables, in general	Wind	Renewables	Wind
Hydropower	Solar	Wind	Biomass

Source: EXIE, 2015.

Examining the media appearances of actors on various levels and comparing them to the most visible *issues*, *contexts* and *energy types private business* sector was the most visible together with Brazil in the observed European media, which echoed the framing of Brazil within the *competitiveness* frame with a focus on *investments*. *Government* actors were also visible – in the news addressing Brazil in the context of energy governance. In the German media in our study, Petrobras and Chevron were both mentioned in addition to the German energy company EON. In the UK case, Petrobras was also mentioned frequently; however, the UN was among the most visible 'other' actors (due to the timing of monitoring). In the observed French press, French domestic energy companies dominated the reportage – a profile that fits the high visibility of France as an actor interacting with Brazil discussed above.

Table 4.5: Context of energy news stories in Brazilian and European media

European media reporting Brazil as an energy actor			**Brazilian media reporting the EU as an energy actor**
German media	**UK media**	**French media**	**Brazilian media**
Economics	Economics	Environment	Politics
Politics	Climate Change	Climate Change	Economics
Environment	Politics	Economics	Climate Change

Source: EXIE, 2015.

In the monitored Brazilian press, the most visible actors appearing together with the EU were *government* actors focussing on the EU in the energy governance context, followed by *private* actors. However, the EU appeared only in general terms; hardly any EU official was mentioned in the Brazilian media under observation when the EU was reported as an energy actor. Arguably, in the energy domain, the EU was presented as an organization devoid of specific recognizable actors.

How do the media findings compare with the results from the interviews and surveys conducted with the EU and Brazilian elites? As discussed above, the main controversy in Brazil-EU energy cooperation is related to biofuel standards and the second generation of biofuels. We demonstrated above that renewables were visible in the media representations, particularly in the Brazilian leading press reporting the EU as an energy actor. Nevertheless, biofuels were much less visible in both European and Brazilian media than initially expected, as discussed above. Also, the topic of offshore safety, which is prominent in the EU-Brazilian energy dialogue, has not been addressed in the observed media reportage. Although other periods of media observation may result in this issue being more prominent, the five-year period of observation surrounding the COP event indicates a certain disconnect between the issues focussed upon in the media and the topics addressed in the official bilateral energy dialogue. This situation is not atypical; elite interactions and official discourses are usually more nuanced and rather complex, whereas media is confronted with the challenge of appealing to a wide readership and 'selling' the news. Encouragingly, there is also evidence of resonances. An EU paper on its strategy towards Brazil frames energy infrastructure and energy efficiency as mutual interests

(Guimaraes/Piefer 2016). This framing echoes the prominence of these two issues in the media of both actors.

Examining the elite actors' motivations to engage in the dialogue illuminates several diverging opinions. The *EU public* actors mentioned the advantages in combating climate change as the main priority for the EU to cooperate with Brazil. This mention was followed by the promotion of private sector cooperation, then of contribution to technology transfer and entry into energy markets. In contrast, securing the energy supply in the EU had the lowest prioritization towards Brazil. Overall, there was little interest in cooperation with Brazil; all motivations were ranked lower if compared with China, India or South Africa, matching a rather low (only approximately 50 per cent) importance given to their bilateral cooperation. It appears that the EU is downgrading and downplaying the potential of its energy cooperation with Brazil (possibly driven by the experience that Brazil has acted somewhat reluctant as a cooperation partner in the past, see Knodt et al. 2015b: 71).

It also appears that Brazil has little interest in entering the European market (other than with biofuels). However, other areas – such as private sector cooperation and the contribution to technology transfer – received a higher priority than combating climate change. Although the EU's main motivation is attached to sustainability, Brazil focusses more on competitiveness and sees the economic and technological benefits as more important.

Respondents from Brazil and the EU viewed securing its own energy supply as the least important motivation for their cooperation (Figure 4.3). Although this view is rather logical in the case of Brazil (it is already largely a self-supplying actor), the EU appears to consider what potential cooperation with Brazil can bring to the EU. Brazil might very soon become a major oil-exporting country. On a different note, Brazil's interest in technology transfer from the EU and in the promotion of private sector cooperation is much higher than is the EU's interest in these two issues. On these issues – together with market entry – in the case of the Brazilian actors, the *public* and *non-state* actors diverged in their views significantly. In the latter case, the *non-state* actors were more in favour of the option of market entry. However, in the case of technology transfer and the promotion of private sector cooperation, they were much more reluctant.

Figure 4.3: Motivations of Brazil and the EU to engage in cooperation on energy issues*

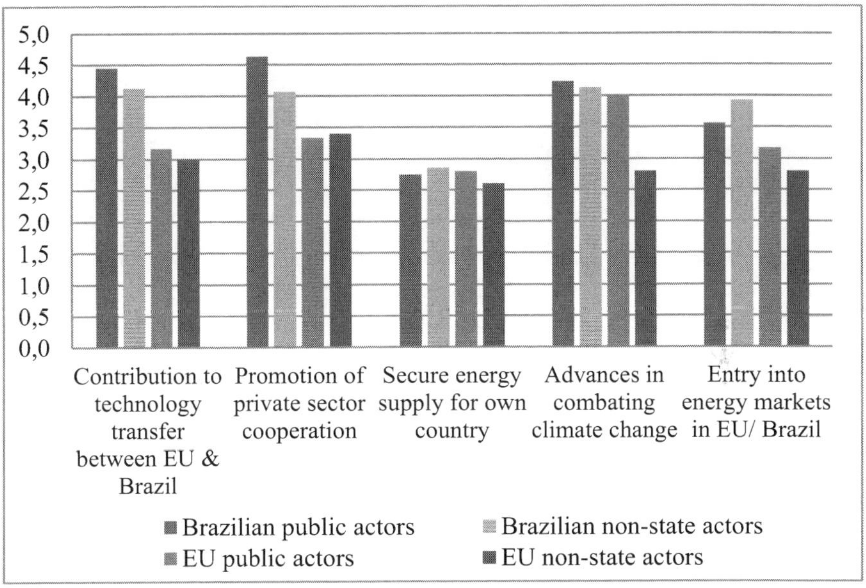

*Means of all answers; 1 = "Strongly disagree"; 5 = "Strongly agree"
Source: EnergyGov, Darmstadt, 2014.

Interviews with stakeholders made clear that Brazilian actors are very keen to increase cooperation with the EU and to establish diverse sectorial dialogues. Respondents highlighted that there is a need for a clarification of mutual interests and that a better exchange of information should occur. There was a call for more openness and less protectionism from the EU side. From the European side, there was a request for more frequent meetings and clear definition of common interests. Arguably, both sides demonstrate their readiness to start a common "story line" in the energy interactions. However, the perceived lack of engagement from the EU side is viewed as hindering this desire for increased cooperation.

4.4.2 Normative Orientation of EU-Brazil Energy Relations in Media and Elite Discourses

Following our earlier argument that norms play an important role in EU energy governance, we focus now on how the EU and Brazil were framed in the media and elite discourses with respect to the different energy *norms*.

Figure 4.4 summarizes the distribution of *normative frames*. A similar image of Brazil is traced in the German and UK media chosen for observation. Keeping in mind energy *issues* and the *contexts* of their representations discussed above, Brazil's main normative frame in these two EU Member States is *competitiveness*. Brazil in general was portrayed as an economic actor in the energy field – a depiction which partly can be associated with Brazil's general drive for economic growth and with its energy matters being shaped by competition (Bain et al. 2016). This portrayal was specifically related to Brazil's discoveries of pre-salt oil and the potential attached to oil exports. It is also about European companies interested in investing in Brazil's energy sector, which again can be reflected in EU non-state actors' positive perception of the energy dialogue. The second most visible frame for the UK and German media was *sustainability*. In the French case, *sustainability* was the most visible energy frame (visible through the above-discussed energy *issues* and *contexts*). This framing was linked to an image of Brazil as an 'environmental power', to its extensive use of hydropower, and finally to its active engagement in the UN climate negotiations. *Security of supplies* was the least visible frame across the three European cases (with German leading press providing a slightly higher visibility to this frame than French and UK observed media). A low visibility of the frame *security of supplies* added to Brazil's framing as a self-sufficient energy actor in the European opinion-forming leading press.

Security of supplies was also not the frame typically associated with the EU in the Brazilian newspapers. A low visibility of this framing of the EU in Brazil 'could be explained by the fact that Brazil is not a major energy exporter for the EU' (Guimaraes/Piefer 2016). The EU was primarily framed within the *sustainability* frame, followed by competitiveness. The portrayal of the EU as a sustainable actor shows a strong emphasis on the role of the EU in relation to renewables (also seen in our discussion on the energy types in Brazil's EU 'energy' sample) and the potential role the EU could play in Brazil's energy policy towards more sustainability. The EU was also framed within competitiveness, with articles addressing the EU in economy-related contexts and in general competitive terms. Although the

EU was predominantly framed as an economic actor in the Brazilian media, the EU as an energy actor was framed in terms of sustainability.

Figure 4.4: Energy frames of Brazil and the EU in European and Brazilian media

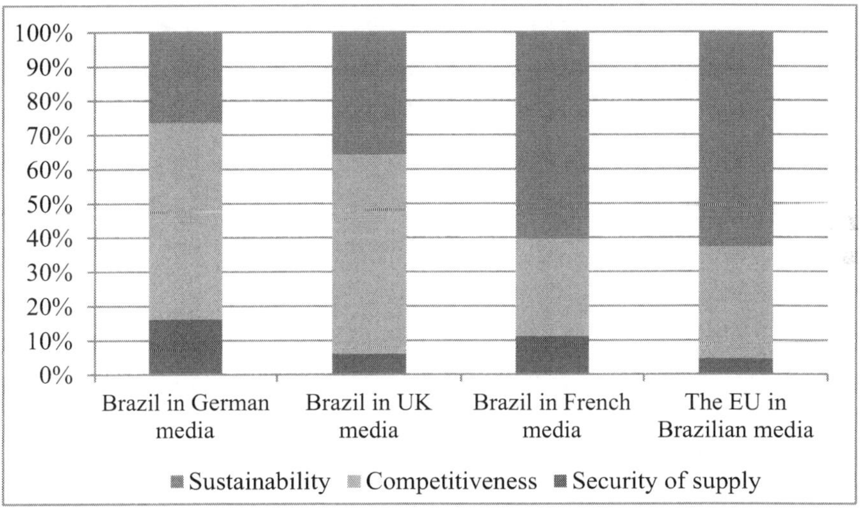

Source: EXIE, 2015.

The elite survey revealed that different energy frames were prioritized by policy- and decision-makers. The majority of Brazilian actors valued *security of supplies* as the most important frame in Brazil-EU energy cooperation. *Sustainability* was considered the second most important frame, whereas only 10 per cent valued *competitiveness* as the most important frame. Keeping in mind that these results show the perception of their *co-operation* – not the framing of the individual actors as in the media – these results indicate some divergences between elite and media discourses. Although the EU was framed most frequently by the media within the *sustainability* frame, *security of supplies* is the leading norm in the eyes of the Brazilian actors for their bilateral cooperation. This norm might indicate that in more popular mass media discourses, the EU is (stereo)typically framed in light of sustainable energy politics, whereas interest in cooperation voiced by Brazilian elites and stakeholders is much more focussed on securing its energy supply. While the EU frames renewable energies, one of the key areas of cooperation in the dialogue, as *sustainability,* Brazil sees it as *security of supplies*. It is however also important to add that *security of supplies* was largely interpreted as access to energy technology (Ribas/Schaeffer 2015: 185) and less so as access to energy autonomy, which is the interpretation by European actors (Knodt et al. 2015c: 334). This interpretation can be explained by the fact that Brazil is considered much less dependent on energy imports than the EU.

Figure 4.5: Energy frames of Brazil-EU cooperation by Brazilian and EU stakeholders*

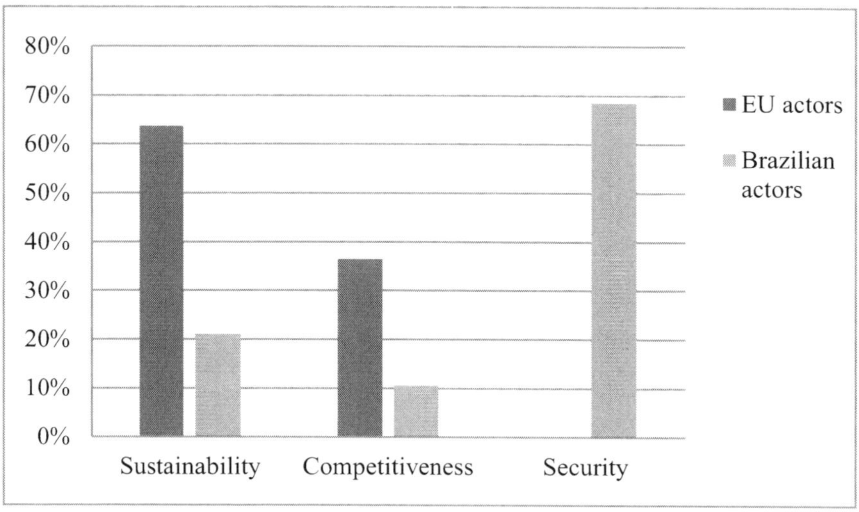

*Percentage of respondents ranking the respective frame highest in energy dialogues
Source: EnergyGov, Darmstadt, 2014.

Conversely, European actors value *sustainability* as the most important norm in their cooperation with Brazil, followed by *competitiveness*, whereas *security of supplies* is not chosen at all as an important norm in bilateral cooperation. The priority of *sustainability* found among the EU stakeholders matches the Brazilian media frames of the EU as an energy actor. However, only the French media prioritized *sustainability* as the dominant frame in portraying Brazil. Although *security of supplies* is interpreted different ways by the EU and Brazilian actors, *competitiveness* and *sustainability* are both understood similarly. In particular, the three-fold understanding of *sustainability* (social, ecological and economic) by elites involved in the dialogue promises to provide an important ground to the development of common narratives (Knodt et al. 2015c: 334), as discussed above. Overall, however, the results from the interviews

> reveal a critical difference in the normative background that predetermines the political interaction on energy issues between the EU and Brazil as dialogue partners (Ribas/Schaeffer 2015: 185).

4.4.3 Mutual Perceptions as Dialogue Partners in Media and Elite Discourses (Evaluations and Roles)

An important factor in the EU-Brazilian energy dialogue is the *evaluations* Brazil and the EU assign each other in perceptions of each other. Across all observed newspapers in the three EU Member States, the majority of the articles evaluate Brazil in a neutral manner, with clear negative or positive evaluations being hardly visible (Figure 4.6). Such an evaluation pattern was found in other cases in this book and should be of no great surprise. We observed a quality press that prides itself on a balanced approach to reporting. However, analysing the borderline evaluation – negative-to-neutral and neutral-to-positive – we observe that Brazil was evaluated by the French and German newsmakers in a more positive than negative light. In the German media, the dominant frame of *competitiveness* presented Brazil in a positive light as a potential place for investments. In contrast, China was also reported by the German media within the *competitiveness* frame but from a negative angle (see Chapter 5). In the UK media, the dominant frame of *competitiveness* attracted more negative than positive evaluations. These negative stories portrayed Brazil and its energy markets in a non-competitive matter in comparison to other energy markets, e.g., China. Interestingly, Brazil was portrayed differently in the French media. The French press framed Brazil as a competitive actor engaging in offshore drilling and developing green energies.

In the Brazilian press, there were more articles containing an evaluation of the EU as an energy actor than articles in which the EU was reported from a neutral perspective. Overall, the EU in general was portrayed in a rather positive tone, which is particularly true when the EU was evaluated as a sustainable energy actor. Hence, although the EU was not a very visible actor in Brazilian media, when it appeared, it was presented in a positive light. This presentation did however change when the EU-Brazilian energy interaction was evaluated. In those articles, the negative tone outweighed the positive. Furthermore, there was a visible change over the years. Although the EU was evaluated more positively in 2009 (during the Copenhagen Climate Summit), the tone became more negative in the following years. Some of this evaluation was connected to the EU's challenged performance at the climate summits (Guimaraes/Piefer 2016).

Figure 4.6: Evaluation of Brazil and the EU in European and Brazilian media

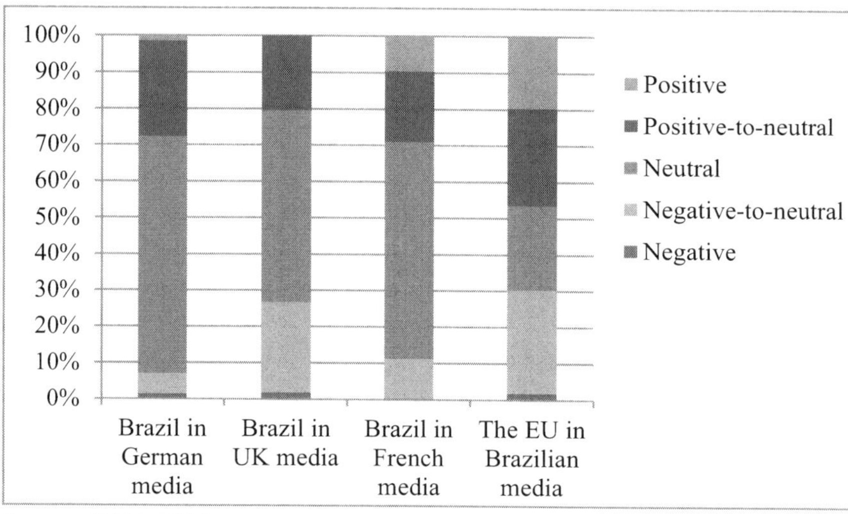

Source: EXIE, 2015.

In the elites' perceptions, the EU and Brazilian actors perceive Brazil as a dialogue partner similarly. Both groups saw Brazil as being open for mutual learning in the dialogue, possessing compromise-building qualities and acting with an open agenda. The EU actors perceived Brazil as more of an agenda-setter than Brazil perceived itself (Ribas/Schaeffer 2015, 186-187) (Figure 4.7).

Brazilian *public* actors had a very positive self-image of Brazil's role as a *dialogue partner* in energy cooperation. That self-image appears to derive from the country's growing role in international arenas and its status as a regional power, which is reflected in the perceptions of the Brazilian actors of their openness for mutual learning in bilateral cooperation and strong interest in the EU's perspectives. European actors shared these perceptions. The same holds true for the Brazilian *compromise-building* qualities and *open agenda*. Interestingly, the EU actors shared the perception of Brazil's contributions to the dialogue. They even asserted a more active role than Brazil did in initiating topics and placing them on the agenda (Ribas/Schaeffer 2015: 186). In the perception of the EU's properties as a *dialogue partner*, the Brazilian and European actors did not converge similarly. In particular, the Brazilian actors perceived the EU as not playing with an open agenda. There appears to be a degree of mistrust from the Brazilian side.

As mentioned above, in the Brazilian media observed in our study, the EU was evaluated in negative terms in the EU-Brazil interactions. This evaluation matches the Brazilian actors' negative perceptions of the EU as a dialogue partner (Figure 4.8). Brazilian actors perceive the EU as being less open to mutual learning. However, the greatest discrepancy is the perception of the open agenda. The EU sees itself as having a rather open agenda; in contrast, Brazil views the EU as acting with a "hidden agenda" (Knodt et al. 2015b: 68). Such different perceptions of how the EU acts in the dialogue, particularly if Brazil is examining the EU suspiciously, can hinder further cooperation.

Figure 4.7: Perception of Brazil's properties as a dialogue partner*

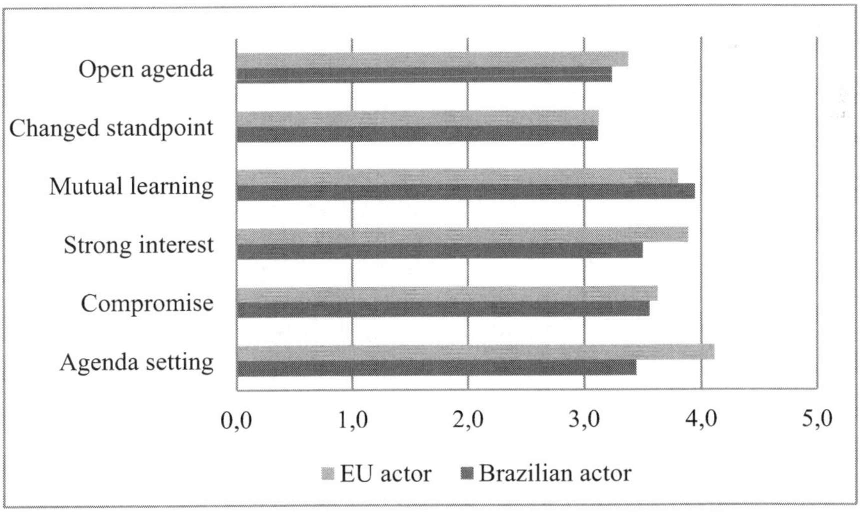

*Means of all answers; 1 = "Strongly disagree"; 5 = "Strongly agree"
Source: EnergyGov, Darmstadt, 2014.

Figure 4.8: Perception of the EU's properties as a dialogue partner*

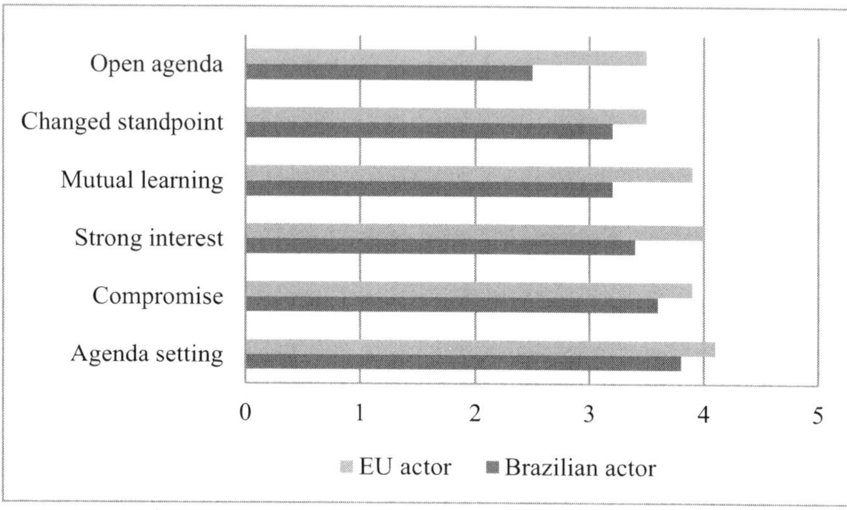

*Means of all answers; 1 = "Strongly disagree"; 5 = "Strongly agree"
Source: EnergyGov, Darmstadt, 2014.

4.5 Conclusions: Lessons Provided by EU-Brazil Energy Cooperation

Brazil is likely to become the fifth-largest economy in the next two decades because it possesses an internal market almost of the size of the EU. The EU acknowledged Brazil as one of its closest strategic partners in terms of normative orientation and foreign policy goals and upgraded bilateral relations – outside the Mercosur framework – to a Strategic Partnership in 2007. However, Brazil's economic and political global rise has reoriented its foreign policy – traditionally focussed on the US and the EU – to increasing "BRICSalization" and South-South cooperation (Gratius 2012; Santander 2015). Brazil is a self-confident cooperation partner for the EU, with clear visions of how the energy dialogue can serve its own broader national interests. Normative orientations and mutual perceptions provide explanatory perspectives, which allow shedding light on how the EU and Brazil construct, interpret and actually shape their relationship and the political orientations that pervade external energy governance.

Our analysis of the EU-Brazil energy dialogue – together with the mutual perceptions – demonstrates that Brazil-EU energy cooperation has not gained overall prominence, and its potential remains to be seen. Moreover,

Brazilian actors recognize that they have reached out more to the EU than has the EU to them. One strong example in the period of our analysis is their attempts to certify Brazil's second generation of biofuels according to EU standards (by engaging in trilateral cooperation projects in Africa). However, generally, the EU is not considered to be among the most important energy partners for Brazil. Our study traced that bilateral relations with EU Member States are perceived to be more important.

Another obstacle to a more informed and active dialogue is a low visibility of each other as mutually beneficial energy actors in the leading media discourses on both sides. Each had a limited media profile of the other as an energy policy actor in the period of observation that was expected to draw attention to energy matters. This media framing appears to differ from the opinions of the stakeholders involved in EU-Brazilian energy cooperation. Informed and socialized, public actors from both sides think that this cooperation influences their own energy policy, even when the sides are not at the same positive level (with more than 80 per cent of the Brazilian but only 50 per cent of EU public actors perceiving the cooperation to influence their own energy policy). It appears that the influential press on both sides reflected only partially the priorities assigned by public and non-state actors to the Brazil-EU energy dialogue, potentially leading to gaps in public opinion concerning forming views on external energy cooperation.

We found that in the energy sector, Brazil sends out messages of its own and does not necessarily echo the EU's international norm set. Energy is predominantly considered a domestic and internal issue. For Brazil, hydropower and biofuels have been the major renewable energy sources. Controversies with the EU over biofuel standards exist, and Brazil's stand on hydropower was one reason for the country not to join the International Renewable Energy Agency (IRENA). Both issues therefore form part of Brazilian diplomatic activities, for example its pronounced biofuels diplomacy in Africa. Yet despite Brazil and the EU sending out different messages and acting as normative agents in their respective spheres of influence, there are many opportunities to forge win-win scenarios for external (European) investors and internal (Brazilian) market stakeholders. The EU should continue to foster debates, exchanges and ongoing dialogues to better understand the intricacy of the Brazilian energy market and its many institutions to offer the EU's comparative advantage, in terms of service, logistics, technology, human capital, and respond timely to opportunities (e.g., auctions, new laws, mergers and acquisitions, and bids).

To conclude, Brazil and the EU assign different importance to their bilateral dialogue in the energy field, which is a difficult starting point for closer cooperation. We argue that mutual perceptions and images reveal a strong potential to develop a common narratives. Such common 'story lines' can become a story in which the two partners are the two protagonists trusting each other, acting in a future-oriented scenario focussed on sustainable energy and bringing mutually beneficial economic outputs. The failure to create a shared energy narrative means that the EU will move faster to the periphery of Brazil's energy interests and that closer energy cooperation with Brazil will remain a dream.

Chapter 5
A Long-Term Partner or a Mistrusted Outsider? EU-China Mutual Perceptions as Energy Actors

5.1 Introduction

The 2015 EU-China Summit celebrated the 40th anniversary of bilateral relations between the two partners. The Summit was marked by breakthroughs on several previously contested issues. Willingness to cooperate was displayed on highly disputed Intellectual Property Rights and climate change (European Commission 2015e). Importantly for our research, the two sides agreed on the Statement on Climate Change, an area of cooperation closely linked to energy matters in the dialogue between China and the EU. Both parties demonstrated their willingness to take steps towards development of low carbon emissions and cooperation on emissions trading (facilitated by China's plans to introduce a nationwide carbon emissions trading system by 2020). Positioning their cooperation in the discourse of the then upcoming UN Climate Summit in Paris, China and the EU stressed that they "commit to work together to reach an ambitious and legally binding agreement" (European Council 2015: 2). Both subsequently signed the Paris Agreement, which is yet to be ratified. It remains to be seen whether such cooperation will eventuate – the two actors took different positions at the previous climate summits. However, for the EU, such a common commitment would be of importance, particularly at a time when the EU's significance and influence in international politics is perceived to be decreasing.

China and the EU are the world's largest importers of natural resources, causing both of them to be highly dependent upon external suppliers.[48] This dependence means that the energy sector of both actors is significantly challenged and pressured to support urgent changes in production and consumption. These challenges will remain closely linked to climate change concerns and actions for the foreseeable future. The growing pressures might lead to increased competition between the two actors in their quest for resources. However, shared challenges might entail a true potential for closer

48 For example, by 2030, the EU and China are predicted to import more than 80 per cent of their oil (Lee et al. 2015: 2).

cooperation. Notwithstanding the promising rhetoric during the 2015 Summit, reality indicates that close cooperation in energy and climate sectors between the two remains wishful thinking; "Despite the imperative for closer collaboration on energy and climate change, EU-Chinese relations have ebbed and flowed much since 2007" (Lee et al. 2015: 6). Instead, China seeks closer ties with other actors, such as the US, with whom China agreed on a "Joint Announcement on Climate Change and Clean Energy Cooperation" (IEA 2015a: 50). Focussing on the energy sector, China's most recent official policy papers on China-EU cooperation give only minimal attention to this area vis-à-vis other issue areas such as economic and financial cooperation (Lai/Shi 2016). This deficit of attention in the energy sector could be emblematic; some scholars argue that over time, the EU is gaining less attention from China. This change is not only due to the Eurozone sovereign debt crisis and changes in the Chinese foreign policy priorities; China is choosing to focus less on multipolar multilateralism and more on bilateral ties (Lee et al. 2015: 3) and, consequently, on bilateral cooperation with EU Member States rather than the EU (Piefer et al. 2015a: 42-43).

The aim of this chapter is to understand the mutual perceptions of the EU and China on energy policy. Analysing the understandings of external energy governance executed by the EU and China, what mutual perceptions exist between the two actors? What controversies are registered when the two sides are "imagining" each other as energy actors? This chapter starts with an analysis of "reality", examining China's energy profile and governance. The chapter then turns to the realm of images and perceptions, exploring media framings of the EU's energy governance in the Chinese newspapers vis-à-vis European media representations of China as an energy actor. As discussed in Chapter 1, European media in our research is represented by a pan-European source, the former *European Voice* (today *POLITICO)* and leading newspapers from the EU's "Big 3" – Germany, France and the UK. The chapter also analyses the elite perceptions of the ongoing EU-China Energy Dialogue and finishes with insights into how to promote better understanding of EU-China energy relations factoring reflections on mutual perceptions.

5.2 China's Energy Policy

The last two decades have marked a substantial increase in China's energy consumption and a continuously widening gap between China's energy consumption and production. China has been a net energy importer since 1993. Today, its energy consumption accounts for over one-fifth of the world's total. In 2013, China not only was the largest global coal consumer and importer but also overtook the US as the world's largest oil importer (IEA 2013: 55, 61-62, 67). Importantly, China's energy sector continues to display ongoing dependence upon coal (Figure 5.1). In 2009, the volume of China's coal imports more than tripled from one year earlier (*China Daily*, 10.2.2010). This growth is with the background of China having the third largest coal reserves, worldwide. A huge local availability of coal in China means an abundant, secure and low-cost local supply; however, such heavy reliance on fossil fuels contributes to China's huge greenhouse gas emissions. In fact, China has become the world's largest emitter of CO_2, having overtaken the US in 2007 (*The Guardian*, 19.6.2007). Consequently, China's energy consumption and policy are no longer exclusively domestic issues but rather issues of global concern (Zha/Lai 2015: 129). Because of the acknowledgement of the serious air pollution problems in the last two years, China eased off its coal consumption and achieved a standstill and even a reduction since 2014. 'Coal demand in China is sputtering as the Chinese economy gradually shifts to one based more on services and less on energy-intensive industries', explained the Annual IEA Coal Report 2015 (IEA 2015b). The Report continued, stating that 'New Chinese hydro, nuclear, wind and solar are also significantly curtailing coal power generation, driven not only by energy security and climate concerns but also by efforts to reduce local pollution' (IEA 2015b). The Report concluded that the global coal market is under pressure, in particular because of the Chinese economic restructuring (IEA 2015b).

Beyond coal, oil and natural gas, resources in China remain limited – thus, their low share in the country's energy mix. Non-fossil sources of energy are also low in China's energy profile. The development of non-fossil energy is however recent and costly in China. Renewables are dominated by hydropower. If hydropower is subtracted, the remaining renewables (e.g., solar, biomass and wind) constitute only two per cent of the energy mix (Figure 5.1).

Confronting the two-prong challenge of ensuring energy security and curbing climate change requires strong governance structures in China (Kong 2011). The country's role as a net importer of energy has shaped China's self-perception in terms of its high-energy insecurity. China sees energy resources as concentrated with other actors – in the Middle East, Russia, Central Asia and Africa. This vision has informed China's energy-related foreign policy, which since the 1990s has redirected its attention towards new partners not previously prioritized. Paradoxically, energy remains a peripheral issue for the Chinese government (Zha 2013). The Chinese government had even decided to abolish its Ministry of Energy in 1993, the same year in which China turned into a net importer of crude oil (Zha/Lai 2015: 131).

Figure 5.1: China's energy consumption (2015)

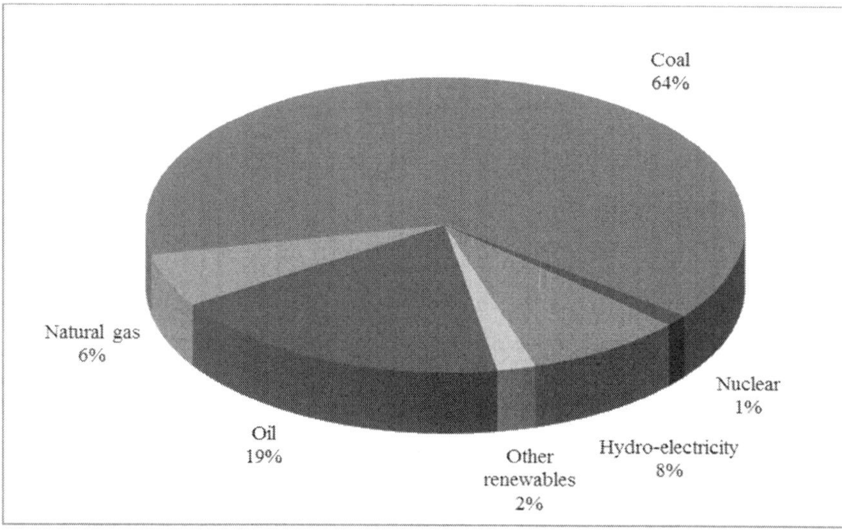

Source: BP Statistical Review of World Energy 2016.

Energy governance in China is complex and fragmented, with overlapping competencies (Downs 2008; Vaclav 1981; Leung 2011). The fragmentation of the national energy administration was at its peak between 1993 and 2003. The fragmentation has increased in speed, particularly since the National Coal Industry Bureau and the National Petrochemical Industry Bureau were revoked and their responsibilities distributed to other ministries. The major change in China's energy governance came with the shift in government in 2003, when such leaders as Hu Jintao and Wen Jiabao brought new visions and policy approaches into China's governance because of their creation of study groups and seeking informed advice (Meidan et al. 2009: 592, see also Knodt et al. 2010).

In 2003, the National Development and Reform Commission (NDRC)[49] was founded. The NDRC is an agency that reports directly to the State Council in different policy areas of economic and social development, including energy. Within the NDRC, the Energy Bureau is responsible for energy matters. It was created to centralize planning and control in one institutional framework. However, the Energy Bureau has suffered from a lack of authority. To overcome this lack, the Chinese government created the National Energy Leading Group (NELG) in 2005, composed of 13 members from the NDRC and other key ministries, including consultation links with think tanks.[50] Currently, the NELG is in charge of energy strategies and major policies, the development and conservation of energy resources, energy security and emergency responses, and energy cooperation with foreign organizations (Yu 2010: 2163). The subordinate ministerial State Energy Office (SEO) provides the administrational support, whereas the NDRC Energy Bureau retains its functions on policy implementation. Nevertheless, it appears that the NELG is not able to escape the influences of the national oil companies (NOCs) or ministries (particularly the NDRC) (Knodt et al. 2010). The failure since 2008 to establish an Energy Ministry – which could have enhanced leverage on energy policy decisions – is clear evidence of NDRC's strength and power (Meidan et al. 2009: 595).

The sustainable use of energy was introduced as a new key priority for China's energy policy following the institutional changes in 2003 described above (Yu 2010: 2161; Knodt et al. 2010). In 2003, the State Electricity Regulatory Commission (SERC) also took charge of electricity issues. SERC was responsible for the united electricity regulatory system and electricity-trading mechanisms. SERC was later merged with the National Energy Administration (NEA, vice-ministerial level), which was established in 2008 under the jurisdiction of the NDRC. With this recent reform, NEA's mandate covers formulation and implementation of energy development plans and industrial policies, regulation of energy sectors, promotion of en-

49 NDRC was the predecessor of the state Planning Commission (SPC) founded in 1952, which was renamed the State Development Planning Commission (SDPC) in 1988.

50 For the energy policy field, the Development Research Centre of the State Council and the NDRC Energy Research Institute in particular are relevant. They produced the two most authoritative reports on the main priorities for China's energy policy in 2004 at the request of Wen Jiabao: the National Energy Strategy and Policy Report (Beijing: Development Research Center, 2004) and the Medium and Long Term Energy Conservation Plan (Beijing: NDRC 2004).

ergy system reform, and leading China's participation in international energy cooperation. Noteworthy is that former leaders in SERC became the leadership of the current NEA after the SERC-NEA merger (Zha/Lai 2015: 132). In January 2010, another attempt to overcome the fragmentation was made, and the National Energy Commission (NEC) was created. It is headed by the Premier. The linkage with the NEA is achieved by assigning the head of the NEA as the NEC deputy. The other nineteen members include a variety of Chinese ministers. NEC's main goal is to formulate a comprehensive and coordinated national energy strategy. Its daily work was undertaken by the NEA. However, thus far, NEC has functioned on a crisis-driven basis (Zha/Lai 2015: 132).

The fragmentation in China's energy governance is also due to other ministries and national agencies holding power in a number of energy-related matters. One important player in the field is the Ministry of Science and Technology (MOST). It is in charge of the technology, innovation, and research and development-related aspects of energy. State-owned energy enterprises (i.e., nearly all other state-owned enterprises) are under the jurisdiction of the state-owned Assets Supervision and Administration Commission (SASAC). The Ministry of Commerce (MOFCOM) is responsible for all energy-related trade. The State Administration of Coal Mine Safety is responsible for the regulation and monitoring of safety in coal mining. This responsibility brings an overlap of competencies in a wide range of areas among the specialized ministries, the NEA and the NDRC. In the 12th Five-Year Plan on Energy Development, published by the State Council in January 2013, this issue is acknowledged. The Plan proposes a "division of labour" table; within it, other than for financial issues, the NDRC remains the main leader of the responsible ministries with one issue (Zha/Lai 2015: 133).

Because energy business is in the hands of state-owned firms, they also play an important role in China's energy governance. The following firms are among the main local actors: State Grid Corporation of China (State Grid); the three Oil Giants – China National Petroleum Corporation (CNPC), China Petrochemical Corporation (Sinopec) and China National Offshore Oil Corporation (CNOOC); and the major power-generators – China Huaneng, China Datang Corporation (CDT), China Guodian Corporation, China Huadian Corporation and China Power Investment Corporation (CPI) (Zha/Lai 2015: 133).

The Chinese energy governance system is stretched over several levels (central, province, and municipal). Decisions with respect to goals and regulations on energy are made at the highest level by the central government.

Provincial and municipal governments are responsible for implementation. However, implementation at those levels suffers delays and discontinuity due to other priorities such as budget and industry protection (Zha/Lai 2015: 133).

Such high fragmentation and division of competences within the Chinese energy governance system cannot avoid influencing China's external energy relations and hence the EU-China Energy Dialogue, which is explored more closely in the following section.

5.3 EU-China Energy Dialogue

The energy dialogue between China and the EU has a long tradition and is significantly advanced in comparison to the EU's other energy dialogues with external partners. The dialogue is based on more than 30 years of cooperation history initiated by the EU-China Trade and Economic Cooperation Agreement in 1985 and started with cooperation in basic energy science. Beginning in 1994, the EU and China initiated biannual energy conferences between the European Commission and the Chinese Ministry of Science and Technology. In 2005, the energy dialogue was initiated with the NEA, and six key issues of cooperation between the EU and China were identified: renewable energies, smart grids, energy efficiency in the building sector, clean coal, nuclear energy and energy law. Energy issues are also discussed during the annual high-level summits, entering the dialogue structure with a special focus on energy security and urbanization (DG Energy 2013, cited in Piefer et al. 2015a: 39).

The year 2012 marked promising developments and visible progress in China-EU energy cooperation. The first China-EU High-Level Meeting on Energy occurred in May that year. For the first time, the EU Commission plus 27 energy ministers of the EU Member States met with Chinese representatives in this format to enhance cooperation on energy issues. The EU-China Partnership on Urbanization and the Joint Declaration on Energy Security were important outputs of this summit. They were the first documents that were agreed upon by all 27 Member States and the European Commission on the one hand and the Chinese officials on the other hand. The fact that a dialogue on energy security has been initiated between China and the EU provides evidence that the EU has recognized the importance of geopolitics related to energy in general and with China in particular. One of the most recent examples of the EU's interaction with Chinese partners in the energy sphere is their discussion on Central Asian energy resources and the role of Russia in the region (Zha et al. 2011). Engaging China in international energy governance is also part of the political agenda of the EU, i.e., into the IEA and ECT. Commissioner Oettinger mentioned this direction in his speech in the European Parliament in May 2012. In addition, China is interested in negotiating with global energy markets. The 2013 EU-China Summit agreed on the 'EU-China Agenda 2020', which included six points on energy cooperation (in the chapter on 'Sustainable Development' [EEAS 2013]). Importantly, both the EU and China remain committed to reinforcing their cooperation on energy issues, placing a special emphasis on global energy security in the bilateral energy dialogue (Piefer et al. 2015a: 39-40). This commitment from the EU is visible in the 'new EU strategy on China' (motivated by the EU's need for its own strategy towards China [European Commission 2016a: 2]); "The EU and China [...] have a common interest in transparent, well-regulated and open energy markets to ensure improved energy security" (European Commission 2016a: 16). In this strategy, China is viewed as a cooperation partner in the development of "a more modern, inclusive and effective global energy architecture" (Ibid.; emphasis in original). In this respect, the EU supports an embeddedness of China in the IEA. In addition, the EU is aiming to support China in several current energy challenges, including China's transition towards a low carbon economy, its establishment of a nationwide emissions trading system and undergoing domestic energy reforms (covering energy efficiency, energy sustainability and resource efficiency). Cooperation on energy infrastructure projects in third countries and joint research on clean energy technologies are viewed as further key areas by the EU (European Commission 2016a: 16). In June 2016, an 'EU-China Roadmap on Energy Cooperation (2016-2020)' was agreed upon, focussing on the enhancement of mutual trust in energy cooperation, on market-related energy issues and on cooperation in the management of the energy system (including both the supply and the demand side) (European Commission 2016b). The EU-China Energy Roadmap is based on recommendations from the EU-China Clean Energy Centre (EC2 2015) and includes environmental and climate issues.

The EU-China energy dialogue is the only one of the EU-BICS dialogues that has resulted in the joint implementation of energy-focussed projects. One example is the EU-China Clean Energy Centre (EC2), which was initiated in 2010 by the European Commission and the NEA together with MOFCOM. The main aim of EC2 is to offer support to Chinese government officials in the clean energy sector through capacity building, policy advice and provision of services in technologies. The list of the EC2's focus areas includes clean coal technology, sustainable biofuels, renewable energy sources, energy efficiency in energy consumption, and sustainable and efficient distribution systems. Joint implementation in the EC2 is managed by Chinese-European project teams for each of the above-mentioned focus areas. They jointly agree on setting goals and means to achieve final results (EC2 2014). EC2 remains a unique example of an energy relations facilitator between the EU and China (Piefer et al. 2015a: 40).

To assess the interaction structure of the EU-China energy dialogue, our team performed a network analysis exploring the perceived importance of many actors participating in the dialogue and views on how they exchange information and interact with each other. The analysis of the network structures shows that the Chinese actors are considered the most important by all of the actors involved in the network. Among these are the MOFCOM, the NDRC, the NEA and the Ministry of Foreign Affairs (MFA).[51] The NEA was found to be seen as one of the main partners in the energy dialogue, with the European Commission calling NEA its "natural partner in energy cooperation" (European Commission 2014a). It was expected that MOST would be another key partner. However, it did not rank high in the importance network (Piefer et al. 2015a: 40). Only the European Commission's Directorate-General for Energy (EC DG Energy) called MOST its oldest Chinese partner in energy cooperation (European Commission 2014d), but it appears that MOST was perceived as losing its importance. A peripheral position of the Ministry of Housing and Urban Rural Development (MoHURD) was another surprising finding. MoHURD is the partner in the Urbanization Partnership; thus, it was anticipated to be a central and important actor (Piefer et al. 2015a: 40).

Evaluating the responses to our survey question about the importance of the EU COMs, DG Energy was mentioned among the top five as the only EU actor. DG Energy appeared not only in the importance network analysis but also in the exchange network analysis. It was considered a broker and the most important actor in the exchange network. In the network picturing regular exchange, the Delegation of the European Union to China was a key actor in the 'broker' function together with DG Energy. DG Climate was also mentioned. As a permanent representation of the EU in China, the Delegation can often be the first contact with the EU for Chinese stakeholders to find a contact in Brussels (Piefer et al. 2015a: 41-42).

51 As discussed above, the NEA has undergone a recent restructuring, being merged with SERC. This change occurred after our survey; thus, this analysis explores both actors separately but keeps administrative changes in mind.

Because business and market access interests are central for China-EU energy cooperation, the private sector naturally plays an important role and is prominently represented in the network. In the Chinese case, state-owned companies (SOCs) are central actors, with standards and policies being harmonized by the government. They generally have more power than other non-state actors do because they are backed by public money and have the best conditions to operate in third countries. The China State Power Grid (CSPG) and China National Petroleum Group (CNPG) have been among the most central actors in the exchange network. According to our interviews, the EU Chamber of Commerce in China (EUCCC) in Beijing is also central for the representation of European non-state actors' interests, although it does not feature as prominently in the network analysis. It appears that within the working groups, the EUCCC was seen to be serving as a gatekeeper for European companies, through which they gain access to the dialogues and can shape lobby activities. The EUCCC informs them of developments concerning market access and, in its energy working group, advises on best strategies to engage with the Chinese authorities (Interviews Brussels, February 2012; Beijing, March 2012). Furthermore, business summits are organized in parallel with the summit meetings (which are held without non-state actor participation) to benefit from the fact that all relevant stakeholders are already meeting in the same place (Piefer et al. 2015a: 42).

A glimpse at an aggregated version of our network data on importance and exchange indicates the EU's acute interest in cooperating with China in the energy field. The EU considers the Chinese public and non-state actors and European non-state actors important and exchanges information with them. However, the Chinese public actors attribute greater importance to the Chinese non-state actors and exchange information primarily with them and European non-state actors. Arguably, Chinese interest is very high in technology transfer and exporting its renewable energy technologies to other world regions, including the European market. Thus, private sector cooperation is favoured over public sector cooperation and exchange. Those findings match with the media findings discussed later in this chapter.

The EU-China energy dialogue has evolved considerably in the years since its inception. Despite different political priorities, there is evidence of increased interest in this dialogue from both sides. There are a growing number of cooperation areas, a consistent number of high-level participants (including the EU Energy Commissioner and NEA Administrator), EU-Member State Coordination (witnessed by the High Level Meeting on Energy in 2012), and the establishment of joint centres and implementation of concrete projects. However, although the EU-China energy dialogue stands out in comparison to other EU energy dialogues, China still prefers cooperation with EU Member States in the energy field. This cooperation is often referred to in China as 'another cup of tea'. China tends to address the EU Member States rather than the EU when considerable gains and financial flows are expected because the Member States are perceived to have more to offer (interviews in Beijing and Brussels, February-May 2012, cited in Piefer et al. 2015a: 42-43).

Germany is China's most important trading partner out of all EU Member States, with the German share of EU trade with China constituting 29 per cent (Federal Foreign Office 2016). The same holds true for investment. Since July 2010, China is no longer considered a developing country, entitled to receive Official Development Assistance (ODA) from Germany. Instead, Germany and China have converted their relationship into a strategic partnership (Bundesregierung 2014). Like the EU strategic partnership with China, the German-Chinese strategic partnership includes a chapter on energy dialogue. The dialogue occurs in the German-Chinese Forum for economic and technological cooperation. Two action groups are responsible for energy issues. In the first group, the "AG Energy", the German Federal Ministry for Economic Affairs and Energy (BMWi) and the Chinese NEA discuss renewable energies. In the second group (AG Energy Efficiency), the BMWi and the NDRC work on energy efficiency and strategies for energy saving. In October 2014, the Forum agreed on a common action plan on innovations in which both groups formulated their energy strategies and pledged commitment to the intensification of the collaboration.

Currently, the agenda of the China-Germany energy dialogue is headed by such issues as energy efficiency, biogas, e-mobility and climate protection. The Bundesministerium für Verkehr, Bau und Stadtentwicklung – BMVBS (now Bundesministerium für Verkehr und digitale Infrastruktur – BMVI) had signed a common declaration on cooperation on sustainable mobility, energy efficiency and emission reduction and innovative transport technology with the Chinese Ministry for Science and Technology. With respect to the two latter issues, the German Ministry of Environment has signed a declaration with the Chinese MOST to intensify cooperation in environmental issues and a declaration of intent with the Chinese Ministry for Environmental Protection to expand the Chinese-German environmental partnership. The agricultural ministries of the two countries have signed a Memorandum of Understanding on biogas cooperation. E-mobility has become a major field of cooperation in which German ministries such as

Transport and Digital Infrastructure and Education and Research are involved. Also linked to the EU-China energy dialogue is the German-Chinese strategic partnership in energy issues; technical cooperation in energy efficiency and low-CO_2 urban construction are of great interest to the two countries.

The Chinese government is interested in the German Energiewende and keen on learning about best practices and sorting out possibilities for investment, such as the investment of the China State Grid Corporation in Desertec Industrial Initiative in 2013. The China State Grid Corporation is very active in approaching all German research institutes and universities addressing the Energiewende. At the same time, the two countries are competitors on solar panels and RE technologies (Westphal 2015: 95-96).

Energy cooperation between the UK and China is relatively new, with the first UK-China high-level energy dialogue meeting held only in 2010. The focus in the bilateral relations is on low carbon energy, including among other components exchanges of technologies, low carbon development, emissions trading and services (Zhang 2015). This focus is intended to secure the supply of energy, to prevent climate change and to boost business cooperation and investment opportunities on low carbon technologies (Kim 2015: 103-104). In this field, the transfer of carbon capture and storage (CCS) technology is considered the first example of successful cooperation between China and the UK. Furthermore, the UK's own energy reforms, namely moving from coal to gas, are of interest to China due to China's own high reliance on coal in its energy mix (discussed above). The UK also supports China in enabling a more eco-friendly coal consumption (Ibid.: 104-105). Another area of cooperation is nuclear power development. Here, China actively seeks closer ties with the UK. In October 2015, a strategic investment agreement was signed between China General Nuclear Power Corporation (CGN) and Électricité de France (EdF) (the French electricity giant (owned primarily by the French government) that owns and operates almost all nuclear power plants in the UK). This agreement was part of Xi Jinping's agenda during his visit to the UK. This agreement will provide certain financial support to new British nuclear power plants, e.g., at the nuclear power station Hinkley Point. Such participation of a Chinese state-owned company who is taking stakes in nuclear power plants in Europe is a very new and predictably controversial phenomenon. On the one hand, it enables future UK developments in domestic nuclear power production and boosts economic opportunities for China in this field. On the other hand, it has triggered many critical voices concerned with security issues. Here, an open investment environment appears to clash with national security interests (Nakano, 2015). In 2016, Amec Foster Wheeler, a British engineering company, and China National Nuclear Corporation (CNNC), China's other major nuclear power company, agreed on mutual cooperation (both are known to address high temperature reactors) (World Nuclear News 2016). A third central area of China-UK collaboration is climate change and renewable energies. In 2013, the Offshore UK-China Wind Co-operation project was launched. Its aim is to create an offshore wind energy industry able to compete with other energy producing industries. Thus far, the costs tend to be higher than the expected benefits (Kim 2015: 105). These concrete measurements of closer cooperation between the two actors are argued to lead to a rather positive image of the UK as an energy partner in China. This image contrasts with the past; previously, the UK was viewed as an actor lacking concrete actions in its energy interactions with China (Kim 2015: 106).

Rather predictably, energy cooperation between France and China focusses primarily on matters surrounding nuclear energy. Most recently, in May 2016, the French Foreign Minister Jean-Marc Ayrault and the Chinese Premier Li Keqiang confirmed their commitment to closer cooperation between China and France, including cooperation in the field of nuclear energy (Xinhua 2016). The agreement to cooperate on the peaceful use of nuclear energy is not new, however – it dates back to an agreement between the two countries in 1982, which was the first agreement ever for China in this field (Yi 2014). Since then, closer ties have been established in this area, with the agreement in 2010 initiating an encompassing partnership covering all stages of the nuclear fuel cycle, followed by a joint statement on civil nuclear energy cooperation in 2015. This cooperation is a result of the French industry's strong and ongoing involvement in the Chinese nuclear energy power sector. Over the last decade, French nuclear companies such as Areva, Alstom and EDF have been key actors in China's construction of nuclear power plants. Importantly, one of the pillars in China-France energy cooperation is nuclear safety (France Diplomatie 2016). China and France also cooperate in the field of climate change; they launched a joint presidential statement on climate change (it was agreed upon in the margins of the climate summit in Paris in 2015). Finally, the French Development Agency has been involved with China since 2004 through the framework of a partnership with China's Ministry of Finance and National Development and Reform Commission (NDRC). The aim of this engagement is to support China's transition to a low-carbon and environment-friendly economy. In total, 24 projects have been implemented since 2004 (France Diplomatie 2016). During Hollande's first visit to Beijing in 2013, China and

France agreed on bilateral energy cooperation in the areas of urbanization, industrial energy saving and renewables (Yi 2014).

Energy cooperation between China and the EU is multifaceted, multi-leveled and complex. It exists on the EU's supranational level and on the level of its Member States. Our analysis is evidence that the latter level of interactions often brings more specific outcomes than do China's engagements with the EU.

5.4 EU-China Energy Perceptions in Media and Elite Discourses

This chapter has thus far discussed the reality of the EU-China energy relations. It appears that with China and the EU being among the major energy consumers in the world, the two can become competitors for resources. However, shared concerns are also believed to build grounds for cooperation. With the EU recognizing the importance of China as a global energy actor and a key energy collaborator, it is important to understand how China imagines and perceives the EU in this sphere. Dominant images and perceptions trickle into the policy realm, informing and shaping it. The same holds true for the Chinese side. It is important for China to understand European perceptions of China's energy governance to evaluate China's standing with its European partners. For example, China recognizes the EU as the global leader in the area of sustainable use of energy[52] – a vision that can inform policy directions and interactions between various stakeholders in China.

As detailed in Chapter 1, in addition to our network analysis that explicated mutual perceptions among elites in both China and the EU, we assessed mutual visions coming through the respective media discourses. To remind our readers, in China, we observed daily coverage of the EU (on its own and interacting with BICS) in the *People's Daily* (government-owned newspaper) and the *21st Century* (business daily). In Europe, we observed representations of China (on its own and in interaction with the EU and BICS) in the *European Voice* (currently *POLITICO*), and in the German, British and French presses. Most articles on energy matters in China and in Europe – reporting on the EU in China and on China in the European media

52 The EU introduced the concept in the 1990s as an important norm for the EU. China officially introduced the concept to its domestic policy in 1994 (China's Agenda 21, Lai/Shi 2016; Knodt et al. 2016).

– were written by local journalists, suggesting a potential for a more extensive local 'anchoring' of global energy matters and actors. In our Chinese sample, the *People's Daily* relied entirely on local sources when reporting the EU as an energy actor. The business paper *21st Century* sample had only one article from a non-local respondent over five years. European media exhibited a similar preference for local sources. In the French sample, only one article was from a non-local source. The UK and German media were somewhat more open to the use of non-local sources (approximately 6 per cent of the sample in each case were of international origin).[53]

Overall, we discovered a major difference in how the European and Chinese media frame each other. China is by far the most visible actor among BICS in the monitored German, French and UK media, and in the pan-European *European Voice*. In contrast, the EU enjoys only a modest visibility in the monitored Chinese press. When reported, the EU receives much more attention in the Chinese press as an economic and political actor than as an energy one (Lai/Shi 2016). The total sample from the two Chinese newspapers covers 1633 articles reporting energy issues and referencing the EU and/or Brazil, India, China and/or South Africa. However, in this extensive sample, the EU as an energy actor is visible in only 87 articles, or only 5 per cent of the Chinese sample of energy-focussed news (Figure 5.2).

In contrast, when we examine the European media, significant attention is given to China in the context of energy-related news. In our sample, China was the most visible in the monitored UK newspapers, in which energy news stories referencing China appeared in 45 per cent of the total sample. China was observed in 32 per cent of the total energy sample in Germany and in 25 per cent of the sample in France. The *European Voice*, a pan-European weekly, had the lowest share of references to China in the "European" sample of our analysis – 6 per cent. However, this rather high visibility of China in absolute numbers in the European press was mitigated by a dominant minor perspective on China as an energy actor. This perspective was observed in more than one-half of the sample in the UK and Germany, whereas French reportage placed more emphasis on China (Figure 5.2). In contrast, in China, a higher share of news featured the EU with more intensity. The *People's Daily* addressed the EU from a major perspective in more than one-half of the EU sample. These two patterns of visibility – a higher volume but with lesser intensity vis-à-vis a lower volume but with

53 The UK sample was also special because it featured a high number of non-acknowledged articles (46 over five years).

higher intensity – suggest that the visibility of both actors in the energy sphere is somewhat challenged for both the EU in Chinese media and China in the European media. An assumption that media visibility of an actor translates into perceived salience of that actor informs this research.

Figure 5.2: Visibility of the EU and China in Chinese and European media

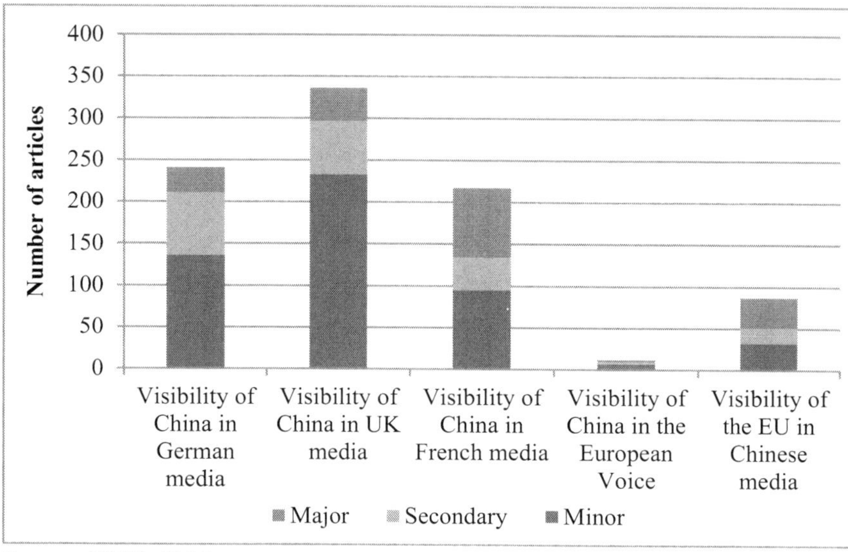

Source: EXIE, 2015.

To compare visibility of the EU and China in each others' media, we also examined other actors appearing in the EU-China energy context. In both Chinese newspapers, the EU 'energy' sample, China, rather predictably, was presented as the most prominent actor appearing together with the EU. The second most visible energy actor was the US, who enjoyed a remarkable visibility in contrast to other actors, particularly in *The 21st Century*, followed by Russia in both cases (Table 5.1). India, Brazil, South Africa and individual EU Member States are almost invisible in the EU energy-specific sample. These results are consistent with the appearance of energy actors in the total Chinese 'energy' sample, in which China was by far the most visible energy actor reported. Media observation points to media's very strong domestic focus on energy policy rather than a focus on China within global energy governance or consideration of other international energy actors (Lai/Shi 2016). With the US being a more prominent energy actor than the EU in the total 'energy' sample, it is safe to suggest that local media reflect a policy vision in which China has a stronger focus on the US than on the EU. France, Germany and the UK all appeared in the observed Chinese media but with lesser numbers than the EU itself. However, note that Member States were not specific search words in the analysis and were accounted for only when they were reported in the news referencing the EU. In the EU-specific sample for both the *People's Daily* and *The 21st Century*, the UK is slightly more visible than either Germany or France.

Table 5.1: The most visible 'other' actors appearing together with China and the EU in the media

European media reporting China as an energy actor				**Chinese media reporting the EU as an energy actor**	
German media	**UK media**	**French media**	**The European Voice**	**The People's Daily**	**The 21st Century**
US	US	US	EU	China	China
Germany	UK	France/ India	US	US	US
EU	India	EU	Russia	Russia	Russia

Source: EXIE, 2015.

Media visibility patterns echo the perceptions traced among the Chinese elites. With energy being a policy field with shared competences in the EU, EU Member States play a crucial role concerning energy policy, including external energy policy, and it was recognised by the Chinese respondents. In our research, 85 per cent of the interviewed stakeholders viewed Germany as "very important" or "important". Thus, it was recognized as the most significant EU Member State for China's energy policy. The other two important Member States were the UK and France. Germany was considered a crucial cooperation partner with respect to renewables, particularly solar and wind. France was mentioned in relation to nuclear energy. The UK was considered an important partner in general, without specifications (Zha/Lai 2015: 141). Furthermore, Denmark was often referenced due to its competencies in wind power. Close attention to France and Germany in the Chinese perceptions is reinforced by the strong presence of French and German energy companies in China. Respondents stressed that Chinese actors were more accustomed to – and even often preferred – bilateral cooperation with Member States than with the EU. It was argued that those bilateral cooperation projects were more tangible than the cooperation between the EU and China. They are also considered more flexible and efficient, not least due to the perceptions that such bilateral cooperation often has a specific focus (Ibid.: 138).

In the case of *The European Voice*, an EU-focused publication, the most visible energy actors appearing together with China were the EU, the US and Russia. In the other monitored European media, the US, the most visible actor appearing together with China, was even more a visible actor than was the EU or its individual Member States (Table 5.1). The US was reported in the energy-specific contexts and in relation to climate change negotiations. The US was much more visible in the UK sample, showing the UK's ongoing strong orientation towards its cross-Atlantic partner.

The second most visible actor in energy interactions with China in the German, French and UK reportages was the respective country itself. This is a predictable high profile because the leading papers in our sample are leading national voices, rendering a strong location-specific message in their reportage. They also tend to assign more attention to their own states' affairs vis-à-vis the EU, which might explain why these newspapers emphasize energy cooperation between their state and China, then between the EU and China. Respectively, the EU was the third most visible actor in energy addressing China in the observed French and German media, and the fourth in the UK case.

India was the third most visible energy actor addressing China in the UK media (also in the French media, in which it shared third place with the EU) and the fourth was Germany. China and India were shown to face similar challenges in the energy field, related to the need to combat climate change and pollution linked to coal consumption and to supply their huge populations with sufficient energy. Both actors have often been reported as blocking international climate negotiations and adopting a role of defending the interests of the developing countries. The latter was specifically visible in India's reports (see Chapter 6).

Our media findings on the EU's and China's visibility as energy actors echo our observations of the elites' opinion towards the EU-China energy dialogue. The EU *public* and *non-state* actors interviewed in our study unanimously agree that EU-China cooperation is important. However, Chinese actors' views differ from those of their European counterparts; 21 per cent of the interviewed Chinese non-state actors disagree that this relationship is important, whereas 40 per cent of the Chinese public actors do not evaluate the EU-China cooperation as important (EnergyGov, Darmstadt, 2014). Chinese respondents often view the dialogue with the EU as lacking concrete projects and the bilateral cooperation with EU Member States as being more important and efficient. In addition, one third of the interviewees highlighted that the dialogue (although it was initiated in 1994) only became important after 2000, with the specific focus on renewable and clean energy (Zha/Lai 2015: 138-139).

Examining the perceived effect of the dialogue on Chinese energy policy reveals, however, that Chinese actors (particularly, *public* actors) do view the dialogue as having an actual effect (83.3 per cent) despite the rather negative perception of the dialogue, as seen above. The EU actors also perceive the dialogue as affecting Chinese energy policy; however, *public* actors are more reluctant in this recognition than are *non-state* actors. Although 75 per cent of EU *non-state* actors perceive such an effect, only 50 per cent of EU *public* actors agree on this aspect. Opinions on the effect on EU energy policy diverge between the two actor groups. Perceptions of non-state actors on both sides match (with 50 per cent of EU actors and 55 per cent of Chinese actors perceiving an effect on EU energy policy); however, the opinions of Chinese and EU *public* actors are reversed. Importantly, 83 per cent of the Chinese *public* actors perceive the dialogue as affecting EU energy policy; conversely, only 17 per cent of EU *public* actors are of the same opinion, showing clear mismatched perceptions of the effects of the dialogue on EU energy policy (EnergyGov, Darmstadt, 2014).

5.4.1 Topics of EU-China Energy Perceptions in Media and Elite Discourses

Assessment of the general media visibility of the EU and China as energy actors in terms of volume and intensity of representation is further complemented by our analysis of the visibility of different *issues* and *types* of energy in the respective media discourses. Patterns and priorities in reporting energy *issues* (Table 5.2) reveal that energy issues allocated to China in the German and UK media were very similar; the issues of *energy policies/governance* and *investments* were among the top three reported by media in connection with China. In the observed French media, *energy policies/governance* was also among the top three reported issues. However, *investments* as an issue received less attention in France. *Emissions* was the third most visible issue in the German press under observation and the fourth in the UK press. In contrast, it was the most visible energy issue in the monitored French media. The issue of energy *prices* in connection with China was the second most visible in the UK and is the fourth and fifth in German and French media, respectively.

European reporters' strong focus on *energy policies/governance* and *emissions* can be explained by the timing of the analysis around the COPs and China's involvement at these summits (and the topic of emissions was related to pollution, in general). However, of interest is the appearance of the theme of *investments* – an issue that demonstrates media reflections on the connection between energy, business and companies. In the observed European media, China was presented either as a potential place of investment or as an investor itself.

In the French media, China's *energy access* was the second most visible energy issue and third most visible in the *European Voice* reportage, in which *energy infrastructure* was the most visible energy issue. Media appearance of these two issues reflects recognition by Europeans of China's challenges in supplying its population with energy. Importantly, the normative energy triangle surfaces through the media visibility of these issues; *emissions* can be connected to sustainability, *investments* and *prices* to competitiveness, and *energy access* and *infrastructure* issues to security of supplies.

China press coverage of the EU prioritizes different energy *issues*. Only occasionally do these issues intersect with the issues in the European media on China. The issue of *energy saving* was visible in both Chinese newspapers. Linked to it was the issue of *energy efficiency* – one of the three most visible in the *People's Daily*. In contrast, in the European media studied here, *energy efficiency* ranked as the fifth (UK) and eighth (Germany and France) most visible, indicating a peripheral status of this issue in the eyes of European newsmakers, with the exception of the *European Voice*, in which *energy efficiency* ranked as the second most visible energy issue. This media profile of the EU in our sample suggests that Chinese newsmakers are most interested in the EU for its technologies to save energy and to make energy use more efficient – themes that echo the top priorities of the Chinese energy policy discussed above. The issue of *climate change* appeared in the business daily *The 21st Century*, paralleling the issues of *emissions* and *energy policies/governance* in the European media. One of the most telling discoveries is that in the *People's Daily*, one of the main agenda-setters in China, the most-mentioned energy issue related to the EU was *cooperation*. Here, the Chinese media differs from other BICS media discussed in this volume who do not prioritize this issue in their respective reportages. In China, the *cooperation* profile of the EU was in place when media reported visits and meetings of the political VIPs and when cooperation in technology transfer and joint projects was in view.

Table 5.2: Visibility of energy issues in European and Chinese media

European press reporting China as an energy actor				**Chinese press reporting the EU as an energy actor**	
German media	**UK media**	**French media**	**The European Voice**	**The People's Daily**	**The 21st Century**
Energy policies/ Governance	Energy policies/ Governance	Emissions	Infrastructure	Cooperation	Energy saving
Investments	Prices	Energy access	Energy efficiency/ Investments	Energy saving	Climate change
Emissions	Investments	Energy policies/ Governance	Energy access	Energy efficiency	Investments

Source: EXIE, 2015.

Our analysis now turns to the most reported *types* of energy (Tables 5.3 and 5.4). When the Chinese newspapers report the EU's energy actions, the top three *types* of energy mentioned are 'clean energy', 'renewable energy' and 'new energy',[54] respectively. The same three types of energy topped the reportage of EU-China energy interactions. In contrast, the top three types of energy mentioned by the observed Chinese media when describing the energy actions of China were all non-renewable sources: coal, oil and gas. Lai/Shi (2016) commented on this difference:

> The contrast here is clear. Whilst the EU was framed as an actor who was working with the renewables, which are green and have lots of economic potential, China was portrayed as still using 'unclean' and old energy sources.

If we compare the most visible types of energy according to the split *renewables* vs. *non-renewables* (see Tables 5.3 and 5.4), we observe many similarities. In the context of *non-renewables*, in the eyes of each other, the EU

54 All three are mentioned as general terms in the Chinese media when referring to renewables and are used without distinctive meanings.

and China are linked to almost the same types of fossil fuel. This linking is no surprise, because oil, gas and coal are the three main fossil fuel sources for both actors. One exception here is nuclear energy, which was a topic reported differently across the EU Member States' media and by the Chinese vs. European press. In the *People's Daily* and in French media, it is the third most visible energy type and the fourth in the UK media. In the *European* Voice, it is the second most visible type (however, it is important to keep in mind the low numbers for this sample). In contrast, German press deprioritized this energy type when China was reported in the energy context. Arguably, these differences reflect diverging domestic policies on nuclear energy. Although Germany is currently phasing out its nuclear energy, it is the main electricity source in France, and the UK is investing in this source, constructing new power plants (and accepting investments from China, as discussed above). For China, nuclear energy is one type of energy in which the Chinese side is seeking cooperation with the EU and its Member States. Hence, the emphasis on this type of energy in the *People's Daily* reflects the interest of the Chinese government in cooperating more closely with the EU on nuclear energy.

Examining the *renewable types* of energy reported in the newspapers, the differences between the Chinese and European coverage of energy matters are more visible (Table 5.4). When European media reported China as an energy actor, it linked its representations to such types as *solar*, *wind,* and *renewables in general* (one article in the *European Voice* mentions *clean energy*). The observed Chinese media tends to use different terms such as *new energy*, *clean energy* and *renewables in general*. In *The 21st Century* coverage, *solar* energy is the second most frequently mentioned term in relation to the EU as an energy actor. Arguably, *new energy* and *clean energy* can be connected to *solar* and *wind* as energy types. However, that Chinese newsmakers prefer using different terms is an important finding, specifically in designing recommendations for how to improve the dialogue between the EU and China on energy matters.

Table 5.3: Visibility of non-renewable energy types in European and Chinese media

European media reporting China as an energy actor				**Chinese media reporting the EU as an energy actor**	
German media	**UK media**	**French media**	**The European Voice**	**The People's Daily**	**The 21st Century**
Oil	Oil	Oil	Gas	Gas	Oil
Gas	Gas	Gas	Nuclear	Oil	Coal
Coal	Coal	Nuclear	Coal	Nuclear	Gas

Source: EXIE, 2015.

Our analysis also examined the energy reportage in a wider *context*, i.e., which general themes were the most visible when the EU reported on China as an energy actor and China reported on the EU. The context of *economics* was among the two top dominant *contexts* in both the European and Chinese media under observation (in the *European Voice*, the position of *economics* as the second most dominant context is shared with *politics*) (Table 5.5). Hence, energy matters are communicated primarily as a means for economic interactions and gains. These findings echo our findings on energy *issues* (Table 5.2), in which *investments* and *prices* were observed among the most reported energy issues.

Table 5.4: Visibility of renewable energy types in European and Chinese media

European media reporting China as an energy actors				**Chinese media reporting the EU as an energy actor**	
German media	**UK media**	**French media**	**The European Voice**	**The People's Daily**	**The 21st Century**
Renewables	Solar	Solar	Solar	New energy	New energy
Solar	Renewables	Renewables	Wind	Clean energy	Solar
Wind	Wind	Wind	Renewables/ Clean energy	Renewables	Renewables

Source: EXIE, 2015.

Reportage of energy matters in the context of *climate change* and *environment* was another visible grounding in both the European and Chinese media in their framings of each other. Visibility of these dimensions is undeniably influenced by the timing of observation. The context of *politics* was also among the three most visible in both Chinese and European media. In fact, for the French press in our study and the Chinese party-owned newspaper, it is the most dominant context in representing China and the EU, respectively. Finally, contextualizing energy matters in terms of *development* was almost invisible in both cases (only the *People's Daily* had this theme as the fourth most visible).

Adding to our analysis of *issues*, *contexts* and *energy types*, we also assessed the visibility of actors on other levels. Assessment of the visibility of government vs. other actors can be instrumental in honing energy diplomacy between the EU and China, which is increasingly characterized by the involvement of multiple stakeholders (Chaban/Knodt 2015). Predictably, *government actors* were among the most visible – they received special attention in the Chinese party-owned newspaper. In the *People's Daily*, these actors were mostly profiled in the news stories that framed energy actions in political contexts. *Private business actors* were visible in *The 21st Century* business paper and in all three European countries. In the observed French media, the energy companies (Areva, EDF) were reported more frequently than were official actors. The UK press in our study also frequently reported *international organizations* in its energy-related stories. Among most visible *EU actors* mentioned both in China and in Europe were the actors related to the European Commission, an institution in the EU addressing energy issues.

Arguably, commonalities found in how the *issues*, *types* and thematic *contexts* of China as an energy actor are framed in the influential European press and how the EU is framed in the Chinese media suggest potential for a meaningful dialogue on energy cooperation. However, our analysis also found a number of diverging frames. As discussed above, the EU-China energy dialogue is characterized by a set of key areas of cooperation, such as energy efficiency, renewables, smart grids, energy security and urbanization. Media analysis demonstrated that not all of these topics are visible in the observed media reportage. In both the European and Chinese presses, *renewables* received attention from the newsmakers (referenced either as a generic term or as a specific type of renewable, see Table 5.4). In contrast, *energy security* was visible only in the European media reporting China (Table 5.2). The Chinese media, however, were not reporting the EU from this perspective. *Energy efficiency* is among the key official areas of cooperation; yet it was not prioritized in the observed European media when they reported China or EU-China energy cooperation (one exception was *The European Voice*). In contrast, the Chinese media directly addressed this issue in the *People's Daily* and, indirectly, in terms of *energy saving* in both Chinese newspapers.

Table 5.5: Context of energy news stories in European and Chinese media

European media reporting China as an energy actor				**Chinese media reporting the EU as an energy actor**	
German media	**UK media**	**French media**	**The European Voice**	**The People's Daily**	**The 21st Century**
Economics	Economics	Politics	Climate change	Politics	Economics
Politics	Climate change	Economics	Politics, external/ Economics	Economics	Climate change
Environment	Politics	Environment	Safety	Development/ Environment	Politics

Source: EXIE, 2015.

Notably, reportage of energy matters in the context of *urbanization* was hardly visible in both the European and Chinese media; the two Chinese newspapers in our analysis dedicated only seven articles to addressing this issue in the periods of observation across five years, whereas there were five articles in the UK sample, three in the German and one in the French (there was no mentioning of *urbanization* in *The European Voice*). This very low profile is surprising. Energy in the context of urbanization is one of the core areas of cooperation that gained increased attention at the official level (e.g., the EU-China Urbanisation Partnership Forum and the EU-China Dialogue on Smart Cities), and it was expected to capture media interest in the period surrounding the UN climate summits. In contrast, it is *investments* that were highly visible in the European and Chinese presses under observation. Each discourse framed the Other as a potential place for investments or as a potential energy counterpart in financial terms.

These findings indicate that the official dialogue between the EU and China on energy is somewhat detached from the media framings of China-EU energy relations. With leading press being among the most powerful opinion-makers on international partners in the energy field in a given society, the mismatches in framing may indicate potentially challenging areas of communication and cooperation, especially those areas that involve non-government actors.

Comparing media findings with analysis of elite opinion, we observe that both European and Chinese *public* actors considered advances in *combating climate change* the main motivation for the bilateral energy dialogue. Although this elite view parallels media emphasis on this topic, the study of elite opinion did not occur in the periods surrounding the COPs. Both Chinese and European actors consider cooperation in the area of renewables fruitful, which fits with both the motivations and the findings from the media analysis. *Technology transfer* was considered equally important for cooperation for the Chinese public actors. However, the issue of *securing energy supply for own country* did not elicit unanimous reactions; divergence can be seen in the perceptions of non-state actors. EU *non-state* actors perceived this issue as least important; conversely, Chinese *non-state* actors considered this area the most important motivation. In addition, the *promotion of private sector cooperation* is viewed differently. Although the EU *public* actors considered this area the second most important motivation for energy cooperation, Chinese *public* actors rated this option low, in fact the least important among the different motivations. Additionally, the EU *non-state* actors saw *entry into the energy market* as a significant motivation, whereas both European and Chinese *public* actors viewed this issue as less important. This last finding echoes the results of media analysis, in which *investments* were framed as a visible energy issue.

The EU *public* actors, additionally, mention *urbanization*, *energy efficiency* and *carbon capture storage* (CCS). *CCS* issue had a low visibility in the media coverage on both sides, and it does not have a prominent profile in the EU-China energy cooperation rhetoric. In contrast, *urbanization*, also a hardly visible matter in the media coverage, was claimed to be an official area of cooperation. Finally, *energy efficiency*, one of the key areas in cooperation, was mentioned by EU *public* actors, whereas European media overlooks *energy efficiency* in its reportage of EU-China energy cooperation.

Figure 5.3: Motivations of China and the EU to engage in cooperation on energy issues*

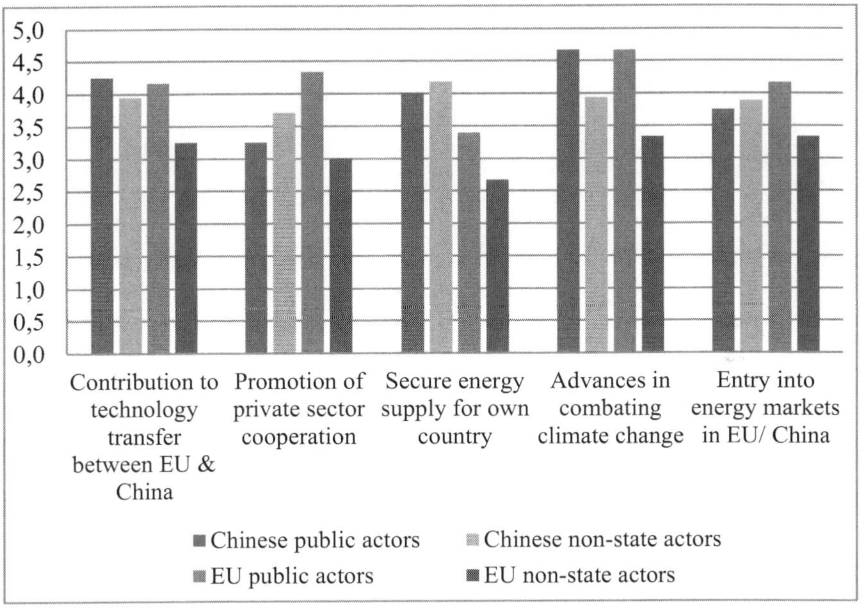

*Means of all answers; 1 = "Very unimportant"; 5 = "Very important"
Source: EnergyGov, Darmstadt, 2014.

Resonances in meanings and priorities between public, non-state and media discourses in the EU and China highlight issues that have already captured the imaginations of the two partners in terms of priorities and shared grounds. These issues could be used to facilitate and advance current dialogue. Dissonances suggest that those areas will continue to present challenges in understanding each other and effecting cooperation. Stakeholders on both sides stress that China and the EU have not yet fully explored their potential for cooperation (EnergyGov, Darmstadt, 2014).

The realization of this under-used potentials and dissonances drives the recommendations for the EU-China energy dialogue (Knodt et al. 2015b). Both sides admitted a need to launch more concrete projects and avoid "vague talk" (EnergyGov, Darmstadt, 2014). Concrete projects were requested in the areas of clean energy, renewables and technology, with several actors also noting the cooperation area on security of supplies. A shared vision of the interviewed stakeholders was that the EU and China are the two largest energy importers; thus, together, they could more significantly influence the energy market concerning supply and prices. However, both Chinese and European respondents agreed that this result is possible only if there is a better coordination of actions between the two actors. It was also noted that cooperation on energy and environment must be better interlinked. Both sides stated that the EU needs better coordination among its Member States and that it must "speak with one voice" towards China. A few voices in the EU interviewed elites wanted China to become a "true and fair market economy" to cooperate with the EU more productively, which shows that the EU remains eager to influence (or "help" as it itself states) the political system of China, whereas China wants cooperation with the EU on an equal basis (EnergyGov, Darmstadt, 2014). Moreover, Chinese actors were found to perceive a general lack of trust and understanding among the actors concerning energy matters, particularly from EU-side actors towards China. This perception inevitably brings tensions to the EU-China dialogue on energy and presents a challenge to EU-China energy cooperation.

5.4.2 Normative Orientation of EU-China Energy Relations in Media and Elite Discourses

As discussed in Chapter 3 of this book, energy policy is driven by the three fundamental normative frames of *sustainability*, *competitiveness* and *energy security*. The perceived normative orientations in the energy sphere are traced here in media and elite discourses in both China and the EU.

European newspapers under observation did not present a unified pattern in China's framing as an energy actor. Although *competitiveness* was the dominant frame of China in the German media, *competitiveness* and *sustainability* were equally visible in the UK media, and *sustainability* was the dominant frame in the French press. The *European Voice* did not prioritize any particular frame in its representations of China (Figure 5.4).

The frame of competitiveness – so visible in the UK and German case – is indicative of Europe's perception of China's drive for economic growth, the country's subsequent need for energy, and the predominant economic contexts for energy matters and competition (Bain et al. 2016). Visibility of the *sustainability* frame in the French case is partially but not only related to the timing of the analysis (around the COPs). The French press in our study also focussed on the issue of pollution related to coal consumption and development of renewable energies. In the UK, the *sustainability* frame was often mentioned in a negative context, i.e., China not taking necessary steps towards more sustainability or blocking efforts towards sustainability, including China's actions during international climate negotiations. The focus on security of supplies in the observed German and French media framed China as an actor who must fulfil its energy demand and satisfy its "energy hunger".

Figure 5.4: Energy frames of China in European media

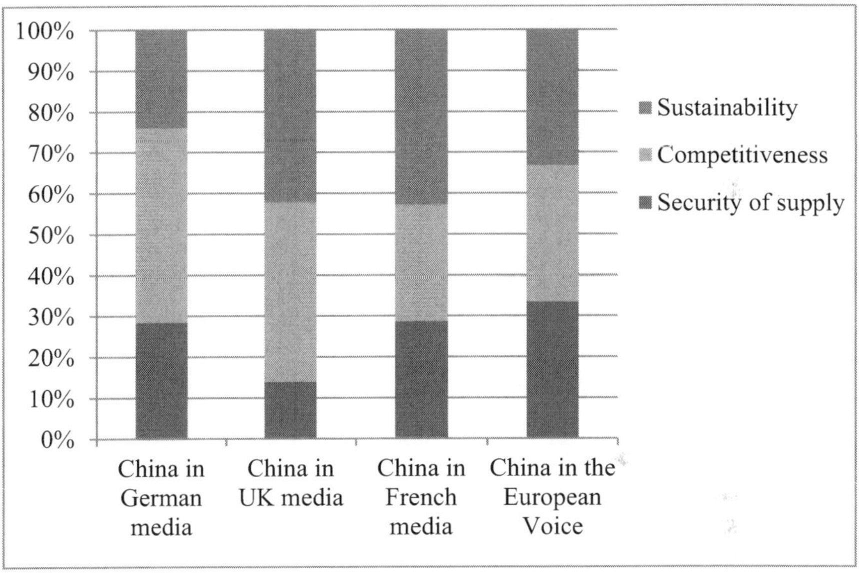

Source: EXIE, 2015.

In the Chinese newspapers, the EU was largely framed in terms of *sustainability* (Figure 5.5). This framing existed for both monitored newspapers, with the *sustainability* frame being more visible in the business daily. *Competiveness* was the second most visible frame in both papers, followed by *security of supplies*. Priority assigned to the *sustainability* frame relates to the EU's strong focus on sustainable energy development (Lai/Shi 2016), that is, commitment to renewables and priorities assigned to the energy issues traditionally linked to sustainability: energy saving, energy efficiency and combating climate change.

Figure 5.5: Energy frames of the EU in Chinese media

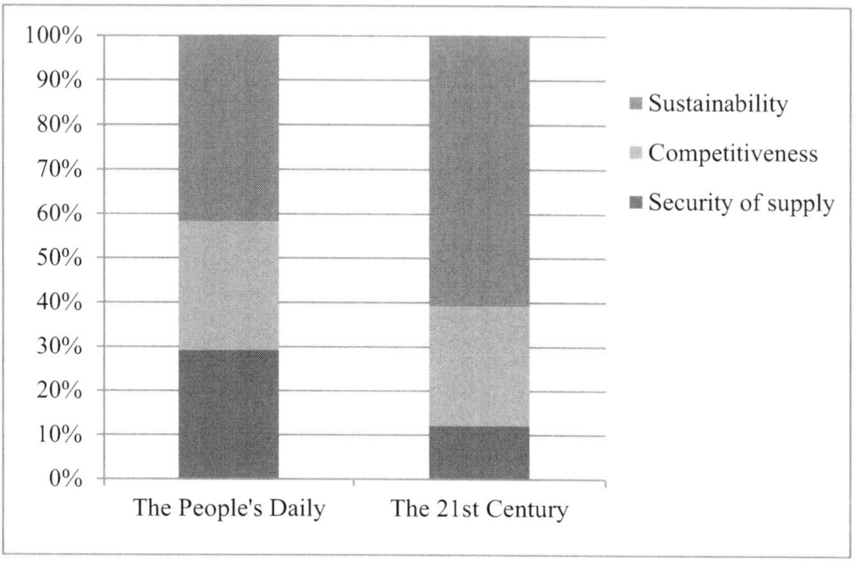

Source: EXIE, 2015.

In the analysis of the stakeholders' opinion, the interviewees were asked to rank the energy normative frames of *sustainability*, *security* and *competitiveness* in terms of importance in the dialogue and choose between different understandings/interpretations of each norm. The resulting findings informed us about the perceptions of the normative background that feed into political interactions between the EU and China in energy governance. Over one half of the EU actors valued *sustainability* as the most crucial norm in its relations with China, whereas *competitiveness* and *security of supplies* were valued significantly less (Figure 5.6).

We found that the visions of normative orientations in the energy dialogue do not match between the EU and Chinese elites. *Security of supply* is the frame widely preferred by the Chinese respondents leading in their perceptions of the EU-China dialogue, whereas the EU respondents chose the *sustainability* frame. The focus on *security of supply* in China fits with its official political discourse on energy policy (see Section 5.2 of this chapter) and reflects a high priority given to energy security. Our findings also note that European actions in the energy field are guided by a liberal understanding of energy governance, which increasingly interprets *sustainability* as *energy efficiency*, whereas China would categorize *energy efficiency* under the *security* norm. These findings suggest that the EU might factor China's priorities on *security of supply* into the EU-China energy dialogue if it is committed to establishing more-common ground. For instance, the EU might strengthen its message on a heightened relevance of renewable energy sources in the context of how these sources will guarantee China security of supply. Encouragingly, the EU-China negotiations provide evidence of a long-standing cooperation with a strong focus on *sustainability* issues (e.g., the above-discussed creation of the Europe-China Clean Energy Centre [EC2] [Knodt et al. 2015c: 332-333]).

Figure 5.6: Energy frames of China-EU cooperation by Chinese and EU stakeholders*

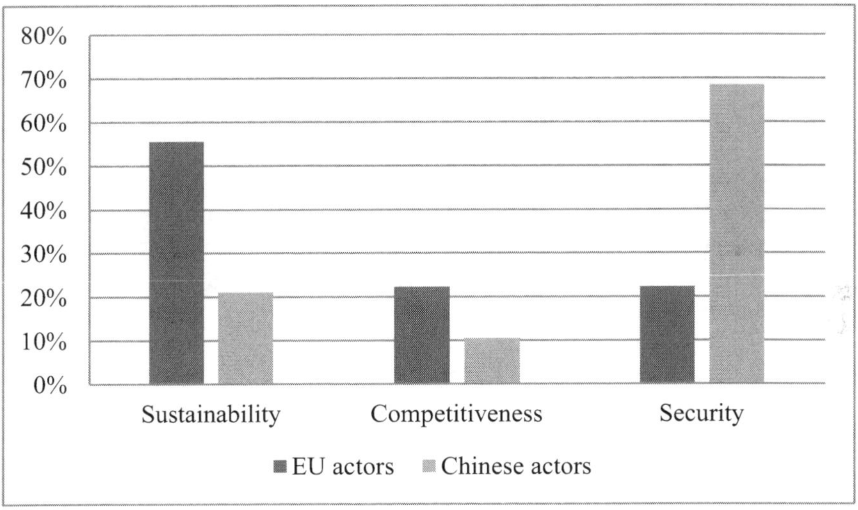

*Percentage of respondents ranking the respective frame highest in energy dialogue
Source: EnergyGov, Darmstadt, 2014.

Echoing media profiles of the EU as an energy actor in the European and Chinese media, EU actors ranked the *sustainability* norm highest in the dialogue. In contrast, the Chinese elites ranked the *security of supply* norm the highest in the dialogue. The fact that the EU is considered a sustainable actor in the Chinese media but is viewed in terms of security of supplies by Chinese public actors is not necessarily a contradiction. Although the EU as an actor is presented from a sustainability viewpoint by the media, the interest of the Chinese government lies in its cooperation with the EU focussed on security of supplies; this focus is a high priority in its domestic energy policy.

5.4.3 Mutual Perceptions as Dialogue Partners in Media and Elite Discourses (Evaluations and Roles)

The next dimension of our analysis explores the extent to which the two actors perceive each other's willingness and ability to cooperate with each other. One important indicator of these visions comes from the media data – the evaluations assigned to the EU as an energy actor in the Chinese media and to China in the European media in our sample. In the elite interviews and the survey, our respondents were asked to assess different roles of the EU and China, for instance, "being an agenda-setter" or "playing with a hidden agenda". The two indicators of evaluations and roles are argued to identify the emotive charges of mutual perceptions and visions of agenda-setting qualities, compromise-building skills and diplomatic attitudes critical for negotiations (including initiatory activities, trade-offs, and open vs. hidden agendas (Knodt et al. 2015c: 335).

In all observed European media, China was evaluated in a predominantly neutral manner, with clearly positive or negative evaluations hardly being visible (Figure 5.7). Such a neutral style of reporting could be a hallmark of the European quality press, who claim objective information-oriented reportage. Respectively, our analysis considered less clear-cut categories *positive-to-neutral* and *neutral-to-negative* to analyse more closely the evaluation of the actors (following Bain et al. 2016). Considering these nuanced portrayals, China as an energy actor was evaluated with a more negative than positive tone in the UK and French presses, and with a positive tone in the German media. The *European Voice* presented a balanced distribution between these nuanced categories. Negatively flavoured evaluations in the German media are often related to the depictions of China's competitive character, particularly concerning renewables, in which China was cast in the image of an "enemy" to the German solar industry. As mentioned above, in the UK media, negativity often appeared in the *sustainability* frame, with China described as lacking in actions as a sustainable actor and being destructive in the course of the COP negotiations. The same counts for the French media – a significant number of articles with a clearly negative evaluation of China were in the context of the climate summits, with China hindering the conclusion of an agreement at the COPs. Another negatively coloured theme was China's dumping of solar panels on EU markets (similar to German media reportage). In Germany, the positively coloured images of China were primarily linked to economics, e.g., China being an attractive place for investments, China itself investing in renewables, and being on the path to become a "world market leader in green technologies" (*Süddeutsche Zeitung*, 09.12.2010).

Figure 5.7: Evaluation of China in European media

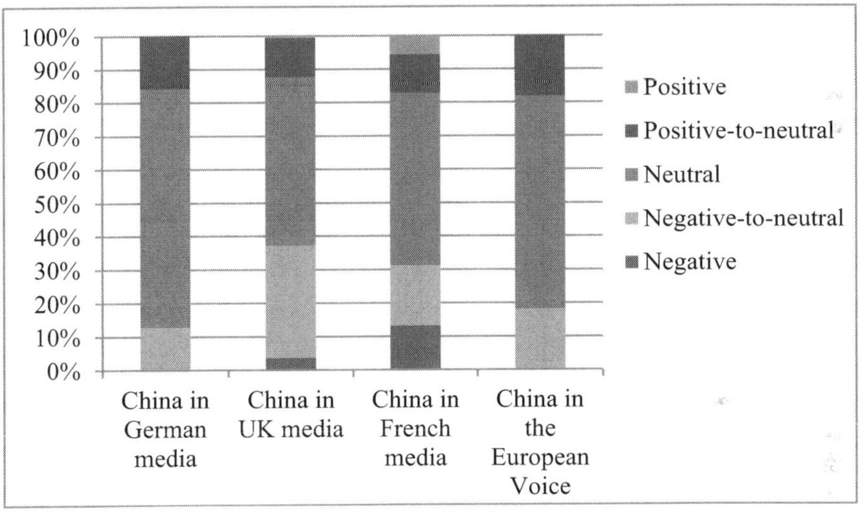

Source: EXIE, 2015.

A neutral tone dominated the portrayals of the EU as an energy actor in both Chinese newspapers. When evaluations occurred, they demonstrated a noticeable difference between the party-owned newspaper vis-à-vis the business daily (Figure 5.8). While *People's Daily* evaluated the EU from a rather positive standpoint, *The 21st Century* did not have a single article that presents the EU in a positive light in our periods of observation. It appears that the official opinion of the EU in China rendered by the party newspaper is more positive than the opinion of the business daily. The articles reporting the EU with a negative connotation addressed the topics of international climate negotiations, emissions and the solar dispute between the EU and China. Note that China was evaluated in the same articles in a neutral tone (with the exception of one article). Positive evaluations assigned to the EU by the *People's Daily* were largely in the context of the China-EU summits and the progress made in cooperation on clean energy and energy saving (Lai/Shi 2016).

Figure 5.8: Evaluation of the EU in Chinese media

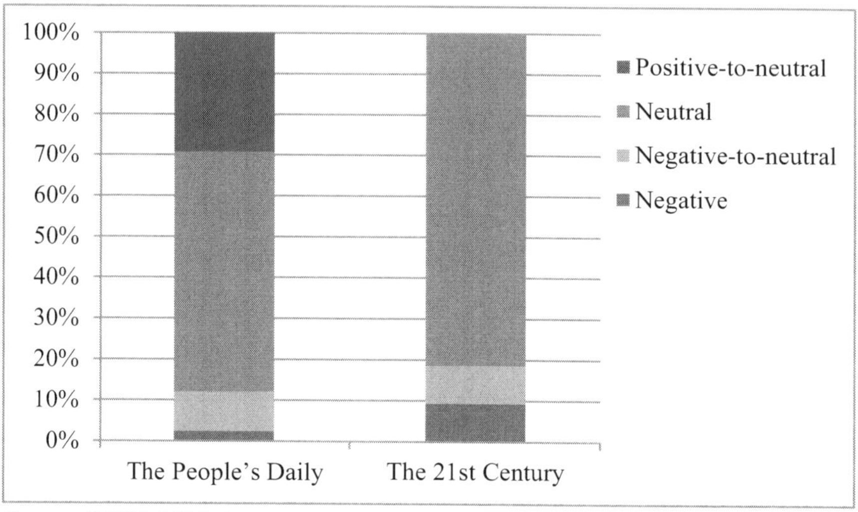

Source: EXIE, 2015.

Evaluations surfacing in media discourses show that the European side, in general, is more critical towards China as an energy actor than China is towards the EU. This media pattern is echoed by elite opinion. Positive portrayals of the EU in the *People's Daily* parallel Chinese elite opinion; the elite see the EU in a positive light concerning mutual learning and the EU's openness to compromises. The EU was perceived to raise awareness, contribute to sustainable energy development and share its expertise in this field (Lai/Shi 2016). The self-perceptions of the EU are even more positive (Figure 5.9). The EU actors themselves tend to view the EU as an active agenda-setter and emphasize the EU's high compromise-building qualities. They also see the EU as taking an interest in other negotiation partners, i.e., being open to learning. This overwhelmingly positive self-image is however slightly less supported by *non-state* actors, who also stress that the EU has been increasing pressures on emerging powers during the course of negotiations (EnergyGov, Darmstadt, 2014).

Figure 5.9: Perception of the EU's properties as a dialogue partner*

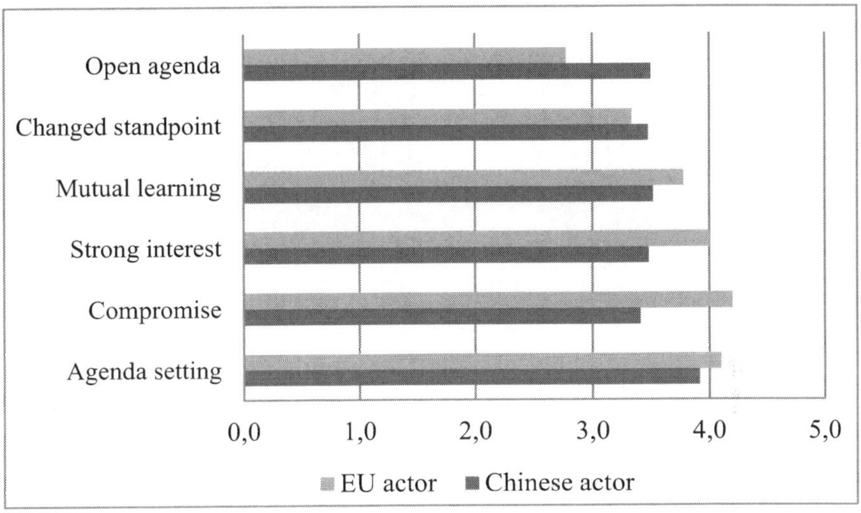

*Means of all answers; 1 = "Strongly disagree"; 5 = "Strongly agree"
Source: EnergyGov, Darmstadt, 2014.

Perceptions of China in the EU-China energy dialogue by the Chinese and European actors converge only on some aspects (Figure 5.10). Chinese elites see China's involvement in the EU-China energy dialogue as being rather transparent. In contrast, the EU considers China playing with a "hidden agenda". Furthermore, China sees itself willing to compromise, whereas the EU considers China as an actor less inclined towards compromises (Figure 5.10). Such diverging perceptions may undermine the feeling of trust between the two actors (Zha/Lai 2015: 139).

Chinese interviewees noted that in the energy sphere, China has more to learn from the EU than vice versa, a point especially pertinent in the areas of technology, energy management and regulation. Several respondents mentioned misunderstandings and misperceptions between China and the EU. The EU side is seen as questioning China's long-term strategic intentions and viewing Chinese enterprises as competitors. The solar panel trade dispute serves as the most telling example. Respondents also agreed that due to different stages of development in the economic and energy spheres, the interests of the EU and China differ. The various communication mechanisms established were viewed as positive attempts to help the situation. However, the interviewees demanded more and better communication. Another frequently named problem was the lack of openness of the Chinese and EU energy markets to foreigners, particularly the former market. Hence, trade frictions were perceived as likely to increase. Restrictions on market access are, according to the interviewees, hindering the flow of technological innovations and expertise. Blocking European companies from entering the Chinese energy market means that European advanced technology and skills are also blocked from reaching China. Many European enterprises already reluctant to sell their technology to China are aware of this issue. Interviewees remarked that such market access problem could only be settled at the EU level, between the EU and the Chinese government (Zha/Lai 2015: 140).

Figure 5.10: Perception of China's properties as a dialogue partner*

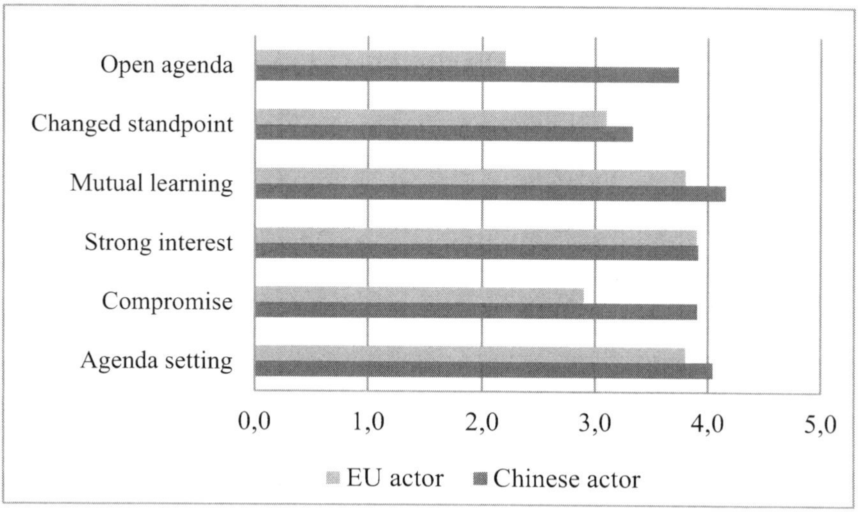

*Means of all answers; 1 = “Strongly disagree”; 5 = “Strongly agree”
Source: EnergyGov, 2014, Darmstadt.

Chinese interviewees noted that in the energy sphere, China has more to learn from the EU than vice versa, a point especially pertinent in the areas of technology, energy management and regulation. Several respondents mentioned misunderstandings and misperceptions between China and the EU. The EU side is seen as questioning China’s long-term strategic intentions and viewing Chinese enterprises as competitors. The solar panel trade dispute serves as the most telling example. Respondents also agreed that due to different stages of development in the economic and energy spheres, the interests of the EU and China differ. The various communication mechanisms established were viewed as positive attempts to help the situation. However, the interviewees demanded more and better communication. Another frequently named problem was the lack of openness of the Chinese and EU energy markets to foreigners, particularly the former market. Hence, trade frictions were perceived as likely to increase. Restrictions on market access are, according to the interviewees, hindering the flow of technological innovations and expertise. Blocking European companies from entering the Chinese energy market means that European advanced technology and skills are also blocked from reaching China. Many European enterprises already reluctant to sell their technology to China are aware of this issue. Interviewees remarked that such market access problem could only be settled at the EU level, between the EU and the Chinese government (Zha/Lai 2015: 140).

5.5 Conclusions: Lessons Provided by EU-China Energy Cooperation

Being among the world's largest energy consumers and being the world's leading energy market players, the EU and China are facing the need to maximize their energy cooperation. However, our research notes that under the current mechanisms, mutual exchanges, visions of each other and levels of trust are far from optimal.

The China-EU energy dialogue, the oldest and most advanced of the EU-BICS dialogues, has resulted in the joint implementation of many projects. Energy efficiency, renewable energies, energy security and urbanization are the topics that the EU and China have jointly agreed to address despite existing controversies (e.g., over intellectual property rights). However, the long tradition of the dialogue is not reflected in the network structure or media reportages on either side. In fact, the Chinese-EU actors' network is not yet dense and centralized, and the media profile is relatively modest in the period of observation that was expected to raise the visibility of each other in the energy field (In particular, the EU's energy profile in Chinese media is low, and China as an energy actor frequently appears as only a minor actor in the European media). In the network analysis, Chinese actors dominate the network. Only one EU actor (DG Energy) is considered the most important actor in the exchange network, and the EU Delegation and DG Energy are recognized as playing an important 'broker' role. All other European actors are viewed as playing a marginal role. It appears that fragmented energy governance structures in both the EU and the Chinese government are causing a loose and rather decentralized network. Due to the crosscutting nature of the energy policy, there are many Directorate-Generals and Chinese ministries involved in policymaking in the energy field. This polyphony makes an efficient and effective handling of the EU-China energy dialogue a difficult task (Zha/Lai 2015: 130).

Our analysis shows that a move to reach and communicate with a partner comes more from the EU actors than from the Chinese actors. Chinese actors show far less interest in the EU – because it was valued as being of low importance to the dialogue by Chinese public actors. These perceptions resonate with the leading media framings of energy actors and issues; China is far more visible as an energy actor in the European media than is the EU in the Chinese press. Moreover, China clearly values bilateral cooperation with EU Member States more highly than with the EU. It is difficult for the EU to achieve bilateral energy cooperation with China because of the different policy mixes and thus energy strategies and interests in the Member States, as in the case of the diverse nuclear polices among the EU Member States, an area in which China picks the individual Member State that suits its interests best.

Normative orientations and mutual perceptions provide explanations and allow shedding light on how the EU and China construct, interpret and shape their relationship and the political orientations that pervade external energy governance. Our multifaceted empirical analysis indicates that China has not yet viewed the EU as a prominent global energy player or a major energy partner. Indeed, China was found to be rather internal-looking in energy issues. Its strong internal motivation to reduce its reliance on fossil fuels and curb environmental damage inflicted by fossil fuels makes China particularly interested in the EU's advancements in sustainable energy development. Existing dialogue and cooperative projects between the two sides prioritize such aspects as energy efficiency, renewable energy and clean coal technology. In terms of norms of sustainable energy development, the EU was recognized by China as an advanced norm-setter. A strong will is observed from the Chinese side to learn from the EU in these areas; however, as *The Economist* (2010) stated:

> The Chinese no longer want to be passive recipients of information from the outside world; they want to shape the information for consumption at home and abroad (Lai/Shi 2016).

The EU can count some success in its energy interactions with China – for example, concerning promotion of the sustainable development norm, which is the EU's most-prioritized norm in the China-EU energy dialogue. However, the EU thus far appears not to have received China's message, namely its primary interest in and concern with respect to energy security. The same holds true for the European media in our study, which were found to frame China largely through the *competitiveness* norm. Such misperception of the normative orientation of the cooperation partner and a normative mismatch in the dialogue can result in severe problems and major miscommunications. It is important to stress that it is not a "simple process of EU actively exporting norms in the input end and China passively receiving such norms as the output" (Lai/Shi 2016). Over the decades of energy cooperation between China and the EU, China has clearly adopted some ideas and practices (promotion of energy efficiency and a renewable energy industry) but rejected others (e.g., protection of private business). As a high official from the EU Delegation Office in Beijing says, 'the EU cannot make China change; China only changes something when it itself wants to do so' (Author interview, 22 October 2013, cited in Lai/Shi, 2016). He mentions the example of energy efficiency, which the EU has been preaching to China for years without much change in China's energy policy. However, as soon as the Chinese central government discovered its own interest in this issue, many energy efficiency projects were integrated into the final period of China's 11th Five-Year Plan (2006-2010) (Lai/Shi 2016). The newest developments in reaction to the COP 21 in Paris related to joint statements on Climate Change closely linked to energy matters in the dialogue between China and the EU seemed to give new impulse for the long-term relation and may be another step of confidence building.

Chapter 6
Overlooked Partner or Budding Counterpart? EU-India Mutual Perceptions as Energy Actors

6.1 Introduction

Miguel Arias Cañete, European Commissioner for climate action and energy, presenting at the 2016 EU-India Summit in Brussels, enthusiastically noted:

> [a]s a major world player, India is a crucial partner for the EU on energy and climate matters. I look forward to deepening our already fruitful relationship with this new partnership. Together, the EU and India can boost energy security and fight climate change through a clean and sustainable energy system (European Commission 2016d).

This Summit demonstrated to the world a commitment to revitalize EU-India bilateral relations. Both parties declared their mutual vision of being "global partners and the world's largest democracies" and "reaffirmed their commitment to strengthen the EU-India Strategic Partnership based on shared values and principles" (European Council 2016a: 1). The Summit also represented a breakthrough in EU-India energy relations: both partners adopted the 'Joint Declaration between the EU and India on a Clean Energy and Climate Partnership'. The Declaration outlines the EU and India's commitment to continue dialogue and cooperation on clean energy, energy efficiency and climate action (Joint Declaration 2016). Importantly, it is clearly linked to the 2015 Paris Agreement. The EU's hopes for a renewed climate dialogue with India include reinforced energy cooperation, primarily on renewable energy sources, and the promotion of clean energy generation and increased energy efficiency. India is a fast-growing economy with a sizable and rapidly increasing population – conditions that indicate its rising demand for energy. India is not only one of the world's largest energy consumers but also a large market for both conventional and non-conventional energy technologies. Predictably, the EU considers its engagement with India in the energy field to be essential. For India, the EU is also a promising partner due to the EU's technical expertise in general and in the areas of solar power, cross-border pipelines and nuclear power in particular. India's energy policy shows a trend of shifting towards the use of renewable energies in response to the COP 21 in Paris. Even before the Summit, India's climate vision outlined its intention to follow "a cleaner path than the one followed hitherto by others at a corresponding level of economic development" (cited in IEA 2015c: 3).

Considering the latest joint declarations by the EU and India and their seemingly shared visions and intentions in the field of energy and climate, the aim of this chapter is to identify and assess mutual perceptions the two have about each other as energy actors – when they imagine each other acting independently and in collaboration. It traces where the elite perceptions and media images of one another resonate and where they clash. It explores how images and perceptions reflect the controversies and shared ground between India and the EU and how they contribute to the EU-India dialogue in the context of external energy governance.

6.2 India's Energy Policy

India's energy consumption has nearly doubled since 2000, bringing India into the group of the world's largest energy consumers. This consumption is linked to India's rapid economic rise; in 2010, India's GDP grew by 10 per cent. Despite some decline in recent years, the GDP growth rate remained 7.6 per cent in 2015 (WBG 2016b). Hence, the potential for further rapid growth in energy consumption is enormous (IEA 2015c: 11), and India's economy desperately requires securing substantial growth in primary energy and electricity supplies. Moreover, there is an urgent need for a reliable infrastructure to ensure supply for growing energy demands. India's energy strategy focuses primarily on utilizing all available domestic resources to obtain optimal output, including hydropower, oil and gas, nuclear energy, biofuels and other renewable energies (Knodt et al. 2010). Despite current efforts towards a more diverse and sustainable energy mix, fossil fuels will continue to be a crucial part of India's energy mix; coal accounts for 58 per cent of its energy consumption (Figure 6.1), and 70 per cent of power generation is coal based (EIA 2013). Coal is likely to remain the leading energy source because India possesses abundant coal resources and is able to secure competitive prices on it. According to the IEA, a

> large expansion of coal output makes India the second-largest coal producer in the world, but rising demand also means that India becomes, before 2020, the world's largest coal importer, overtaking Japan, the European Union and China (2015: 13).

Importantly, the sector of renewables is growing fast, particularly in the areas of solar and wind energies; however, it is not without negative environmental and social impacts. Nuclear power is also gaining an increasing share in India's energy mix (Joshi/Ganeshan 2015: 151).

Figure 6.1: India's energy consumption (2015)

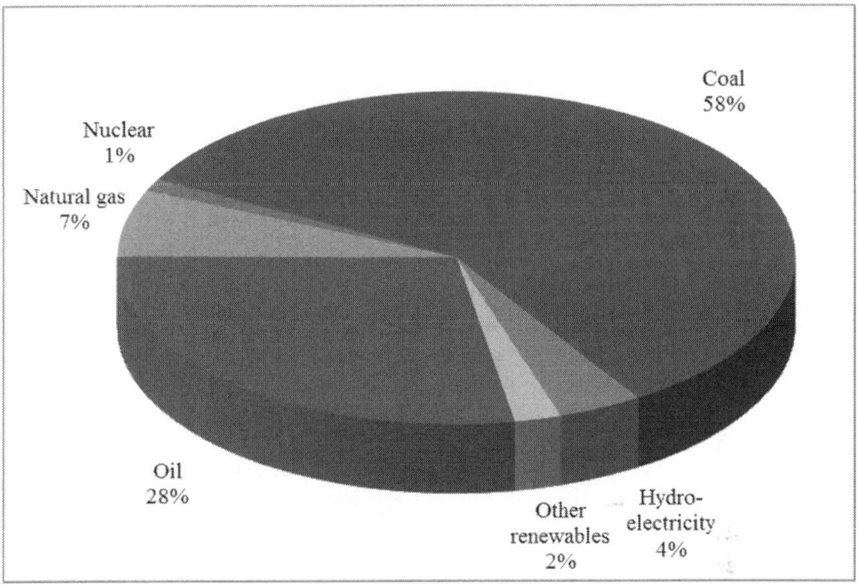

Source: BP Statistical Review of World Energy 2016.

One of the unique characteristics of India's energy governance – particularly in light of India's economic growth – is a close link between securing energy access and aspects of development. A combination of increasing domestic energy demand and limited domestic supply leads to a debate on energy security and energy poverty. Energy poverty is defined here as a

> lack of access to modern energy services, including both electricity and clean cooking facilities (that is, fuels and stoves that do not cause indoor air pollution) (Jaeger/Michaelowa 2015: 236).

Problematically, approximately 25 per cent of India's population lacks access to electricity, and 66 per cent use traditional biomass for cooking (Ibid.: 237). The country aims to guarantee a secure, affordable and sustainable supply of energy in its social development policy. In its 2006 Integrated Energy Policy, the Indian Planning Commission delineated India's energy security objectives for the next few decades. The objectives include a promise to supply energy to all Indian citizens and produce safe and convenient energy at competitive prices at all times (Planning Commission 2006; see also Joshi/Gansehsan 2015: 151).

In this context, energy security appears to be a strong candidate to frame India's energy governance. India's preference to explore and exploit domestic oil, gas and particularly coal resources and to expand domestic energy production through new nuclear plants indicates that India is striving to be energy independent and self-reliant. However, there remains an ongoing debate over whether India's goal should be "energy independence" or "energy security" (Betz/Hanif 2010: 12-13). Both appear difficult to achieve because India is becoming more vulnerable and dependent upon foreign energy sources due to its rapid economic growth (Knodt et al. 2010).

The Indian energy governance system is a complex and fragmented multi-level system that reflects India's status as a federal state. The Planning Commission, the Department of Atomic Energy, the Bureau of Energy Efficiency and the four energy ministries – the Ministry of Power, Ministry of Coal, Ministry of New and Renewable Energies (MNRE) and Ministry of Petroleum and Natural Gas – each play a major role. Furthermore, independent regulatory authorities for electricity, oil and gas and coal have been established in the last decade (Dubash 2011: 68). Coordination among these various bodies is challenging, although the Planning Commission (now the National Institution for Transforming India [NITI Aayog]) strives to assert control over the other actors. Furthermore, state-owned enterprises (SOEs) are important actors in Indian energy policies, with Coal India Limited, the national Oil and Natural Gas Commission and the State Electricity Boards being the most important (Ibid.: 69). State-owned Coal India Limited is the largest coal-producing company in the world, the second-largest employer in the world and the largest employer in the country (Coal India Homepage 2012 cited in Knodt et al. 2012). The creation and execution of a more coherent energy policy has for decades been one of the objectives of India's government. The Planning Commission was established in 1950. Issuing the Integrated Energy Policy document in 2008 was another major step. A Cabinet Resolution on 1 January 2015 replaced the Planning Commission with the National Institution for Transforming India (NITI Aayog) to facilitate the implementation of the Resolution. In its first year of existence, on 1 October 2015, NITI Aayog submitted India's Intended Nationally Determined Contribution (INDC) to advance India's energy and environmental policies. The INDC clearly aims at pursuing a more climate-friendly and cleaner path for India, including commitments to increase the share of non-fossil fuel power sources to 40 per cent and to reduce emissions intensity by 33-35 per cent (measured against the 2005 baseline), both by 2030. It also oversees the India Energy Security Scenarios, launched in 2015.[55]

The current Indian administration, which came into office in 2014, is also attempting to solve the vertical cooperation problem in energy governance. India is a federal system in which regional and local entities play an important role in energy policy in addition to the national institutions. In the energy area, the central government has exclusive competence over mineral and oil resources and nuclear energy. States have jurisdiction over natural gas infrastructure, water issues, taxation on mineral rights and the consumption/sale of electricity. Both national and federal actors share power on electricity. The new administration is now promoting a model of co-operative federalism – also used in federal Germany's energy system – to coordinate these different levels. It includes devolution developments, which are coupled with a higher regional share of hydrocarbon revenues in some cases to enable the regional level to participate financially in energy transformation processes. It also introduces a wider set of regional responsibilities to speed the implementation and approval of the state-level clearances required for investment projects (IEA 2015c: 42).

6.3 EU-India Energy Dialogue

The signing of the Strategic Partnership Agreement with India in 2004 indicated a widening of the EU's 'new' focus on Asia, which until then had been almost exclusively on China. Previously, the rising Indian subcontinent had, to a certain extent, been neglected by the EU. This attitude was not perceived well in India and led to anti-European sentiments fed by colonial and early post-colonial legacies and discourses (Jaffrelot 2006; Piefer et al. 2015a: 47). The earlier attempts to negotiate an India-EU Association Agreement failed due to the EU's classification of all South Asian countries as "non-association" partners (Abhyankar 2009, cited in Joshi/Gansehsan 2015: 153). In 1980, two Commercial Cooperation Agreements were signed between the EU and India. The early 1990s brought a more active political dialogue, with the signing of a political cooperation

55 The Indian government has developed an energy scenario-building tool – Indian Energy Security Scenario (IESS) 2047 – intended to explore the potential of future scenarios for India. http://www.indiaenergy.gov.in/iess/news_details.php [10.08.2016].

statement (1993), a Joint Political Statement (1994) and a Cooperation Agreement (1994), all of which helped to broaden the relations between the two partners (Joshi/Gansehsan 2015: 153).

The reality of a multipolar globalizing world challenged the EU to become more aware of India as a potential strategic partner. It pushed the EU to address miscommunications with India and to focus closely on the diplomatic balance between India and China as the Union's key partners in Asia (see Chapter 2). It also led to enhanced cooperation in several sectors, including closer engagement in the energy and climate fields. These two fields are now among the main fields of cooperation in the strategic partnership agreement (Bava 2007; Noronha/Sharma 2009). It is only logical that the framework of the Strategic Partnership, formulated in November 2004, included the political decision to initiate an energy dialogue. Its key priorities are the development of clean coal technologies, increasing energy efficiency and savings, promoting environmentally friendly energy sources and assisting India in energy market reforms (DG Energy 2010). The 'EU-India Energy Panel for dialogue and cooperation on energy issues' was created as a formal instrument of cooperation in 2005. Since its inception in 2006, regular meetings of the panel and its working groups have been held. The four working groups on Coal/Clean Coal Technology, Renewable Energy/Energy Efficiency, Petroleum/Natural Gas and Fusion/ITER report directly to the panel, and the proceedings are jointly discussed.

Because coal is the main source of energy production in India, great importance is attributed to the associated working group (e.g., it has held more frequent meetings than have the other groups). At first glance, the priority assigned to this dialogue group might not appear to be in line with the EU's priorities on climate change and renewable energy. However, interviews we conducted in our project in New Delhi (September 2013) justified the rationale behind this heightened attention to the Coal/Clean Coal Technology Working group. Coal will remain the leading energy source in India in the immediate future. Respondents believed that engaging on dialogue and cooperation on clean coal technologies represents a promising start; this energy sector will continue to have a major influence on India's overall energy situation (in contrast to other sectors). A significant effect can be achieved by cleaning up the energy produced from coal (which is where the greatest Indian interest lies) (Piefer et al. 2015a: 47-48).

In contrast, the Working Group on Renewable Energy and Energy Efficiency exhibits very little activity. Although both India and the EU emphasize the importance of sustainability in the rhetoric of their energy dialogue, this emphasis has hardly been reflected in the working group's activities, with only sporadic meetings having occurred. The focus of the group was on relevant exchanges among academics, researchers and business stakeholders. Additionally, the group facilitates sharing experiences on running public awareness campaigns, standard setting for energy-using products, developing technologies on energy efficiency and establishing efficiency standards for buildings. Photovoltaic, solar thermal, wind energy, biomass combustion and gasification, and biofuels are areas of collaboration in research and development. However, despite the large range of areas of cooperation, the outputs of this Working Group remain limited, which might be explained by the fact that renewable energy as a topic in EU-India cooperation is primarily situated in the development cooperation portfolio, which has been phased out. Moreover, cooperation in these fields traditionally occurs though strong cooperative ties between India and several EU Member States, such as Germany and Spain. Nevertheless, the EU and India agreed on a Joint Work Programme on Energy, Clean Development and Climate Change adopted at the EU-India Summit held in Marseille in 2008. Most recently, these issues have been enhanced by the success of COP 21, with many countries adopting the Paris Agreement on Climate Change in December 2015. In their 'Joint Declaration between the EU and India on a Clean Energy and Climate Partnership', the two partners stated that they recognize their common interest in promoting clean energy generation and increased energy efficiency for climate action and the positive contribution that clean energy generation and increased energy efficiency can make to global energy security (European Council 2016a: 1)

In November 2011, at the 6th EU-India Energy Panel held in New Delhi, both energy partners agreed to extend the dialogue. Regular exchanges on energy security matters, enhancing the security of supply, and coordination of positions in international organizations and initiatives on energy were the new areas of cooperation. These areas also included EU-India coordination on relations with Russia, Turkmenistan and other Central Asian countries. Energy security is even mentioned as one of the objectives of the new Clean Energy and Climate Partnership agreement. Interestingly, the strategy on energy security incorporates the question of nuclear power, which is discussed in the Working Group on Nuclear Fission. This has been made clear through India's active participation in the ITER project[56] on fusion research since 2005. In addition, the Euratom-India Agreement on Fusion Energy Research was concluded in 2009. However, civil nuclear cooperation on nuclear fission has not seen progress, not least due to bilateral cooperation in this area between India and EU Member States such as France and the UK.

At the EU-India Summit in February 2012, the energy agenda was refocused to spur progress in seven new priority areas, which were embedded in the 'Joint Declaration for Enhanced Cooperation on Energy' (Joint Declaration 2012). The Declaration reiterated the importance of development and deployment strategies for clean energy production, inter alia, clean coal technologies and advanced coal mining. Both partners agreed to improve the energy efficiency of products and energy efficiency in the building sector. Cooperation on renewable energy sources and the development of smart grids was decided and a focus established on energy safety (nuclear and offshore drilling safety). The EU and India endeavour to advance the development of fusion energy as one future sustainable energy source. Thus, the energy dialogue between the EU and India has great potential to become more dynamic; interest in enhanced cooperation is repeatedly voiced by both sides. However, personnel constraints – in the sense of limited and frequently changing staff – on both sides and the phasing-out of development cooperation with India are obstacles in this area. In the future, these efforts will be incorporated under the Energy Panel, but the question of how to replace budgets that are no longer available remains. Interviewed stakeholders hoped that the new Partnership Instrument would provide bridge funds (Piefer et al. 2015a: 48) because development is now addressed by the new Clean Energy and Climate Partnership agreement. Meetings of the EU-India Energy Panel and its working groups have a strong business orientation, and the working groups are instrumental in paving the way for cooperation between European and Indian energy firms. In the new initiative on Clean Energy and Climate Partnership, a stronger link to civil society and stakeholders is visible.

Here, we analyse the perceptions of interactions and exchanges of the actors involved in the EU-India energy dialogue and their importance of

56 ITER (the Latin word for 'the way') is an international consortia of researchers from China, the European Union, India, Japan, Korea, Russia and the United States engaged in a 35-year collaboration to advance fusion science and technology for future fusion power plants (https://www.iter.org).

each other (traced with the help of a social network analysis). First, the Indian importance and exchange networks are among the less dense networks of the four cases considered in this book. The density of the importance network is only 0.14, compared with 0.29 for Brazil (discussed in Chapter 4). The density of the Indian exchange network is 0.10 (it is the second lowest after China; see Chapter 5). The centrality of the importance network is also low. It ranks in last place – 15.4 (tied with South Africa; see Chapter 7). The degree of centrality in the importance network is 13.7, a middle position, comparable with Brazil (Piefer et al. 2015a: 49).

In the importance network, perceptions revealed that there not a single European actor was considered one of the five most important actors (which is similar to other cases in this book). DG Energy was considered the second-most important actor in the exchange network (similar to the Chinese case). The EU Delegation in India and DG Energy were rated among the five most important brokers in the exchange network, with the EU Delegation also being the most important broker. The results of the aggregated network analysis point to the perceptions of far fewer exchanges among actors of different groups than in the other three dialogues. Indian *public* and *non-state actors* were viewed as engaging in regular reciprocal exchanges, and EU *non-state actors* were largely viewed as addressing the EU. The exchanges between the Indian *public sector* and EU *non-state* actors and between Indian *non-state* actors and EU *public* actors were perceived to be very low (actually below the average of the Indian network). Moreover, the EU was viewed as only addressing the Indian *public* actors, but not vice versa. In terms of importance, the picture is more balanced, but the EU *public* actors still appear to be in a rather remote position compared with their Indian counterparts. The EU *public* actors viewed the Indian *public* actors as important, but not vice versa. All sides appear to consider the Indian *public* actors important and attempt to gain access to them (Piefer et al. 2015a: 48-49). Both Indian and EU respondents emphasized that more-concrete projects should be included in the dialogue (Interviews New Delhi, September 2013). In their opinion, the dialogue is more like a 'talk-shop', lacking specific projects with clear goals and implementation procedures. This opinion was particularly held when the EU was compared with bilateral initiatives towards India by EU Member States. One example was the Indo-German Energy Forum, a dialogue platform with concrete joint projects. When asked why there are no joint projects between the EU and India similar to the EU-China energy dialogue, respondents from both sides highlighted a persistent mismatch in expectations; the EU expects concrete inputs from India on what India wants, whereas India expects the EU to develop concrete proposals for what it could offer – a 'catch 22' situation. Due to the lack of human resources on both sides to follow up and engage in discussions with various stakeholders, no concrete proposals have materialized thus far. For the energy dialogue to remain relevant, this issue must be overcome. There is a great willingness on the Indian side to contribute funds to support potential joint projects. For example, one interviewee in New Delhi (September 2013) suggested that the EU and India could jointly finance and establish an India-EU Energy Policy Centre in which not only the EU's but also Member States' expertise on, for example, energy policies and regulations could be exchanged with interested Indian partners. Stakeholders' perceptions also revealed a shared understanding of the challenge in addressing constituent parts of their polities – with the EU being a 28-Member State organization and India being a federal state. Perceptions featured recognition of the complex coordinative challenges both actors face – with dispersed ministerial structures in India and the complex structure of the EU's Directorates-General and agencies. Furthermore, it appears to be unclear to the Indian stakeholders what added value cooperation with the EU provides in comparison to cooperation with its Member States. This aspect is not unique to the dialogue with India, but Indian interviewees were clearly asking about specific EU value added (Piefer et al. 2015a: 50).

Moving up from energy relations to the larger picture, there are general tensions between the EU and India concerning closer economic cooperation. Some of these tensions affect the ongoing negotiations over the parties' bilateral free trade agreement (FTA) (see Chapter 3). The FTA agreement might affect energy cooperation; issues of 'green energy' and 'clean energy' are a part of the FTA negotiations and covered in a special section. Effectively, the FTA should cover the elimination of tariff and non-tariff barriers to clean energy technologies as part of a general liberalization strategy for environmental services. This approach would, for example, affect investment conditions in the Indian energy sector. Here, FDI regulations do not allow 100 per cent foreign capital, but are restricted to 74 per cent (Sawhney 2008: 19). Furthermore, much pressure exists, particularly from the EU and Germany, to install an intellectual property rights regime that would go even beyond the WTO's TRIPS agreement (*The Hindu* 2013, quoted in Piefer et al. 2015a: 50). As long as the EU-India FTA negotiations are experiencing a series of standstills due to different liberalization schedules and the long-standing dispute on investment conditions and IPR, agreements in the energy sector will be thwarted, and the delay might hinder more substantial cooperation. This problem also affects questions of technology transfer to the extent that IPR issues such as licensing and patenting are affected (Piefer et al. 2015a: 50).

In the EU, Germany plays a crucial role for India. Of all EU Member States, it ranks second in imports from India and first in exports to India (Eurostat 2014). At the heart of German-India energy relations is the Indo-German Energy Forum, viewed by the Indian elite respondents as a successful model for energy interactions (Interviews EnergyGov in New Delhi, September 2013). The Forum was created in 2006 by Indian Prime Minister Manmohan Singh and German Chancellor Angela Merkel to enhance cooperation in the fields of energy security, energy efficiency, renewable energy and investment in energy projects. Currently, planning and implementation are collaborations between Indian Ministries and the German Development Organization GIZ (Gesellschaft für Internationale Zusammenarbeit). Participants in the dialogue are the Indian and the German Governments, public institutions and the private sector. The latest – 6th – German-Indian Energy Forum (13 February 2015) in New Delhi focussed primarily on renewable energies, demand-side energy efficiency and low-carbon growth strategies. Although the Forum started in 2006, a bilateral Indo-German Energy Programme (IGEN) has been in place since 2003. IGEN supported the implementation of the Indian Energy Conservation Act, adopted in 2001, and served as another example of successful cooperation between the two countries. In 2008, another bilateral programme was created that was intended to support concrete cooperation projects that emerge from the dialogue. The connection has two dimensions. On the one hand, the bilateral cooperation projects provide inputs in the form of identifying clusters of problems and searching for possible solutions on the ground. On the other hand, the dialogue's results are transferred to the bilateral programmes to promote their implementation. The results thus far demonstrate several successes emerging from this approach. One example is the joint effort on the construction of green energy corridors in India, which is supported by Germany with an allocation of 1 billion EUR through the banking group Kreditanstalt für Wiederaufbau (KfW).

The UK and India also cooperate in the energy field; however, energy was initially discussed in a general context of bilateral relations with a focus on technology transfer and investments. Energy was not treated as a separate area of cooperation, a change that occurred due to the civilian nuclear accord signed in 2010 to enhance nuclear energy cooperation (Kim 2015: 106). After the UK-India Summit in November 2015, bilateral energy relations were strengthened and intensified through a 'Joint Statement on Energy and Climate Change' (Department of Energy and Climate Change

2015). This document evinces the willingness for closer cooperation in the field of climate change and shared commitments ahead of the then-upcoming UN Climate Summit in Paris (Ibid.: 2). Tellingly, in Paris, the UK-India climate and energy partnership was showcased at the Indian Pavilion. The then British Prime Minister Cameron and Prime Minister of India Modi agreed on regular meetings at the ministerial level to advance current cooperation projects and explore the potential for cooperation. Both actors signed a Memorandum of Understanding to enhance cooperation on electricity market reform, energy efficiency, offshore wind energy, solar, smart grids, energy storage and off-grid renewable energy services (Ibid.). The energy market in India is of particular concern to the British private sector because the Indian government has set a price ceiling for energy (particularly on natural gas), a move that hinders UK companies in turning a profit but protects consumers (Kim 2015: 107). In the Joint Statement, these aspects are to be combined to "promote energy security and economic growth and deliver a cost-effective low carbon transition" (Department of Energy and Climate Change 2015: 4). It remains to be seen whether the announced reforms of the Indian gas market will boost UK investments. At the ministerial level, it is expected that UK-India energy relations will receive less attention in the aftermath of Brexit and Cameron's resignation.

Nuclear energy is at the core of the energy relations between India and France, with France being the first country to sign a civil nuclear agreement with India (2008). In 2009, a Memorandum of Understanding was signed between the two partners to pave the way for six nuclear reactor units in Jaitapur (in progress) (Kumar 2013). France's expertise in this field makes it an attractive partner for India. Conversely, France expects significant economic benefits and to gain a global ally in the nuclear power energy field from this partnership. France strongly supports India's efforts to become part of the global export control regime. To both actors, nuclear energy is of great importance for ensuring energy security and combating climate change. Following the UN Climate Summit in Paris, India and France sought to implement the Paris Agreement through cooperation in sustainable development and energy, covering governments, regions, cities and companies. This approach was emphasized in their Joint Statement from January 2016 during Hollande's visit to New Delhi during the 67th Republic Day celebrations. Both partners are also members of the International Solar Alliance (ISA) (2015), seeking to enhance the use of solar energy on a global scale and cooperating on joint research, development, financing and technical innovation. French companies are heavily engaged not only in the field of nuclear energy but also in the area of renewable energy. Additionally, the French Development Agency (AFD) is a strong supporter of India's development of cleaner and more efficient energy (e.g., through technical assistance in the establishment of Smart Cities in India). Although France and Germany continue to provide financial development assistance to India, such development cooperation was phased out in the UK in 2015. As discussed above, the EU's development cooperation with India is also being phased out, and renewable energies are no longer being financed through DG DevCo (Piefer et al. 2015a: 48).

6.4 EU-India Energy Perceptions in Media and Elite Discourses

The observed divergence between the rhetoric of the EU-India energy dialogue and the results of our network analysis invites us to assess the mutual perceptions of each actor as energy actors in various discourses. This section details our analysis of mutual perceptions found in media and elite discourses.

Observed press coverage (2011-2013, surrounding the annual Conferences of the Parties to the UNFCCC [COP]) demonstrated that the EU had minimal visibility in the Indian media in general and as an energy actor in specific. During three years of analysis (of one month of each year; see Chapter 1), only 135 articles reported on the EU and/or its institutions, largely in the frame of economics. A minor degree of intensity further undermined the EU's limited visibility. In our 'EU' sample in Indian media, the EU was reported in the energy field in only one article. India's 'energy' sample in the three years of analysis accounted for 337 articles. Barely 9 per cent of this sample addressed the EU in the context of energy. This low profile shows that the EU was not presented to the Indian public as a crucial energy actor or a visible energy partner of India. Moreover, when reported on in the context of energy, the EU was largely addressed from a minor perspective (Figure 6.2). The peripheral visibility of the EU's interactions with India as an energy actor was further emphasized by the considerably more pronounced visibility of other actors, specifically China and the US. This lack of media visibility for the EU in India echoes the findings obtained by previous studies on perceptions of the EU in India (Chaban/Elgström 2014: 178; Jain/Pandey 2015; Olivier/Fioramonti 2010). In our research, Indian media reporting on the EU as an energy actor relied heavily on domestic Indian sources – with a visible input for the Times News Network, India's largest media conglomerate. The European media considered in our study – when reporting on India – also extensively used their respective local sources. The UK coverage of Indian energy matters featured the largest number of non-local sources – 11 out of 114, with two additional articles being of mixed origin. However, this share is relatively small. The nature of news sources suggests the potential for grounding of the respective reporting of one another in local contexts and discourses. A failure to consult the other party's news sources also indicates the possibility that the nuances and priorities of the other's energy matters are overlooked.

Figure 6.2: Visibility of the EU and India in Indian and European media

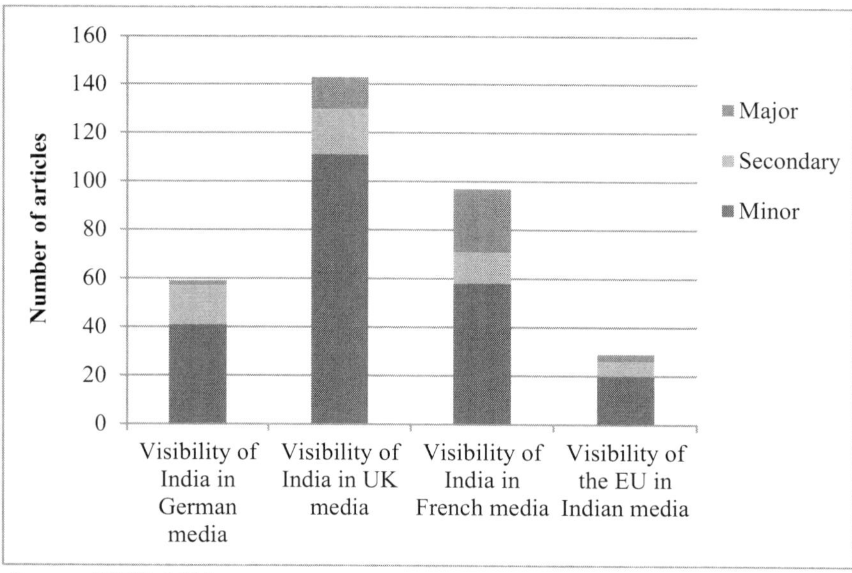

Source: EXIE, 2015.

Assessing the visibility of India as an energy actor in European media (this sample is described in Chapter 1), India presented a modest profile in both the German and French press. In the observed German media, reports that referenced India represented 8 per cent of the total 'energy' sample, whereas in the French press, the corresponding coverage was 11 per cent. However, India's degree of visibility differs between the two EU Member States. Although German media in our sample reported on India as a major actor in only two articles, 26 articles (27 per cent of the India-specific sample) in the French media framed India as the central actor of the news story. Although India was not featured as a major energy actor/partner in the UK media, it remains considerably more prominent when compared with its characterization in the German and French media (19 per cent of the UK 'energy' sample). The historical ties between India and the UK and the activation of the energy dialogue in recent years (discussed above) are among the first explanations for why India may be more visible as an energy actor in the UK reportage. Overall, the European media observed in this study were more interested in reporting on China as an energy actor than on India (see Chapter 5). In the *European Voice*, a pan-European newspaper typically read by EU practitioners and scholars, India as an energy actor appeared in only three articles during our period of observation (as a minor actor in two articles and as a secondary actor in one article). *The European Voice* sample, due to its minimal size, is not included into our analysis below.

In our analysis, we also compared the media visibility of India and the EU to the visibility of other actors in the energy field that interact with the two sides. In the three European samples of Germany, France and the UK, China was the most visible energy actor mentioned together with India. The high visibility of China in this case adds another piece of evidence in support of our argument of China being framed by leading presses around the world as the most prominent energy actor and interlocutor (either promising or challenging). European newsmakers made a visible link between India and China in the energy field – both actors were often reported as the two 'emerging powers' with rising energy demands and increasing CO_2 emissions. The two were therefore also often presented in tandem when climate negotiations were discussed in the press. The US appeared as the second most visible energy actor together with India in the three European cases. Each respective country – France, Germany and the UK – appeared as the third most visible actor, surpassing the visibility of the EU in their respective country samples (Table 6.1). Even Brazil was more reported than the EU in the three European cases.

These findings indicate that EU-India energy relations did not appear to be a high priority for the three European countries' influential presses. This low media profile might influence the perceptions of the public and elites who read these leading papers that EU-India energy relations are of peripheral importance. Moreover, although the visibility of the respective countries among the most visible actors is predictable – domestic context and concerns are always a priority for leading national newspapers – paradoxically, the European press chose to focus on Indian energy relations with external actors (China and the US first) rather than with the EU. This particular media profile framed India as being eager to engage on energy matters with other, external-to-the-EU actors.

We must not forget that this profile exists against the background of India's low visibility (specifically in the German and French samples). The EU's attempts to invest in and bring more attention to its energy relations with India did not resonate with German and French newsmakers and may potentially contribute to a muted awareness and vague perceptions of the EU-India energy dialogue in these two countries. The observed UK media evidenced a somewhat higher visibility of India (arguably linked to the UK's historical ties with India), but the reportage was still detached from India-EU relations (perhaps not a very surprising finding given the outcome of the Brexit referendum in 2016).

In the observed Indian media, when they reported on the EU as an energy actor, India itself was the most visible actor mentioned together with the EU. In fact, there was only one article in the sample in which India did not appear when the EU was mentioned. This framing indicates a strong 'local hook' when the EU is presented as an energy actor. The US was the second most visible actor together with the EU, and China was the third.

Table 6.1: The most visible 'other' actors appearing together with India and the EU in the media

European media reporting India as an energy actor			**Indian media reporting the EU as an energy actor**
German media	**UK media**	**French media**	**Indian media**
China	China	China	India
US	US	US	US
Germany	UK	France	China

Source: EXIE, 2015.

In the interviews conducted with European and Indian actors directly involved into the EU-India dialogue – *public* and *non-state* – all actors stated that they view the dialogue as important. This shared view points to a great interest in the EU-Indian energy dialogue and even a readiness to invest in intensifying energy cooperation. However, as discussed above, there is lukewarm commitment and a lack of progress on both sides of the dialogue.

Examining the perceived impact of the dialogue, neither EU nor Indian actors considered that the EU-Indian dialogue affects EU energy policy. While 83 per cent of the Indian actors did not view the dialogue as influencing EU energy policy, 75 per cent of the EU actors were of the same opinion (EnergyGov, Darmstadt, 2014). Examining the sub-groups, the results differ. All EU *non-state* actors and Indian *public* actors viewed the dialogue as having no real effect on European energy policy, whereas Indian *non-state* actors and EU *public* actors appeared to be slightly more optimistic. Here, 40 per cent of EU *public* actors and 33 per cent of Indian *non-state* actors perceived the dialogue as having an effect.

In contrast, EU *public* actors and Indian *non-state* actors have different evaluation of the effect of the dialogue on Indian energy policy. Sixty per cent of the EU *public* actors and 67 per cent of the Indian *non-state actors* viewed the dialogue as having an effect, whereas only 33 per cent of *EU non-state actors* and Indian *public* actors perceived such an effect. These perceptions of EU and Indian *public* actors of a low overall impact on one another's energy policy match the lack of engagement in the actual energy dialogue.

Neither the EU nor India received substantial visibility as an energy actor in the other's media. The content analysis of reported *issues, types* and *contexts* discussed below reveals a number of common patterns (and major differences) that contribute to our discussion about how images and perceptions can facilitate (or obstruct) energy dialogues.

6.4.1 Topics of EU-India Energy Perceptions in Media and Elite Discourses

In the German media under observation, India was largely mentioned in connection with *energy policies/governance* (Table 6.2). This finding is connected to the period of observation around the annual COPs: India appeared largely as a minor actor and mostly in the context of the UN climate negotiations together with other actors. The thematic framing of India was similar in the monitored UK and French media. In the UK press, *emissions* and *energy policies/governance* were the most visible energy issues in reporting on India. In the French case, *emissions* were by far the most visible energy issue related to India. These energy issues are both closely connected to the theme of sustainability and the attempt to find global solutions to climate change.

Investments in the German media represented the second most visible energy issue, which indicates German interest in the potential of the Indian energy market as an investment target for German companies in the energy sector. In the UK media, *energy efficiency* was the third most visible energy issue. This focus reflects the UK's interest in linking with India, which is prioritizing its search for a more efficient energy system. Specifically, the coverage examined the role that European actors (specifically the UK) could play in this area. Note that *cooperation* was also a visible energy issue in the UK media (being the fourth most visible energy issue), which can count for (potential) cooperation in climate politics and energy efficiency. In the French and German media in our study, we saw security of supplies being reflected in the articles addressing the themes of *energy access* and *energy infrastructure*.

The focus on *energy access* dominated the observed Indian media overall. It was also the most frequently mentioned energy issue in connection to the EU. This media framing demonstrates India's strong need for and focus on securing energy and its current challenges in ensuring a reliable energy supply for its vast population and rural areas. Because of the need to address this issue, there is a prevalent interest towards the EU as a cooperation partner. *Prices* was the second most visible energy issue reported, followed by *investments*. Both are related to the *competitiveness* norm; however, *prices* are also connected to the *security of supply* norm. The period of observation around the COP did not appear to affect the visibility of the issues in Indian media, biasing them towards sustainability themes.

In summary, we observed a significant difference in how the two actors present each other in the monitored media. European influential press chose primarily to focus on the role of India in relation to international climate negotiations – a topic that Europe finds important for itself. Leading Indian media were more concerned with addressing the country's immense domestic challenge of acquiring a secure energy supply (which was only partly reflected in German and French media). Thus, the EU was framed primarily as a potential economic partner specifically in the area of energy supply. Our analysis demonstrates that the two sides chose to present and perceive in one another in the areas and issues that were important to them, not to the interlocutor – a pattern we already observed in the cases of Brazil and China and will see in the case of South Africa in this volume. These visions of the Other – filtered through a self-focussed perspective – are potentially an obstacle to meaningful energy dialogue between India and the EU, especially if they are not listened to by both sides and incorporated into interactions.

Table 6.2: Visibility of energy issues in European and Indian media

European media reporting India as an energy actor			**Indian media reporting the EU as an energy actor**
German media	**UK media**	**French media**	**Indian media**
Energy policies/governance	Emissions	Emissions	Energy access
Investments	Energy policies/governance	Energy infrastructure	Prices
Energy access	Energy efficiency	Energy Access	Investments

Source: EXIE, 2015.

Assessing the coverage of energy in general, we tracked the visibility of non-renewable *energy types* assigned by the observed European and Indian press to each other (Table 6.3). *Oil* and *gas* were overall the most frequently mentioned non-renewable energy types, which came as a surprise – we initially expected *coal* to predominate. The only exception was France, where *nuclear energy* clearly dominated the media discourse on energy, reflecting the great importance of nuclear power in France's own energy mix. Moreover, nuclear power is an area central to the energy cooperation between France and India discussed previously. *Coal* and *nuclear power* were among the most reported in the observed German and UK media (in the UK case, *nuclear power* was the fourth most visible energy *type*). In contrast, when Indian newspapers in our sample reported on the EU as an energy actor, *coal* appeared in only two articles and *nuclear power* was not mentioned at all. This is despite the fact that coal is the most important energy source in India, nuclear power is gaining greater attention in the effort to secure the domestic energy supply, and the activities of the working group on coal are the most active in EU-Indian energy cooperation, as discussed above. Furthermore, while a longer period of observation may yield greater visibility for the EU in the context of *coal* and *nuclear power* energy types, the EU's low media visibility in relation to these *types* in our period of observation may have conveyed a message that the EU is not 'imagined' as a cooperation partner in these areas. It might also indicate that India considers nuclear cooperation with individual EU Member States to be more fruitful than cooperation with the EU. As discussed above, the UK and France in particular are actively cooperating with India in the field of nuclear energy.

Table 6.3: Visibility of non-renewable energy types in European and Indian media

European media reporting India as energy actor			Indian media reporting the EU as an energy actor
German media	**UK media**	**French media**	**Indian media**
Oil	Oil	Nuclear	Oil
Coal/Gas	Gas	Oil	Gas
Nuclear	Coal	Gas	Fossil

Source: EXIE, 2015.

In all three EU Member States, reports on India referencing *renewable* energy types were much less visible than were the reports on *non-renewables*. This difference is even more pronounced in the Indian media: while *non-renewables* were mentioned in almost three-quarters of the articles reporting on energy-related matters and the EU, *renewables* appeared in less than one-fifth of the articles in our Indian sample. Neither influential Indian press nor the European media under observation portrayed the EU and India as actors cooperating extensively in the area of renewables. However, we want to remind our readers that the data were collected before the latest shifts in Indian policy towards renewable sources of energy. When *renewables* were reported on, *wind* and *solar* power attracted the most media attention across the borders, together with *renewables in general* (Table 6.4). Hence, although India and the EU are not presented as great cooperation partners on renewables, the types of *renewables* prioritized by the media were the same in both locations.

Our next point of analysis is dedicated to the *contexts* within which the EU and India were framed as energy actors in the respective media. The three main *contexts* were *economics*, *climate change* and *politics* (Table 6.5). Although *economics* was the most visible *context* in both German and Indian media in our study, *climate change* dominated the energy discourse in the UK, and *politics* was the most visible in the French media coverage of India. The dominance of the *economics* context in the observed media echoed the high priority placed on economic relations between the EU and India (Joshi/Ganeshan 2015: 149). *Climate change* being the second most visible context and the visibility of the *environment* in the French media were related to the period of our analysis around the annual COPs and indicated the strong interconnection between these policy fields. Climate change cannot be combatted without addressing the ongoing dominance of fossil fuels. *Development* as a context was hardly visible in the monitored German and French media, which is surprising considering the official development assistance towards India from Germany and France. In contrast, the *development* context appeared in 21 articles in the UK case, making it the fourth most visible dimension. India had been receiving overseas development assistance from the UK until 2013, which has arguably influenced the visibility of this context (Bain et al. 2016). The Indian media in our sample had *development* as the third most visible context for the EU energy representation. However, the total number of articles is very low in the Indian case; thus, the actual visibility of the articles referencing the EU in the *development* context is minimal.

Table 6.4: Visibility of renewable energy types in European and Indian media

European media reporting India as energy actor			**Indian media reporting the EU as an energy actor**
German media	**UK media**	**French media**	**Indian media**
Renewables, in general	Wind	Renewables in general/ Solar	Solar
Wind	Solar	Wind	Wind/Renewables, in general
Solar	Renewables, in general	-*	Green energy

*No other energy type is mentioned more than once
Source: EXIE, 2015.

The visibility of *issues*, *contexts* and *energy types* was closely linked to the visibility of the actors at different levels. In the German media under observation, *private business* actors were the most prominent actors when India was reported as an energy actor, followed by *governmental* actors. In contrast, *academics*, *international organizations* and *NGOs* were much less visible. This gallery of actors in the German media demonstrates recognition of the role of companies in energy-related matters. The appearance of *business* actors also echoes the visibility of *investments* as a leading energy issue and *economics* as a leading context, as discussed above. Among the *governmental* actors, many German actors were mentioned; however, Indian governmental actors were almost invisible (only two articles mentioned the former Indian Prime Minister Manmohan Singh). In the monitored UK media, the *governmental* actors were the most prominent when India was reported as an energy actor, followed by *international organizations*. This pattern in actors' visibility reflects the UK press's prioritization of *emissions* and *climate change* in energy-related reportage. The difference between German and UK reportages highlights a strong focus of the German media on India's economic potential in energy-related matters vis-à-vis the UK media's dominant concern with India's role in relation to international climate negotiations. In the observed French media, both *governmental* actors and *private companies* were visible in the Indian 'energy' sample. Among the private companies, Areva and EDF were the most prominent actors, particularly Areva, reflecting its involvement in India's expansion of nuclear power. Among the most visible *governmental* actors were former French president Sarkozy (2007-2012) and the former Indian Prime Minister Manmohan Singh. In the Indian press in our study, *state-owned businesses and oil companies*, including the Indian ONGC and other international oil companies, appeared in only two articles during our period of observation.

Table 6.5: Context of energy news stories in Indian and European media

European media reporting India as energy actor			**Indian media reporting the EU as an energy actor**
German media	**UK media**	**French media**	**Indian media**
Economics	Climate change	Politics	Economics
Politic	Economics	Environment	Politics
Climate change	Politics	Climate change	Development

Source: EXIE, 2015.

The visibility patterns of various *issues*, *contexts* and *energy types* – and the actors associated with them – provide further evidence supporting our key argument in this volume – in reporting on the Other (or relations with the Other), the Self sets this reportage in issues and contexts that matter locally, prioritizing them. Below, we compare media frames to the elite perceptions identified in the course of interviews and the survey. Perceptions of the motivations for EU-India energy dialogue are very different among Indian *public* actors vs. EU *public* actors (Figure 6.3). The former linked their view on motivation to a high interest in technology transfer. The area of special interest for Indian *public actors* was energy efficiency and clean energy technologies to achieve cleaner production of coal. However, this focus was only partially echoed by the EU actors. Although EU *public* actors appeared to be most interested in combating climate change, EU *non-state* actors were most interested in technology transfer, market entry and the promotion of private sector cooperation. These perceptions indicate that the dialogue could benefit from a stronger focus on technology transfer and better-articulated support for European interests in market entry and private technology cooperation by the EU (Knodt et al. 2015c: 338). Conversely, EU *public* actors showed an extremely high interest in combating climate change. We must bear in mind that the elite data, like our media data, were collected before the latest move in Indian policy-making towards renewable energies. Future research may examine whether there is a change in elite perceptions after the COP 21 in Paris. We hypothesize that after the 'Joint Declaration between the EU and India on a Clean Energy and Climate Partnership' (European Council 2016a), greater motivation may be observed on the Indian side.

Figure 6.3: Motivations of India and the EU to engage in cooperation on energy issues*

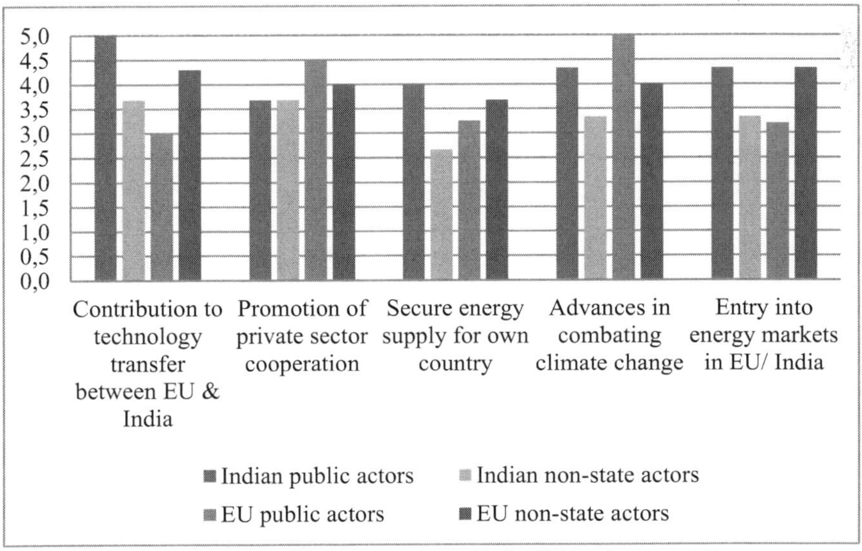

*Means of all answers; 1= "Very unimportant"; 5= "Very important"
Source: EnergyGov, Darmstadt, 2014.

Beyond being major trading partners, India and the EU do not depend upon energy trade because the two do not trade energy supplies. In this light, entry into their respective markets and the promotion of private sector cooperation do not appear as strong motivations. In particular, the EU *public* actors did not show high motivation in this area. In contrast, they appeared to be motivated by the promotion of the private sector.

With future energy supplies being a top concern for India's energy policy, it is telling that India's stakeholders did not regard cooperation with the EU as being important. This perception could indicate that India's stakeholders do not view the EU as an essential partner in supplying energy to India. This opinion among Indian elites differs from the Indian media under observation, which mentioned *energy access* as the most dominant energy *issue* when looking towards the EU.

6.4.2 Normative Orientation of EU-India Energy Relations in Media and Elite Discourses

We now turn to how India and the EU frame and perceive one another in terms of the three *normative energy frames*: *sustainability*, *security of supplies* and *competitiveness* (see the Introduction and Chapter 3 for their definitions). Different normative frames are in the limelight of media attention in India and in Europe when the two portray one another as energy actors (Figure 6.4). Although India was largely framed within the *security of supplies* frame in the German press in our sample, the main focus on India in the UK media was *sustainability*. The dominance of *sustainability* in the UK related to the reports on international climate negotiations and India's role in creating a negotiation bloc as a means of applying political pressure on Western actors. In contrast, the observed German media framed India as an actor concerned with rising energy demands. The term "energy hunger" appeared rather frequently in the German press when India was reported (Bain et al. 2016). In both European countries, *competitiveness* was also somewhat visible and was more so in the UK. This frame emerged when India's economic potential in energy relations was emphasized. In the French media monitored in our study, the framing of India as an energy actor was almost equally divided between *security of supply* and *sustainability* (with a minor lead for the former frame). This correlated with the most frequently reported energy *issues* of emissions, energy infrastructure and energy access. Some of the reportage on India in the *sustainability* frame related to its actions at the annual COPs; however, a number of articles in the French press reported on India's interest in facilitating nuclear energy in its energy mix and on the involvement of Areva in the construction of two nuclear reactors in India (Bain et al. 2016). Nuclear energy was presented by the French media as ensuring a cleaner energy mix and a reliable energy supply for India's vast population. This media framing of nuclear energy resonates with the official positions of France and India on their nuclear energy cooperation, as discussed earlier in this chapter. In the observed Indian press, framing of the EU as an energy actor in terms of *sustainability* was the most visible of the three frames, while *competitiveness* was the least visible frame.[57]

Figure 6.4: Energy frames of the India and the EU in European and Indian media

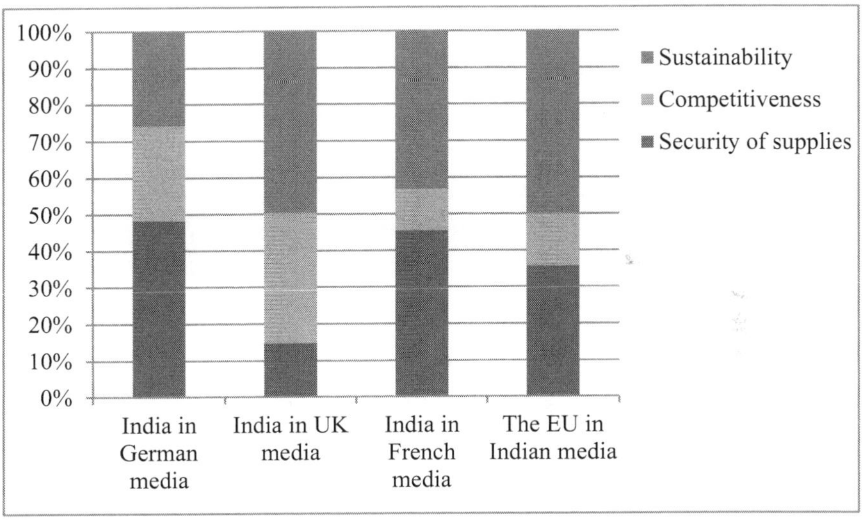

Source: EXIE, 2015.

Indian stakeholders ranked both *sustainability* and *competitiveness* as important. This balanced perception may indicate an early reflection of the emerging orientation towards renewables in India. The first steps in this direction were policy instruments in the first decade of the century, such as the 'National Tariff Policy of 2006', which mandates that State Electricity Regulatory Commissions purchase "a minimum percentage of electricity

57 However, we would like to be cautious with this conclusion and remind our readers that the sample of the observed Indian press reporting the EU was very small.

from renewable sources" and "launching the Jawaharlal Nehru National Solar Mission in 2009" (Joshi/Ganeshan 2015: 163). The emphasis on *sustainability* is argued here to be not only connected to the gradual expansion of renewables in India but also indirectly connected to the low value attributed to *securing energy supplies* visible in our survey data. However, in the qualitative interviews, *security* was highlighted much more than in the survey data.

Figure 6.5: Energy frames of India-EU cooperation by Indian and EU stakeholders*

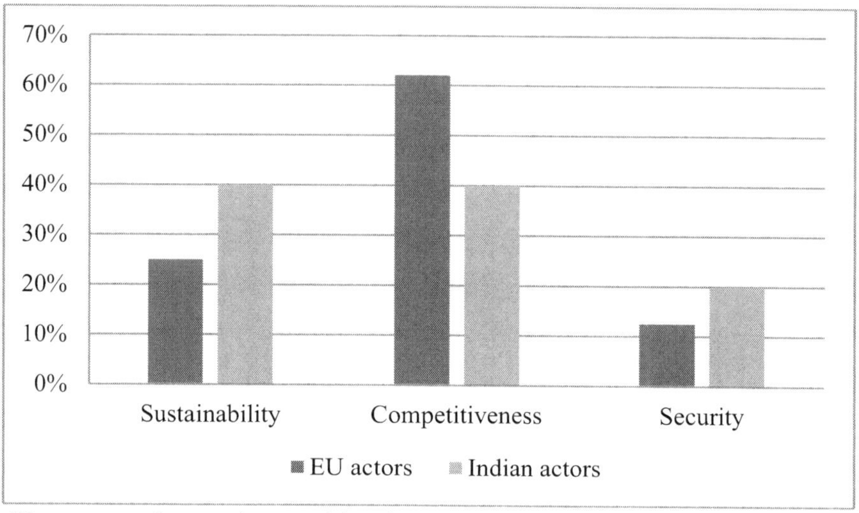

*Percentage of respondents ranking the respective frame highest in energy dialogues
Source: EnergyGov, Darmstadt, 2014.

6.4.3 Mutual Perceptions as Dialogue Partners in Media and Elite Discourses (Evaluations and Roles)

Our analysis of mutual perceptions now turns to *evaluations* assigned by the EU and Indian media to each other in their energy dialogue and to the perceived roles and characteristics of each other. The former dimension was assessed using media discourse, and the latter was traced in the responses to in the elite interviews and the survey.

In the European media in our study, a neutral tone predominated in the portrayals of India in the three country-specific samples (Figure 6.6); however, when evaluations appeared, positive evaluations were less visible than negative. A substantial share of negative evaluations of India in the three cases appeared in the news reporting on India's destructive involvement in the climate change negotiations.

Figure 6.6: Evaluation of India and the EU in European and Indian media

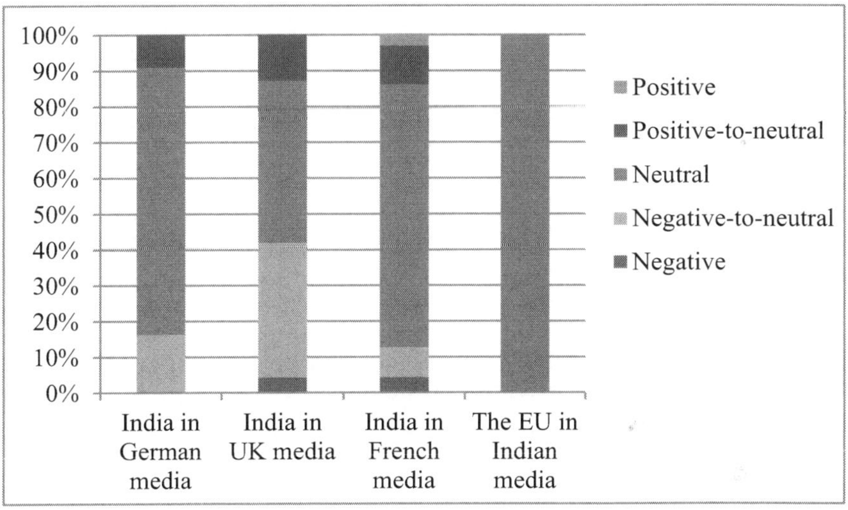

Source: EXIE, 2015.

In the monitored German press, the articles reporting India from a negative perspective presented India in the context of the COPs and India's ever-rising energy consumption followed by an increase in CO_2 emissions in India. Of particular interest is one article that addressed India's ambitions to invest in and expand its nuclear energy and protests from a civil society movement against nuclear energy in the Southern state of Tamil Nadu. The role of foreign investors was discussed in the context of severe concerns regarding the Indian authorities' ability to manage the security and safety standards of nuclear energy technology (*Der Spiegel*, 19.11.2012). This and other articles framed China and India as competing actors in this field. These rivalries were often framed in terms of geopolitical controversies and competition for natural resources. In the French case, negative and negative-to-neutral stories on India also focussed on India's problematic involvement in the annual COPs. Although the French press observed in our study also had several positive stories on India in relation to climate change, negative evaluations led when this issue was reported. It is noticeable that there were no negative stories on India connected to its expansion of nuclear energy in the French sample – only positive ones, indicating France's interest in this development and its positive overall views on nuclear energy, in contrast to those in Germany. The UK media featured the most negative views in our sample. In the British press, negative images of India appeared in the reportages addressing COP 18 in Doha (2012), the construction of new coal power plants, and safety issues concerning nuclear power plants in India.

The Indian media in our study presented the EU as an energy actor from an exclusively neutral perspective. Previous analyses of the EU's images in the Indian media also reported that Indian media portrayed the Union almost exclusively in neutral terms (Chaban/Elgström 2014: 179).

Figure 6.7: Perception of India's properties as a dialogue partner*

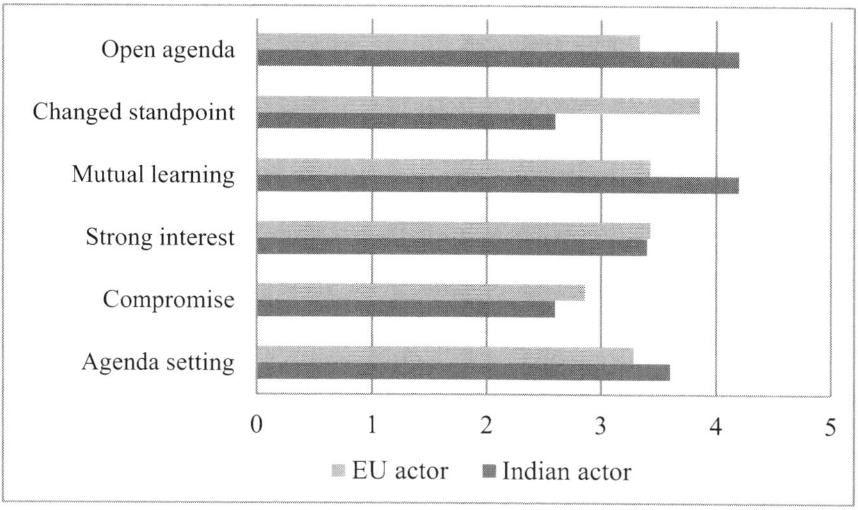

*Means of all answers; 1 = "Strongly disagree"; 5 = "Strongly agree"
Source: EnergyGov, Darmstadt, 2014.

Complementing the media analysis, we analysed elite interviews and a survey intended to identify properties assigned to the EU and India as dialogue partners by stakeholders involved in EU-India energy dialogue. A number of critical differences between the views of the two partners were observed.

The main difference concerned how the EU and Indian stakeholders perceived India as a dialogue partner (Figure 6.7). Although Indian respondents considered India acting with an open agenda in this dialogue, the EU actors perceived India as acting with a hidden agenda. The same holds true for the perception of India being open to mutual learning. European actors perceived the Indian side to be less willing to engage in learning processes. In contrast, Indian respondents saw themselves as being open to mutual learning. Interestingly, the EU actors also viewed Indian interlocutors as not insisting on but as changing their position, whereas the Indian dialogue partners did not perceive themselves as having changed positions.

Figure 6.8: Perception of the EU's properties as a dialogue partner

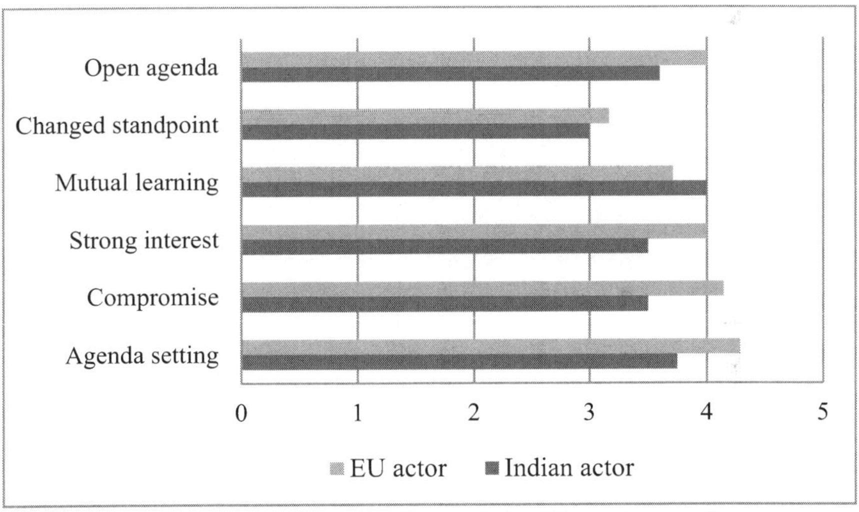

*Means of all answers; 1 = “Strongly disagree”; 5 = “Strongly agree”
Source: EnergyGov, Darmstadt, 2014.

Regarding perceptions of the EU held by both European and Indian actors, European actors saw the EU as challenging India’s position and increasing pressure on Indian partners during the dialogue and negotiations (Figure 6.8). They also saw themselves as having more influence on agenda-setting, in contrast to how Indian stakeholders’ perceptions. Moreover, the EU actors perceive themselves as being more willing to compromise than the Indian actors did. Surprisingly, the Indian actors attributed to the EU a greater willingness to engage in and openness to mutual learning than the EU actors perceived about themselves. Overall, European and Indian actors' perceptions did not differ as much when they judged the EU's properties as a dialogue partner vis-a-vis when they considered India as a dialogue partner.

Our analysis leads to the conclusion that a rather negative perception of India exists on the European side (both in the media and among elites). This perception might hinder otherwise promising cooperation between the two partners.

6.5 Conclusions: Lessons Provided by EU-India Energy Cooperation

The COP 21 in Paris and the EU-Indian discourse following the summit revitalized EU-Indian energy relations. Even before this landmark meeting, both sides agreed that the energy dialogue required improvement. It appears that a formerly overlooked partner is becoming a budding counterpart. Although the dialogue was initiated in 2004, both parties still consider it to be in its initial phase. The EU actors stated that there is a need for greater commitment from their side and a general need for more frequent high-level meetings and more active low-level cooperation between those meetings to achieve concrete results. In addition, they noted that the mutual interests and the goals of the energy dialogues should be clarified (Madhura/Ganeshan 2015: 165). Thus, as with other cases of bilateral energy cooperation in this volume, views on EU-Indian energy cooperation are characterized by a high interest in undertaking cooperation, but actual cooperation still lacks quality and substance.

Ultimately, both European and Indian elites viewed bilateral EU-Indian energy cooperation as being important. However, this view is not reflected in either the European or Indian media under observation during a period that was expected to raise each others' energy profiles. This point is specifically confirmed in the cases of influential German, French and Indian newspapers. The low visibility of the EU in the Indian media parallels the finding that the majority of the Indian *public* actors did not consider EU-India energy cooperation to actually affect Indian energy policy. Hence, such cooperation might not appear to be an important topic for local newsmakers to report. The same picture can be found in the perceptions of the EU-Indian dialogue. The network analysis showed that EU actors in the network were considered marginalized and in a rather remote position. Indian actors were perceived to be more important and attractive for the EU than vice versa.

Differences in the perceptions of the dialogue can also be observed regarding different topics of the cooperation. In the eyes of Indian actors, greater cooperation in the area of technology transfer is needed. This vision matches the high priority assigned to this aspect in the dialogue. Steps towards increased technology transfer are already acknowledged in the dialogue – both Indian and European actors view cooperation on renewables and particularly on clean coal technology as being fruitful. Interestingly, this vision was not reflected in the media during our period of observation, a period that was expected to heighten the visibility of such topics. Clean coal was not among top reported issues in either India or Europe. In the German media, clean coal technologies were only mentioned in one article; the UK media mention them in only two articles. It was also striking to see that coal as an energy source was only mentioned in two articles in our Indian media sample focussing on the EU – and clean coal technologies did not appear at all. In addition, cooperation on technology transfer, stressed by the Indian elite respondents, was also not a prominent issue in the media. A situation in which core cooperation areas are not communicated by the leading media in the period of observation that is deemed to raise the profile of energy matters presents a challenge for the dialogue in the future. In general, EU-India cooperation on energy issues enjoyed very modest media visibility in contrast to more visible reportage on India's interactions with China and the US.

The same holds true for the topics of renewable energy sources and energy efficiency. Renewables were not a visible energy type in the media, despite the importance given to them in the dialogue and declarations by several actors highlighting that cooperation on renewables is a fruitful aspect of the energy dialogue. Energy efficiency – viewed as a fruitful area of cooperation by several EU public actors – also did not enjoy major visibility in the observed media. It was hardly mentioned in the German, French and Indian press under observation in our study. However, in the UK case, it is the third most visible energy issue. We predict that the newly signed 'Joint Declaration between the EU and India on a Clean Energy and Climate Partnership' (2016) may trigger changes in the framing of EU-India energy relations in various discourses. Future studies are recommended to trace potential evolutions in media representations and elite perceptions.

Finally and significantly, the two sides framed the EU-India cooperation very differently in their media and elite discourses. In the European media, influential German press framed India within the *security of supplies* and less within the *sustainability* or *competitiveness* normative frames. In the observed British media, *security of supply* came in third place, and the *sustainability* and *competitiveness* frames were much more common. EU elites have a very clear perception of the energy dialogue as being framed by *competitiveness* topics. Conversely, in Indian media, *sustainability* and *security of supplies* are the two most widely used frames when reporting on the EU. However, the Indian elites in the EU-Indian energy dialogue frame cooperation primarily in terms of *sustainability* and *competitiveness.* Diverging visions on the normative priorities of the dialogue among elites and non-resonating media and elite discourses present a clear challenge for the success of the dialogue in the future. Hopefully, the newly initiated common discourse on the COP 21 achievements will change the picture.

Chapter 7
Energetic Launch but "Negotiation Fatigue"? Mutual Perceptions of South Africa and the EU as Energy Actors

7.1 Introduction

Maroš Šefčovič, Vice-President and Commissioner for the Energy Union, spoke at the University of Pretoria on his tour through Sub-Saharan Africa in April 2015. His speech was interrupted by several power cuts. Reflecting on the event on social media, he posted:

> The energy disruption in university was a perfect opportunity to discuss with South African students and scholars the tremendous potential in creating a cross-border network of electricity infrastructure, similar to the Energy Union we are building in Europe (Šefčovič 2015a).

Part of Šefčovič's mission to South Africa – in light of the then-upcoming UNFCCC COP 21 in Paris in December 2015 – was to stress the importance of joint efforts between the EU and South Africa in climate change and energy policy. Šefčovič states:

> Both Europe and South Africa are important players in this game; we in Europe are the largest energy importer in the world, and you are a major producing and transit country. Given the major consequences of our respective policies, we are bearing a great responsibility on our shoulders (Šefčovič 2015b).

This aspirational rhetoric appears to be in sharp contrast to the reality of the EU-South African bilateral energy dialogue. Not only does it remain in its early years (it was initiated in 2008), it is characteristically sluggish; after its energetic start, it has rapidly encountered "negotiation fatigue" (EnergyGov, Interview Brussels, May 2012). This outcome is somewhat disappointing, as South Africa is the second largest economy in Sub-Saharan Africa and "the gateway to the African continent" (Draper/Scholvin 2012). Since the end of Apartheid in 1994, the country has been a stable democracy that developed into an upper middle-income country with a significant growth rate. However, South Africa continues to struggle with various problems such as poverty (including energy poverty), unemployment and inequality. To overcome its challenges, the country is interested in development cooperation with the EU. In the field of energy, the main orientations towards the EU are in the areas of technology transfer, specifically clean coal technology (CCT) and carbon capture and storage (CCS). Importantly, South Africa is a crucial partner for the EU's coal imports. At the end of the 1990s/beginning of the 2000s, up to 27 per cent of EU coal imports came from South Africa.

Given the obvious bilateral interests between the EU and South Africa, it is puzzling to observe such slow progress in the energy cooperation between the two. The aim of this chapter is to elaborate the mutual perceptions of the EU and South Africa in the energy policy realm. When do the partners see eye to eye? What controversies exist when the two frame each other as global energy actors? How can the perceptions of the external energy governance of the EU and South Africa in the eyes of each other influence the interactions between the two?

7.2 South Africa's Energy Policy

South Africa's energy sector underwent an intense restructuring process after the end of the Apartheid regime. In 1992, the distribution of electricity remained extremely skewed, both racially and socially. In townships, access to electricity intermittent, and electricity tariffs for neighbourhoods with predominantly black populations were much higher than in white areas. Only 15 per cent of farmworker households had access to electricity (Eberhard/van Horen 1995: 49). Thus, the immediate post-Apartheid aim was to implement countrywide electrification schemes and to restructure state-owned energy companies (of which Eskom is by far the largest). As of 1998, Eskom was converted into a company subject to taxation, and its power stations were restructured into separate independent and competitive companies. The plan is to privatize these companies, with the state holding only partial control over the generation capacity (Greenberg 2006: 32-33). South Africa's first independent power producer was licensed only in 2000.

Together with the objective to transfer the pre-Apartheid energy system, another important objective has been to expand the environmental and climate dimension in South African energy development. Among Sub-Saharan African states, South Africa is by far the most important contributor to CO_2 emissions (IEA 2014: 117). The carbon intensity of the country's electricity production is high because coal is used as the primary energy source for electricity production (Figure 7.1). In just one decade, between 1992 and 2012, South Africa's CO_2 emissions rose by 45 per cent (Maupin 2015: 201). South Africa is responsible for one-third of the CO_2 emissions in Africa (however, Africa as a continent is responsible for only 3 per cent of global CO_2 emissions) (IEA 2013: 64). The government of South Africa states that emissions will peak in 2020-2025, then plateau for several years before declining in the 2030s. The government plans to extend its nuclear power production, expand the amount of renewables, and improve energy efficiency in end-use sectors to achieve a reduction in CO_2 emissions (IEA 2013: 65).

Figure 7.1: South Africa's energy consumption (2015)

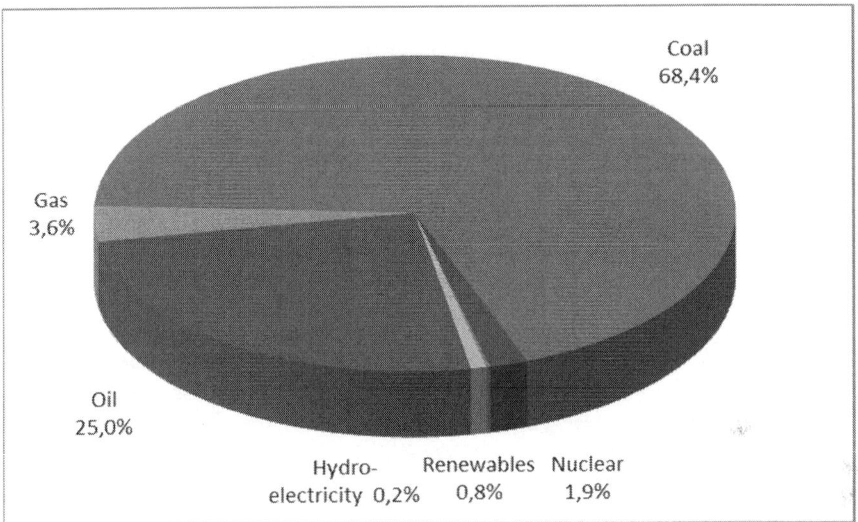

Source: BP Statistical Review of World Energy 2016.

Coal is the main pillar of the South African energy system. It constitutes nearly 70 per cent of the country's energy consumption. Examining the supply side, it accounts for over 90 per cent of domestic electricity supply. However, the position of coal in the energy mix is not as dominant as one might suspect (IEA 2014: 146). South Africa is exporting a high share of its coal to international markets; it is the sixth-largest coal exporter in the world. In the past, South Africa was the main supplier of coal to Europe. However, in 2013, South Africa supplied only 6.8 per cent of the solid fuels (hard coal, lignite, peat and derived fuels) to the EU (Energy Commission 2015: 26), shifting its coal exports towards the Asia-Pacific area with its growing demand. India is one of the new export priorities for South Africa (IEA 2014: 115).

South African coal also accounts for the third-largest source of hydrocarbon liquids in sub-Saharan Africa. Its coal-to-liquids output increases "with the assumed construction of long-discussed additional capacity by Sasol, the South African internationally operating energy company" (IEA 2014: 96). South Africa is also one of very few countries in the world where coal-to-liquids accounts for a significant part of transport fuel (Ibid.: 38).

Most of the coal has been produced in the mature Witbank coalfields in the north-eastern Mpumalanga Province. Because coal production in this location is in decline, South Africa has begun to mine other deposits, such as the Waterberg (near the border with Botswana). The shift in the geography of deposits imposes restrictions on both domestic supply and the export of coal. The fields at the Waterberg are not well connected by rail to the Richard's Bay Coal Terminal, and transport capacity is lacking. The Richard's Bay Coal Terminal has already increased its capacity, but transport capacity from the coalfields to the harbour is a bottleneck (IEA 2014: 115).

After the end of Apartheid, South Africa succeeded in rapidly electrifying its households. As of 2008, governmental programmes (e.g., the National Response to South Africa's Electricity Shortage) had delivered access to electricity for 64-81 per cent of the population (Bekker et al. 2008: 3130-3131). The current electrification rate is 85 per cent, the highest in mainland sub-Saharan Africa. Only approximately 11 per cent of households lack access to electricity, and approximately "4 per cent rely on illegal access (non-paying) or obtain access informally (from one household to another but paying)" (Statistics South Africa, 2013, cited in IEA 2014: 32). However, the energy system has struggled with such fast growth. This rapid electrification has not been supported by sufficient investment in the supply structures and generation capacity. Arguably, the main reason for this mismatch is the failed policy of privatization, which resulted in a lack of generation capacity in the 2000s. The consequence was frequent nationwide power cuts, which occurred primarily in winter and posed a serious challenge for both private households and industry. The year 2008 was marked by a power crisis – a critical juncture that called for the development of infrastructure and changes in the energy mix. This situation explains why Eskom, the public electricity company of South Africa, raised electricity prices (until then, the lowest in Africa). The increase followed the regulations of the South African energy agency (NERSA) to generate capital for investment (Maupin 2015: 198). With South Africa still possessing one of the world's largest coal reserves, the drive for changes in this energy mix is moderate. South Africa's options for a decarbonization scenario are also limited due to significant path dependencies and the relatively low cost of electricity produced by coal, which "remains an asset in societies concerned about the affordability of electricity" (IEA 2014: 15).

Because South Africa prioritized energy independence during the Apartheid era, energy research had concentrated on fossil fuels. In contrast, renewable energies experienced a lack of financial support. To address the domestic energy crisis, the focus was on the long-term expansion of the coal industry. For example, a 60 billion Rand loan was given to Eskom by the government for the construction of new coal power plants (Sebitosi/Pillay 2008: 2514). At the beginning of the 2000s, competitive costs remained too high to offer an alternative to fossil fuels because of the necessarily large investments in basic transmission infrastructure (Sebitosi/Pillay 2008: 2514). However, in 2003, a White Paper on Renewable Energy was published by the South African government. In it, one target for renewable energy was established, namely that 21 per cent of energy production by 2013 should come from renewable sources (this goal has since been increased to 30 per cent by 2030) (Maupin 2015: 196). The White Paper triggered remarkable policy transitions. Among these was the feed-in tariff – an instrument that was initially introduced by the German government to encourage the use of new energy technologies. It was adopted by the South African government. In 2009, South Africa's National Energy Regulation agency (NERSA) announced feed-in tariffs for solar, wind and biomass energy, with subsidies for wind energy that even exceed those in Germany. However, South Africa has decided to turn away from the feed-in tariffs because they led to non-competitive procurement that clashed with the government's public finance and its procurement regulations. In 2011, two large-scale initiatives were begun to unlock the great potential for renewables. First, the South African Renewables Initiative (SARi) was initiated (an international partnership between South Africa, Denmark, Germany, Norway, the UK, and the European Investment Bank) to enhance renewable energy in South Africa. SARi was designed to solve the funding issue and bridge energy, climate and industrial policy to create synergies in promoting, developing and deploying renewable energy capacities (SARi 2011). SARi also sought to obtain financial investments for renewable energy with the Department of Trade and Industry as a key actor. In addition, the Renewable Energy Independent Power Producer Procurement Program (REI4P) was initiated in 2013. Within its framework, potential bidders are to produce 3,725 megawatts from renewable sources (Maupin 2015). Since then, there have been three rounds of bidding, resulting in concrete projects with financial closure (Eberhard et al. 2014: 14-16).

However, electricity demand in South Africa was not developing as predicted. The anticipated growth in demand did not eventuate. In 2012, electricity demand was equivalent to demand in 2006, but the economy had grown at 3 per cent per year over this period (IEA 2014: 147). The government began a new programme to support renewable power projects to meet this challenge while decarbonizing its power production. Since 2011, three bidding rounds have occurred (the first project began in 2013). They resulted in new renewable capacities. Moreover, in 2013, the government updated its main long-term planning document for generation capacity, the Integrated Resource Plan (IRP) for electricity, which also reflected the government's acknowledgement of renewables. The 2011 IRP presented a vision of a long-term diversification of the power mix (IEA 2014: 146-147):

> The update [of the IRP] responds to a new set of circumstances and uncertainties: the likely pace of demand growth, falling technology costs for renewables, the costs of nuclear and of future coal supply, the possible rise of shale gas (a resource that South Africa is estimated to have in abundance) and natural gas discoveries in Mozambique and Tanzania (IEA 2014: 146-147).

The 2013 update of the IRP presents a strategy to diversify the power mix, moving strongly towards low-carbon sources of electricity. The update has shifted the focus of governance instruments away from their concentration on large-scale capital-intensive projects (coal and nuclear plants) that generate excessive capacity and towards smaller, more flexible ventures. The new instruments hold capital and are technologically flexible in a fast-changing energy environment. They are intended "to bring production closer to demand and to reduce transmission and integration costs" (IEA 2014: 148).

Solar and wind energy combined do not even constitute 1 per cent of South Africa's 2015 energy consumption. Nevertheless, the solar sector is particularly promising in large parts of South Africa, whilst potential for wind energy in the Western and Eastern Cape is also present; an increase in renewables was noted in 2015 in comparison to the previous year (BP 2016). Growth in the solar sector in South Africa is strong, whereas the growth in wind is more modest (IEA 2014: 79). With its Integrated Resource Plan to 2030, the South African government has plans to increase its solar and wind capacity. To increase capacity, auctions are already occurring. Only 0.2 per cent of energy consumption in South Africa comes from hydropower, and the government does not plan to significantly increase its hydropower capacity. In contrast, it does import increasing volumes of hydropower from other parts of Southern and Central Africa (IEA 2014: 105).

In 2015, 25 per cent of South African energy consumption came from oil. South Africa imports its oil, primarily from Saudi Arabia (38 per cent), Nigeria (32 per cent) and Angola (12 per cent) (2014) (Observatory of Economic Complexity 2014). Recently, substantial shale gas resources have also been identified in South Africa in the Karoo Basin (Hedden et al. 2013). Shell, Australia-based Challenger Energy and a number of other companies have been awarded exploration licenses. Drilling was halted in 2011 by an exploration moratorium due to environmental concerns about water usage and hydraulic fracturing. Although the Karoo Basin is sparsely populated, in this dry area, many communities rely on groundwater supplies. The moratorium was lifted in 2012 by the government, which proposed new technical regulations to govern petroleum exploration, particularly standards for shale gas exploration and hydraulic fracturing (IEA 2014: 52, 101).

South Africa is the only country in sub-Saharan Africa with a nuclear power plant today; and it has stated its intention to expand nuclear power capacity. In 2014, nuclear energy had a share of approximately 3 per cent of the country's total energy consumption; however, in 2015, this figure dropped to approximately 2 per cent (consistent with an overall decrease in energy consumption noted in South Africa) (BP 2016). Because South Africa is one of the ten largest uranium resource-holders in the world, it would be able to use own resources to achieve this increase (IEA 2014: 60). The South African Nuclear Energy Corporation (NECSA), a state-owned nuclear company, and the National Nuclear Regulator (NNR) play a crucial role in nuclear governance in South Africa (Maupin 2015: 197).

Since 2009, energy governance in South Africa has been situated in the then-established Department on Energy (DoE). Within the new department, governance of energy and mineral resources was separated. DoE is seconded by two regulators, NERSA, in charge of energy-infrastructure price control, and the National Nuclear Regulator (NNR). As stated above, state-owned companies play a crucial role in South African energy policy. The South African electricity sector is dominated by the state-owned enterprise Eskom, which produces 96 per cent of South Africa's electricity (Eberhard et al. 2014: 5), whilst private companies only produce approximately 2 per cent. Additionally, Eskom owns and operates the national transmission system (Pegels 2010: 4946). Links between the Department of Minerals and Energy and Eskom are strong. At times, qualified public personnel are the focus of Eskom's recruiters, hindering the procurement of highly qualified staff for the public sector because the private sector pays better salaries. In 2001, it was decided that Eskom's share in power generation should be lowered to 70 per cent, leaving the remaining 30 per cent for private sector participation (Maupin 2015: 196). There is a strong interest from European companies in entering the South African energy market; however, it "is not an overnight operation" (Ibid.: 199) because Eskom's monopolistic position obstructs others from entering that market (Piefer et al. 2015a: 44). In addition, the South African Nuclear Energy Corporation (NECSA), a state-owned nuclear company, and South Africa's national oil company, Petro SA, are important actors in South African energy governance.

7.3 EU-South Africa Energy Dialogue

The energy dialogue between South Africa and the EU was established in 2008 during the first high-level summit between the two partners, together with 12 other sectorial dialogues. The energy dialogue between the two sides is embedded in the Strategic Partnership, as are all other energy dialogues. The Strategic Partnership was signed in 2007 and remains the only one that the EU has signed in Africa. It was and remains funded under the EU's Development Cooperation Instrument (DCI) – although with a significantly reduced amount – from the EU under the new financial framework (2014-2020). In 2013, the EU approved a EUR 100 million infrastructure programme, including support for South African energy, transportation and logistics, water and environment. South Africa is the only one of the four cases in this volume that continues to receive bilateral development assistance. In contrast, Brazil, India and China have phased out traditional development cooperation funds.

In the energy dialogue, CCS and CCT are top issues on the agenda. A working group was established on coal, clean coal and CCS, and an Energy Dialogue Forum was established to oversee the work of these groups and structure the bilateral contacts. In 2012, a Clean Coal Programme was established between the EU and South Africa. In addition to CCS and CCT, bilateral cooperation has been pursued in such areas as energy efficiency, nuclear energy and renewable energy. Initially, Germany and France were particularly interested in discussing nuclear energy issues and CCS prototypes with South Africa. These issues were discussed at the 2013 summit between the EU and South Africa.

After a promising start in 2008, "a period of missed opportunities started" (Piefer et al. 2015a: 44). The reasons for this current slow progress in cooperation – described in Brussels as "negotiation fatigue" (EnergyGov, Interview Brussels, May 2012) – are manifold. As mentioned, there are serious difficulties in entering the South African energy market due to Eskom's monopolistic role. Moreover, a lack of offers from the South African side made it less attractive for foreign energy providers to invest in joint projects. In addition, the EU had not considered energy policy on the African continent a priority. Yet another challenge is a large-scale shift in energy governance personnel on both sides. Cooperation is further aggravated by the fact that bilateral energy cooperation between the EU and South Africa is embedded in a "complicated set of overlapping partnerships" (Maupin 2015: 207). For example, energy topics between the EU and South Africa are also discussed in the EU's dialogue with the Southern African Development Community (SADC). In addition, the negotiation of a regional Economic Partnership Agreement (EPA) (signed in 2014), which should enlarge the EU-South African EPA, hampered the energy dialogue between the partners. Furthermore, South Africa, a key player in the region, is essential to the EU's support for regional energy cooperation, particularly in terms of the Southern African Power Pool (SAPP). EU energy cooperation with South Africa is largely exercised through regional instruments such as the EU-Africa Energy Partnership, EU-Africa Energy Facility and the EU Energy Initiative Partnership Dialogue Facility. As a regional leader, South Africa plays an important role in various forums on regional energy cooperation (Interview Brussels, February 2012; Piefer et al. 2015a: 44).

At the heart of the EU-South African energy dialogue lies the fact that energy policies are viewed through the lens of climate and development policies. This is due to South Africa's high reliance on coal as its primary energy source and on development aid after the end of Apartheid. The EU's dialogue is most active in areas related to coal and CCS, with the working group on clean coal being the only one active in holding meetings in recent years (Piefer et al. 2015a: 44). A debate on nuclear energy – framed in the context of renewable energies and positioned within South Africa's decarbonization strategy – is also taking place. The signing of the European Atomic Energy community (EURATOM)-South Africa Agreement in July 2013 represented a milestone in this discourse, concluding years of negotiations in this field (Council of the European Union 2013). The agreement is focussed on the peaceful use of nuclear energy and expected to lay the foundation for enhanced nuclear cooperation between the EU and South Africa, including research and development. South Africa is also a participant in the European Regulatory Conference on Nuclear Safety (e.g., the Third European Regulatory Conference on Nuclear Safety, which occurred in Brussels in June 2015). Overall, the 2013 EU-South African summit showed that the EU understands and supports the priority placed by South Africa on security of energy supply. During the year of UNFCCC COP 17 in Durban, EU-South African relations also focussed on the clean coal and CCS issue and showed a strong energy-climate nexus. At the EU-South Africa Summit in September 2011, both sides reiterated their support to make the Cancún agreements fully operational (Piefer et al. 2015a: 44). On 22 April 2016, the two parties signed the Paris Agreement on Climate Change at the opening ceremony for signatures in New York (Department of Environmental Affairs 2016/European Commission 2016e).

Although reality presents a rich tapestry of interactions, our research focuses on the perceptions of energy matters and relations. How do EU and South African actors perceive one another when they interact in an energy dialogue? How might these perceptions affect the dialogue? A network analysis was performed to trace elite perceptions. Our analysis shows that the South African importance and exchange networks are the second densest networks (0.17 importance/0.11 exchange) after Brazil (see Chapter 6), with a very high distance. Nevertheless, the South African exchange network has the highest degree of centrality (14.8) among our four cases; South African actors are mostly at the centre of the dialogue (Piefer et al. 2015a: 45).

The network analysis provides evidence that it is primarily South African actors who are considered important in the importance and exchange networks. On the topic of energy cooperation, five South African actors were considered at the top of the importance network: Department of Energy (DoE), Development Bank of Southern Africa (DBSA), Parliamentary Portfolio Committee on Energy (PPCE), Eskom, and the NERSA. In addition, the NECSA and Sasol have prominent places in the perceived importance network and in the exchange network. The EU's DG Trade is listed as an important broker and maintains regular contact with a wide range of South African actors. These findings highlight that issues of competitiveness and market entry are perceived to gain importance, whilst the political side of the dialogue has great potential to improve in the future. DG Energy – similar to the three other cases in this book – is viewed as an important actor in the exchange network, whereas – as in Brazil – no European actor can be seen in the importance network. The EU Delegation to South Africa is viewed as playing an important role as a broker in most of the dialogues. It is followed – at a great distance – by the EEAS. All other European actors occupy marginal positions.

Examining these results from a more abstract level of the network density block matrices, which sorts the actors into the *public* and *non-state* actor categories on each side, the remote position of EU actors becomes even clearer. In terms of the importance network, South African *public* and EU *public* actors mutually considered one another important. Neither the EU nor the South African *non-state* actors attributed importance to the EU, and vice versa, suggesting that the EU must find and project its role when cooperating with political and private sectors. In terms of the exchange network, the EU *public* actors saw themselves addressing South African *public* actors, but this consideration did not appear to be reciprocated by South African *public* actors. European *non-state* actors also saw themselves addressing the EU; however, most of these communications were perceived as not having been answered. South African *non-state* actors and the EU *public* actors reported having had no noteworthy direct contacts. Their communication relies more on brokers (Piefer et al. 2015a: 46). Nevertheless, even when the energy dialogue remains stagnant, South African-EU energy cooperation has definite potential to accelerate and increase, particularly in the areas of CCT and CCS and growing investment opportunities in the South African renewable energy sector.

Beyond the EU-South Africa energy cooperation, trilateral cooperation, energy cooperation with individual EU Member States, other energy actors and fora were among the most visible themes emerging in the interviews and survey tracing elite perceptions of South African actors. In general, South African stakeholders reported favourable attitudes towards bilateral energy relations. This perception parallels reality; South Africa has already signed several agreements with individual EU Member States, neighbouring countries in Africa, and with China, Russia, Algeria, Nigeria, Mauritania, Iran, Korea, Argentina, Cuba and Venezuela (Maupin 2015: 207). South Africa seeks bilateral cooperation with actors close to and far away from its borders to find solutions for its current energy challenges.

South Africa has a number of concrete energy cooperation projects with Germany, France and the UK and South African companies cooperate with various energy companies from across Europe. Hence, individual EU Member States are perceived to be reliable investment partners (Maupin 2015: 202-204). Although South African *public* actors give no clear preference to any specific EU Member State, South African *non-state* actors specifically emphasized the importance of energy cooperation with Germany, the UK and France (EnergyGov, Darmstadt, 2014).

Moreover, Germany, France and the UK recognize the rising economic relevance of South Africa and maintain rather strong bilateral trade relations with South Africa, with Germany being the most important trade partner for South Africa in the EU (Westphal 2015: 96). The UK continues to be the largest source of foreign direct investment, despite declining trade volumes between the two countries (Kim 2015: 108). France considers South Africa a "major economic force" (French Embassy in South Africa 2015), yet this vision appears to be based more on potential developments than on actual numbers.

Energy cooperation between South Africa and Germany began in 1994 as part of Germany's development cooperation with South Africa. Specific cooperation in the energy field is however new, following the establishment of working groups focussing on renewable energy, energy efficiency and affordable energy in 2013 (Westphal 2015: 96-97). Technology transfer and carbon capture and storage are, as mentioned above, further specific areas of cooperation in South African-German energy relations (Maupin 2015: 199). Germany, together with other countries, has been involved in establishing the SARi. Currently, the GIZ is supporting a project called SAGEN on renewable energies and energy efficiency planned to run until 2017 (Westphal 2015: 96-97). It is intended to improve the frameworks of public and private investments in the area of renewable energy and energy efficiency (GIZ 2016).

UK-South Africa energy relations are in their infancy, with rare examples of concrete energy cooperation projects. Among these is the UK-South Africa bilateral forum held in 2011, at which the UK and South Africa agreed on a doubling of bilateral trade with a focus on energy. In addition, the UK International Climate Fund supports the development of carbon capture and storage technology, in which South Africa is among the receiver countries. Finally, in 2014, the British High Commission in Pretoria announced support for a pilot project on emissions trading in South Africa; however, concrete actions have yet to occur (Kim 2015: 108-109).

The main direction of French-South African energy relations is to involve French companies in South Africa's development to advance the goal of a more sustainable and reliable energy supply. In 2014, France and South Africa signed an agreement on the peaceful use of nuclear energy. During the 2016 visit of South African President Jacob Zuma to France, the significant role of French companies in ensuring a sustainable energy mix and their role in the expansion of renewable and nuclear energy in South Africa was stressed (Odendaal 2016). The Green Credit Line Project was initiated in 2012 by the French development agency AFD and the State Secretariat for Economic Affairs of Switzerland (SECO) to enable clean energy projects in South Africa. The credit facility gives loans to renewable energy and energy-efficiency projects. In June 2016, the French multinational electric company Engie signed an agreement with Eskom on the construction of the Kathu Solar Project in the Northern Cape (Moyo 2016).

Although energy cooperation is between South Africa and the three EU Member States is a relatively recent phenomenon, it entails great potential for the respective partners. South Africa strives to overcome its greatest challenges in domestic energy policy, specifically, to provide a reliable energy supply to the whole population and reduce the country's high reliance on coal. European companies strive to obtain promising investment opportunities (based on better access to the South African energy market).

Although the EU and South Africa's interests in and motivations for cooperation match, the dialogue progresses relatively slowly, as discussed above. Stakeholders' differing perceptions of one another's roles in these energy interactions represent one possible explanation for this sluggish uptake. In the next section, we examine in greater detail the mutual perceptions of the EU and South Africa in their respective media and elite discourses and explore how these perceptions might influence energy dialogue between the EU and South Africa.

7.4 EU-South Africa Energy Perceptions in Media and Elite Discourses

As detailed in Chapter 1, the South African and European presses were observed over five years (2009-2013), one month in each year surrounding the period of the annual Conference of the Parties to the UNFCCC (COP). In South Africa, we observed daily coverage of energy matters and of the EU as an energy actor (on its own and interacting with BICS) in the prestigious influential daily *The Star* and in the leading business newspaper *Business Day*.[58] For the list of European newspapers under observation, see Chapter 1. News about South Africa as an energy actor in the European media was largely authored by local, European authors. In Germany, all news reporting South Africa in the energy field was locally sourced, and in the French and UK samples, only one and three articles, were written by non-local authors, respectively (in the latter case, one article was also of mixed origin – a non-local/local source). Such a minimal incorporation of international news sources (let alone South African ones) suggests a higher level of domestic orientation in the respective reporting, even when covering international energy actors, and potentially a Eurocentric position. In the South African press reporting the EU as an energy actor, the sources were more diverse.

58 The South African energy dataset does not detail the energy frames or evaluation of the EU as an energy actor, which explains why these categories could not be included in the following analysis.

Although local sources still dominated when the EU was reported as an energy actor (suggesting a more intense focus on energy matters grounded in domestic discourses), there was a higher share of mixed sources (local with international) and non-local sources than in the European media reporting on South Africa.[59] This diversity reflects the newsgathering practices on a national scale and individual news-sourcing preferences of particular media outlets. Importantly, it also potentially suggests a greater diversity in views and frames in the South African case, with the media reflecting on other than only local foci.

Examining the 'energy' sample, the German press under observation featured South Africa as an energy actor in only 2.9 per cent of the total sample, and the monitored French media in 4 per cent of all reports. The UK media in our study focussed more on South Africa's energy actions (9 per cent of the sample). However, South Africa remains the least visible actor among BICS in the UK press coverage of energy matters. Assessed in terms of intensity of representations, differences are seen among the three Member States' cases (Figure 7.2). South Africa was almost entirely portrayed as a *minor* actor in the German media (only one article addressed South Africa from a *secondary* perspective). In addition, South Africa was reported as an energy actor from a very generic standpoint, without detailed attention to individuals or companies. Only one South African actor was mentioned, the coal and oil company Sasol. In contrast, *major* or *secondary* perspectives were observed in the observed French 'energy' sample when they reported on South Africa as an energy actor; one-quarter of all energy-specific articles in the UK addressed South Africa as the *major* actor. In the *European Voice,* South Africa is reported as an energy actor in only one article over the five-year period of observation; this article discusses the worldwide use of nuclear power after Fukushima and mentions several minor actors, including South Africa (*European Voice*, 29.11.2012).

In the observed South African 'energy' sample, the EU was not portrayed as a visible energy player (Fioramonti 2016). Although total numbers are low, the centrality of EU representations – *secondary* – somewhat raises the visibility of the EU. However, overall low media visibility of each other – in absolute and relative terms – risks translating into a low salience assigned by regular readers to these actors in the energy field.

---

59 Bearing in mind that the South African sample of the EU in energy matters is small, locally sourced news pieces accounted for seven articles, non-local for four, and mixed for three.

Figure 7.2: Visibility of the EU and South Africa in South African and European media

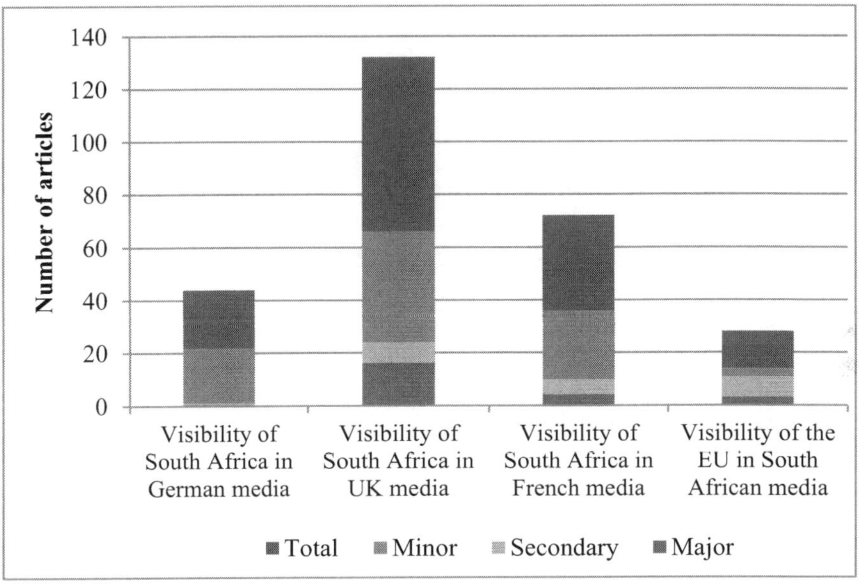

Source: EXIE, 2015.

Examining in greater detail the other energy actors in our European and South African 'energy' samples, we see that China and the US ranked among the three most visible actors appearing together with South Africa and the EU across the South African and the three European media samples. In addition, the findings reveal a strong domestic focus – i.e., on the country of the reportage – in all cases (with the exception of France) and as well show very little attention given to EU-South Africa energy relations in the all observed European media (Table 7.1).

In the South African media, South Africa itself was the most visible actor together with the EU. This shows a strong local perspective and indicates reflection of the EU's impacts on domestic energy governance (Fioramonti 2016). China was the second most visible actor, followed by the US with the UK. Remarkably, no specific EU actors were mentioned. This arguably renders an impression of the EU as an energy actor with unrecognizable leaders in the energy field.

In the UK media in our sample, the US was the most visible actor appearing together with South Africa, followed by China, the UK itself and then Brazil. It is noticeable that South Africa and the EU were hardly ever presented together in the UK media in the energy context. The European Commission was mentioned once as the only EU actor together with South Africa.

In the monitored German media, China was the most visible actor appearing together with South Africa, followed by Germany, the US and India. In almost 70 per cent of the articles, China and South Africa appeared together, revealing an image of China as a visible and vocal actor in international energy issues, both in general and specifically in relation to South Africa. These reports contextualized China's actions in its increasing engagement with Africa and its growing importance to South Africa. The high visibility of Germany with South Africa in the monitored German press is not surprising; it shows a clear domestic grounding given by these leading German newspapers to international energy news. India shared the third place in visibility with the US, and the EU is the fourth most visible actor appearing together with South Africa. The visibility of India alongside South Africa is noticeable because India in general had a low profile as an energy actor in the German media (see Chapter 6). The EU acting together with South Africa enjoyed a modest profile in comparison to other actors. This limited visibility of South Africa-EU energy relations in the leading German press observed in our study potentially contributes to low awareness among its readers about the EU-South Africa energy dialogue.

In the French case, China was again the most visible actor appearing together with South Africa. India was featured as the second most visible actor, even before the US and France itself. France received only limited attention in energy news stories addressing South Africa as an energy actor in the French media. This low profile of France fits in line with the virtually total lack of concrete energy cooperation between the two actors during our period of analysis (2009-2013). The EU was more visible than France was but overall had only a low appearance, being the fifth most visible actor, even less visible than Brazil (the fourth most visible actor).

The opinions of the elites directly involved in the EU-South Africa energy dialogue revealed – rather predictably – more-informed and nuanced perceptions. *Public* and *non-state* actors from the EU and South Africa shared a common opinion that the EU-South Africa energy dialogue – initiated in 2008 – is important. They also shared a view that the EU-South African energy policy dialogue has a perceived effect. However, the impact of the dialogue was viewed differently among respective *public* and *non-state* actors. On average, the majority of South Africa's actors (69 per cent) view the dialogue as influencing South African energy policy; however, its *public* actors remain less convinced. Although 80 per cent of the South African *non-state* actors view this dialogue as influencing their country's energy policy, only 33.3 per cent of South African *public* actors are of the same opinion. Conversely, a majority (66.7 per cent) of both *public* and *non-state* EU actors viewed the dialogue as influencing South African energy policy (Maupin 2015: 200). Perceptions of the influence on EU energy policy reveal different patterns. Although all EU *non-state* actors perceived the dialogue as influencing the EU energy policy, only 33.3 per cent of the EU *public* actors agreed. South African actors saw this differently. Although only 30 per cent of South African *non-state* actors agreed on the effect on EU energy policy, all South African *public* actors perceived it as influencing EU energy policy. In conclusion, *public* actors appeared to have higher opinions of themselves than other actors have of them. Both the EU and South African *public* actors believe that their dialogue does affect the other's energy policy; however, they do not perceive such an effect on their own energy policy.

Table 7.1: The most visible 'other' actors appearing together with South Africa and the EU in the media

European media reporting South Africa as an energy actor			**South African media reporting the EU as an energy actor**
German media	**UK media**	**French media**	**South African media**
China	US	China	South Africa
Germany	China	India	China
US/India	UK	US	US/UK

Source: EXIE, 2015.

In summary, the leading press of the EU's 'Big 3' and of South Africa credited little recognition of the other country as an energy actor in our period of observation. Public actors from both sides viewed the dialogue as having a limited effect on their own energy policy – perceptions that arguably echo a low media profile. However, elites who are informed about and engaged in the dialogue appear to grant one another recognition around the energy dialogue – an encouraging finding for the EU-South Africa energy interactions, coming from stakeholders who address energy matters on a daily basis.

7.4.1 Topics of EU-South Africa Energy Perceptions in Media and Elite Discourses

Examining in greater detail the topics of the EU-South Africa energy relations reported by the media, our analysis shows that different *energy issues* lead in the media representations of each other (Table 7.2). The *sustainability* theme – coming through the reportage of *sustainable development* and *emissions* issues – is among the top three most visible in the German, UK, French, and South African media under observation; however, the priorities differ. For the South African media in our study, *sustainable development* is the leading issue in portraying the EU as an energy actor. In the French press, *emissions* were the top energy issue in the news on South Africa as an energy actor, followed by *energy policies/governance*. In Germany, *energy policies/governance* was the leading issue in the reportage on South Africa in our period of observation (primarily related to the UN climate negotiations), whereas *emissions* and *sustainable development* took second and third place, respectively. In contrast, *investments* were the most visible energy *issue* in the monitored UK press. The visibility of these particular issues – in South Africa and across all four countries – shows some influence of the period of observation – around the UN climate negotiations – but not an exclusive one. In the European media, *investments* were among the top most visible energy issues assigned to South Africa (and the most visible in UK media). The leading focus on *investments* in the European leading press reflects the interest of European companies in entering the South African market. In contrast, this issue was invisible in the South African media looking towards the EU. In the South African press, *cooperation* and *energy access* were among the three leading energy issues. Energy access remains a crucial issue in South Africa, linked not least to the deficiencies in energy infrastructure. Unsurprisingly, this issue gained attention in the observed South African media. Importantly, there was a focus on the EU in relation to this issue because the EU was represented as a promising cooperation partner, able to provide technologies to solve the problems around energy infrastructure. *Access to energy* is an issue of great importance and public awareness in South African energy politics. As discussed above, *sustainable development* and *energy access* are also the issues that dominate South African stakeholders' perceptions of importance. These issues are often interlinked because sustainable development is viewed as necessary to achieve nationwide access to energy; "This aspect is directly linked to the development of new infrastructure to meet the energy needs of millions of South Africans" (Fioramonti 2016).

Table 7.2: Visibility of energy issues in European and South African media

European media reporting South Africa as an energy actor			**South African media reporting the EU as an energy actor**
German media	**UK media**	**French media**	**South African media**
Energy policies/ Governance	Investments	Emissions	Sustainable development
Emissions	Emissions	Energy policies/ Governance	Cooperation
Investments	Sustainable development	Investments	Energy access

Source: EXIE, 2015.

However, some issues that are important areas of cooperation in the South Africa-EU energy dialogue were almost invisible in the respective media. Among those are issues of *CCS* and *clean coal technologies*. In the monitored South African media, these issues were not mentioned at all in the observed five-year period. The German media sampled in our study had only one article mentioning clean coal and one mentioning CCS. In the UK media, there was only one article on clean coal and no articles about CCS. In the French case, only one article mentioned CCS, ignoring the issue of clean coal technologies. This discrepancy between the actual priorities of the EU-South Africa energy dialogue and leading media's representations of it during a period that was expected to raise the profile of the key energy issues is telling. Potentially, a modest media profile given to the key areas of cooperation could influence public awareness of the priorities in the dialogue and of the opportunities that the two partners present to each other.

We now turn to the assessments of the visibility of different *types* of energy – *non-renewable* and *renewable* energy sources (Tables 7.3 and 7.4). Overall, *non-renewable* energy sources dominated news on South Africa as an energy actor in the European newspapers selected for analysis. *Renewable* energy sources were somewhat less visible, however, among the five most visible energy types. The German media appeared to be the most interested in reporting on *renewables* in relation to South Africa; *solar* energy was as visible as *gas*, both being the second most visible energy types. In the observed French media, *coal* and *renewables* shared the third most visible position of energy types when they reported on South Africa, whereas *solar* in the UK media appeared just after *coal*. In comparison, there was a lesser focus on *renewables* in the South African media examining the EU than in the European media examining South Africa. This media portrayal parallels the reality; in which renewables are only slowly gaining attention in South African energy policy.

Note that *coal* in both the German and UK media under observation was the most reported energy source in relation to South Africa (not *gas* and *oil*, which dominate the BIC cases discussed earlier). This media priority might again parallel reality – the UK and Germany are both importing coal from South Africa. In Germany, South Africa is among the five largest suppliers of coal, although the import volume has been decreasing in recent years. In 2014, South Africa accounted for 9 per cent of coal imports in Germany (VDKI 2015). In the UK, imports from South Africa have also decreased in recent years. In 2013, they accounted for less than 1 per cent of total coal imports (Bide et al. 2015; Euracoal 2016). In comparison, the South African media focussed less on *coal* when examining the EU. *Gas*, *oil* and *nuclear energy* were more visible. Gas and oil are of general interest for South Africa in the area of external energy relations because South Africa relies heavily on imports of these energy sources. However, coal remains the main energy source in South Africa, which is reflected in the total 'energy' sample. *Coal* was the most visible energy source reported overall, "with almost 300 articles of the dataset that make reference to coal-based energy" (Fioramonti 2016).

Table 7.3: Visibility of non-renewable energy types in European and South African media

European media reporting South Africa as an energy actor			**South African media reporting the EU as an energy actor**
German media	**UK media**	**French media**	**South African media**
Coal	Coal	Oil	Oil
Gas	Oil	Gas	Gas
Oil	Gas	Coal	Nuclear

Source: EXIE, 2015.

The visibility of *renewable* energy sources in relation to South Africa as an energy actor has a very similar picture across the three European samples in our study (Table 7.4). There are dominant references to *renewables* as a general term, followed by references to *wind* and *solar* energy. In the South African media, *solar* and *wind* energy were also among the most reported *renewable* sources when the EU was reported; however, this reportage attracted very low numbers in general. Despite this low profile, parallels in the portrayals of the most visible *renewable* sources in framing each other suggest a potential for shared grounds in the dialogue.

Table 7.4: Visibility of renewable energy types in European and South African media

European media reporting South Africa as an energy actor			**South African media reporting the EU as an energy actor**
German media	**UK media**	**French media**	**South African media**
Solar	Solar	Renewables, in general	Solar
Renewables, in general	Renewables, in general	Solar	Hydropower
Wind	Wind	Wind	Wind

Source: EXIE, 2015.

Examining the energy *contexts* in the European media, the *economics* context dominated the UK media in representing South Africa as an energy actor (Table 7.5). In contrast, *environment* and *climate change* were the most visible contexts for South Africa in the observed German and French presses. Juxtaposing these observations of *contexts* with the most visible energy *issues* (Table 7.2), we see that issues of *energy policies/governance* and *emissions*, most visible in the German and French media, appeared in the contexts of *climate change* and *environment*, whereas *investments*, the most visible issue in the UK media, matched the leading context of *economics*. The *climate change* context visible in the European media points to the links between *energy* and *climate change* issues built by influential media – a link expected in our research due to the timing of the analysis around the UNFCCC COPs. However, *development* was the most visible context for the EU as an energy actor in the observed South African media. This high visibility of *development* in the South African media in our study reflects the recognition of the ongoing importance of European development aid to South Africa. In contrast, *development* as a context was not a popular one in the monitored German or French newspapers reporting on South Africa (only two articles in each sample portrayed South Africa as an energy actor in the context of *development*). It was, however, a visible dimension in the UK case looking towards South Africa. Mismatches in setting the *contexts* are potentially ripe for misunderstandings of how the partners may imagine each other – the same energy *issue* or *type* might be positioned in a different *context* and assigned a different priority and interpretation.

Table 7.5: Context of energy news stories in South African and European media

European media reporting South Africa as an energy actor			**South African media reporting the EU as an energy actor**
German media	**UK media**	**French media**	**South African media**
Climate change	Economics	Environment	Development
Economics	Climate change	Climate change	Economics
Environment	Development	Economics/politics	Environment

Source: EXIE, 2015.

The visibility of *issues*, *contexts* and *energy types* was linked to the visibility of the actors at different levels. In the UK media in our study, *governmental* actors were occasionally mentioned (primarily in reports on the COPs) – e.g., South African officials were mentioned in a few articles. *Private business* actors were also featured in the reports – a profile that indicates a general focus on business actors in energy reportage and a general interest in investing in South Africa's energy sector. Among South African business actors reported in the UK were concrete companies and individuals connected to energy affairs locally and internationally. Eskom was the most mentioned (eight articles out of 66). Some other South African companies – e.g., Sasol and Riversdale – were also visible. These actors are linked to the energy *issues investments* and *emissions* as well as to the *contexts* of *economics* and *climate change*. In the observed German media, the picture is similar. *Governmental* and *private business* actors are the most predominant, reflecting the energy *issues energy policies/governance*, *emissions*, and *investments*, as well as the *contexts climate change* and *economics*. Interestingly, the observed German sample entailed several German solar companies echoing *solar* power as the leading renewable energy source and indicate the interest of German solar companies to enter the South African energy market. In the French media, *private business* actors, *governmental* actors, and *international organizations* were all visible actors. However, in comparison to the state-level actors, specific companies and other micro-actors had a lower profile. Among the *private business* actors, French companies (Areva, EDF) attracted the most attention. Among the *international organizations*, two were the most visible – the International Energy Agency (IEA) and the UN. Among South African actors, South African President Zuma was reported in three articles. The visibility of *governmental* actors and *international organizations* actors echoes the visibility of *emissions and energy policies/governance* as *energy issues and* the *contexts* of *environment* and *climate change*, while the low profile of *private business actors* is connected to the lower reportage on economic energy *issues* in the observed French media. The observed South African media paid limited attention to specific actors, with some rare references to *governmental* and *business* actors, as well as *international organisations*.

Turning now to the elite perceptions and, specifically, towards the perceptions and motivations of the different actor groups, we observed that there is one issue concerning which the EU and South African actors have a strikingly different motivation to join the bilateral energy interactions (Figure 7.3). Reflecting on the motivation to *secure energy supplies* for the EU or South Africa, the South African elite actors chose it among the three top motivations for South Africa. In contrast, it was the least important motivation for the EU actors.

For the South African stakeholders, advances in *combating climate change* and the contribution of cooperation to *technology transfer* between the EU and South Africa were the top motivations to join the bilateral dialogue. In these three options, we do not see a large variation between *public* and *non-state* actors. Again, we would assume that climate change and the importance of coal for the country are closely interlinked concerning motivations for the dialogue. South Africa has pledged its commitment to fight climate change through its domestic energy policy and in its international efforts. The launch of the domestic SARi (during the COP 17 in Durban 2011) and the REI4P with the focus on solar and wind further illustrates this motivation. Both partners highly value technology transfer and the motivation to secure energy supplies for their own citizens. This vision can accommodate South Africa's desire for cooperation on securing its own energy supplies as, e.g., energy infrastructure measures can be understood as instruments to enhance the security of the energy supply.

Figure 7.3: Motivations of South Africa and the EU to engage in cooperation on energy issues*

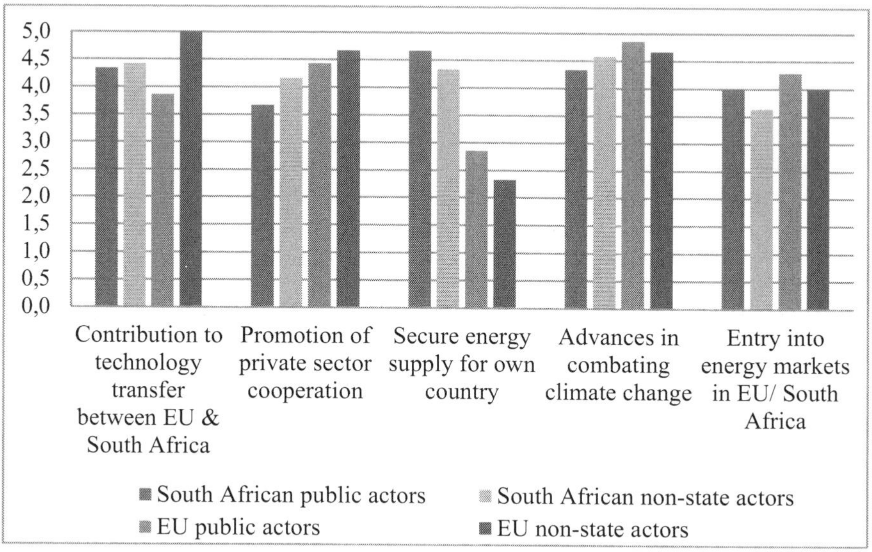

*Means of all answers; 1= "Very unimportant"; 5= "Very important"
Source: EnergyGov, Darmstadt, 2014.

For the EU stakeholders, the advances in combating *climate change* are the most important reason for *public* and *non-state* actors' perceptions to converge. The promotion of *private sector cooperation* is the second most pronounced motivation for both *actor* types in the EU. A major difference is visible in the perception of the contribution to *technology transfer* between the EU and South Africa. For *non-state* actors in both polities, this is the most pertinent explanation of their interest in the bilateral dialogue. However, for the EU *public* actors, this motivation ranks only in fourth place. Except for a low-ranked *secure energy supply* option chosen by EU actors, the *entry into energy markets* in the EU or South Africa appears to be a less important motivation for all actors in the dialogue.

The finding of diverging motivations for the South Africa-EU dialogue can be interpreted in several ways. It is possible that

> South Africa's interest in enhancing security of supply might be matched by the European interest in improved access for the private sector; increasing FDI activities in South Africa's renewable energy sectors might be a first step (Knodt et al. 2015c: 338);

thus, the motivations complement each other well.

A comparison of media and elite perceptions makes it clear that the issue of *security of supplies* resonates in both South African discourses – media and elite. The same accounts for cooperation on measures for preventing *climate change*. On the EU side, *combating climate change* is the leading motivation for cooperation with South Africa. This concern is also reflected in the European media's focus on *emissions* and *governance* in this field. The focus on *investments* and *economy* prioritized by the European media is only partly reflected among the elites, and in the European motivations, *market access* ranked rather low.

7.4.2 Normative Orientation of EU-South Africa Energy Relations in Media and Elite Discourses

In our study, we also assessed media and elite discourses with respect to the three normative frames of *security of supplies*, *sustainability* and *competitiveness* in mutual perceptions.[60]

In the cases of the UK and France, *sustainability* was a dominant media frame of South Africa as an energy actor (Figure 7.4). In both cases, it constituted more than 50 per cent of the energy news sample. The priority assigned to this frame is connected to the timing of the research – around UNFCCCs COPs (and specifically to the 2011 UN climate conference held in Durban). In the German media, we note an almost equal distribution of representations across the three frames; it appears that South Africa was not associated with a specific energy frame in the eyes of German newsmakers. However, compared with the French and UK media, *security of supplies* attracted greater attention in the German media. *Security of supplies* was the second most visible frame in the observed French press, addressing international investments of French companies, among others, in nuclear energy and the construction of the first solar energy plant in South Africa. The UK press in our study gave *competitiveness* the second most visible position, which is in line with the high visibility of the *investments* issue. However, it is important to bear in mind that the sample of the European news referencing South Africa as an energy actor is rather small, as discussed previously.

60 As highlighted, data on energy frames of the EU in South African media are missing.

Figure 7.4: Energy frames of South Africa in European media

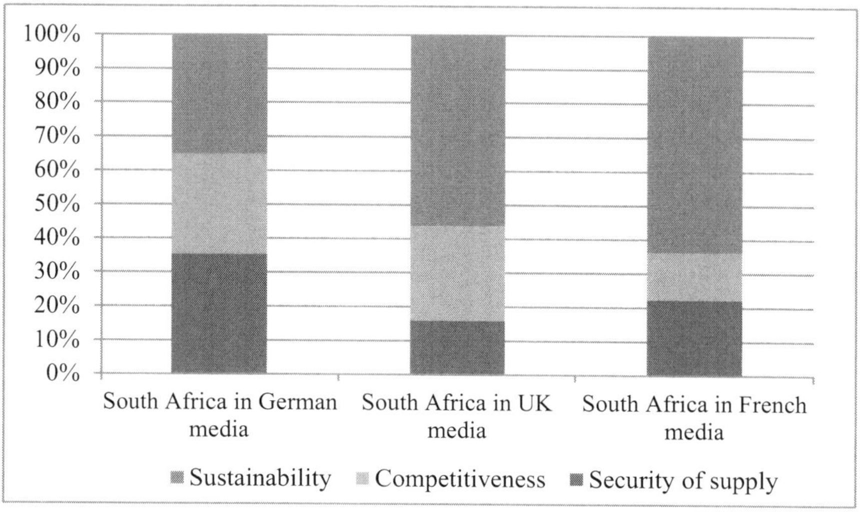

Source: EXIE, 2015.

Elite perceptions of the EU-South African energy dialogue analysed in terms of normative frames (Figure 7.5) revealed that both EU and South African actors ranked *security of energy supply* as the most important frame in EU-South Africa energy cooperation. This topic was did not register as a leading motivation for EU actors to participate in the dialogue. However, the EU actors acknowledged this frame as being central to the dialogue because of the South African focus on energy security.

The other frames, such as *sustainability* and *competitiveness,* were perceived to be in distant second and third place. Whereas the EU actors ranked *sustainability* as their second choice, the South African actors ranked *competitiveness* as the second most important frame. The monopolistic role of Eskom in the South African energy market can be one explanation for why *competitiveness* featured relatively low among EU actors. It is expected that the importance of this frame will grow over time as European interests in entering the renewable energy market in South Africa rise (Knodt et al. 2015c: 333).

Figure 7.5: Energy frames of South Africa-EU cooperation by South African and EU stakeholders*

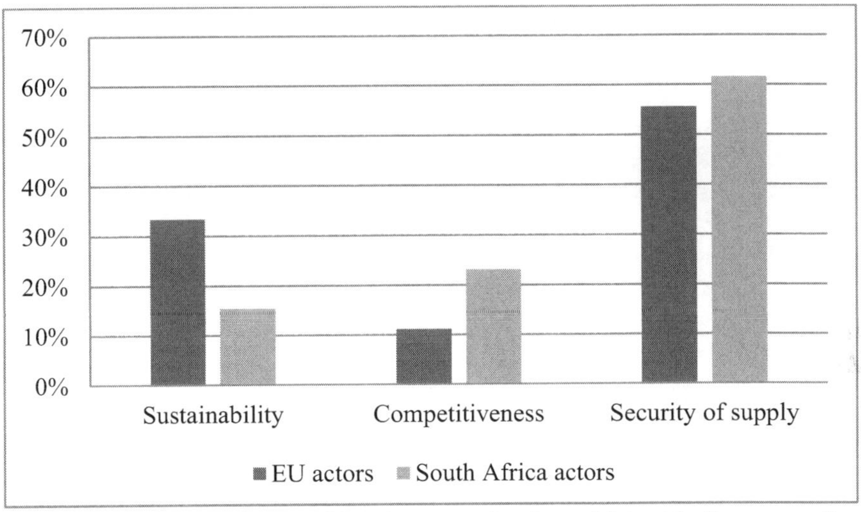

*Percentage of respondents ranking the respective frame highest in the energy dialogue
Source: EnergyGov, Darmstadt, 2014.

Interpretations of the *competitiveness* frame reveal that both South African and EU actors consider the role of the renewable energy sector to be the most important. However, South Africa also highly values energy-intensive industry. This is due to its heavy industry and the minerals sector (Knodt et al. 2015c: 334). South African and EU actors both referred to *sustainability* in the three-fold understanding of social, ecological, and economic *sustainability* (Ibid.), whereas *security of supplies* was to some extent interpreted differently. All South African respondents considered access to energy technology to be an important aspect, followed by security of supply for industry and agriculture. Conversely, EU public actors valued security of supply for individual households highest, thus revealing discrepancies in interpretations. EU non-state actors saw both security for industry and agriculture and access to energy technology as important, echoing the perceptions of South African actors. Despite some differences, the gap between the EU and South Africa's mutual perceptions in terms of normative frames is not particularly significant, with both actors seeing technology transfer as an important area for bilateral cooperation.

7.4.3 Mutual Perceptions as Dialogue Partners in Media and Elite Discourses (Evaluations and Roles)

In this section, we examine in greater detail the mutual *evaluations* assigned by observed European media to South Africa[61] and trace the elite perceptions of *roles* of each other. A *neutral* tone dominated South African portrayals as an energy actor in the monitored European media (Figure 7.6). This pattern parallels the evaluation patterns of Brazil, India and China in the European media discussed in other chapters. The UK and French reports, however, featured more articles with pronounced evaluations of South Africa as an energy actor (this resonates with the overall volume and intensity of South Africa's representations in these media). In the UK media observed here, news stories portraying South Africa were rather polarized, whereas a *positive* tone led in the French press.

Figure 7.6: Evaluation of South Africa in European media

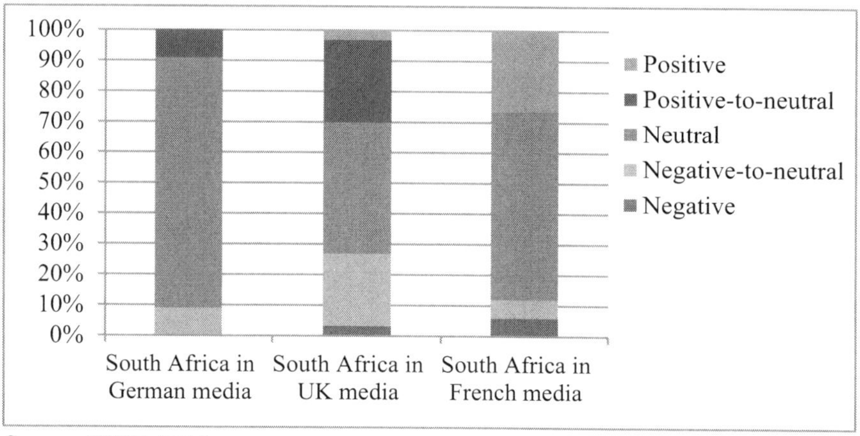

Source: EXIE, 2015.

The *negative-to-neutral* stories in the UK media addressed South Africa's energy challenges concerning its energy mix, energy supply and energy efficiency, whereas the *positive-to-neutral* stories among others South Africa's role in combating climate change, its aim to reduce the amount of coal in its energy mix and its use of biofuels.

61 As highlighted, data on media evaluations of the EU in South Africa are missing.

Figure 7.7: Perception of South Africa's properties as a dialogue partner*

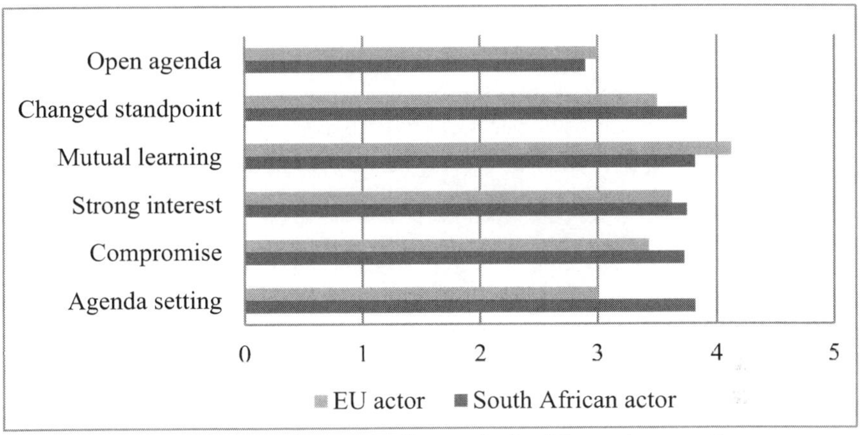

*Means of all answers; 1 = "Strongly disagree"; 5 = "Strongly agree"
Source: EnergyGov, Darmstadt, 2014.

Positive stories in the French media addressed diverse issues, such as, the involvement of South Africa at the UNFCCC COPs, the construction of solar plants and the production of energy from methane in South Africa.
In the elite discourse, South African actors and EU actors assessed the perceptions of each other's *roles* in the energy dialogue (Figures 8.7 and 8.8). Importantly, South Africa sees itself as being an *agenda setter* – more so than the EU perceives South Africa to be. The same holds true for policy trade-offs, in which South Africa considers itself to trade off energy policy issues against issues in other policy areas (Maupin 2015: 204).

Both actors perceive the EU to be a strong agenda-setter in the dialogue. However, whereas EU actors perceived the EU to have an open agenda, South African actors stated that the EU was playing with a hidden agenda (Knodt et al. 2015b: 68). Although the EU actors perceived the EU to be willing to change positions during negotiations, South African actors agreed less on this aspect. Such differences in the perceptions of each other as a dialogue partner can hinder a fruitful dialogue. Of major concern are the differing visions of agenda setting, particularly with respect to open vs. hidden agenda. Such perceptions can lead to mistrust among dialogue partners.

Figure 7.8: Perception of the EU's properties as a dialogue partner*

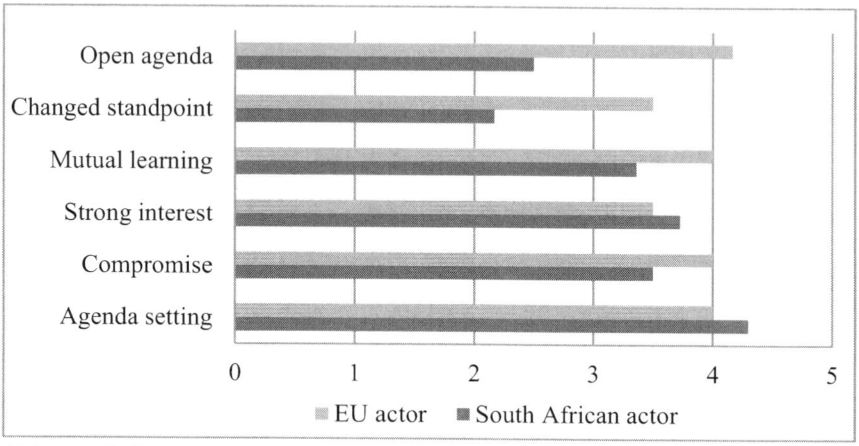

*Means of all answers; 1 = “Strongly disagree”; 5 = “Strongly agree”
Source: EnergyGov, Darmstadt, 2014.

7.5 Conclusions: Lessons Provided by EU-South Africa Energy Cooperation

South Africa is the second-largest economy in Sub-Saharan Africa and an important trading partner for the EU. Particularly in energy, it is a crucial partner for the EU’s coal imports. Thus, it is perplexing that the EU-South African bilateral energy dialogue appears to be muddling through currently despite its energetic start in 2008.

The visibility of South Africa in the observed European media and of the EU in the monitored South African media was extremely low during the period of observation which was expected to lift the profile of energy-related matters and actors. In contrast to the media representations, *public* and *non-state* actors from the EU and South Africa shared a common opinion that the EU-South Africa energy dialogue is important. However, EU and South African *public* actors believe that their dialogue does influence the other’s energy policy, not their own.

In the influential South African media reporting on the EU, *sustainable development*, *cooperation* and *energy access* were the three leading energy issues. They appear to create an image of the EU as a ‘helping hand’ in solving one of the major problems facing the country – energy security –

sustainably and through cooperation. Even at present, energy access remains a critical challenge for South Africa, one linked to the development of new infrastructure to meet the energy needs of many South African citizens. Different from South African visions, the leading presses of the European 'Big 3' were dominated by their view of South Africa as a country struggling with the negative environmental side effects of its main energy resource – coal. South Africa was also framed by European media in our sample as an attractive place for European investments. As such, the two countries' dominant media portrayals of each other did not overlap.

The European media's orientation towards the themes of economic cooperation and investment corresponds to the visibility of coal (presented as a very important non-renewable energy source). With respect to renewable energy sources, the observed European and South African newspapers most frequently referenced solar. In addition to economics, the European newsmakers stressed the themes of climate change and environment (not least due to the timing of the observations around UNFCCC COPs).

A different picture appears with respect to the perceived dominant frame of the EU-South African dialogue. Here, both EU and South African actors agree that *security of supply* is the dominant frame in the dialogue.

Evaluating their partners, the European media portrayed South Africa as an energy actor from a predominantly neutral viewpoint. The elites appear to be more sceptical in their mutual perceptions. Whereas the South African actors perceived the EU as acting with a hidden agenda, the Europeans saw the South Africans setting the agenda. In a mismatched perception, South Africans believed that the Europeans set the agenda. Such perceptions are argued here to have the potential to lead to problems for the dialogue, not least due to the mutual perception that the other side is mistrustful.

Chapter 8
Comparing Mutual Perceptions of the EU and BICS in Energy Policy

This book started with an argument that bilateral cooperation of the EU and Brazil, India, China and South Africa (BICS) is important in global energy governance. The literature addressing governance agrees that the architecture of global energy governance is challenged; it builds on highly fragmented structures (Baccini et al. 2011), including regional (e.g., IEA) and resource-based (e.g., OPEC, IEA, IRENA) organizations. In this problematic structure, the EU's energy relations with BICS are further challenged by the EU's poor performance in the bilateral EU-BICS dialogues (Knodt et al. 2015). One reason for this performance is the EU's communication mode with 'emerging powers'; it appears that the EU is very good at 'talking at' instead of 'talking with' its external partners, including energy-related communications (Chaban et al. 2016). The EU's one-way projection of interests, norms and values risks alienating global partners. In contrast, developing a dialogue-led, two-way interaction between equal partners is recognised as promising and stressed by EU Global Strategy (EEAS 2016a).

Coming from a constructivist research perspective, the book focussed on perceptions and images as key elements in the external reception process. It conceptualized perceptions and images as important explanatory factors in understanding nuanced interactions between the EU and the four BICS in energy policy. We asked what mutual perceptions both sides hold of each other, what controversies are highlighted by those perceptions and how mutual perceptions could influence the reactions of policy- and decision-makers towards each other. A set of research questions outlined in the Introduction led analysis presented in this book. Our conclusions bring together the answers discussed in the country chapters in a comparative summary.

Answering the questions about the emerging powers' views on the EU and the 'mirror' perceptions (views of the BICS coming from Europe), we summarise in a comparative mode the multiple visions of each other as actors in the global energy governance. In this section, we focus initially on the media visibility of issues, types and contexts of each other and proceed with a comparison of these factors with the elite perceptions of motivations to engage in cooperation on energy issues. Answering the question about perceived dominant normative frames and their hierarchies in the bilateral energy dialogues, we continue with a discussion about the frames of the EU and BICS as energy actors, comparing media findings vis-à-vis elite ones. We also compare the extent to which the European and BICS actors in respective energy dialogues perceive each other's willingness and ability to cooperate with each other. We focus particularly on the comparison between evaluations assigned to the EU as an energy actor in the BICS media and BICS in the European media. We offset these findings against the perceived roles of the EU and BICS in the energy dialogue, traced through elite interviews and the survey. Throughout this chapter, we also answer our final research question – how these systematic insights into mutual perceptions and comparisons are be useful for the policy- and decision-makers involved in the energy interactions.

8.1 Topics of EU-BICS Energy Perceptions in Media and Elite Discourses

For the media analysis, this book observed BICS and European presses over five years (2009-2013), one month each year surrounding the period of annual UNFCCC COP. With volume and intensity being the key visibility measurements, Figure 8.1 summarizes the energy-related news that reported on respective BICS countries in the European selected newspapers and the EU in the respective BICS media – when the actors in question were reported from a *major* perspective (i.e., either the EU or the BICS were a main actor in a news story).[62]

In the three European presses, the most visible country – the most voluminous in reportage and often framed as a major topic – was China (with the French newsmakers being the most inclined to frame China as a main energy actor). Were we to include the articles with secondary and minor intensity patterns, China would have an even higher numbers of appearances (but this larger sample would also feature a dominant perspective of China as a minor energy actor in the German and UK media). South Africa was the least visible BICS country in terms of intensity in representation. In the German leading newspapers, South Africa did not even appear in the major centrality category, but was predominantly portrayed as a minor actor.

62 Although *The European Voice* was a part of our study, it is not in this summary for comparative reasons. With the exception of the Chinese case, Brazil, India and South Africa were reported as energy actors in only one or two articles over five years, making their cases not comparable.

Figure 8.1: Number of articles respective BICS media reporting the EU

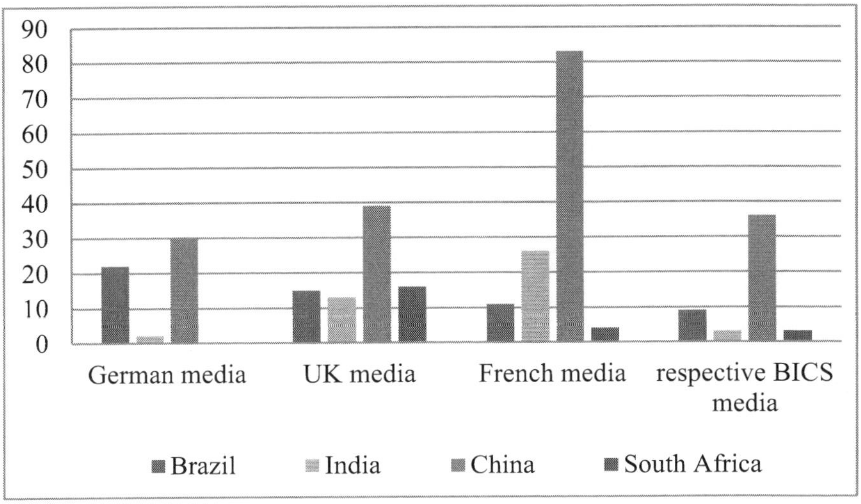

Source: EXIE, 2015.

Assessing images of the EU in the respective BICS presses, there was a higher share of news in China that featured the EU with more intensity. In contrast, the EU was barely visible as a major topic in South African, Indian and Brazilian reportage of energy matters. In general, (not only in the energy field), the EU had a low media profile in leading South African and Indian presses. This low interest appears to be reciprocal – South Africa and India are the least visible as major energy actors in the European media under observation (with the single exception of France, in which India was more visible in energy reportage).

It appears that the leading newspapers of the EU's 'Big 3' and BICS credit each other with low profiles when reporting each other as major energy actors. China was one exception. Influential European and BICS presses framed China not only as the most visible energy actor in its own right, but also as a visible cooperation partner in the energy field. This high media profile is of significance as it presents China as a powerful contestant for the title of the 'most popular' energy diplomacy partner. Reinforced by a more general – and increasingly stereotypical – image of China as a 'rising superpower', it presents a challenge for EU energy diplomacy. In contrast, the EU is seen as being hit by multiple crises.

However, this low media visibility of the EU and BICS as energy actors does not parallel elite perceptions of the respective EU-BICS relations in energy policy. Our elite survey demonstrated that all BICS and EU stakeholders – those who are involved in the institutionalized bilateral energy dialogues – largely consider these dialogues important (Figure 8.2). There was no major difference between either the BICS and the EU or *public* and *non-state* actors. However, two exceptions were observed; the EU elites were somewhat more reluctant to call the EU-Brazil dialogue important, and the Chinese actors were more sceptical to call the EU-China dialogue important.

Figure 8.2: Perceived importance of EU-BICS cooperation on energy issues since 2007 (percentages of actors)

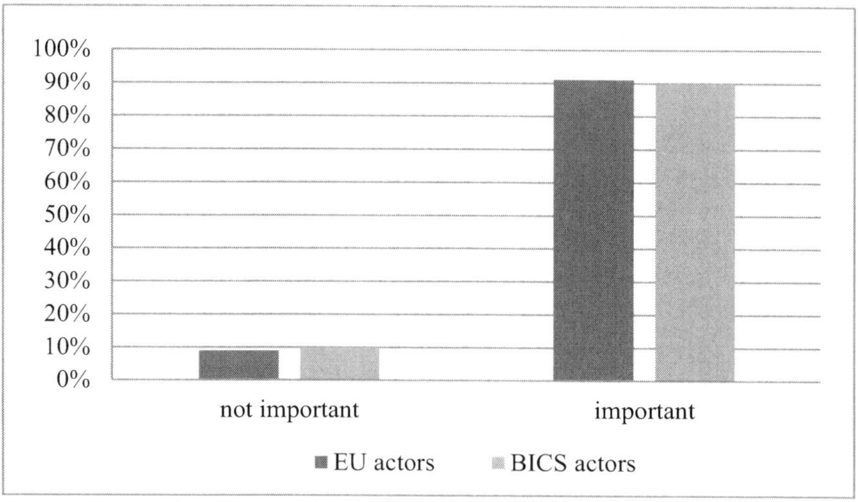

Source: EnergyGov, Darmstadt, 2014.

The *impact* of the dialogue on BICS and EU energy policy was perceived differently. In nearly all cases, the effect of the dialogue on the respective BICS national energy policy was perceived to be higher than the effect on the EU's energy policy (Figure 8.3). The only exception is the perceptions of the Brazil-EU dialogue, in which the EU actors perceive a slightly higher effect on its own energy policy than on Brazil's policy. Importantly, in the South African and Indian cases, the perception of the effect on the EU's energy policy is substantially lower than in the case of Brazil and China. We argue that South Africa and India, the two economically 'weaker' emerging powers in our sample, appear to be perceived by the EU and by themselves as being less influential than the two 'stronger' countries Brazil and China. The perceptions of the effect in the Brazilian case are much more balanced. Notably, the perceived effect in the case of the EU actors in the China-EU energy dialogue is extremely low.

Figure 8.3: Perceived effect of the dialogue on EU and BICS energy policy*

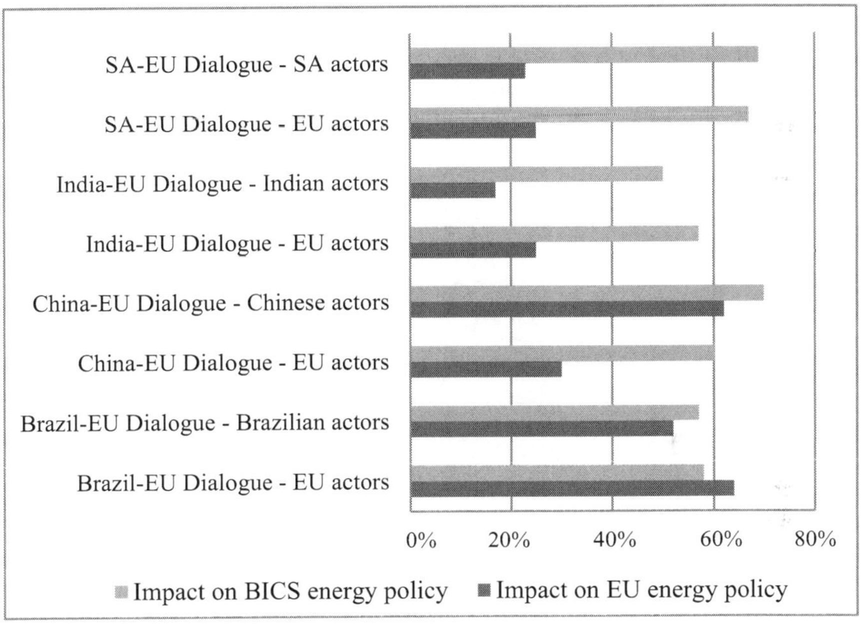

*Percentages of the actors
Source: EnergyGov, Darmstadt, 2014.

Focussing on the Brazilian and Chinese cases, we can nevertheless detect differences between the two. In the EU-Brazilian case, the EU actors are much more convinced that the dialogue has an impact on the EU energy policy in comparison to the Chinese-EU energy dialogue. Brazilian actors are also much more reluctant to see an impact on the EU's and their own energy policies than are the Chinese actors. This might be explained by the fact that the Brazil-EU energy dialogue is in its initial phase, whereas China-EU energy cooperation has a long history. Brazil and the EU have cooperated and held dialogues on specific topics of interest for both sides, but these interactions never addressed the 'essentials' of each other's energy systems.

Assessment of the general media visibility of the EU and BICS as energy actors in terms of volume and intensity of representation and the perceived importance and impact of the respective EU-BICS energy dialogue in the eyes of the elites is further complemented by our analysis of the visibility of different *issues* and *types* of energy in the respective media discourses.

Here, we present the synopsis of the findings, selecting *policy-related* issues visible in the selected newspapers in the period of observation that was expected to raise the profile of the energy-related matters. In this summary, we leave out the *process-related* issues such as 'energy governance' or 'cooperation'. Table 8.1 shows the most visible *energy policy issues* detected in the respective media.

Table 8.1: Visible energy issues in the media (only energy policy-related)

	German media reporting respective BICS	**UK media reporting respective BICS**	**French media reporting respective BICS**	**Respective BICS media reporting the EU as an energy actor**
Brazil	Investment	Emissions/ Investment	Emissions	Emissions/ Investment Energy Infrastructure
India	Investment	Emissions	Emissions	Energy access
China	Investment	Prices	Emissions	Energy saving
South Africa	Emissions	Investment	Emissions	Sustainable development

Source: EXIE, 2015.

German press (Table 8.1) reported on nearly all BICS with a stress on *investments* in the energy field. Only when South Africa is reported do the German media preferred to report more about *emissions*. However, this policy issue was closely followed by the *investment* issue. In contrast, the French media assigned priority to the respective BICS in the context of *emissions*. Some of these media emphases in France were linked to the *sustainability* frame visible due to the timing of the observation. However, these emphases also appeared in the context of the overall French energy policy orientation towards nuclear energy reflected by the leading French press. Nuclear energy was introduced as contributing to the fight against climate change and towards clean air policy. The UK case was a mixed case. The issues of *investments/prices* as well as *emissions* were the most visible policy-oriented issues in the UK media. Importantly, none of the European media cases has a highly visible discussion on *energy savings*, *energy access* or *sustainable development*. None of these issues ranked first.

Media portrayals of the EU's energy policy issues by the BICS media showed a list of topics very different from the European list. Once again, we observe a divide between how Brazil and China framed the EU vis-à-vis how India and South Africa framed it. *Emissions*, *investment* and *energy infrastructure* were leading issues in EU media representations in the Brazilian case and *energy saving* in the Chinese case. In contrast, Indian and South African media show an orientation towards *development* issues when framing the EU – such as the EU actions in the context of *energy access* in India and *sustainable development* in South Africa.

South Africa also portrayed the EU in the context of *energy access* (energy access remains a crucial issue in South Africa, linked not least to the deficiencies in energy infrastructure). Access to energy is an issue of great importance and public awareness in South African energy politics. Perhaps unsurprisingly, in the South African media case, the EU was represented as a promising cooperation partner, able to provide technologies to solve the problems around energy infrastructure. *Sustainable development* and *energy access* were also the issues that dominated the South African stakeholders' perceptions of importance and were often interlinked because sustainable development is considered necessary to achieve nationwide access to energy. "This aspect is directly linked to the development of new infrastructure to meet the energy needs of millions of South Africans" (Fioramonti 2016).

The issue of *energy saving* was visible in the Chinese newspapers. The media representation of the EU suggests that Chinese newsmakers were most interested in the EU for its technologies to save energy and to make energy use more efficient, which requires technologies and investment. The topics of *energy saving* and *infrastructure* found in the BICS selected newspapers fit with the orientation of Germany and the UK concerning investment in China and Brazil. To provide one example, the issue of *investments* dominated the German reportage of Brazil as an energy actor in the observed period, with almost one-half of the articles mentioning Brazil related to investments. This perspective adds to the image of Brazil as a potential market for business interests and appears to reflect on the latest developments of the wind sector in Brazil as the fastest growing source of electrical power in Brazil. The most recent Ten-Year Energy Expansion Plan of the

Brazilian Ministry of Mines and Energy[63] is of special interest for Germany and the UK. In another example, the Federal Ministry of Economy and Energy has launched an information event on 'Onshore Wind energy in Brazil' in September 2016 within the framework of its 'Export Initiative Renewable energies' to boost German investments in Brazil's wind energy infrastructure.[64]

The most visible policy issue of *emissions* in the reportages of India and South Africa in the European leading newspapers also points to the fact that both 'emerging' countries remain highly dependent upon coal as an energy source and must address its emission problems. This leads us to the question of which *types* of energy were the most visible in the respective media when they reported on each other as energy actors. The data are analysed according to the two categories – *non-renewable* and *renewable* types of energy sources (Tables 8.2 and 8.3).

Table 8.2: Non-renewable energy types in the media

	German media reporting respective BICS	**UK media reporting respective BICS**	**French media reporting respective BICS**	**Respective BICS media reporting the EU as an energy actor**
Brazil	Oil	Oil	Oil	Gas
India	Oil	Oil	Nuclear	Oil
China	Oil	Oil	Oil	Gas/Oil
South Africa	Coal	Coal	Oil	Oil

Source: EXIE, 2015.

Specifically, examining *non-renewable* energy *sources* (Table 8.2), *gas* and *oil* are the two most visible energy types for all actors when they report each other as energy actors. This media priority is not a surprise, because these two sources remain the most used fossil fuels to produce energy in general.

63 http://www.mme.gov.br/documents/10584/3642013/03+-+Energy+Expansion+in+Brazil+Investiment+Opportunities+(PDF)/97e49acb-ee22-4c98-ad80-c70056288e89;jsessionid=EA174D8159C21B7C94B25A59F05C52EC.srv155?version=1.1 [24.08.2016].

64 http://www.erneuerbare-energien.de/EEE/Redaktion/DE/Veranstaltungen/2016/Infoveranstaltungen/iv-brasilien-wind.html [26.08.2016].

In the case of Brazil, European newspapers chosen for observation concentrated exclusively on oil when reporting Brazil as an energy actor. This specific media profile was greatly influenced by the discovery of the pre-salt oil that catapulted Brazil into the group of oil producing countries. *Gas* was more visible than *oil* when the EU is reported by Brazilian media. At first glance, this finding is surprising because natural gas plays only a modest role in Brazil's energy mix (accounting for less than 12 per cent of the domestic energy supply and 7.2 per cent of the country's final energy consumption). This is due to the

> predominant role of hydroelectricity in Brazil's power generation, the country's relatively undeveloped gas infrastructure, government subsidies for LPG (liquefied petroleum gas) and the monopoly of Petrobras, which contributes to balancing the supply of competing fuels – natural gas and low-value fuel oil (Gomez 2014: 1-2).

However, the dry seasons since 2012 caused energy production shortages from their hydropower generation. Brazil had to import LNG (liquefied natural gas) to meet the needs of its gas-fired power plants. From this perspective, the expansion of the gas share in the Brazilian power mix becomes an important topic for the Brazilian media when they report energy matters in general and the EU within them.

The focus on *nuclear* energy in the case of Indian and French media observed in our study is arguably a reflection of their own domestic energy matters and mixes. There is an increasing importance of nuclear power in India's energy mix, and in this context, nuclear power is an area central to the France-India energy cooperation. Moreover, France was the first country to sign a civil nuclear agreement with India (2008). In 2009, a Memorandum of Understanding was signed between the two partners to pave the way for six nuclear reactor units in Jaitapur (in progress).[65] France's expertise in this field makes it an attractive partner to India. Conversely, France expects significant economic benefits and the gaining of a global ally in the nuclear power energy field from this partnership. France strongly supports India in its aim to become part of the global export control regime. To both actors, nuclear energy is of great importance to ensure energy security and to fight climate change.

Note that *coal* in both the German and UK media is the most reported energy source in relation to South Africa. This media priority seem to parallel the reality – the UK and Germany both import coal from South Africa.

65 http://thediplomat.com/2013/02/france-and-india-deepen-ties/ [05.07.2016].

Turning to the *renewable* types of energy prioritized in the respective media, our summary below (Table 8.3) left out such generic categories as 'renewables in general', 'new energy', 'green energy' and 'clean energy' and focussed on particular types of renewable energy sources.

Table 8.3: Renewable types of energy in the media (without category renewables in general)

	German media reporting respective BICS	**UK media reporting respective BICS**	**French media reporting respective BICS**	**Respective BICS media reporting the EU as an energy actor**
Brazil	wind	wind	solar	wind
India	wind	wind	solar	solar
China	solar	solar	solar	solar
South Africa	solar	solar	solar	solar

Source: EXIE, 2015.

The influential presses in the EU and BICS tend to focus on *solar* and *wind* types of renewables. S*olar* dominated the EU's portrayals in the Chinese, Indian and South African cases. *Wind* was most visible in the reporting of BICS in the German and UK media.

A more visible media profile of the EU in terms of *wind* energy in the Brazilian case appears to reflect the latest positive developments of the wind sector in Brazil. These developments are also of special interest in Germany and the UK, when the report on Brazil.

In the Indian case, wind and solar are competing renewables in the country's energy mix. However, India's solar power potential is considered larger than its wind potential because "installed wind capacity grows at less than one-half the pace of solar" (IEA 2015d: 131). It is also a question of costs because both energy installations must be imported. The costs for solar are less than are the costs for wind. Nevertheless, German and UK firms are highly interested in selling wind turbines to India, particularly for offshore installation. Arguably, offshore wind parks would be one solution for India to solve its land acquisition issues, but an expensive one.

In the next segment of our analysis, we identify the most visible *contexts* within which the EU-BICS energy relations are framed in the respective newspapers (Table 8.4). The main contexts were *economics*, *climate change, development* and *politics*.

Table 8.4: Contexts of mutual representations in BICS and EU media

	German media reporting respective BICS	UK media reporting respective BICS	French media reporting respective BICS	Respective BICS media reporting the EU as an energy actor
Brazil	Economics	Economics	Environment	Politics
India	Economics	Climate Change (followed by Economics)	Politics	Economics
China	Economics	Economics	Politics	Politics/Economics
South Africa	Climate Change (followed by Economics)	Economics	Environment	Development

Source: EXIE, 2015.

The *climate change* context visible in the European media points to the links between *energy* and *climate change* issues reported by the media – a link expected in our research due to the timing of the analysis around the UNFCCC COPs. However, it was not an exclusively visible context.

BICS energy reportage in the German and UK presses in the selected period of observation was actually dominated by the *economic* context, which corresponds with the most visible policy-related issue of *investment and prices* we discussed previously. In contrast, in their reportage of BICS as energy actors, the French media focussed much attention on *environment* and *politics*, which corresponds to the above-discussed priority assigned to the issue *emissions*.

Importantly, the context of *development* did hardly appear in the European media reports of BICS as energy actors in our sample over five years. This lack of visibility of this context in the coverage of India and South Africa as energy actors is telling – EU Member States continued to perform development policy measures in the energy field in the observed period.[66] Considering the scale of Germany's and France's official development assistance (and specifically towards India), not seeing the leading presses of these EU states acknowledge development cases is also of note. A *development* context, however, did appear in 21 articles in the UK media and was the fourth most visible context. India was receiving overseas development assistance from the UK until 2013; this has arguably influenced the visibility of the context (Bain et al. 2016).

Turning to BICS presses, only South Africa showed *development* as the most visible context when referring to the EU as an energy actor. This might be explained by the fact that of the four BICS, only South Africa continues receiving development aid assistance from the EU. Most EU energy projects and measures are financed through development programmes because DG Energy of the EU Commission has limited budget for cooperation programmes with third countries. In this light, it is logical that the local media were framing the EU as an actor of development aid when speaking about the EU as an energy actor. *Development* appeared as the third most visible context in Indian media energy-related coverage of the EU, with *economics* appearing to be the most visible context there.

Following the discussion of the most visible energy *issues*, *types* and *contexts* in leading presses, we assess the most visible motivations to engage in cooperation with each other shared by the elites involved in the EU-BICS energy dialogues. These motivations were identified in the course of interviews and the survey. Actors show very different motivations (Table 8.5). The table lists top motivations of the public actors and the second most visible motivation (in the cases in which they are closely ranked).

A key finding shows that the EU *public* actors have the same motivations for all EU-BICS dialogues: first, to cooperate with BICS as energy actors to combat climate change, and second, to promote private sector cooperation. The latter motivation appears to resonate with the European media framing of the energy matters in EU-BICS relations and the three EU Member States' interests as presented in the media.

66 Please, note that our periods of observation were limited to one month around UN climate summits. A longer period of observation may result in some visibility of the development issues.

Table 8.5: Motivations to engage in cooperation on energy issues

	BICS public actors on motivations to engage with the EU	**EU public actors on motivations to engage with respective BICS**
Brazil	private sector cooperation technology transfer	climate change private sector cooperation
India	technology transfer	climate change private sector cooperation
China	climate change technology transfer	climate change private sector cooperation
South Africa	secure energy supply technology transfer	climate change private sector cooperation

Source: EnergyGov, Darmstadt, 2014.

For BICS *public* actors, technology transfer was one of the top two motivations. In India, public actors prioritized technology transfer so much that all other motivations are considered far behind it (and thus not listed in Table 8.5). Specifically, for the EU-India dialogue, the motivations of the EU and Indian stakeholders are highly divergent. The area of special interest for Indian public actors is energy efficiency and clean energy technologies, prioritized to achieve a cleaner production of coal. India had an acute interest in technology transfer; however, this interest is only partially reciprocated from within the EU. To the EU, the promotion of private sector cooperation was the second most important point of interest; thus, the dialogue could benefit if technology transfer gained more attention and if European interests in market entry and private technology cooperation were backed more articulately. Certainly, issues such as the absorptive capacity of the Indian energy sector might be a point of concern. However, we must keep in mind that the data were collected before the latest shift in the Indian policy towards renewable energies. Future research should examine if there is a possible change in elite perceptions after COP 21 in Paris. We hypothesize that after the 'Joint Declaration between the EU and India on a Clean Energy and Climate Partnership' (European Council 2016), higher motivations might be observed on the Indian side.

In Brazil, private sector cooperation received a high priority, producing an impression that economic and technological benefits are considered more popular motivations than is the issue of combating climate change. In the EU-Brazil dialogue, the motivations were partly convergent because the EU and Brazil share the interests of promoting private sector cooperation.

In the case of the EU-China energy dialogue, we also find converging interests. The two share a political interest in combating climate change. Moreover, the EU's interest in promoting private sector cooperation might match very well China's interest in technology transfer (not least, if pending licensing issues can be solved to everyone's satisfaction).

Finally, the EU-South African dialogue initially appears to be driven by quite divergent motivations. However, South Africa's high interest in enhancing security of supply might be matched by European interests in private sector cooperation; the growing FDI activities in South Africa's renewable energy sectors could be a first indicator.

8.2 Normative Orientation of EU-BICS Energy Relations in Media and Elite Discourse

Following our earlier argument that norms play an important role in EU energy governance, we focus now on how the EU and BICS were framed in the media and elite discourses with respect to the different normative energy frames – *competitiveness, sustainability* and *security of supply*. We have analysed in this book the frames in the media analysis (Table 8.6) and in elite opinions (collected with the help of the survey instrument and interviews) (Table 8.7).

Table 8.6: Energy frames of BICS and the EU in media

	German media reporting respective BICS	**UK media reporting respective BICS**	**French media reporting respective BICS**	**Respective BICS media reporting the EU as an energy actor**
Brazil	competitiveness	competitiveness	sustainability	sustainability
India	security of supply	sustainability	security of supply/sustainability	sustainability
China	competitiveness	competitiveness	sustainability	sustainability
South Africa	security of supply/sustainability	sustainability	sustainability	-

Source: EXIE, 2015.

Remarkably, all BICS newspapers under observation[67] prioritised framing of the EU as an energy actor within *sustainability* (Table 8.6). Although the timing of the media analysis around the UNFCCC COPs and the EU's role at the COPs could be one explanation, this framing also reflected a broader 'green image' of the EU as a normative energy actor. This media finding is of special interest – elite frames discussed below do not show such a unanimous emphasis.

The monitored German and UK newspapers demonstrated an already familiar divide between their framing of Brazil and China on the one hand and India and South Africa on the other hand. Whereas the former group is framed through *competitiveness*, India and South Africa were framed through the prism of their national problems (e.g. the lack of security of supply in India and South Africa noted by the German media, or India's challenged sustainability reported by the UK media). The French media is consistent with the *sustainability* frame when reporting BICS as energy actors, adding the frame of *security of supply* in the Indian case.

The next step compares media data with the opinion of the elites. Chapters 4-7 provided detailed information concerning the normative orientations and mutual perceptions of the participants in the energy dialogues that allows us to assess the political interactions of the dialogue partners. Concerning normative orientations, we asked our interviewees to rank the aspects of *sustainability*, *security of supply* and *competitiveness* and choose between different possible understandings of each norm. This helped us to discover more about the shape and structure of each normative triangle and thus the normative background that predetermines political interaction within energy governance. Our findings note that 'liberal' and 'green' motivations become closely interwoven in the European stakeholders' normative orientations. However, comparing the normative orientations of the EU actors with the orientations of the BICS actors shows a different pattern displaying a high variance of normative orientations (Figure 8.4). This major difference in normative framing in the four surveys on EU-BICS energy relations might be explained by the differing political agendas of European official institutions and actors interacting with each BICS in the energy field. Obviously, the EU does not perform as a coherent normative actor promoting the same energy norm in each of the four dialogues. The norm hierarchy of the EU changes according to the context of the respective dialogue. In addition, the normative orientations between the EU and BICS in

67 Note that South African sample had some missing data for frame identification.

the dialogue do not always show the same orientation. In the cases of China and Brazil, the normative orientations by EU vis-à-vis BICS actors on the energy dialogues did not match. In contrast, in the cases of India and South Africa, all of the European and BICS normative orientations matched quite well.

In the case of China, we find *security of supply* to be the widely preferred frame by Chinese actors, whereas the EU prefers the *sustainability* frame in this dialogue. Here, in light of China's priority given to the security of energy supplies, the EU may consider reframing its messages to China to search for more common grounds on which political dialogue could be based. This might for instance imply a focus on the potential of renewable energy for guaranteeing security of supply. Such framing may find rich grounds in already existing EU-China cooperation that strongly focusses on *sustainability* issues – e.g., the creation of the Europe-China Clean Energy Centre (EC2), energy law cooperation or the energy sub working-group on energy-efficient buildings as a part of the energy dialogue.

In the EU-Brazil dialogue, normative orientations of the two actors are, as stated above, viewed as diverging. Whilst the *security of supplies* frame appears to be most important for the Brazilian actors in the dialogue, the *sustainability* frame has the strongest weight for the EU actors, and *security of supplies* does not appear at all. It is likely that the strong focus of the Brazil-EU energy dialogue on renewable energies is viewed as one aspect of energy security by Brazilian actors and framed within sustainability ambitions by the EU side. Due to Brazil's green energy mix with over 45 per cent renewable energies, further investments in wind and solar energy are considered a measure to enhance energy security due to the excellent climatic conditions for wind and solar energy and not as a measure to enhance sustainability. However, a normative disconnect between the EU and Brazil exists in interpreting the *sustainability* frame with reference to the licensing of Brazilian second-generation biofuels. Whereas Brazil aims for EU certification of its second-generation biofuels, the EU does not consider its sustainability standards to have been fulfilled.

Figure 8.4: Energy frames of BICS-EU cooperation by BICS and EU actors in elite opinion*

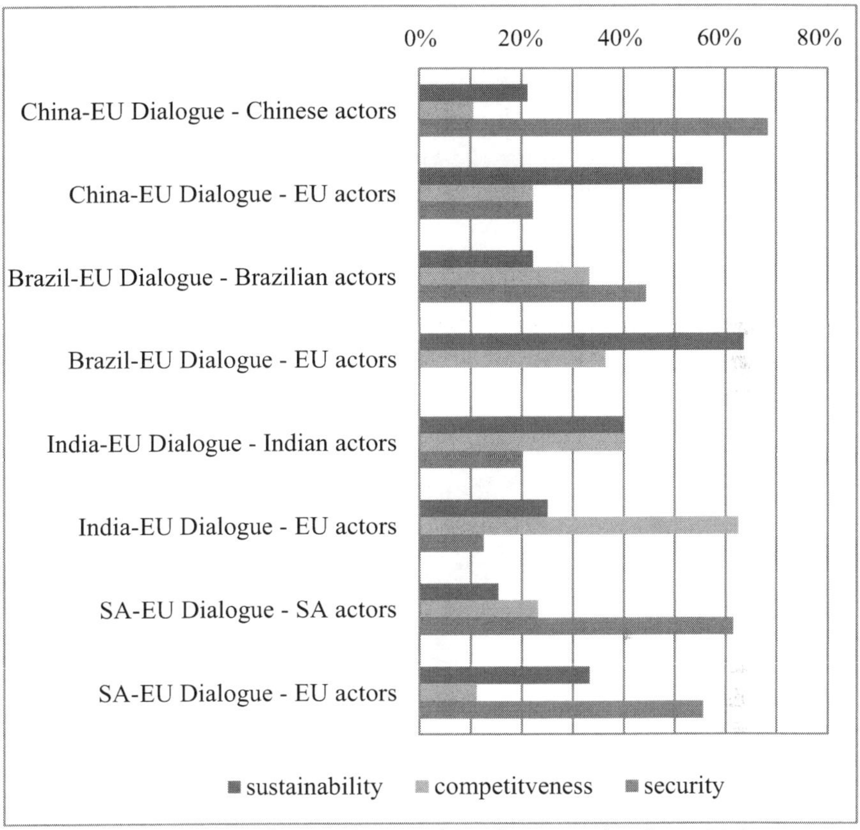

*All actors: percentage of respondents ranking the respective frame highest
Source: EnergyGov, Darmstadt, 2014.

The Indian case is one of the two cases in which the normative orientations overlap. The Indian and European normative configurations match relatively well, with *competitiveness* and *sustainability* considered the most important frames, followed by *security of supply*. Here, EU and Indian actors show similar orientations, a fact that might facilitate cooperation if considered as a point of reference within political communication. Competitiveness plays a very important role, which can be explained by growing European interest in market entry and enhanced energy cooperation with India. The ongoing EU-India FTA negotiations might also influence this orientation. For EU officials, this is obviously a situation in which the impetus to enhance competitiveness is more important than sustainability or security concerns.

In the EU-South Africa energy dialogue, the orientations match – both actors here share a preference for *security of supply* as a guiding frame for energy policy-making. This could be considered an important normative basis for intensifying the dialogue, in light of developing common solutions for security of supply and for battling energy poverty. *Energy security* as the most important issue in the EU-South African dialogue certainly does not point to the occurrence of a highly competitive struggle over resources. This underlines the high importance the EU devotes to *security of supply* issues in the South African case. At the same time, in a country driven by energy path dependencies with the state-owned energy enterprise Eskom as a single monopolist and only few private energy providers, *competitiveness* is of minor importance for the EU as long as this solid structure is changing slowly. However, a growing interest in obtaining access to the South African energy market for renewables technologies can be observed, and it is likely that the frame of *competitiveness* will gain in importance in the future.

8.3 Mutual Perceptions as Dialogue Partners in Media and Elite Discourses (Evaluations and Roles)

Our conclusions also explore to what extent the EU and the BICS perceive each other's willingness and ability to cooperate with each other. One important indicator of these visions comes from the media data – the evaluations assigned to the EU as an energy actor in the BICS media and to BICS in the European media. In the elite interviews and the survey, our respondents were asked to assess different roles of the EU and BICS (for instance, "being an agenda-setter" or "playing with a hidden agenda"). The two indicators of evaluations and roles are argued to identify emotive charge of mutual perceptions and visions of agenda-setting qualities, compromise-building skills and mutual learning (Knodt et al. 2015c: 335).

Table 8.7 sums up the respective evaluations of BICS and the EU assigned by the newsmakers in our period of observation – from negative-to-neutral and neutral-to-positive. In the German and French media in our sample, BICS tend to be evaluated in a predominantly neutral manner, with clearly positive or negative evaluations hardly visible (Table 8.7). Such a neutral style of reporting could be a hallmark of the European quality press, who claim objective fact-oriented reportage. Importantly, our analysis considered less clear-cut categories *positive-to-neutral* and *neutral-to-negative* to analyse more closely the evaluation of the actors (following Bain et al. 2016). In France, we observed slightly more negative assessments of China and Brazil, in contrast to a slightly more positive tone in the case of Brazil. The UK media portrayals of BICS as energy actors were the least neutral in the sample. Here, we find clear tendencies towards negative (or even both directions, as in the South African case) evaluations.

Table 8.7: Evaluations of BICS and the EU in the respective media

	German media reporting respective BICS	**UK media reporting respective BICS**	**French media reporting respective BICS**	**Respective BICS media reporting the EU as an energy actor**
Brazil	neutral	neutral (with slight tendency to negative)	neutral (with slight tendency to positive)	positive
India	neutral	neutral (with tendency to negative)	neutral	neutral
China	neutral	neutral (with tendency to negative)	neutral (with slight tendency to negative)	neutral
South Africa	neutral	neutral (with tendency in both directions)	neutral (with slight tendency to negative	-

Source: EXIE, 2015.

In the Brazilian case, the majority of the European articles evaluated Brazil in a neutral manner, with clear negative or positive evaluations being hardly visible. However, in the UK press reporting Brazil as an energy actor, the dominant frame of *competitiveness* attracted more negative evaluations than positive. These negative stories portrayed Brazil and its energy markets as non-competitive in comparison to other energy markets, e.g., China. Interestingly, the French press in our study framed Brazil remarkably differently – as a capable competitive actor, particularly in offshore drilling and developing green energies.

In the Brazilian press, there were more articles containing some evaluation of the EU as an energy actor than articles in which the EU was reported from a neutral perspective. Overall, the EU was portrayed in a rather positive tone. This was particularly the case when the EU is evaluated as a sustainable energy actor. The EU was not a very visible actor in the Brazilian media, but when it appeared, it was presented in a positive light. However, this presentation did change when EU-Brazilian energy interaction was evaluated. In those articles, the negative tone outweighed the positive. Furthermore, there was a visible change over time. Although the EU was evaluated more positively in 2009 (during the COP 15 in Copenhagen), the tone becomes more negative in the following years. This change in evaluation is partly connected to the EU's challenged performance at the climate summits (Guimaraes/Piefer 2016).

In the Indian case, the European press reported India as an energy actor in a more negative tone. This is mostly linked to the reportage on India's role and less constructive involvement in the annual climate summits. The German and UK presses also spoke about concerns with respect to India's nuclear policy and related safety issues.

Indian media in our study presented the EU as an energy actor from an exclusively neutral perspective. This finding is in line with previous media analyses of the EU images in the Indian media – those also observed that Indian media portrayed the Union almost exclusively in neutral terms (Chaban/Elgström 2014: 179).

China was evaluated in a more negative than positive tone in the UK and French presses. In the UK media, negativity often appeared in the *sustainability* frame, with China described as lacking in actions as a sustainable actor and being destructive in the course of the COPs negotiations. The same counts for the French media – a significant number of articles with a clearly negative evaluation of China were linked to its reluctance to combat climate change, hindering the conclusion of an agreement at the COPs. Another negatively coloured theme was China's dumping of solar panels into EU markets.

A neutral tone dominated the portrayals of the EU as an energy actor in both Chinese newspapers. When evaluations occurred, they demonstrated a noticeable difference between the party-owned newspaper vis-à-vis the business daily. Although *People's Daily* evaluated the EU from a rather positive standpoint in our period of observation, *The 21st Century* did not have a single article presenting the EU in a positive light. It appears that the official opinion of the EU in China rendered by the party newspaper is more positive than the opinion of the business daily. Positive evaluations assigned to the EU by the *People's Daily* were primarily in the context of the China-

EU summits and the progress made in cooperation on clean energy and energy saving (Lai/Shi 2016). The business daily addresses the EU from a negative viewpoint regarding the COPs, emissions and the solar dispute between the EU and China.

The UK and French reports of South Africa in our sample featured more articles with pronounced evaluations (this resonates with the overall volume and intensity of South Africa's representations in these media). In the UK newspapers under observation, news stories portraying South Africa were rather polarized, whereas the *positive* tone led in the French media. The *negative-to-neutral* stories in the UK media addressed South Africa's energy challenges concerning its energy mix, energy supply and energy efficiency, whereas the *positive-to-neutral* stories among others addressed South Africa's role in the fight against climate change, its aim at reducing the amount of coal in its energy mix and its use of biofuels. *Positive* stories in the French media addressed diverse issues, among others, the involvement of South Africa at the UN climate summits, the construction of solar plants and the production of energy from methane in South Africa.

Another important dimension in our analysis is tracing the mutual perceptions of the partners undertaking the dialogue. Mutual perceptions of the actors are an important explanatory factor; they provide evidence of how the dialogic partners view each other's political interactions, agenda-setting qualities, and consensus-building activities (Chaban et al. 2009; Lucarelli/Fioramonti 2010; Knodt et al. 2015). In this summary, we examine the mutual perceptions of the political and administrative elites. The mutual perceptions display to what extent the actors are willing and able to cooperate and which neuralgic points must be clarified to come to terms for cooperative policymaking. To explore how the actors perceive each other's behaviour as dialogue partners, we asked our respondents to assess different properties, for instance, "being an agenda-setter" or "playing with a hidden agenda" (for more properties, see Figure 8.5). This comparative summary allows further conclusions how to facilitate the quality of bilateral energy cooperation and negotiate strategies for optimizing energy cooperation.

In their self-perception, the EU public actors (Figure 8.5) tend to view the EU as an active agenda setter, emphasizing high compromise-building qualities and an interest in the other negotiation partner, which is also visible in the openness for mutual learning. This very positive self-image must be set against the BICS' perceptions of the European actors. The public actors in the four emerging powers agreed that the EU acts as an agenda setter; at the same time, the EU is also willing and able to learn from the BICS side. Although they do not consider the EU a dominant promoter of interests, they do note that the EU is not particularly eager to compromise or change its positions. In addition, they would not subscribe to the claim that the EU is acting with an open agenda. Instead, some respondents from India and China stated that the EU was occasionally acting with a 'hidden agenda'. Importantly, the self-perceptions of each BICS were that they have an open agenda, whereas the EU view this property rather critically. The same holds true for compromise (see Figure 8.6).

Figure 8.5: Perception of the EU's properties as a dialogue partner*

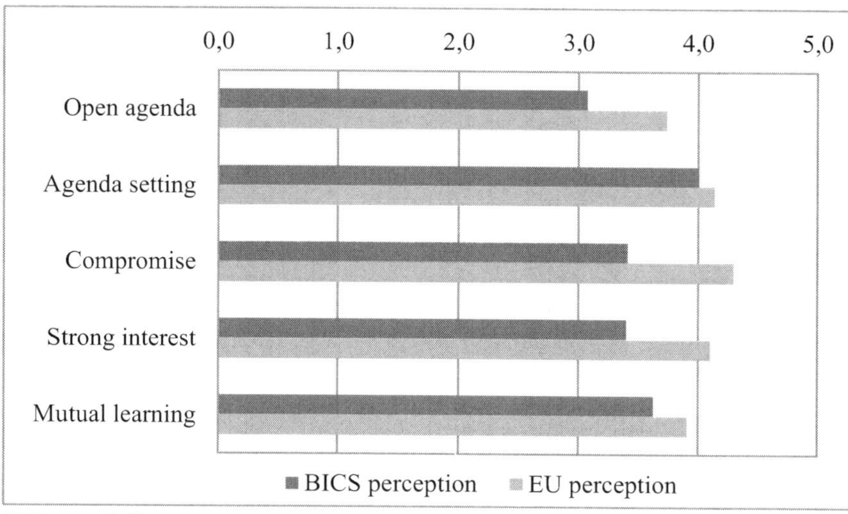

*Means of all answers; 1 = "Strongly disagree"; 5 = "Strongly agree"
Source: EnergyGov, Darmstadt, 2014.

The perceptions of the partners match when referring to how they view the BICS as agenda setters, possessing a strong interest and ability to change a position. The BICS perceive each other in a slightly more positive light with respect to being able to undertake mutual learning. The European public actors stress that the BICS experienced increased political pressure and made use of policy trade-offs in the dialogue. Because this perception could weaken private actors' confidence in the negotiations, it might be an important task for EU and BICS public actors to prevent further irritations during the process.

Figure 8.6: Perceptions of BICS' properties as a dialogue partner*

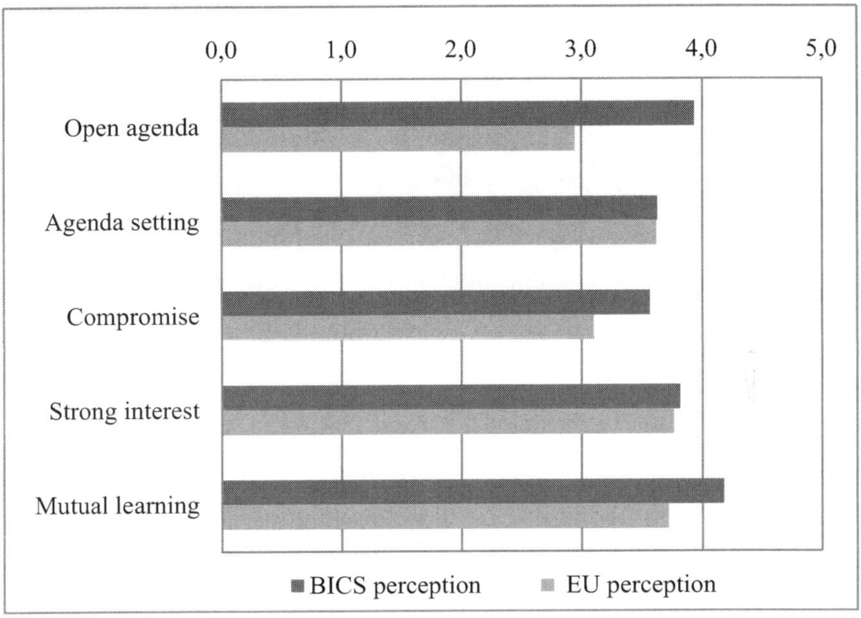

*Means of all answers; 1 = "Strongly disagree"; 5 = "Strongly agree"
Source: EnergyGov, Darmstadt, 2014.

Brazilian public actors have a very positive self-image of Brazil's role as a dialogue partner in energy cooperation, highlighting Brazil's openness for mutual learning within bilateral cooperation and its strong interest in the EU perspective, also noting the country's compromise-building qualities and open agenda. Interestingly, the EU actors share the perception of Brazil's contributions to the dialogue. They even assert a more active role for Brazil than does Brazil in initiating topics and placing them on the agenda (Ribas/Schaeffer 2015). Within the perception of the EU's properties as a dialogue partner, the Brazilian and European actors do not converge similarly. In particular, the Brazilian actors perceive the EU as not playing with an open agenda. Thus, there appears to be a potential for mistrust from the Brazilian side.

Concerning the perceptions of the EU by both European and Indian actors, European actors view the EU as challenging India's position and increasing pressure on Indian partners in the dialogue and negotiations. They also view themselves as having more influence on the agenda setting in contrast to how the Indian stakeholders would perceive the situation. At the same time, the EU actors perceive themselves as more willing to compromise than the Indian actors would admit. In an interesting twist, the Indian actors attribute more willingness and openness to the EU for mutual learning than the EU actors perceive about themselves. Overall, the perception between European and Indian actors does not differ as much when judging the EU's properties as a dialogue partner as when judging India as a dialogue partner.

A few Chinese interviewees elaborated and stated that in the energy aspect, China had more to learn from the EU than vice versa, particularly in technology, energy management and regulations. Numerous respondents mentioned the misunderstandings and misperceptions between China and the EU. These misunderstandings could indeed link back to the lack of trust between the two actors. The EU side suspects China's long-term strategic intentions and see Chinese enterprises as competitors. The solar panel trade dispute served as an example. Because they are at different stages of development in economic and energy aspects, the interests of the EU and China differ. The various communication mechanisms established were viewed as positive attempts to help the situation. However, the interviewees demanded more and better communication. Another frequently named problem was the lack of openness of the Chinese and EU energy markets to foreigners, particularly the former. Hence, trade frictions increase. Restrictions on market access also hinder the flow of technology and expertise. Blocking European companies from entering the energy market means that European advanced technology and skills are also blocked from reaching China; many European enterprises are already reluctant to sell their technology to China. Interviewees remarked that such market access problems could only be settled at the EU level, between the EU and the Chinese government.

In the case of South Africa, both actors perceive the EU to be a strong agenda-setter in the dialogue. However, although EU actors perceive the EU to have an open agenda, South African actors stated that the EU was playing with a hidden agenda (Knodt et al. 2015b: 68). Although the EU actors perceive the EU to be willing to change positions during negotiations, South African actors agree less on this aspect. Such differences in the perceptions of each other as dialogue partners can hinder a fruitful dialogue.

To conclude, of major concern are the differing mutual visions of agenda setting – particularly concerning open vs. hidden agenda. Such perceptions can lead to mistrust among the dialogue partners.

Conclusion
Studying Mutual Perceptions of EU-BICS Energy Co-operation: Lessons Provided

Our findings allow us to comment on the quality of bilateral energy cooperation and suggest recommendations to develop strategies to optimize energy cooperation. In terms of *visibility,* we found that leading presses of the EU's 'Big 3' and the BICS credit only little recognition to each other as energy actors in the period of observation that was expected to boost the mutual energy profiles. The only exception is China. However, this relative lack of media visibility did not seem to be detrimental for the mutual perceptions as energy partners in the eyes of the dialogue-participating elites. Here, BICS and the EU are considered important communication partners, and the bilateral energy dialogues are perceived as important by 90 per cent of all the elite respondents. Concerning the question of the impact on national energy policy, all actors perceive the impact on the BICS partner as higher than on the EU (with the exception of the Brazil dialogue). Still, low visibility patterns should be of concern to the EU's burgeoning energy diplomacy. Leading news media's influences on public and elite views are cumulative. Cumulative effect of media means that certain meanings of the EU and BICS as energy actors, spread and activated by influential media, may present either an opportunity or challenge for EU energy diplomacy both short- and long-term. This is true when it comes to designing the EU external action towards the BICS as well as justifying investments into energy diplomacy towards BICS with domestic audiences in the Member States.

Analysis of the *visibility* in terms of energy *issues*, *types* of energy and *contexts* of mutual representation and of the *emotive charge*, we observe interesting patterns in the European sample. The German and UK media framed energy matters and BICS within them similarly, whereas the French media largely diverged. German media reporting respective BICS cases showed a clearly economic orientation and framed energy issues within *competitiveness*. In contrast to the common popular impression of Germany being the 'green' country of the 'Energiewende', the media under observation did not reflect that profile when BICS were concerned. In contrast, the French media showed a much stronger orientation towards the *sustainabil-*

ity frame, but with a nuclear 'twist'. Whereas German media prioritized *investments* as a leading energy issue in all cases, French media preferred to speak about *emissions*. Earlier, we have cautioned our readers not to interpret the topic of *emissions* as being solely linked to the *sustainability* frame. The French media's talk about emissions should be considered in the context of France's advocacy of nuclear energy towards BICS countries (as discussed previously in the case of India). Finally, the German and UK media prioritized the context of *economics*, whereas the French media was much more oriented towards the *environment*.

These findings point the key role of local factors and priorities in shaping images of each other as energy actors. The national variations were considered in our media analysis. Despite the large world-scale event of the climate summits being a focal point in our press sampling, the *local* domestic concerns led in the coverage and framing of energy matters, not the global ones. The locally 'hooked' images were the most visible. For instance, differences in the visibility of energy *types* in the portrayals of the Other by the respective media could be explained by the local national energy industry orientation. The German media, for example, prioritized solar in the reports on China and South Africa. Solar industry in the case of China is a large issue for Germany, and South Africa invests more in solar than in other renewables.

Another major finding appearing through media and elite opinion analyses is a divide in perceptions of the economically stronger and powerful emerging powers (such as China and Brazil) on the one hand and 'weaker' ones (such as India and South Africa) on the other hand. This divide emerged in the perception of the impact of the EU-BICS dialogue and the EU's perception of the BICS. In the case of the 'weaker' countries, elite actors perceived a weaker impact on the EU's energy policy from the respective EU-BICS energy dialogues than in the case of the stronger emerging powers. Remarkably, both sides, the EU and the emerging powers, perceived the same impact. The framing of energy in the selected media also testified to this divide. In the German and UK media, we discovered the divide between the frames of Brazil and China on the one hand and India and South Africa on the other hand. The former pair is framed within *competitiveness* (which corresponds to the economical orientation towards those countries). The latter pair is framed through their national problems discussed earlier).

The divide could also be detected in how the BICS frame and perceive energy issues – and within them the EU as an energy actor. The 'stronger' China and Brazil reported more on *investment*, *energy infrastructure* and *energy savings*. In contrast, India and South Africa perceived the EU in relation to the topics of *energy access* and *sustainable development*.

When asked why they cooperate in the energy dialogue, EU and BICS public actors' perceptions largely diverge. Whereas the EU in all BICS cases was seen to be motivated most by fighting climate change and trying to enforce private sector cooperation, the main issue for all BICS themselves was technology transfer. The difference in perceptions suggests if the EU wants to play a more important role in the EU-BICS energy dialogues, it must commit to interesting cooperation projects that resonate with local visions and priorities. Our analysis of BICS perceptions also found attractive the EU's role as a 'moderator' of the EU Member States and EU energy governance towards BICS.

Our research concludes that successful cooperation requires primary identification and understanding of the areas of common interest. For example, the EU's energy outreach towards China should be informed by the recognition of China's desires for tangible cooperation to secure its energy supplies sustainably. Chinese stakeholders urged more concrete cooperation instead of 'talk shop'. Notably, China prefers state-to-state cooperation with individual EU Member States because reaching bilateral agreements with an individual EU country and implementing these agreements into concrete actions is easier and faster. Moreover, several stakeholders noted that China enjoyed better leverage when the EU is divided in a negotiation (Piefer et al. 2015b: 350-351).

Another finding is the detected problem of latent mistrust and diverging mutual perceptions as cooperation partners. In their self-perception, the EU public actors tend to view the EU as an active agenda setter. In particular, they emphasize the EU's high compromise-building qualities and recognize the EU's interest in the other negotiation partner, a property that is also visible in the openness for mutual learning. Certainly, this is a very noble and elevated self-image, but for a reality check, it must be juxtaposed with the perceptions BICS have about the European actors. BICS actors mostly agree that the EU acts as an agenda-setter but also hope that the EU, at the same time, is willing and able to learn from the BICS side. Although they largely do not consider the EU a dominant promoter of interests, they also note that the EU is not that flexible in terms of compromise seeking or changing a stand. The EU was viewed as acting with a hidden agenda. Reciprocating this vision from BICS, European actors showed a lack of trust towards the BICS partners (Knodt et al. 2015c: 336-337).

We discovered that stereotypical expectations to find the EU's self-images as a "sustainable", "green" and "technologically advanced" actor were supported only partially. Our analysis of EU energy policy (formulated and projected internally and externally) shows that the EU itself has competing frames inside the EU. All selected BICS media prioritised framing of the EU as an energy actor through the *sustainability* frame. This is partially due to the timing of the media observation (around the UNFCCC COPs and the EU role in the COPs) as well as a reflection of a broader stereotypical 'green' image of the EU as a normative energy actor. However, other frames in the BICS reportage of the EU were not that far in their visibility from the *sustainability* frame. A diverse media portraits of the EU in normative terms may be a reflection of the EU's energy-related actions that do not always promote *sustainability* as a dominant norm. The EU's shifting normative priorities were also picked up by the BICS elites directly engaged in the energy dialogues. As such, elite perceptions—both in the EU and in BICS – also featured a diversity of frames, where *sustainability* was not necessarily the leading one.

Importantly, there was no unanimity in normative visions endorsed for BICS by the European press under observation. Normative framing of energy matters and BICS as energy actors in the European media varied according to national media and according to BICS reported on. Concerning elite perceptions in 'stronger' vs. 'weaker' emerging powers, normative framing attributed to the other by the EU and by the respective BICS varies in the Chinese and Brazilian cases and converges in the cases of India and South Africa. Awareness of diverging and converging normative interpretations becomes a key for a successful dialogue on norms and values between the EU and its partners worldwide. A more subtle and horizontal approach (in contrast to top-down Eurocentric communication), attuned to differing normative visions, might result in more-viable collaborative solutions for both sides. It is important to highlight that at least some of the BICS have also become 'normative powers' in their regions of influence willing to actively shape international discourses on a normative basis. This is on the background of their advocacy for a paradigm shift towards a multipolar world order and away from a Eurocentric vision. In addition to China, we think here of Brazil. Similarly, Brazil has reoriented its foreign policy – traditionally focussed on the US and the EU – to increasing "BRICSalization" and South-South cooperation (Gratius 2012; Santander 2015: 186-187).

In conclusion we argue a true challenge for EU energy diplomacy is a mutual lack of trust from both sides engaged in the dialogue (found out in our survey of elite perceptions in BICS and the EU). The external perception (appearing in the energy-specific discourses) is resonating with a detected lack of trust appearing within the EU (this time due to the recent multiple political, social and economic crises). This negative resonance in the perceptions of missing trust is of concern, as it could affect development of and support for EU energy diplomacy inside the EU and beyond its borders. Importantly, for the EU its energy diplomacy is a part of a "joined-together external action" (EUGS 2016: 49) that also includes, in the eyes of the EEAS, cultural diplomacy and economic diplomacy. Keeping this comprehensive vision in mind, negative understandings appearing in energy diplomacy risk to negatively impact other diplomatic dialogues.

Potentially – and perhaps ideally – the global arena is presenting the EU a new chance to raise its reputation as a diplomatic energy actor. The unclear position of the new US administration (circa 2017) on fighting climate change and committing to the Paris Agreement, the EU may revisit and reclaim its leading role in international community, capitalising on the emerged consensus and striking new lines of cooperation with global powers, including energy field. Future research will demonstrate if this opportunity on a multilateral level has been utilised by the EU's energy diplomacy practitioners, and specifically those who work with BICS in bilateral dialogues.

To advance future EU-BICS energy dialogues, the following points appear to be the key ones. First, the dialogue is important. Both BICS and the EU have invested time and effort to chisel better approaches to this dialogue. They have tried mechanisms with different representatives, different government levels and different time intervals. It is important for the two sides to build on existing platforms and initiatives, assess past successes, and learn from each dialogue. This is even more important in the fragmented global energy environment that currently exists. A great array of ill-connected actors suggests multiple simultaneous dialogues and competition for attention. As such, an assessment of the successes and failures of existing dialogue mechanisms should be conducted prior to any new dialogue propositions. This is in addition to regular surveys of mutual perceptions in multiple discourses, if a true energy diplomacy advocated by the EU's new Global Strategy is to take place. Moreover, duplication should be avoided, which demands better coordination between different government institutions and between the EU and its Member States. Most BICS actors in our survey suggested more-concrete actions at the BICS-EU level with reference to the more-tangible outcomes at the state-to-state level between EU Member States and BICS. Specifically, for the EU, respondents urged the

EU to avoid duplicating the work of the individual Member States in BICS and to clarify and demarcate the roles between the EU and the Member States (EnergyGov, Darmstadt, 2014).

Positioning our research within the "third wave" of the NPE analytical approach, we followed this wave's call to examine structural changes in international relations for the EU as a normative global actor (energy actor in our case), contest normative power Europe ontologically and epistemologically, and question its intrinsic Eurocentricity (see Whitmann 2013: 186). For the EU as a normative actor at the global level, energy policy is an interesting case because this policy is characterized by extreme institutional segmentation and fragmentation, with energy issues being addressed by over two dozen international organisations. Bilateral discourses remain the main, highly competitive international platform for interactions (illustrated by the South-South cooperation or the China-US relation in energy and climate change). Thus, in the foreseeable future, the EU's bilateral energy-related interactions with third states will be the place to project normative visions on the global level, outside/in addition to a multilateral arena. From an ontological point of view, our analysis demonstrated that the EU in its external energy governance does not promote the same norm in all the bilateral relations. From the three norms identified in energy governance – *sustainability*, *security of supply* and *competitiveness* – the EU prioritises and projects different norms as the most important in different EU-BICS energy dialogues. This means that the EU is sending different normative messages, depending on the cooperation partner and the context. But, in adapting to respective contexts, the EU does not seem to be listening to its partners. We demonstrated in this book how some strategic partners assign higher value to the norms that are not prioritised by the EU, or even ignore the EU's normative framing of the dialogue. The partners also lack clear visibility of the EU. This modest (and often vague) energy profile against the clash of normative orientations between the two partners is of concern to the EU's budding energy diplomacy. In epistomological terms, a systematic consideration of interactions between norm-senders and norm-receivers contributes to the NPE theorisation, not lastly to overcome the Eurocentric bias within this approach. The filter of external recognition and construing it perceptions utilised in our analysis is a valid tool to assess if the EU's global partners are 'receiving' messages that the EU seeks to transmit. Yet, with a dialogue being a two-way process, it is important not to have the EU as the only norm 'exporter'. Emerging powers of BICS have its own domestic agendas, demands and pride. Increasingly, they request not to be treated as a passive norm-receivers but as equal partners. Only through a true dialogue based on respectful and attentive listening can the EU identify common interests with its partners. The EU must learn to speak 'with' its partners instead of speaking 'at' them (Chaban et al. 2016).

The insights into the BICS self-perceptions could be instrumental when (and if) the EU revises its Strategic Partnerships with the respective countries to address true strategic values. Our research suggests that the energy sector is an area in which the EU can carve out its value added, particularly for Brazil and China. Perceptions analysis advocated by this book could be helpful in identifying which demands and priorities BICS have in their own eyes, what the EU can offer, what perceptions of European demands exist in BICS, and what BICS think they can offer to the EU. If the EU is serious about horizontal, equal and strategic partnerships that open up creative space for innovative cooperation modalities, then openness towards mutual learning and the building of trust is essential.

Bibliography

Agência Nacional de Energia Elétrica (A ANEEL) 2016: A ANEEL, 03.05.2016, available at: http://www.aneel.gov.br/ [13.10.2016].

Algieri, Franco 2008: It's the system that matters. Institutionalization and making of EU policy towards China, in: Shambaugh, David/Sandschneider, Eberhard/Hong, Zhou (eds.): Perceptions, policies and prospects. London: Routledge, pp. 65–83.

Allen, David/Smith, Michael 2015: The EU, the US and India. Strategic diplomacy and great power politics, in: Smith, Michael/Keukeleire, Stephan/Vanhoonacker, Sophie (eds.): The Diplomatic System of the European Union. Evolution, change and challenges. Oxon/New York: Routledge, pp. 164–180.

Allen, David/Smith, Michael 2012: Relations with the Rest of the World, Special Issue, in: Journal of Common Market Studies 50, pp. 162–177.

Andonova, Liliana/Chelminski, Kathryn 2016: Emergence of a Regime Complex for Clean Energy: The Critical Role of Legitimacy, Graduate Institute Geneva, Working Paper.

Aydin-Düzgit, Senem 2015: Social-Constructivist and Discursive approaches to European Foreign Policy, in: Kalland Aarstad, Aasne/Drieskens, Edith/Jørgensen, Knud Erik/Laatikainen, Katie/Ben Tonra, Ben (eds.): Handbook of European Foreign Policy. Los Angeles: Sage, pp. 137–151.

Baccini, Leonardo/Lenzi, Veronica/Thurner, Paul W. 2011: Global Energy Governance: Bilateral Trade and the Diffusion of International Organizations. Paper presented at the 2011 EPSA Annual Conference, 16-18 June 2011, Dublin, Ireland.

Bäckstrand, Karin/Elgström, Ole 2013: The EU's Role in Climate Change Negotiations: From Leader to "Leadiator", in: Journal of European Public Policy 20, pp. 1–18.

Bain, Jessica/Greenland, Berengere/Knodt, Michèle/Nielsen, Louise 2016: A Polyphonic Marketplace: Images of EU External Energy Relations in British, French and German Media Discourses, in: Chaban, Natalia/Knodt, Michéle/Verdun, Amy (eds.): External Images of the EU: Energy Power Across the Globe, Special Issue of Comparative European Politics, published online first: DOI:10.1057/cep.2016.16.

Ball-Rokeach, Sandra/DeFleur, Melvin 1976: A dependency model of mass-media effects, in: Communication Research 3(1), pp. 3–21.

Bava, Ummu Salma 2007: New Powers for Global Change? India's Role in the Emerging World Order, FES Briefing Paper 4. New Delhi: Friedrich Ebert Foundation.

Bekker, Bernard/Eberhard, Anton/Gaunt, Trevor/Marquard, Andrew 2008: South Africa's rapid electrification programme: Policy, institutional, planning, financing and technical innovations, in: Energy Policy 36(8), pp. 3125–3137.

Bersick, Sebastian/Bruter, Michael/Chaban, Natalia/Iglesias, Sol/Lenihan, Ronan (eds.) 2012: Asia in the Eyes of Europe: Images of a Rising Giant. Baden-Baden: Nomos.

Bertelsmann Stiftung 2006: World Powers in the 21st Century, 06.12.2013, available at: www.cap.lmu.de/download/2006/2006_GPC_Survey_Results.pdf [13.10.2016].

Betz, Joachim/Hanif, Melanie 2010: The Formation of Preferences in Two-level Games: An Analysis of India's Domestic and Foreign Energy Policy, GIGA Working Paper 142. Hamburg: German Institute of Global and Area Studies.

Bide, Tom/Brown, T.J./Hobbs, S.F./Idoine, N. 2015: United Kingdom Minerals Yearbook 2014, British Geological Survey. Open Report, OR/15/043.

Bieling, Hans-Jürgen 2014: Die BRIC(S) in der globalen politischen Ökonomie: Weltordnungspolitische Perspektiven der Europäischen Union, in: Nölke, Andreas/May, Christian/Claar, Simone (eds.): Die großen Schwellenländer. Ursachen und Folgen ihres Aufstiegs in der Weltwirtschaft. Wiesbaden: Springer VS, pp. 377–394.

Björkdahl, Annika/Chaban, Natalia/Leslie, John/Masselot, Annick (eds.) 2015: Importing EU norms? Conceptual Framework and Empirical Findings. New York/London: Springer.

Brand, Alexander 2012: Medien – Diskurs – Weltpolitik, Wie Massenmedien die Internationale Politik beeinflussen. Bielefeld: transcript.

Brecher, Michael 1968: India and World Politics, Krishna Menon's View of the World. New York/Washington: Frederick A. Praeger Publishers.

British Petroleum (BP) 2016: BP Statistical Review of World Energy, 20.07.2016, available at: http://www.bp.com/content/dam/bp/pdf/energy-economics/statistical-review-2016/bp-statistical-review-of-world-energy-2016-full-report.pdf [14.10.2016].

Bull, Hedley 1977: The Anarchical Society: A Study of Order in World Politics. Basingstoke: Palgrave Macmillan.

Bundesministerium für Umwelt, Naturschutz, Bau und Reaktorsicherheit (BMUD) 2015: Brazilian German Joint Statement on Climate Change, available at: http://www.bmub.bund.de/fileadmin/Daten_BMU/Download_PDF/Klimaschutz/klimakonsultation_deutschland_brasilien_en_bf.pdf [08.09.2016].

Bundesministerium für wirtschaftliche Zusammenarbeit und Entwicklung (BMZ) 2016: Brasilien. Strategie und Zusammenarbeit, available at: https://www.bmz.de/ de/laender_regionen/lateinamerika/brasilien/zusammenarbeit/index.html [08.09.2016].

Burke-Kennedy, Eoin 2016: EU bows to pressure and removes beef from Mercosur trade deal. IFA salutes move by Brussels to withdraw beef from table of trade talks, 11.05.2016, available at: http://www.irishtimes.com/business/agribusiness-and-food /eu-bows-to-pressure-and-removes-beef-from-mercosur-trade-deal-1.2643753 [14.10.2016].

Bundesregierung 2014: Gemeinsame Erklärung zum Besuch von Staatspräsident Xi: Schaffung einer umfassenden strategischen Partnerschaft zwischen Deutschland und China, available at: https://www.bundesregierung.de/Content/DE/Pressemittei lungen/BPA/2014/03/2014-03-28-gemeinsame-erklaerung.html [20.10.2016].

Carta, Caterina/Morin, Jean-Frédéric (eds.) 2014: EU Foreign Policy through the Lens of Discourse Analysis: Making Sense of Diversity. Farnham/Burlington: Ashgate.

Chaban, Natalia 2016: How to work with media content, in: Stetter, R./Lee, S. (eds.): Asia-Europe Public Diplomacy Handbook, Singapore: ASEF, forthcoming.

Chaban, Natalia/Elgström, Ole 2014: The Role of the EU in an Emerging New World Order in the Eyes of the Chinese, Indian and Russian Press, in: Journal of European Integration 36(2), pp. 170–188.

Chaban, Natalia/Elgström, Ole/Gulyaeva, Olga 2017: Russian Images of The European Union, Before and After Maidan, Foreign Policy Analysis. Oxford: Oxford University Press.

Chaban, Natalia/Holland, Martin 2015: EU External Perceptions: from innovation to an established field of study, in: Kalland Aarstad, Aasne/Drieskens, Edith/Jørgensen, Knud Erik/Laatikainen, Katie/Ben Tonra, Ben (eds.): Handbook of European Foreign Policy, Los Angeles: Sage, pp. 672–686.

Chaban, Natalia/Holland, Martin 2010: The EU in the eyes of Asia: Motivation and methodology, in: Asia Europe Journal 8(2), pp. 127–131.

Chaban, Natalia/Holland, Martin (eds.) 2014: Communicating Europe in the Times of Crisis: External Perceptions of the European Union. Houndmills: Palgrave McMillan.

Chaban, Natalia/Holland, Martin (eds.) 2013: Lisbon and the Changing External Perceptions of the EU: Visions from the Asia-Pacific, Special Issue, in: Baltic Journal of European Studies 3(3).

Chaban, Natalia/Holland, Martin (eds.) 2008: The European Union and the Asia-Pacific: Media, Public and Elite Perceptions of the EU. London/New York: Rout-ledge.

Chaban, Natalia/Holland, Martin/Ryan, Peter (eds.) 2009: The EU through the Eyes of Asia: New Cases, New Findings. Singapore/London: World Scientific.

Chaban, Natalia/Knodt, Michèle 2016: International Structures and External Perceptions: Projecting and Receiving the EU as a Global Energy Governance Actor in the Eyes of Emerging Powers (Brazil, India, China), in: Costa, Oriol/Kissack, Robert/Barbé, Esther (eds.): EU Policy Responses to a Shifting Multilateral System, Basingstoke: Palgrave MacMillan, pp. 201–223.

Chaban, Natalia/Knodt, Michèle 2015: EU Energy Diplomacy towards BICS: The Role of EU External Images as a Global Energy Actor, International Conference "The EU and Emerging Powers", April 2015, Brussels.

Chaban, Natalia/Knodt, Michèle/Verdun, Amy (eds.) 2016: External Images of the EU – Energy Power Across the Globe, in: Comparative European Politics, published online first, available at: http://www.springer.com/social+sciences/political+science/journal/41295 [01.10.2016].

Chaban, Natalia/Magdalina, Ana-Maria 2014: External Perceptions of the EU during the Eurozone Sovereign Debt Crisis, in: European Foreign Affairs Review 19(2), pp. 195–220.

Chaban, Natalia/Masselot, Annick/Vadura, Katharina (eds.) 2015: Rising' Asia and 'Normative Power Europe', New Perspectives in the Dialogue on Norms and Values, in: Asia-Europe Journal 13(3), pp. 233–239.

Chaban Natalia/Pardo, Sharon 2015: Normative Power Europe and Perceptions as Cultural Filters: Israeli Civic Studies as a Case-Study, in: Pardo, Sharon (ed.): Normative Power Europe Meets Israel: Perceptions and Realities, Lanham MD: Lexington Books, pp. 39–54.

Chaban, Natalia/Kelly, Serena/Holland, Martin 2015: Perceptions of Normative Power Europe in the shadow of the Eurozone debt crisis: public perspectives on European integration from the Asia Pacific, in: Björkdahl, A./Chaban, N./Leslie, J./Masselot, A. (eds.): Importing EU norms? Conceptual framework and Empirical findings, New York/London: Springer, pp. 57–77.

Chaban, Natalia 1997: The Concept "Politics of Sovereign Ukraine" in its Verbal Embodiment (on the materials of "The New York Times" publications), PhD Thesis, Ministry of Education of Ukraine.

Chan, Kenneth 2010: Images, visibility and the prospects of soft power of the EU in Asia: the case of China, in: Asia Europe Journal 8(2), pp. 133–147.

Cohen, Bernard Cecil 1967: The Press and Foreign Policy. Princeton: Princeton University Press.

Cottam, Martha L. 1992: Recent Developments in Political Psychology, in: Cottam, Martha L./Chih-yu, Shih (eds.): Contending Dramas: A Cognitive Approach to International Organizations, New York: Praeger.

Coulon, Anne 2006: EU-India Understandings on Major Global Political Issues: Where do we Stand?, in: Voll, Klaus/Beierlein, Doreen (eds.): Rising India – Europe's Partner? Foreign and Security Policy, Politics, Economics, Human Rights and Social Issues, Media, Civil Society and Intercultural Dimensions, Berlin: Weißensee Verlag, pp. 340–350.

Council of the European Community 1968: Directive imposing an obligation on Member States to maintain minimum stocks of crude oil and/or petroleum products, (68/414/EEC), No. L308/14, Brussels 23 December 1968.

Council of the European Union 2016: Council Conclusions on EU Strategy on China. 11252/16. Brussels.

Council of the European Union 2014: 7th EU-Brazil Summit. Joint Statement. 6930/14. Brussels.

Council of the European Union 2013: Sixth South Africa-European Union Summit. Joint Communiqué. 12592/13. Pretoria.

Council of the European Union 2011: V European Union-Brazil Summit. Joint Statement. 15084/11. Brussels.

Council of the European Union 2010: EU External Relations. Brussels. 14 September 2010 PCE 186/10.

Council of the European Union 2005: The India-EU Strategic Partnership. Joint Action Plan. 11984/05 (Presse 223). Brussels.

Department of Energy and Climate Change 2015: UK-India joint statement on energy and climate change.

Der Spiegel 2012: Indien. Bomben und Wachstum. Trotz des Desasters im japanischen Fukushima setzt Neu-Delhi auf ein gigantisches Atomprogramm. Die Regierung lässt auch Reaktoren bauen, die in anderen Ländern umstritten sind, 19.11.2012.

Der Spiegel 2016: EU-Bürger. Privat ganz zufrieden, politisch frustriert, 07.08.2016.

Diez, Thomas 2005: Constructing the Self and Changing Others: Reconsidering `Normative Power Europe', in: Journal of International Studies 33(3), pp. 613–636.

Diez, Thomas 2013: Normative power as hegemony. Cooperation and Conflict 48, pp. 194–210.

Directorate General Energy (DG Energy) 2010: EU-India Relations, available at: http://ec.europa.eu/energy/international/bilateral_cooperation/india_en.htm [28.10.2014].

Doty, Roxanne 1993: Foreign policy as social construction: a post-positivist analysis of US counterinsurgency policy in the Philippines, International Studies Quarterly, 37(3): pp. 297–320.

Downs, Erica S. 2008: China's New Energy Administration: China's National Energy Administration will struggle to manage the energy sector effectively, China Business Review, November/December, pp. 42–45.

Draper, Peter/Scholvin, Sören 2012: The Economic Gateway to Africa? Geography, Strategy and South Africa's Regional Economic Relations, SAIIA, Occasional Paper No. 121, September 2012.

Dreger, Jonas 2014: The European Commission's Energy and Climate Policy: A Climate for Expertise? Houndsmills et. al., Palgrave Macmillan.

Dubash, Navroz K. 2011: From Frame Taker to Frame Maker? Indian Energy Governance in Global Context, Global Policy, 2, pp. 66–79.

Eberhard, Anton/Van Horen, C. 1995: Poverty and power-energy and the South African state. Cape Town: UCT Press. London: Pluto Press.

Eberhard, Anton/Kolker, Joel/Leigland, James 2014: South Africa's renewable energy IPP Procurement Program: Success factors and lessons. Washington: World Bank Group, May 2014, available at: http://www.gsb.uct.ac.za/files/PPIAFReport.pdf [20.05.2017].

Elgström, Ole 2006: EU Foreign Policy as Others See It – Images of the EU as an International Negotiator, Statsvetenskaplig tidskrift 108(2).

Elgström, Ole 2007a: Outsiders' Perceptions of the European Union in International Trade Negotiations, in: Journal of Common Market Studies 45, pp. 945–967.

Elgström, Ole 2007b: The European Union as a Leader in International Multilateral Negotiations – a Problematic Aspiration?' International Relations, 21, pp. 445–458.

Elgström, Ole 2008: Images of the EU in EPA negotiations: Angel, Demon – or Just Human?' European Integration Online Papers, 12, available at: http://eiop.or.at/eiop/index.php/eiop/article/view/2008_005a [06.12.2013].

Elgström, Ole 2010: Partnership in Peril? Images and Strategies in EU-ACP Economic Partnership Agreement Negotiations', in: S. Lucarelli and L. Fioramonti (eds.), External Perceptions of the European Union as a Global Actor, London: Routledge.

Elgström, Ole/Chaban, Natalia 2015: To study external perceptions of the EU: A conceptual approach, in: Muller, M./Bachmann V. (eds.) Looking in from the Outside: Perceptions of the EU in Eastern Europe and Sub Saharan Africa, Palgrave-McMillan, 2015, pp. 17–33.

Emmanouilidis, Janis A. 2012: Europe's Role in the Twenty-First Century, in: Renard, T./Biscop S. (eds.): The European Union and Emerging Powers in the 21st Century: How Europe Can Shape a New Global Order, pp. 83–105, Surrey, England: Ashgate Publishing Limited.

Empresa de Pesquisa Energetica (EPE, Energy Research Office) 2012: Brasil: Renováveis para o desenvolvimento (Brazil: Renewables for Development), Rio de Janeiro, available at: http://www.epe.gov.br/MeioAmbiente/Documents/Cartilha%20EPE%20-%20Riomais20.pdf [16.12.2013].

Empresa de Pesquisa Energetica (EPE Energy Research Company) 2013: Balanço Energético Nacional 2013 – Ano base 2012: Relatório Síntese, Rio de Janeiro, available at: https://ben.epe.gov.br/downloads/S%C3%ADntese%20do%20Relatório% 20Final_2013_Web.pdf [18.12.2013].

Enerdata 2016: Global Energy Statistical Yearbook, available at: https://yearbook.enerdata.net [11.08.2016].

Entman, Robert 1993: Framing – Toward Clarification of a Fractured Paradigm, in: Journal of Communication 43(4), pp. 51–58.

Entman, Robert 2003: Cascading Activation: Contesting the White House's Frame After 9/11, Political Communication 20(4), pp. 415–432.

Entman, Robert 2004: Projections of Power: Framing news, Public Opinion, and US Foreign Policy. Chicago and London: University of Chicago Press.

EUBrasil 2015: EU Decides if it is ready to exchange offers with, available at: http://www.eubrasil.eu/en/2015/11/25/eu-decides-if-it-is-ready-to-exchange-offers-with-mercosur/ [20.07.2016].

Euracoal 2016: United Kingdom, European Association for Coal and Lignite, available at: https://euracoal.eu/info/country-profiles/united-kingdom/ [20.07.2016].

EU-Brazil Dialogue Support Facility 2013: available at: http://sectordialogues.org/en [24.05.2013].

EU-China Clean Energy Centre (EC2) 2014: 2014: Europe-China Clean Energy Centre (EC2), available at: http://www.ec2.org.cn [23.10.2014].

EuropeAid 2010: Opinion Polling and Research in the ENPI Countries and Territories (OPPOL), Country report on the opinion poll 1, Ukraine.

EURactiv 2012: Large Countries Oppose EU Gazprom Deals Scrutiny, 12 September 2012, available at: http://www.euractiv.com/energy/largest-eucountries-oppose-gazp-news-514739 [03.06.2014].

European Commission 2016a: Joint Communication to the European Parliament and the Council. Elements for a new EU strategy on China.

European Commission 2016b: EU-China Roadmap on energy cooperation (2016-2020).

European Commission 2016c: Energy in Europe, available at: https://ec.europa.eu/energy/en/energy_newsletter/newsletter-april-2016 [23.05.2016].

European Commission 2016d: Joint Declaration between the EU and India on a Clean Energy and Climate Partnership, available at: http://ec.europa.eu/clima/news/articles/news_20160331 01_en.htm [23.05.2016].

European Commission 2015: A Framework Strategy for a Resilient Energy Union with a Forward-Looking Climate Change Policy, communication from the Commission to the European Parliament, the Council, the European Economic and Social Committee and the Committee of the Regions, COM(2015) 80 final, Brussels, 25.02.2015.

European Commission 2015a: Joint Statement on the Third Round of the EU-China High-Level People-to-People Dialogue. Brussels.

European Commission 2015b: Economic Partnership Agreement (EPA) Between the EU and the Southern African Development Community (SADC) EPA Group. October 2015 Update.

European Commission 2015c: Proposal for a DECISION OF THE EUROPEAN PARLIAMENT AND OF THE COUNCI, on establishing an information exchange mechanism with regard to intergovernmental agreements and non-binding instruments between Member States and third countries in the field of energy and repealing Decision No 994/2012/EU, 2016/0031 (COD), COM(2016) 53 final, Brussels, 16.2.2016.

European Commission 2015d: EU energy in figures, Statistical Pocketbook 2015, available at: http://ec.europa.eu/energy/sites/ener/files/documents/PocketBook_ENERGY_2015%20PDF%20final.pdf [10.06.2016].

European Commission 2015e: EU-China Summit. Press Release.

European Commission 2014: A policy framework for climate and energy in the period from 2020 to 2030', communication from the Commission to the European Parliament, the Council, the European Economic and Social Committee and the Committee of the Regions, COM(2014) 15 final, Brussels, 22.01.2014.

European Commission 2014a: European Energy Security Strategy', communication from the Commission to the European Parliament and the Council, COM(2014) 330 final, Brussels, 28.05.14.

European Commission 2014b: EU-Brazil Fact Sheet. Memo/14/122: Brussels.

European Commission 2014c: Roadmaps for international cooperation. Accompanying the document: Report from the Commission to the European Parliament, the Council, the European Economic and social Committee and the Committee of the Regions. Report on the implementation of the strategy for international cooperation in research and innovation.

European Commission 2014d: Energy from abroad. Stakeholders for EU-China Energy Cooperation, available at: http://ec.europa.eu/energy/international/bilateral_coop eration/china/stakeholders_en.htm [05.11.2014].

European Commission 2013: A 2030 framework for climate and energy policies', Green Paper, COM(2013) 169 final, Brussels 27.3.2013.

European Commission 2013a. Report from the Commission to the European Parliament, the Council and the European Economic and Social Committee, Implementation of the Communication on Security of Energy Supply and International Cooperation and of the Energy Council Conclusions of November 2011. COM/2013/0638 final. Brussels.

European Commission 2013b: A 2030 Framework for Climate and Energy Policy, Green Paper, COM(2013), 169 final, Brussels 27.3.2013.

European Commission 2011: Energy Roadmap 2050', communication from the Commission to the European Parliament, the Council, the European Economic and Social Committee and the Committee of the Regions, COM(2011) 885 final, Brussels, 15.12.2011.

European Commission 2010: Communication from the Commission. Europe 2020. A strategy for smart, sustainable and inclusive growth. COM(2010) 2020 final. Brussels.

European Commission 2010a: Energy 2020. A strategy for competitive, sustainable and secure energy, Communication from the Commission to the European Parliament, the Council, the European Economic and Social Committee and the Committee of the Regions, COM(2010) 639 final, Brussels, 10.11.2010.

European Commission 2008: Second Strategic Energy Review: An EU energy security and solidarity action plan', Communication from the Commission to the European Parliament, the Council, the European Economic and Social Committee and the Committee of the Regions, COM(2008) 781 final, Brussels, 13.11.2008.

European Commission 2007: An energy policy for Europe, Communication from the Commission to the European Council and the European Parliament, COM(2007) 1 final, Brussels, 10.01.2007.

European Commission 2006: Commission proposes to upgrade EU's relations with South Africa to a Strategic Partnership. IP/06/869: Brussels.

European Commission 2006a: A European strategy for sustainable, competitive and secure energy', COM(2006) 105 final, 08.03.06.

European Commission 2005: A stronger Partnership between the European Union and Latin America. Communication from the Commission to the Council and the European Parliament, COM(2205) 636 final, Brussels.

European Commission 2001: Europe and Asia: A Strategic Framework for Enhanced Partnerships, COM(2001) 469 final, Brussels.

European Commission 2000: Report from the Commission to the Council and the European Parliament on the implementation of the Communication "Building a Comprehensive Partnership with China", Brussels, 08.09.2000, COM(2000) final.

European Commission 2000a: Towards a European strategy for the security of energy supply', Green Paper, COM(2000) final, Brussels, 29.11.2000.

European Commission 1998: Communication from the Commission. Building a Comprehensive Partnership with China, Brussels 25.3.1998, COM(1998) 181 final.

European Commission 1997a: The Energy Dimension of Climate Change, Communication, COM(97), 196 final, Brussels 14.5.1997.

European Commission 1997b: Energy for the Future: Renewable Sources of Energy, White Paper for a Community Strategy and Action Plan, COM(97) 599 final, Brussels 16.1.1997.

European Commission 1995a: For a European Union Energy Policy', Green Paper, Com(94) 659, final 2, Brussels, 23.2.1995.

European Commission 1995b: An Energy Policy for the European Union', White Paper, COM(95) 682 final, Brussels 13.12.1995.

European Council 2016: EU-India Agenda for Action-2020. EU-India Summit. Brussels, 30 March 2016.

European Council 2016a: Joint Statement 13th EU-India Summit, Brussels, 30 March 2016, available at: http://www.consilium.europa.eu/en/meetings/internationalsum mit/2016/03/201603 30-joint-statement-eu-india_pdf [23.05.2016].

European Council 2015: Presidency Conclusions', EUCO 11/15, CO EUR 1, CONCL 1, Brussels, 20.03.15.

European Council 2015: EU-China Summit joint statement, 29.06.15, Brussels.

European Council 2014: Presidency Conclusions', EUCO 169/14, Co EUR 13, CONCL 5, Brussels, 24.10.14.

European Council 2012: Joint Declaration for Enhanced Cooperation on Energy between the European Union and the Government of India, 10 February 2012, available at: http://www.consilium.europa.eu/en/meetings/international-summit/2016/03/ 20160330-joint-declaration-energy-climate_pdf/ [23.05.2016].

European Council 2011: Conclusions of the European Council, 4.02.2011, CO EUR 2, CONCL 1.

European Council 2008. Report on the Implementation of the European Security Strategy Providing Security in a Changing World, Brussels, 11.12.2008, S407/08, Brussels.

European Council 2008b: Presidency Conclusions', 17271/08, CONCL 5, 12.12.2008, Brussels.

European Council 2007: Presidency Conclusions', 7334/1/07, REV 1, CONCL 1, 9 March 2007, Brussels.

European Council 2003: A secure Europe in a better world. European Security Strategy, Institute for Security Studies, Brussels.

European External Action Service (EEAS) 2016a: Shared Vision, Common Action: A Stronger Europe. A Global Strategy for the European Union's Foreign And Security Policy.

European External Action Service (EEAS), 2016b: Factsheet. EU-India relations. Brussels.

European External Action Service (EEAS) 2016c: Joint Press Release. 13th South Africa-European Union Ministerial Political Dialogue (MPD) Meeting. 26.0216. Pretoria, South Africa.

European External Action Service (EEAS) 2015: The EU-China Comprehensive Strategic Partnership. Fact Sheet/Memo. Brussels.

European External Action Service (EEAS) 2013: EU-China 2020 Strategic Agenda for Cooperation.

European External Action Service (EEAS) 2012: Joint Declaration for Enhanced Cooperation on Energy between the European Union and the Government of India', Brussels and Delhi.

European External Action Service (EEAS) 2011: Brazil comes to Brussels: the fifth EU-Brazil Summit, available at: http://eeas.europa.eu/top_stories/2011/300911_en .htm [12.09.2013].

European Strategic Partnerships Observatory (ESPO) 2013: EU-SOUTH AFRICA, available at: http://strategicpartnerships.eu/pays/eu-south-africa/ [12.09.2013].

Eurostat 2014: Comext Database, available at: http://epp.eurostat.ec.europa.eu/newxt web/main xtnet.do [13.11.2014].

Federal Foreign Office 2016: China, available at: http://www.auswaertiges-amt.de/EN/Aussenpolitik/Laender/Laenderinfos/01Nodes/China_node.html#doc474918body Text3 [01.12.2016].

Ferreira-Pereira, Laura C. 2015: EU-Brazil Relations as a Developing Field of Study: State-of-the-Art and Perspectives on Future Research, in: Jørgensen, Knud Erik/Kalland Aarstad, Åsne/Drieskens, Edith/Laatikainen, Katie/Tonra, Ben (eds.): Handbook of European Foreign Policy, Vol. 2, Los Angeles: SAGE, pp. 646–658.

Fierke, Karin Marie 2010: Constructivism, in: Dunne, Tim/Kurku, Milja/Smith, Steve: International relations theories. Discipline and Diversity, Oxford University Press: Oxford, pp. 177–194.

Fioramonti, Lorenzo, 2016: South Africa's perceptions of the EU in energy governance: a partner in decline?, in: Chaban, Natalia/Knodt, Michèle/Verdun, Amy: External Images of the EU – Energy Power Across the Globe. Special Issue. Comparative European Politics, published online first, DOI:10.1057/cep.2016.15.

Fischer, Severin 2009: Die Neugestaltung der EU-Klimapolitik: Systemreform mit Vorbildcharakter?, in: Internationale Politik und Gesellschaft, 2/2009, pp.108–126.

Fischer, Severin 2011: Auf dem Weg zur gemeinsamen Energiepolitik. Strategien, Instrumente und Politikgestaltung in der Europäischen Union, Baden-Baden: Nomos.

Fischer, Severin 2014: The EU's New Energy and Climate Policy Framework for 2030', SWP Comments, 55, Berlin.

Fischer, Severin/Geden, Oliver 2015: Die Grenzen der Energieunion, SWP-Aktuell, 36, Berlin.

Fischer, Severin/Geden, Oliver 2015a: Europäische Energieunion. Für jeden ist was dabei, Neu Zürcher Zeitung, 02.12.2015.

France Diplomatie 2016: France and China. Presentation. French Ministry of Foreign Affairs and International Development, available at: http://www.diplomatie.gouv.fr/en/country-files/china/ [09.06.2016].

French Embassy in South Africa 2015: Economic relations between South Africa and France, available at: http://www.ambafrance-rsa.org/Economic-relations-between-South [20.07.2016].

Früh, Werner 2011: Inhaltsanalyse. Theorie und Praxis, UVK: Konstanz; München.

Geden, Oliver 2007: Energiesolidarität im EU-Reformvertrag, SWP-Aktuell, 34, Berlin.

Gehler, Michael/Gu, Xuewu/Schimmelpfennig, Andreas (eds.) 2012: EU-China. Global Players in a Complex World, Olms: Hildesheim.

German Government 2007: German Presidency. Statement on energy policy', available at: http://www.eu2007.de/en/Policy_Areas/Transport_telecommunications_and_Energy/Energy.html [20.03.2016].

Gesellschaft für Internationale Zusammenarbeit (GIZ) 2016: Mit erneuerbaren Energien und Energieeffizienz in eine nachhaltige Zukunft, available at: https://www.giz.de/de/weltweit/ 17790.html [20.07.2016].

GlobeScan/PIPA 2016: BBC World Service Polls, available at: http://www.globescan.com/clients/case-studies/bbc-world-service.html [30.11.2016].

Goldemberg, José 2007: Ethanol for a Sustainable Energy Future, Science, 315 (5813), pp. 808–10.

Goldemberg, José/Coelho, Suani Teixeira/Guardabassi, Patricia 2008: The Sustainability of Ethanol Production from Sugarcane, Energy Policy, 36(6), pp. 2086–97.

Goldstein, Judith, and Robert O. Keohane. 1993: Ideas and Foreign Policy: An Analytical Framework, in: Ideas and Foreign Policy, (eds.) Judith Goldstein and Robert Keohane, Ithaca and London: Cornell University Press.

Gomes Savaira, Miriam 2012: Brazil's Strategies and Partnerships: The Place of the European Union, in: Perspectives 20(2), pp. 45–62.

Gomez, Ieda 2014: Brazil: Country for the future – or has its time come for natural gas?, Oxford Institute for Energy Studies, University of Oxford, June 2014, OIES Paper: NG 88.

Gratius, Susanne 2012: Brazil and the European Union: between balancing and bandwagoning, ESPO working paper No. 02.07.12.

Gratius, Susanne 2013: The EU and its "strategic partnerships" with the BRICS, Online Publication: Konrad-Adenauer-Stiftung.

Greenberg, Stephen 2006: The State, Privatisation and the Public Sector in South-Africa, Cape Town: African People`s Solidarity Network (SAPSN).

Grevi, Giovanni/de Vasconcelos, Álvaro (eds.) 2008: Partnerships for effective multilateralism: EU relations with Brazil, China, India and Russia, Chaillot Paper (109), Institute for Security Studies, Paris.

Griffiths, Martin 2011: Rethinking International Relations Theory, Basingstoke: Palgrave Macmillan.

Gstöhl, Sieglinde 2009: The Social Dimension of EU Neighbourhood Policies. In: Orbie, J./Tortell, L. (eds.): The European Union and the Social Dimension of Globalization: How the EU Influences the World. London: Routledge, pp. 62–80.

Guimaraes, Carolina/Piefer, Nadine 2016: Brazil: (Future) Green Energy Power and Strategic Power for the EU, in: Natalia Chaban/Michéle Knodt/Amy Verdun (eds.): External Images of the EU: Energy Power Across the Globe, Special Issue of Comparative European Politics, published online first: DOI:10.1057/cep.2016.12.

Gulyaeva, Olga 2016: Challenging the EU's Normative Power: Media Views on the EU in India, in: Chaban, Natalia/Knodt, Michèle/Verdun, Amy (eds.): External Images of the EU: Energy Power Across the Globe, Special Issue of Comparative European Politics, published online first: DOI:10.1057/cep.2016.13.

Gupta, Joyeeta/Grijp, Nicolien 2000: Perceptions of the EU's role, in: Gupta, Joyeeta/Grubb, Michael (eds.): Climate change and European leadership: A sustainable role for Europe, Dordrecht: Kluwer Academic Publishers, pp. 67–82.

Häder, Michael 2006: Empirische Sozialforschung. Eine Einführung, VS Verlag: Wiesbaden.

Hedden, Steve/Moyer, Jonathan D./Rettig, Jessica 2013: Fracking for Shale Gas in South Africa: Blessing or Curse?, Institute for Security Studies Papers, available at: https://www.issafrica.org/publications/papers/fracking-for-shale-gas-in-south-africa-blessing-or-curse [15.09.2015].

Herranz-Surrallés, Anna 2015: An Emerging EU Energy Diplomacy? Discursive Shifts, Enduring Practices, in: Journal of European Public Policy 17 (published online: DOI: 10.1080/13501763.2015.1083044).

Hess, Natalie M. 2013: Understanding the EU's strategic partnerships with Brazil, India and South Africa: Strategic alliances forming part of the strategy of cooperating while competing and Social relationships as foreign policy tools of social power. Ph. D. Universität Hamburg.

Hill, Christopher/Smith, Michael 2011: International Relations and the European Union: Themes and Issues, in: Hill, Christopher/Smith, Michael (eds.): International Relations and the European Union, Oxford University Press: New York, pp. 3–20.

Hira, Anil/de Oliveira, Luiz Guilherme 2008: No Substitute for Oil? How Brazil Developed its Ethanol Industry, Energy Policy, 37(6), pp. 2450–2456.

HM Treasury/Obsorne, George 2015: Chancellor announces closer ties with Brazil on infrastructure and financial services, UK Government, available at: https://www.gov.uk/government/news/chancellor-announces-closer-ties-with-brazil-on-infrastructure-and-financial-services [08.09.2016].

Holland, Martin/Ryan, Peter/Nowak, Alojzy/Chaban, Natalia (eds.) 2007: The EU through the Eyes of Asia. Media, Public and Elite Perceptions in China, Japan, Korea, Singapore and Thailand (Singapore and Warsaw: University of Warsaw).

International Energy Agency (IEA) 2015a: Energy and Climate Change, World Energy Outlook Special Report, Paris: IEA.

International Energy Agency (IEA) 2015b: Medium-Term Coal Market Report 2015. Market Analysis and Forecast to 2020, IEA, Paris.

International Energy Agency (IEA) 2015c: India Energy outlook, World Energy Outlook Special Report, Paris, available at: http://www.worldenergyoutlook.org/media/weowebsite/2015/IndiaEnergyOutlook_WEO2015.pdf, [23.05.2016].

International Energy Agency (IEA) 2015d: Global coal demand stalls after more than a decade of relentless growth, available at: https://www.iea.org/newsroomandevents/pressreleases/2015/december/global-coal-demand-stalls-after-more-than-a-decade-of-relentless-growth.html, [07.06.2016].

International Energy Agency (IEA) 2014: Africa World Energy Outlook. A focus on Energy Prospects in Sub-Sahara Africa, Special Report, OECD/IEA, France, Paris.

International Energy Agency (IEA) 2013: World Energy Outlook 2013, Paris: IEA

Jaeger, Marc Daniel/Michaelowa, Katharina 2015: Energy Poverty and Policy Coherence in India: Frames as Means in Strategic Two-Level Discourse, in: Knodt, Michèle/Piefer, Nadine/Müller, Franziska (eds.): Challenges of European External Energy Governance with Emerging Powers, Farnham: Ashgate, pp. 235–247.

Jänicke, Martin 2013: Accelerators of Global Energy Transition: Horizontal and Vertical Reinforcement in Multi-Level Climate Governance, IASS Working Paper, Potsdam.

Jaffrelot, Christophe 2006: India and the European Union: The Charade of a Strategic Partnership, in: Voll, Klaus/Beierlein, Doreen (eds.): Rising India – Europe's Partner? Foreign and Security Policy, Politics, Economics, Human Rights and Social Issues, Media, Civil Society and Intercultural Dimensions, Weißensee Verlag: Berlin, 329–339.

Jain, Rajendra. K (ed.) 2007: India and the European Union: Building a Strategic Partnership. New Delhi: Radiant Publishers.

Jain, Rajendra 2009: The European Union and China: Indian Perceptions and Perspectives', in G. Wiessala, J. Wilson and P. Taneja (eds.), The European Union and China: Interests and Dilemmas, Amsterdam and New York: Rodopi.

Jain, Rajendra. K. 2015: India's Strategy towards the EU: Shared Values but Elusive Coordinated Policies, in: Hungdah Su (ed.). Asian Countries' Strategies towards the European Union in an Inter-regionalist Context, Taipei: National University of Taiwan Press, pp. 177–196.

Jain, Rajendra. K. 2014a: India-EU Strategic Partnership. Perceptions and Perspectives. NFG Working Paper No. 10. Freie Universität Berlin.

Jain, Rajendra. K (ed.) 2014b: India and the European Union in a Changing World. New Delhi: Aakar Books.

Jain, Rajendra. K/Elsenhans, Hartmut (eds.) 2006: India, the European Union and the WTO. New Delhi: Radiant Publishers.

Jain, Rajendra. K./Pandey, Shreya 2015: Perceptions and Misperceptions: Images of the European Union in India, in: Natalia Chaban and Martin Holland (eds.). Europe and Asia: Perceptions from Afar, Baden-Baden: Nomos/Bloomsbury, pp. 143–170.

Jain, Rajendra. K/Pandey, Shreya 2014: Perceptions and Visibility of the European Union in India: A Study of the Media, Elites, and Public Opinion, in: Jakub Zajaczkowski, Jivanta Schottli and Manish Thapa (eds.). India in the Contemporary World. New Delhi: Routledge, pp. 385–406.

Jain, Rajendra K./Pandey, Shreya 2013: Indian Elites and the EU as a Normative Power, in: Chaban, N. and M. Holland (eds.), Special Issue: Lisbon and the Changing External Perceptions of the EU: Visions from the Asia-Pacific, in: Baltic Journal of European Studies 3(3), pp. 105–126.

Jain, Rajendra K./Pandey, Shreya 2013: Indian Elites and the EU as a Normative Power, in: Baltic Journal of European Studies 3(3), pp. 105–126.

Jain, Rajendra K./Pandey, Shreya 2010: The European Union in the eyes of India, in: Holland, M. and N. Chaban (eds.), Special Issue: Reflections from Asia and Europe: How do we perceive one another?, in: Asia Europe Journal 8(2), pp. 193–209.

Jepperson, Ronald L/, Wendt, Alexander/Katzenstein, Peter J., 1996: Norms, Identity and Culture in National Security. In: Peter J. Katzenstein, ed., The Culture of National Security: Norms and Identity in World Politics . New York: Columbia University Press. pp. 33–72.

Jervis, Robert 1976: Perception and Misperception in International Politics, Princeton: Princeton University Press.

Joint Declaration between the European Union and the Republic of India on a Clean Energy and Climate Partnership, Brussels, 30.03.2016.

Joshi, Madhura/Ganeshan, Swati 2015: India-EU Energy Relations: Towards Closer Cooperation?, in: Knodt, Michèle/Piefer, Nadine/Müller, Franziska (eds.): Challenges of European External Energy Governance with Emerging Powers, Ashgate, pp. 149–171.

Juncker, Jean-Claude 2014: A New Start for Europe: My Agenda for Jobs, Growth, Fairness and Democratic Change. Political Guidelines for the next Commission. Opening Statement in the Plenary Session, Jean-Claude Juncker, candidate for President of the European Commission, Strasbourg, 15 July 2014, http://www.eesc.eu ropa.eu/resources/docs/jean-claude-juncker-politicalguidelines.pdf [20.05.2016].

Kalaba, Mmatlou 2016: Post Brexit: does South Africa have the appetite to strike new trade deals?, the Conversation; available at: http://theconversation.com/post-brexit-does-south-africa-have-the-appetite-to-strike-new-trade-deals-61638 [25.05.2016].

Karlsson, Christer/Parker, Charles/Hjerpe, Mattias/Linnér, Björn-Ola. 2011: Looking for leaders: perceptions of climate change leadership among climate change negotiation participants, in: Global Environmental Politics 11(1), pp. 89–107.

Kavalksi, Emilian 2013: The struggle for recognition of normative powers: Normative power Europe and normative power China in context, in: Cooperation and Conflict 48(2), pp. 247–267.

Keukeleire, Stephan/Bruyninckx, Hans 2011: The European Union, the BRICs, and the Emerging New World Order, in: Hill, Christopher/Smith, Michael (eds.): International Relations and the European Union, Oxford University Press: New York, pp. 380–403.

Keukeleire, Stephan/Delreux, Tom 2014: The Foreign Policy of the European Union. 2nd Edition. Palgrave Macmillan: Hampshire and New York.

Keukeleire, Stephan/Mattlin, Mikael/Hooijmaaijers, Bas/Behr, Timo/Jokela, Juha/Wigell, Mikael/Kononenko, Vadim 2011: The EU Foreign Policy towards the BRICS and other Emerging Powers: Objectives and strategies (Ad Hoc Study), European Parliament, Brussels: Directorate-General for External Policies.

Khasson, Viktorya/Vasilyan, Syuzanna/Vos, Hendrik. 2008: Everybody needs good neighbours: the EU and its neighbourhood, in: Orbie, J. (ed.): Europe's Global Role: External Policies of the European Union. London: Ashgate, pp. 217–238.

Kim, Dan 2015: Britain's Energy Cooperation with Emerging Powers, in: Knodt, Michèle/Piefer, Nadine/Müller, Franziska (eds.): Challenges of European External Energy Governance with Emerging Powers, Farnham: Ashgate, pp. 101–112.

Kilian, Bertil/Elgström, Ole 2010: Still a green leader? The European Union's role in international climate negotiations', Cooperation and Conflict 45(3), pp. 255–73.

Kinnvall, Catarina 1995: Cultural Diffusion and Political Learning: The Democratization of China. Lund: Lund University Press.

Knodt, Michèle 2016: Energy Policy, in: Heinelt, Hubert/Münch, Sybille (eds.): Handbook of EU policies, Edgar Elder publishing, forthcoming.

Knodt, Michèle/Müller, Franziska/Piefer, Nadine (eds.) 2015: Challenges of European External Energy Governance with emerging powers: Meeting Tiger, Dragon, Lion and Jaguar. Farnham: Ashgate.

Knodt, Michèle/Müller, Franziska/Piefer, Nadine 2015a: Introduction, in: Knodt, Michèle/Müller, Franziska/Piefer, Nadine (eds.): Challenges of European External Energy Governance with Emerging Powers. Farnham: Ashgate, pp. 3–15.

Knodt, Michèle/Müller, Franziska/Piefer, Nadine 2015b: Explaining European Union External Energy Governance with Emerging Powers, in: Knodt, Michèle/Piefer, Nadine/Müller, Franziska (eds.): Challenges of EU External Energy Governance towards Emerging Powers, Farnham and Burlington: Ashgate, pp. 57–74.

Knodt, Michèle/Müller, Franziska/Piefer, Nadine 2015c: Understanding EU-Emerging Powers Energy Governance: Form Competition towards Cooperation?, in: Knodt, Michèle/Piefer, Nadine/Müller, Franziska (eds.): Challenges of European External Energy Governance with Emerging Powers, Farnham: Ashgate, pp. 327–343.

Knodt, Michèle/Müller, Franziska/Piefer, Nadine 2012: Rising Powers in International Energy Governance, Paper for DVPW Conference „Politik und Ökonomie in globaler Perspektive: Der (Wieder) Aufstieg des Globalen Südens", 5-7 March 2012, Frankfurt am Main, Germany.

Knodt, Michèle/Müller, Franziska/Piefer, Nadine 2010: Challenges of European External Energy Governance with Emerging Powers: Meeting Tiger, Dragon, Lion and Jaguar, Paper presented at the 7th SGIR (Study Group on International Relations) Pan-European International Relations Conference, Stockholm, 09.-11.09.2010.

Kong, Bo 2011: Governing China's Energy in the Context of Global Governance, in: Global Policy 2(1), pp. 51–65.

Kumar, Sanjay 2013: France and India deepen ties. Visits to New Delhi by Francois Hollande and David Cameron highlight India's growing importance for Europe, The Diplomat, available at: http://thediplomat.com/2013/02/france-and-india-deepen-ties/ [05.07.2016].

Lai, Suet Yi/Shi, Zhiqin 2016: How China views the EU in global energy governance: Norm exporter, Partner or Outsider?, in: Chaban, Natalia/Knodt, Michèle/Verdun, Amy: External Images of the EU – Energy Power Across the Globe. Special Issue. Comparative European Politics, pulished online first. DOI: 10.1057/cep.2016.14.

Laatikainen, Katie Verlin 2015: Introduction: The EU's Bilateral Relations, in: Jørgensen, Knud Erik/Kalland Aarstad, Åsne/Drieskens, Edith/Laatikainen, Katie Verlin/Tonra, Ben (eds.): The SAGE Handbook of European Foreign Policy, Volume 2., Los Angeles: SAGE, pp. 561–569.

Lakoff, George/Johnston, Mark 1980: Metaphors We Live By. Chicago: University of Chicago Press.

Lazarou, Elena, 2015: EU-Brazil cooperation on internet governance and ICT issues. Briefing November 2015. European Parliamentary Research Service: Brussels.

Lee, Bernice/Mabey, Nick/Preston, Felix/Froggat, Antony/Bradley, Siân 2015: Enhancing Engagement between China and the EU on Resource Government and Low Carbon Development, Research Paper, Chatman House.

Legg, Tobias, 2014: Normative Power Europe? The European Union in the Negotiations on a Free Trade Agreement with India, in: European Foreign Affairs Review 19(3), pp. 335–356.

Leung, Guy C.K. 2011: China's Energy Security: Perception and Reality, Energy Policy 39(3), pp. 1330–1337.

Lisbonne-de Vergeron, Karine 2006: Contemporary Indian Views of Europe, London: Chatham House, available at: http://www.chathamhouse.org/publications/papers/view/108304 [06.12. 2013].

Lisbonne-de Vergeron, Karine 2007: Contemporary Chinese Views of Europe, London: Chatham House, available at: http://www.comw.org/cmp/fulltext/0711 vergeron.pdf [06.12.2013].

Lisbonne-de Vergeron, Karine 2011: Chinese and Indian Views of Europe Since the Crisis: New Perspectives from the Emerging Asian Giants, Paris and Brussels: The Robert Schuman Foundation, available at: http://www.robert-schuman.eu/ouvrage.php?num=138 [06.12.2013].

Lisbonne-de Vergeron, Karine 2006: Contemporary Indian Views of Europe. Chatman House.

Livingston, Steven 1997: Clarifying the CNN effect: An examination of media effects according to type of military intervention, available at: http://www.genocide-watch.org/images/1997ClarifyingtheCNNEffect-Livingston.pdf [30.04.2014].

Lucarelli, Sonia 2007: EU Political Identity, Foreign Policy and External Image: The External Image of the European Union', GARNET Working Paper Series 17, available at: http://www2.warwick.ac.uk/fac/soc/garnet/workingpapers/1707.pdf [06.12.2013].

Lucarelli, Sonia 2014: Seen from the Outside: the State of the Art on the External Image of the EU, in: Journal of European Integration 36, pp. 1–16.

Lucarelli, Sonia/Fioramonti, Lorenzo (eds.) 2010: The External Image of the European Union – Phase Two, GARNET Working Paper Series 62, available at: http://www2.warwick.ac.uk/fac/soc/GARNET/workingpapers/6209_alt.pdf [06.12.2013].

Lucarelli, Sonia/Manners, Ian, (eds.) 2006: Values and Principles in European Union Foreign Policy, London: Routledge.

Manners, Ian 2002: Normative Power Europe: a contradiction in terms, in: Journal of Common Market Studies 40(2), pp. 235–258.

Manners, Ian 2006: The European Union as a Normative Power: a response to Thomas Diez, in: Millenium 35(1), pp. 168–180.

Manners, Ian/Whitman, Richard 2003: The "Difference Engine", in: Journal of European Public Policy 10(3), pp. 387–391.

March, James/Olsen, Johan 1989: Rediscovering Institutions. The Organizational Basis of Politics. New York: Free Press/Macmillan.

Maupin, Agathe 2015: South Africa-EU Energy Governance: Tales of Path Dependency, Regional Power, and Decarbonization, in: Knodt, Michèle/Piefer, Nadine/Müller, Franziska (eds.): Challenges of European External Energy Governance with Emerging Powers, Farnham: Ashgate, pp. 195–213.

McCombs Maxwell E./Shaw, Donald L. 1972: The agenda-setting function of mass media. The Public Opinion Quarterly 36(2), pp. 176–187.

McGowan, Francis 1989: The single energy market and energy policy: conflicting agendas?, in: Energy Policy 17(6), pp. 547–553.

McGowan, Francis 2011: Putting energy insecurity into historical context: European responses to the energy crises of the 1970s and 2000s', in: Geopolitics 16(3), pp. 486–511.

Meidan, Michael/Andrews-Speed, Philip/Xin, Max 2009: Shaping China's Energy Policy: actors and processes, in: Journal of Contemporary China 18(61), pp. 591–616.

Men, Jing 2014: Is There A Strategic Partnership between the EU and China?, in: European Foreign Affairs Review 19, Special Issue, pp. 5–18.

Mergenthaler, Stephan 2012: The Development of a Comprehensive Partnership between the European Union and China, in: Gehler, Michael/Gu, Xuewu/Schimmelpfennig, Andreas (eds.) 2012: EU-China. Global Players in a Complex World, Hildesheim: Olms, pp. 253–267.

Merlingen, Michael 2007: Everything Is Dangerous: A Critique of 'Normative Power Europe', in: Security Dialogue 38(4), pp.435–453.

Ministry of Mines and Energy (MME)/Secretariat of Energy Planning and Development (SPE) 2015: Energy Expansion in Brazil – 2024 Investment Opportunities; Office of Strategic Energy Studies, available at: http://www.mme.gov.br/documents/10584/3642013/03+-+Energy+Expansion+in+Brazil+Investiment+Opportunities+(PDF)/97e49acb-ee22-4c98-ad80-c70056288e89;jsessionid=EA174D8159C21B7C94B25A59F05C52EC.srv155?version [24.08.2016].

Ministry of Foreign Affairs 2016a: French Republic, available at: http://www.itamaraty.gov.br/en/ficha-pais/6080-french-republic [08.09.2016].

Ministry of Foreign Affairs 2016b: State Visit of the President of the French Republic, François Hollande, Press release 424, available at: http://www.itamaraty.gov.br/en/politica-externa/diplomacia-economica-comercial-e-financeira/42-diplomacia-publica/notas-a-imprensas/3636-state-visit-of-the-president-of-the-french-republic-francois-hollande [08.09.2016].

Mohan, Raja C. 2006: Prerequisites for Foreign Policy and Security Interactions Between Europe and India, in: Voll, Klaus/Beierlein, Doreen (eds.): Rising India – Europe's Partner? Foreign and Security Policy, Politics, Economics, Human Rights and Social Issues, Media, Civil Society and Intercultural Dimensions, Berlin: Weißensee Verlag, pp. 258–263.

Moyo, Admire 2016: SA, France in green energy partnership. ITWeb, available at: http://www.itweb.co.za/index.php?option=com_content&view=article&id=154161 [12.07.2016].

Müller, Franziska/Knodt, Michèle/Piefer, Nadine 2015a: Conceptualizing Emerging Powers and EU Energy Governance: Towards a Research Agenda', in: Knodt, Michèle/Piefer, Nadine/Müller, Franziska (eds.): Challenges of EU External Energy Governance towards Emerging Powers, Farnham and Burlington: Ashgate, pp. 17–32.

Murray, Philomena 1999: Australian perspectives on the European Union, European Information, in: Journal of the European Information Association 8, pp. 2–5.

Murray, Philomena 2002: Australian voices: some elite reflections on the European Union, in: CESAA Review 29: pp. 5–18, available at: http://www.cesaa.org.au/publi cations.htm [12.07.2016].

Nakano, Jane 2015: The UK-China Civilian Nuclear Agreement, Center for strategic and international studies.

Narlikar, Amrita 2003: International Trade and Developing Countries: Coalitions in the GATT and WTO. London: Routledge.

Neuman, Russel W./Just, Marion R./Crigler, Ann N. 1992: Common Knowledge: News and the Construction of Political Meaning. Chicago and London: The University of Chicago Press.

Nicolaïdis, Kalypso/Whitman, Richard (eds.) 2013: Special Issue on Normative Power Europe, in: Cooperation and Conflict 48(2).

Nielsen, Louise 2014: The relations between the European Union and the BRICS – an analysis of media perceptions in Germany, M.A. Thesis, Frankfurt am Main and Darmstadt.

Noronha, Ligia/Sharma, Devika 2009: Energy, Climate and Security: The Interlinkages, Proceedings of the 2nd Conference organized by The Energy and Resources Institute (TERI) and Konrad-Adenauer-Foundation (KAF). New Delhi: Konrad-Adenauer-Foundation.

Oberthür, Sebastian/Pallemaerts, Marc 2010: The EU's Internal and External Climate Policies: An Historical Overview', in: Oberthür, Sebastian/Pallemaerts, Marc (eds.): The New Climate Policies of the European Union, Brussels: Brussels University Press, pp. 27–64.

Observatory of Economic Complexity 2014: Atlas, available at: http://atlas.media.mit.edu/en/visualize/tree_map/hs92/import/zaf/show/2709/2014/ [12.09.2016].

Odendaal, Natasha 2016: France, South Africa join hands on development. Engineering News, available at: http://www.engineeringnews.co.za/article/france-south-afri ca-join-hands-on-developme nt-2016-07-11 [20.07.2016].

Oehler-Şincai, Iulia Monica 2011: The Strategic Character of the cooperation relationship between the EU and the BRIC countries, in: Romanian Journal of European Affairs 11(2), pp.31–44.

Oliver, Gerrit/Fioramonti, Lorenzo 2010: The emerging 'global south': the EU in the eyes of India, Brazil and South Africa, in: Sonia Lucarelli/Lorenzo Fioramonti: External Perceptions of the European Union as a global actor, New York: Routledge, pp. 105–19.

Pegels, Anna 2010: Renewable Energy in South Africa: Potentials, Barriers and options for Support, in: Energy Policy 38(9), pp. 4945–4954.

Piefer, Nadine/Knodt, Michèle 2012: Role Options in Triangular Cooperation, in: Langendorf, Julia/Piefer, Nadine/Knodt, Michèle/Müller, Ulrich/Lazáro, Lena (eds.): Triangular Cooperation: A Guideline for Working in Practice, Baden-Baden: Nomos, pp. 159–184.

Piefer, Nadine/Knodt, Michèle/Müller, Franziska 2015a: EU and Emerging Powers in Energy Governance: Exploring the Empirical Puzzle, in: Knodt, Michèle/Müller, Franziska/Piefer, Nadine (eds.): Challenges of European External Energy Governance with Emerging Powers, Farnham: Ashgate, pp. 34–53.

Piefer, Nadine/Knodt, Michèle/Müller, Franziska 2015b: Policy Recommendations for Enhanced EU-Emerging Powers Energy Cooperation, in: Knodt, Michèle/Piefer, Nadine/Müller, Franziska (eds.): Challenges of European External Energy Governance with Emerging Powers, Farnham: Ashgate, pp. 345–354.

Press Release Database 2013: Commission moves forward on climate and energy towards 2030, 27 March 2013, Brussels.

Planning Commission 2006: Integrated Energy Policy: Report of the Expert Committee. New Delhi: Government of India.

PPMI, NCRE, NFG 2015: Analysis of the perceptions of the EU and the EU's policies abroad. Commissioned by European External Action Service (EEAS).

Regulation (EU) No 234/2014, 11.3.2014. OF THE EUROPEAN PARLIAMENT AND OF THE COUNCIL of 11 March 2014 establishing a Partnership Instrument for cooperation with third countries, in: Official Journal of the European Union, Brussels.

Renard, Thomas/Grevi, Giovanni (eds.) 2012a: Hot Issues, Cold Shoulders, Lukewarm Partners: EU Strategic Partnerships and Climate Change, ESPO Report. Madrid: FRIDE.

Renard, Thomas/Grevi, Giovanni 2012b: Introduction, in: Renard, Thomas/Grevi, Giovanni (eds.): Hot Issues, Cold Shoulders, Lukewarm Partners: EU Strategic Partnerships and Climate Change, ESPO Report, Madrid: FRIDE, pp. 5–9.

Renard, Thomas 2010: Strategy Wanted: The European Union and the Strategic Partnerships, Security Policy Brief 13. Brussels: Egmont.

Renard, Thomas 2011: The Treachery of Strategies: A call for true EU Strategic Partnerships, Egmont Paper 45, Brussels: Egmont.

Renard, Thomas/Biscop, Sven (eds.) 2012a: The European Union and Emerging Powers in the 21st Century. How can Europe Shape a New Global Order. Farnham, Ashgate.

Renard, Thomas/Biscop, Sven 2012b: Introduction, in: Renard, Thomas/Biscop, Sven (eds.): The European Union and Emerging Powers in the 21st Century. How can Europe Shape a New Global Order, Farnham: Ashgate, pp. xv–xviii.

Rettman, Andrew 2010: Ashton designates six new 'strategic partners'. EU Observer, 16.09.2010, available at: https://euobserver.com/institutional/30828 [20.07.2016].

Reuters 2016: Dilma Rousseff will not attend Rio Olympics torch ceremony opening. The Guardian, online, 26.07.2016, available at: https://www.theguardian.com/world/2016/jul/26/dilma-rousseff-rio-olympics-torch-ceremony-michel-temer [20.10.2016].

Ribas, Aline/Schaeffer, Roberto 2015: Brazil-EU Energy Governance: Fuelling the Dialogue through Alternative Energy Sources, in: Knodt, Michèle/Piefer, Nadine/Müller, Franziska (eds.): Challenges of European External Energy Governance with Emerging Powers, Farnham: Ashgate, pp. 173–194.

Rüger, Carolin 2012: Europäische Außen- und Sicherheitspolitik – (k)ein Thema für die Öffentlichkeit? Die außen- und sicherheitspolitische Rolle der EU im Blickwinkel von öffentlicher Meinung und Medien, Baden-Baden: Nomos.

Santander, Sebastian 2015: The EU and Brazil in a changing world. Strategic Partners or Competitors?, in: Smith, Michael/Keukeleire, Stephan/Vanhoonacker, Sophie: The Diplomatic System of the European Union, Evolution, change and challenges, Oxon and New York: Routledge, pp. 181–196.

South African Renewable Initiative (SARi) 2011: The Southern African Renewable Initiative, available at: https://sarenewablesinitiative.files.wordpress.com/2011/12/sari_declaration_of_intent_011211-as-printed.pdf [12.11.2016].

Sautenet, Antonie 2012: The EU's Strategic Partnerships with Emerging Powers: Institutional, Legal, Economic and Political Perspectives, in: Renard, Thomas/Biscop, Sven (eds.): The European Union and Emerging Powers in the 21st Century. How can Europe Shape a New Global Order, Farnham: Ashgate, pp. 123–145.

Sawhney, Aparna 2008: India-EU Trade and Investment Agreement: Environmental Services Sector Study, New Delhi: Indian Council for Research on International Economic Relations, available at: http://wtocentre.iift.ac.in/EU%20BTIA/EU%20BTIA/Report%20on%20Environmental%20Services%20India-EU%20BTIA.pdf [29.10.2014].

Saxer, Marc 2012: Multilateralism in Crisis? Global Governance in the Twenty-First Century, in: Schimmelfennig, Frank 2001: The community trap: liberal norms, rhetorical action, and the Eastern Enlargement of the European Union, in: International Organisation 55(1), pp. 47–80.

Scheipers, Sibylle/Sicurelli, Daniela 2008: Empowering Africa: Normative Power in EU-Africa Relations, in: Journal of European Public Policy 15(4), pp. 607–623.

Schmidt, Vivien Ann 2008: Discursive institutionalism: the explanatory power of ideas and discourse, in: Annual Review of Political Science 11, pp. 303–326.

Schneider, Volker/Janning, Frank/Leifeld, Philipp/Malang, Thomas (eds.) 2009: Politiknetzwerke. Modelle, Anwendungen und Visualisierungen. Wiesbaden: VS Verlag.

Sebitosi, A.B./Pillay, P. 2008: Grappling with a half-hearted policy: The case of renewable energy and the environment in South Africa, in: Energy Policy 36(7), pp. 2513–2516. DOI:10.1016/j.enpol.2008.03.011.

Secrieru, Stanislav 2010: Russia's Mainstream Perceptions of the EU and its Member States SPEC Policy Papers, available at: http://iep-berlin.de/wp-content/uploads/sites/2/2014/09/SPES_Policy_Papers_2010_Secrieru.pdf [24.05.2012].

Šefčovič, Maroš 2015a: African Energies – Part II, available at: https://ec.europa.eu/commission/commissioners/2014-2019/sefcovic/blog/african-energies-part-ii_en [14.05.2016].

Šefčovič, Maroš 2015b: Speech at the University of Pretoria, South Africa, 16 July 2015, available at: https://ec.europa.eu/commission/commissioners/2014-2019/sefcovic/announcements/speech-university-pretoria-south-africa_en [14.05.2016].

Selianko, Iulii/Lenschow, Andrea 2015: Energy policy coherence from an intra-institutional perspective: Energy security and environmental policy coordination within the European Commission, in: Neuhold, Christine/Vanhoonacker, Sophie (eds.): Dynamics of institutional cooperation in the European Union: Dimensions and effects, in: European Integration online Papers (EIoP) 19(1), Special issue, pp. 1–29.

Shambaugh, David/Sandschneider, Eberhard/Hong, Zhou 2008: From honeymoon to marriage: prospects for the China-Europe relationship, in: Shambaugh, David/Sandschneider, Eberhard/Hong, Zhou (eds.): China-Europe Relations. Perceptions, policies and prospects, London: Routledge, pp. 303–337.

Shen, Wenwen 2015: The Diffussion of EU Norms to China. The Case of Tibet, in: Björkdahl, Annika/Chaban, Natalia/Leslie, John/Masselot, Annick (eds.): Importing EU Norms. Conceptual Framework and Empirical Findings, London/New York: Springer.

Shimko, Keith, L. 1991: Images and Arms Control. Ann Arbor: University of Michigan Press.

Sjursen, H. 2006: The EU as 'normative' power: how can this be?, in: Journal of European Public Policy 13(2), pp. 235–251.

Smith, Michael 2013: Beyond the Comfort Zone: Internal Crisis and External Challenge in the European Union's Response to Rising Powers, in: International Affairs 89(3), pp. 653–671.

Sreberny-Mohammadi, Annabelle/Nordenstreng, Kaarle/Stevenson, Robert/Ugboajah, Frank (eds.) 1985: Foreign News in Media: International Reporting in 29 Countries, in: Reports and Papers on Mass Communication 93, Paris: UNESCO.

Stumbaum, May-Britt/Gippner, Olivia/Lutz, Anja/Mohan, Garima/Zhao, Jizhou 2015: Does Europe Matter? The EU as a Security Actor in the Asian Century, NFG Final Report, Berlin: FU Berlin.

The Brazilian National Agency of Petroleum, Natural Gas and Biofuels (ANP) 2016: Competências da ANP, available at: http://www.anp.gov.br/ [03.05.2016].

The Hindu 2013a: India EU FTA Talks Gain Momentum, available at: http://www.thehindu.com/business/Economy/indiaeu-fta-talks-gain%20momentum/article4623470.ece [29.10.2014].

The Hindu 2013b: India-EU FTA talks likely to hit roadblock, available at: http://www.thehindu.com/business/Economy/indiaeu-fta-talks-likely-to-hit-roadblock/article4695909.ece [29.10.2014].

The International Renewable Energy Agency (IRENA) 2015: Renewable Energy Policy Brief: Brazil. Abu Dhabi: IRENA.

The World Bank Group (WBG) 2016a: Brazil. Overview, available at: http://www.worldbank.org/en/country/brazil/overview [22.06.2016].

The World Bank Group (WBG) 2016b: GDP growth (annual %). Overview per country. India, available at: http://data.worldbank.org/indicator/NY.GDP.MKTP.KD. ZG?locations=IN [09.08.2016].

Tsuruoka, Michito 2006: How external perspectives of the European Union are shaped: endogenous and exogenous sources', Paper prepared for the 20th World Congress of the International Political Science Association, Fukuoka, Japan.

United Nations Framework Convention on Climate Change 2015: available at: http://unfccc.int/meetings/paris_nov_2015/meeting/8926.php [30.11.2016].

U.S. Energy Information Administration (EIA) 2015: Brazil. Overview; available at: https://www.eia.gov/beta/international/analysis.cfm?iso=BRA [22.06.2016].

U.S. Energy Information Administration (EIA) 2013: Today in Energy. India's economic growth is driving its energy consumption, available at: https://www.eia.gov/todayinenergy/detail.cfm?id=10611 [09.08.2016].

Vaclav, Smil 1981: Energy Development in China: The Need for a Coherent Policy, in: Energy Policy 9(2), pp. 113–126.

Van der Loo, Guillaume 2016: The Dutch Referendum on the EU-Ukraine Association Agreement: Legal options for navigating a tricky and awkward situation, CEPS Commentary.

Van Vooren, Bart 2012: EU External Relations Law and the European Neighbourhood Policy. A paradigm for Coherence. Oxon/New York: Routledge.

Vaz, Alcides Costa 2014: Brazil's strategic partnerships: origins, agendas and outcomes. Egmont Working Paper 9.

Verein der Kohlenimporteure e.V. (VDKI) 2015: Jahresbericht 2015. Fakten und Trends 2014/2015, World Bank.

Vines, Alex 2013: UK and South Africa: A Relationship Worth Maintaining, Chatman House, available at: https://www.chathamhouse.org/media/comment/view/194212 [30.10.2016].

Westphal, Kirsten 2015: Germany's Energy Cooperation with Emerging Powers: Internationalizing the Energiewende?, in: Knodt, Michèle/Piefer, Nadine/Müller, Franziska (eds.): Challenges of European External Energy Governance with Emerging Powers, Farnham: Ashgate, pp.87–100.

Whitman, Richard 2013: The neo-normative turn in theorising the EU's international presence, in: Cooperation and Conflict 48(2), pp. 171–193.

Whitman, Richard G./Rodt, Annemarie P. 2012: EU-Brazil Relations: A Strategic Partnership?, in: European Foreign Affairs Review 17(1), pp. 27–44.

Williams, Glyn/Meth, Paula/Willis, Katie 2009: Geographies of Developing Areas: The Global South in a Changing World. Abingdon/New York: Routledge.

Wiessala, Georg/Wilson, John/Taneja, Pradeep (eds.) 2009: The European Union and China: Interests & Dilemmas. European Studies – An Interdisciplinary Series in European Culture, History and Politics 27, Amsterdam/New York: Rodopi.

Winand, Pascaline/Vicziany, Marika 2015: Introduction: the problem of EU–India relations, in: Winand, Pascaline/Vicziany, Marika/Datar, Poonam (eds.): The European Union and India. Rhetoric or Meaningful Partnership?, Cheltenham: Edward Elgar, pp. 1–13.

Winand, Pascaline/Vicziany, Marika/Datar, Poonam (eds.) 2015: The European Union and India, Rhetoric or Meaningful Partnership?, Cheltenham: Edward Elgar.

World Nuclear News 2016: British firms extend cooperation with China. World Nuclear Association, 07.04.2016, available at: http://www.world-nuclear-news.org/C-British-firms-extend-cooperation-with-China-0704165.html [09.06.2016].

Wissenschaftlicher Beirat der Bundesregierung Globale Umweltveränderungen WBGU 2011: Welt im Wandel: Gesellschaftsvertrag für eine Große Transformation, Hauptgutachten, Berlin, available at: http://www.wbgu.de/hauptgutachten/hg-2011-transformation/ [12.02.2016].

Xinhua 2016: Chinese premier meets French FM, 17.05.2016, available at: http://news.xinhuanet.com/english/2016-05/17/c_135366566.htm [09.06.2016].

Yi, Ju 2014: Five Decades of Sino-French Relations: Foundations for a New Relationship. China Institute of International Studies.

Yuan, Hang/Orbie, Jan 2015: The Social Dimension of the EU-China Relationship. A Normative and Pragmatic European Approach?, in: European Foreign Affairs Review 20(3), pp. 337–356.

Zhang, Jiawei 2015: News Analysis. China-Britain energy cooperation boosts low-carbon development, Xinhua, English News, 25.10.2015, available at: http://news.xinhuanet.com/english/2015-10/25/c_134747773.htm [09.08.2016].

Zha, Daojiong/Lai, Suet Yi 2015: China-EU Energy Governance: What Lessons to be Drawn, in: Knodt, Michèle/Piefer, Nadine/Müller, Franziska (eds.): Challenges of European External Energy Governance with Emerging Powers, Farnham: Ashgate, pp. 129–147.

Zha, Daojiong 2013: China's Perspective: The Search for Energy Security, in: Tellis, Ashley J./Mirski, Sean (eds.): Crux of Asia: China, India, and the Emerging Global Order, Washington DC: Carnegie Endowment for International Peace, pp. 209–220.

Zha, Daojiong/Gill, B/Melvin, N/Duchâtel, Mathieu 2011: Framing an EU-China Dialogue on Energy Security. Stockholm International Peace Research Institute and the School of International Studies. Peking University. Paper prepared for workshop at the Energy and Research Institute, National Development and Reform Commission, Beijing, China. 31 October 2011, available at: http://file.eu-chinapdsf.org/Intranet/PDSF1/Energy_Security_draft_paper.pdf [05.03.2013].

Zhang, Li 2011: News Media and EU-China Relations, Basingstoke, U.K.: Palgrave Macmillan.

Zhou, Hong 2007: Chinese perspective on Lisbon Strategy, in: Asia-Europe Journal 5(3), pp. 357–365.

Zongze, Ruan 2008: China-EU-US relations. Shaping a constructive future, in: Shambaugh, David/Sandschneider, Eberhard/Hong, Zhou (eds.): China-Europe Relations. Perceptions, policies and prospects, London: Routledge, pp. 287–300.